The European Union Trade Mark

A Practical Guide

Mark Holah and **Patricia Collis**

Authors
Mark Holah
Patricia Collis

Managing director
Sian O'Neill

The European Union Trade Mark: A Practical Guide
is published by
Globe Law and Business Limited
3 Mylor Close
Horsell
Woking
Surrey GU21 4DD
Tel: +44 20 3745 4770
www.globelawandbusiness.com

Printed and bound by Gomer Press

The European Union Trade Mark: A Practical Guide
ISBN 9781909416666

FSC
www.fsc.org
MIX
Paper from responsible sources
FSC® C114687

Table of contents

Preface

This book is written as a practical guide for those using, or seeking to use, the EUTM system. It takes full account of the reforms introduced in 2016, highlighting key changes introduced by these reforms as well as those reforms that are not due to come into force until 1 October 2017.

One of the changes introduced by the reforms was the change in name from Community Trade Mark, or CTM, to European Union Trade Mark, or EUTM. For ease of reference, the term 'EUTM' is used throughout this book, even when referring to CTMs.

Wherever possible, we have avoided references to legislation and case law in the text of the book. There is a 'Further reference' section at the end of most chapters indicating where additional information or detail can be obtained if required.

A number of abbreviations are used throughout this book. The first time each such term is mentioned in the book, it is set out in full, followed by the abbreviation. As this work is intended to be a practical user guide, all abbreviations are also set out in the Glossary, with details of the term that has been abbreviated. Many of these abbreviations are in the form of initialisms (such as 'EUTM' for European Union Trade Mark), and are widely used in the trade mark industry. Abbreviated terms that are not in the form of initialisms can easily be identified by the use of capital letters (such as 'Union', for European Union).

This book is organised into eight parts, starting with a general introduction to the EUTM system, followed by sections dealing with each stage in the life cycle of an EUTM registration. The areas of appeals and enforcement are then discussed, before we look at particular features of the EUTM system and finally the International Registration system.

During the writing of this book, a referendum was held in the UK, the outcome of which was that the public voted in favour of leaving the European Union. No steps have yet been taken to begin the formal process of withdrawal, and it is expected that this process will not be completed until at least early 2019. In the interim, the UK remains a full member of the European Union and EUTM rights continue to apply to the country.

Glossary

The Agreement
The Madrid Agreement (1892).

Benelux
The union of Belgium, Luxembourg and the Netherlands.

Boards of Appeal
The operating divisions of the European Union Intellectual Property Office (the Office) responsible for dealing with, and taking all decisions relating to, appeals filed against the decisions of the other operating divisions of the Office, as well as those of any new body or individual appointed by the President of the Office.

Cancellation Divisions
The operating divisions of the European Union Intellectual Property Office responsible for dealing with, and taking all decisions relating to, invalidity actions, revocation actions and requests to transfer registrations obtained by agents or representatives without the true proprietor's consent

CJEU
The Court of Justice of the European Union, previously known as the European Court of Justice, comprising both the Court of Justice and the General Court.

The Commission
The executive of the European Union, which represents the general interests of the European Union as a whole.

The Council
The Council of the European Union, which represents the governments of the Member States of the European Union and consists of one national minister from each Member State.

CPVR
Community Plant Variety Right, a right the registration of which gives a breeder the exclusive right to produce a plant variety within the European Union.

CTM
Community Trade Mark, the name used for a European Union Trade Mark prior to 23 March 2016.

ECJ
The European Court of Justice, the previous name of the Court of Justice of the European Union. Decisions given by the ECJ are referred to in this book as having been given by the Court of Justice of the European Union for ease of reference.

EEA
The European Economic Area, which comprises the Member States of the European Union together with Iceland, Liechtenstein and Norway.

EUTM
European Union Trade Mark, known as the Community Trade Mark prior to 23 March 2016.

EUTM Court
European Union Trade Mark Court, a court in which actions based on European Union Trade Mark registrations and applications can be brought.

Implementing Regulation
The rules put in place to implement the European Union Regulation that governs the European Union Trade Mark system. The current Implementing Regulation is Commission Regulation (EC) No 2868/95 of 13 December 1995.

IP
Intellectual property

IPO
Intellectual Property Office.

IR
International Registration.

Languages of the Office
The five official languages of the European Union Intellectual Property Office. These are (in alphabetical order): English, French, German, Italian and Spanish.

Languages of the Union
The 24 official languages of the European Union. These are (in alphabetical order): Bulgarian, Croatian, Czech, Danish, Dutch, English, Estonian, Finnish, French, German, Greek, Hungarian, Irish, Italian, Latvian, Lithuanian, Maltese, Polish, Portuguese, Romanian, Slovak, Slovenian, Spanish, Swedish.

Member State
One of the (currently 28) countries that are members of the European Union.

Nice Classification
The international classification system established by the Nice Agreement Concerning the International Classification of Goods and Services for the Purposes of the Registration of Marks (1957).

The Office
The European Union Intellectual Property Office, previously known as the Office for Harmonisation in the Internal Market (Trade Marks and Designs) or the OHIM.

Office Guidelines
The Guidelines for Examination of European Union Trade Marks, available at: https://euipo.europa.eu/ohimportal/en/trade-mark-guidelines.

Office of Origin
The Intellectual Property Office of the 'home' application or registration relied on as the base right for an International application filed under the Madrid Protocol.

Opposition Divisions
The operating divisions of the European Union Intellectual Property Office responsible for dealing with, and taking all decisions relating to, oppositions filed against European Union Trade Mark applications.

Paris Convention
The Paris Convention for the Protection of Industrial Property (1883).

PDO
Protected Designation of Origin, which gives protection to agricultural products and foodstuffs that are produced, processed and prepared in a given geographical area using recognised know-how. Protection comes from registration with the Commission, and is only granted if consumers expect that products bearing the name fulfil this criterion.

PGI
Protected Geographical Indication, which gives protection to agricultural products and foodstuffs that are closely linked to a particular geographical area, with at least some part of the production, processing or preparation of the product taking place in that area. The protection comes from registration with the Commission.

The Protocol
The Madrid Protocol (1995).

RCD
Registered Community Design.

The Register
The register maintained by the European Union Intellectual Property Office containing the details of and information relevant to European Union Trade Marks.

The Regulation
The European Union regulation that governs the European Union Trade Mark system. The current version of the Regulation is Regulation (EC) No 207/2009 of 26 February 2009, as amended by Regulation (EU) No 2015/2424 of 16 December 2015.

TM Directive
The Trade Marks Directive, the European Union directive that indicates the rules each Member State must implement into their national laws. There have been three versions of this directive, published in 1988, 2008 and 2015. In this book, the term 'TM Directive' is used to cover all three versions.

TMDN
The European Trade Mark and Design Network, a body created to establish a more co-ordinated and cohesive trade mark and design system across the European Union. For more information, see www.tmdn.org.

TSG
Traditional specialities guaranteed, which gives protection to terms indicating that an agricultural product intended for human consumption or foodstuff has a traditional composition or has been produced according to a traditional production method. Protection comes from registration with the Commission.

Union
The European Union.

Union Treaty
The international treaties that set out the constitutional basis and operation of the European Union. The core treaties are the Treaty of Rome (1958) and the Maastricht Treaty (2002), as amended by the Treaty of Lisbon (2009).

UPOV
The International Union for the Protection of New Varieties of Plants. Registration of a plant variety under this system gives a breeder the exclusive right to produce that variety in countries that are members of this system.

Vienna Classification
The international classification system relating to the figurative elements of marks established by the Vienna Agreement Establishing an International Classification of the Figurative Elements of Marks (1973).

WIPO
The World Intellectual Property Office, which describes itself as "the global forum for intellectual property services, policy, information and cooperation". This body administers the International Registration system under the Madrid Agreement and Madrid Protocol.

WTO
The World Trade Organization, which aims to ensure that global trade flows as smoothly and freely as possible. For more information, see https://www.wto.org.

Chapter 1: Introduction to the Union and the EUTM system

1. Introduction

The European Union Trade Mark ('EUTM') system is a unique trade mark registration system. It has allowed brand owners to obtain protection throughout the entire European Union ('Union') by means of a single registration since it was first introduced back in 1996.

Although detailed consideration of the structure and operation of the Union are beyond the scope of this book, this chapter provides some high-level background on the Union and the creation of the EUTM system.

2. An overview of the Union

The Union is a political and economic union that, when it was first created as the European Economic Community in 1958, comprised just six Member States. Since then, membership has grown considerably. There are now 28 Member States and this number is expected to rise further over time.

2.1 Creation of Union legislation

Union legislation is created by three institutions:

- *the Parliament* – which represents the Union's citizens and is made up of more than 750 members directly elected from the Member States;
- *the Council* – which represents the Union's governments and consists of one national minister from each Member State. The members of the Council are not fixed and the minister involved in any particular instance is normally the minister responsible at national level for the topic under discussion; and
- *the Commission* – which represents the interests of the Union as a whole. It has 28 members, one from each Member State.

All legislation within the Union is initiated by the Commission. The process begins with the Commission sending a proposal to the Parliament. This proposal is considered by both the Parliament and the Council, who can accept, amend, or reject it. Once the Parliament and the Council approve the text of a proposal, the legislation is published.

2.2 Forms of Union legislation

Union legislation takes three different forms:

- *Regulations* – these are directly applicable. Once published, a regulation becomes law and is binding throughout the Union and so must be complied with by all the Member States;

- *Directives* – these are directly effective. Once published, the Member States must amend their national laws to comply with a directive by a specified date; and
- *Decisions* – these relate to specific circumstances and are directly effective once published.

It should be noted that regulations are quite separate from, and technically not affected by, directives. Directives impact upon the laws of the individual Member States, whereas regulations automatically have effect throughout the entire Union. While Member States are given a specific amount of time (usually years) to implement directives into their national laws, regulations come into effect and must be complied with throughout the Union as soon as they are published.

2.3 The Court of Justice

The Union operates through many different institutions, including those discussed above. Another institution of key relevance to the EUTM system is the Court of Justice of the European Union ('CJEU'). This body is responsible for ruling on the interpretation and application of the Union Treaty and Union law. It comprises the General Court and the Court of Justice, the highest courts in the Union legal system. Both the General Court and the Court of Justice routinely hear trade mark cases, including both appeals from the Boards of Appeal and references from the national courts of the Member States seeking guidance on the interpretation of Union trade mark law.

3. Harmonisation of trade mark rights in the Union

One of the key aims of the Union is the development of a single internal market, which guarantees free circulation of goods, people, capital, and services within the Union; these are known as 'the four freedoms'.

There is a clear conflict between the free movement of goods and services within the Union and the normal operation of national intellectual property ('IP') rights, including trade mark rights. For example, if the same trade mark is owned by a different proprietor in each Member State, each individual proprietor is potentially able to use national trade mark law to prevent all the other proprietors importing goods into its Member State, thus hindering the free movement of those goods through the Union. As a result, the harmonisation of IP laws within the Union has been discussed for as long as the Union has been in existence.

There are two prongs to the attempts to harmonise trade mark law in the Union:

- *The amendment of national laws:* to harmonise the provisions that most directly affect the functioning of the internal market. This does not apply to all provisions: it has never been the intention that all national laws relating to trade marks, or other IP rights, would be exactly the same. The harmonisation approach led to the implementation of the original version of the Trade Marks Directive, the full name of which was Council Directive No 89/104/EEC, to approximate the laws of the Member States relating to trade marks. This directive was adopted on 21 December 1988 and has subsequently been repealed. The Trade Marks Directive is referred to in this book as the 'TM Directive'; and

- *The creation of a unitary trade mark right:* to have a single right giving uniform protection throughout the Union. Such a right was first introduced with the implementation of the original EUTM Regulation, the full name of which was Council Regulation (EC) No 40/94 of 20 December 1993 on the Community trade mark. This regulation has subsequently been repealed. The EUTM Regulation is referred to in this book as the 'Regulation'.

The latest version of the TM Directive came into force on 13 January 2016. It made some fundamental changes to trade mark law in the Union, most of which the Member States are required to implement within three years, by January 2019. However, there some provisions, such as the requirement that all Member States allow cancellation actions to be brought before their national IP offices ('IPOs') (rather than having to go to court), that do not need to be implemented into national law for seven years.

4. Creation of the EUTM system

The original version of the Regulation came into force on 15 March 1994. At that time, and until the latest version of the Regulation came into force on 23 March 2016, an EUTM was called a Community trade mark (CTM). For ease of reference, the term 'EUTM' is used throughout this book, even when discussing situations that arose before the name change.

The effective date of the first EUTM applications was 1 April 1996. Although it was possible to file EUTM applications from 1 January 1996, all applications filed on or before 1 April 1996 were treated as if filed on 1 April 1996. As a result, there are no EUTM registrations giving EU-wide rights prior to 1 April 1996, subject to priority claims (which are discussed in Chapter 5) and seniority claims (which are discussed in Chapter 24).

The EUTM system was the subject of fairly substantial reforms with the introduction of the latest version of the Regulation in 2016. Not all the changes set out in this regulation came into force on 23 March 2016, however. A number of changes will not come into force until 1 October 2017; these provisions are noted where relevant.

5. The nature of EUTM registrations

An EUTM registration is, by its very nature, a unitary Union-wide right, otherwise it would not serve the purpose of promoting a single internal market within the Union. The effect of this is that an EUTM registration is an 'all or nothing' right. To obtain an EUTM registration, the relevant trade mark must be acceptable and capable of registration in every Member State. If there is a reason why a particular trade mark cannot be registered in any given Member State, it is not possible to obtain an EUTM registration for that trade mark.

As a result of the unitary nature of an EUTM registration, it is not possible for ownership to be split by territory: the owner (or owners) must be the same across the entire Union. This applies both when an EUTM application is filed and when an

EUTM application or registration is assigned: only the entire application or registration (in terms of territory) can be transferred (see Chapter 16 for discussion).

6. The interaction of the EUTM system with national trade mark rights

The EUTM system is not intended to replace, or even compete with, the registration systems that exist at national level in the Member States. Rather, these systems are intended to complement each other. There are some instances when an EUTM registration is more appropriate and others when national registrations are more appropriate, or even necessary if there is a problem with obtaining an EUTM registration. This is discussed in Chapter 3.

At the national level, filing an EUTM application is equivalent to filing a national application. This means that, within the Member States, EUTM applications and registrations give the same rights as national applications and registrations. This is true whether an application is filed directly with the Office or as a Union designation of an International Registration ('IR') (as to which, see Chapter 32).

The EUTM system is a fully autonomous legal system with its own rules. It is extra-jurisdictional in nature, quite independent from any rules set out in national law. As a result, decisions made at national level within the Member States are not binding on the European Union Intellectual Property Office ('the Office'). Having said that, the laws of the Member States and the EUTM system are harmonised to a large degree, so that in most cases it is intended (and expected) that the same decision will be given on the basis of identical facts.

In any event, there is a strong interaction between the EUTM and national trade mark systems. Earlier national rights can be used to oppose or cancel EUTM applications and registrations (and vice versa) (see Chapter 12 for discussion). Further, actions for infringement of EUTM registrations are brought before the national courts of the Member States (as to which, see chapters 21 and 22).

7. What territories are covered by an EUTM registration?

An EUTM registration gives rights in all Member States. Rights in any individual Member State are, however, only effective from the date of accession to the Union of that Member State.

As a result, EUTM registrations give rights in the current Member States with effect from the following dates:

1 April 1996 (when the EUTM system started) – Austria, Belgium, Denmark, Finland, France, Germany, Greece, Ireland, Italy, Luxembourg, the Netherlands, Portugal, Spain, Sweden and the UK;

1 May 2004 – the Czech Republic, Cyprus, Estonia, Hungary, Latvia, Lithuania, Malta, Poland, Slovenia and Slovakia;

1 January 2007 – Bulgaria and Romania; and

1 July 2013 – Croatia.

EUTM registrations also give rights in certain territories that have special relationships with Member States. For example, an EUTM registration automatically extends to the Canary Islands (which is part of Spain), Madeira and the Azores (both of which are part of Portugal) and Réunion (which is part of France).

In addition, some dependent territories have introduced local legislation so that EUTM registrations give rights within those territories. For example, local legislation means that EUTM registrations automatically give protection in the Falkland Islands. It is also possible to extend EUTM registrations to give protection in the Cayman Islands.

It is clear that most dependent territories are not covered by the EUTM system. For example, EUTM registrations do not automatically give rights in Bermuda, Greenland, the Faroe Islands, the British Virgin Islands, Aruba or French Polynesia.

Finally, it should be borne in mind that not all European countries are part of the Union. EUTM registrations give no rights in many territories that are often referred to as being 'in Europe', including Andorra, Iceland, Lichtenstein, Monaco, Norway, Russia, San Marino, Switzerland, Turkey and the Vatican City.

8. Enlargement of the Union

Before a new Member State is accepted into the Union, the country in question (referred to as a 'candidate country') must satisfy a number of conditions. A key part of this is that the candidate country must agree to adopt, implement and enforce all the current rules of the Union (known as the acquis). The acquis is split into 35 different chapters, one of which relates to IP. As a result, no candidate country is accepted into the Union unless it satisfies the Commission that it would be able to comply with the provisions of the Regulation.

The basic rule is that all EUTM registrations and applications are automatically extended to, and effective in, new Member States as soon as they join the Union. There are, however, some more complicated transitional rules to be considered.

Where an EUTM application is pending on the date of accession of a new Member State, the application cannot be refused on the basis of an objection relating to that State. This is because objections are judged as of the filing date of the EUTM application, at which point the new Member State was not part of the Union. For example, an application filed on 30 June 2013 (the day before Croatia joined the Union) could not be refused on the basis that the mark was not distinctive in Croatia on that date.

Where a Union-wide objection is raised against an application, the objection need only be overcome as regards the Member States that were part of the Union at the filing date. Therefore, if acquired distinctiveness is relied upon, this only needs to relate to those Member States that were part of the Union at the filing date. To continue with the example given above, if the mark was arguably non-distinctive in both Croatia and Slovenia, proof that the objection was incorrectly raised in relation to Slovenia would be enough to overcome the objection.

As a result of these transitional rules, it is technically possible for an EUTM registration to give rights in a country in which the relevant mark should not be capable of registration. However, this anomaly is necessary to ensure the unitary nature of the EUTM system is maintained. The only exception is where it is proved that the EUTM application was filed for the sole purpose of obtaining rights in a non-registrable mark, in which case the application would have been filed in bad faith. However, proving this is likely to be very challenging and there do not appear to be any instances of registrations being invalidated on this basis.

For applications filed after the date of accession of a new Member State, objections will be raised that are relevant to that state, even if the priority date of the EUTM application is earlier than the accession date. If, in the example given above, the EUTM application had been filed on 1 July 2013 rather than 30 June 2013, an objection could have been raised that the mark was not distinctive in Croatia, irrespective of any priority claims.

As noted in section 7 above, EUTM applications and registrations cannot give rights in a Member State that predate that state's accession to the Union. Where an EUTM application or registration is converted into national applications, the conversion date cannot be before the date of accession of that Member State (as to which, see Chapter 25). For example, if an EUTM registration dating from 1 January 2003 were withdrawn and converted into national applications in Italy, Slovenia and Croatia, the effective filing date of the converted applications would be 1 January 2003 in Italy, 1 May 2004 in Slovenia and 1 July 2013 in Croatia.

It is also possible to claim seniority from national registrations in a new Member State as of the date of accession of that state (see Chapter 24). This can lead to the unusual situation where seniority can be claimed from a national registration that actually post-dates the EUTM registration. For example, if a proprietor owns an EUTM registration from 1996 and a Romanian registration from 2000, seniority can be claimed from the Romanian registration. This is possible because the EUTM registration only gives rights in Romania from that state's accession date of 1 January 2007.

When a new Member State joins the Union, the rules relating to languages, professional representation and translations (see Chapter 2), together with the possibility for the national IPO of the new state to join the national search system (see Chapter 4), automatically apply to that state as of its accession date.

9. Contraction of the Union

No Member State has ever left the Union, though following the result of the referendum held on 23 June 2016 in the UK, it seems likely that the UK will leave the Union within the next few years.

It is unclear what would happen to existing EUTM rights if a Member State did leave the Union. As EUTM rights are Union-wide rights, they would clearly cease to have effect in a country after it had left the Union.

It seems very unlikely, however, that all rights in existing EUTM registrations and applications would simply be lost in the departing country. Instead, it is much more likely that there would be some mechanism to allow EUTM registrations and applications to be turned into national registrations and applications in the departing Member State so that rights would not be lost. The structure and operation of this transfer mechanism would be a matter of national law in the departing Member State and, as a result, is beyond the scope of this book.

Further reference

This chapter contains only a brief and simplistic summary of the operation of the Union. For more information, a good starting point is the Commission website, at www.ec.europa.eu.

Further information can also be obtained from:

- The online guidelines on current trade mark practice on the Office's website (referred to in this book as the Office Guidelines) – Part A, Section 9
- Regulation – Article 165

Chapter 2: The Office

1. Introduction

The European Union Intellectual Property Office (the 'Office') is based in Alicante, Spain, and has over 1200 staff from across the Union and beyond. It is responsible for administering the EUTM system and currently processes over 100,000 EUTM registrations annually.

In addition, the Office administers a Union-wide design registration system (the Registered Community Design ('RCD') system); around 75,000 RCDs are currently registered each year.

The Office is also involved in an increasingly wide range of activities and works closely with a number of other bodies and institutions, including the European Observatory on Infringements of Intellectual Property Rights (the 'Observatory') and the European Trade Mark and Design Network ('TMDN'). Together, these entities provide very useful tools and information, work towards ensuring consistency of practice and help to promote and protect IP rights in the Union.

2. The status and structure of the Office

The Office is a 'body of the Union' with its own legal personality and is represented within the Union by an appointed President.

According to the Regulation, each Member State must give the Office "the most extensive legal capacity accorded to legal persons under their laws; it may, in particular, acquire or dispose of movable and immovable property and may be a party to legal proceedings".

The Office is managed as follows:

- *the President* – who is responsible for the overall functioning of the Office, which includes implementing the Office's budget. The President is appointed for renewable five-year terms;
- *the Executive Director* – who is responsible for managing the Office. This includes a very wide range of tasks and responsibilities set out in the Regulation, not least "taking all necessary steps ... to ensure the functioning of the Office". The Executive Director is accountable to the Management Board and is appointed for a five-year term, which can be renewed only once (so that no Executive Director can be in place for more than 10 years);
- *the Management Board* – which is responsible for overseeing the management of the Office by the Executive Director and, once they have been approved, adopting the various programmes carried out by the Office pursuant to its

obligations. The Management Board consists of representatives from each Member State, the Commission and the Parliament. The chairperson of the Management Board is elected for a four-year term, which can be renewed once;

- *the Budget Committee* – which is responsible for overseeing, agreeing and (once approved) adopting the annual budget of the Office; and
- *the operating divisions* – these are responsible for the day-to-day work of the Office. There are currently five operating divisions and the President has the power to appoint new units or individuals at any time, particularly where a decision needs to be taken that does not fall within the competence of the existing operating divisions. The tasks and responsibilities of the Office's current operating divisions can be briefly summarised as follows:
  - *Examiners* – who are responsible for dealing with, and taking all decisions relating to, EUTM applications, other than those decisions for which the Opposition Divisions are responsible;
  - *Opposition Divisions* – which are responsible for dealing with, and taking all decisions relating to, oppositions filed against EUTM applications;
  - *the Department in charge of the Register* – which is responsible for the upkeep of, and taking all decisions relating to, entries in the Register, as well as maintaining the list of Professional Representatives;
  - *Cancellation Divisions* – which is responsible for dealing with, and taking all decisions relating to, invalidity actions, revocation actions and requests to transfer registrations obtained by agents or representatives without the true proprietor's consent; and
  - *Boards of Appeal* – which are responsible for dealing with, and taking all decisions relating to, appeals filed against the decisions of the operating divisions referred to above, as well as those of any new body or individual appointed by the President.

One potential new body referred to specifically in the Regulation is the Mediation Centre which, if established, could be used by parties involved in any proceedings before the Opposition Divisions, the Cancellation Divisions or the Boards of Appeal. At the time of writing, the Office only offers a mediation service during appeal proceedings.

3. The aims and objectives of the Office

The Regulation sets out the following tasks of the Office:

- administering and promoting the EUTM system;
- administering and promoting the RCD system;
- promoting convergence of practice and tools across the Union in co-operation with national IPOs. This is achieved through the Office's involvement in the TMDN. The Regulation sets out the subject-matter that the Office is to cover through its work in this area, including "the development of common examination standards" and "the creation of common or connected databases and portals for Union-wide consultation,

search and classification purposes" (the latter is achieved through the Office's involvement in the TMView and TMClass databases);
- working with national authorities, the private sector and the institutions of the Union in the fight against infringement of IP rights. This is achieved through the Office's involvement in the Observatory. This obligation comes from Regulation (EU) No 386/2012 on entrusting the Office with tasks related to the enforcement of intellectual property rights, which lays down other responsibilities for the Office, such as "improving understanding of the value of intellectual property" and "enhancing knowledge of best public and private sector practices to protect intellectual property rights"; and
- carrying out certain tasks in relation to orphan works (ie, copyright works the owner of which cannot be determined or contacted) as identified in Directive 2012/28/EU on certain permitted uses of orphan works. Discussion of this Directive and the Office's associated tasks are outside the scope of this book.

4. How the Office works: general principles followed in proceedings

In all proceedings, the Office follows general principles of Union law on such issues as non-discrimination and equal treatment (ensuring all parties are treated fairly) and sound administration (ensuring decisions are proportionate and reached in a fair, sensible and consistent manner).

This is backed up by the requirement that, where there is no specific procedural provision in the Regulation (or other acts adopted pursuant to it), the Office must take into account principles of procedural law generally recognised in the Member States.

Every decision made by the Office must be in writing and clearly indicate both the division/department and the specific officials responsible for the decision. In addition, all decisions must set out the facts and fundamental legal considerations on which they are based.

The facts and evidence which the Office can take into account in reaching a decision in any given case depend on the nature of the proceedings:

- in *ex parte* proceedings (ie, those involving only one party), including the examination of EUTM applications, the Office carries out its own research into the relevant facts; whereas
- in *inter partes* proceedings (ie, those involving two or more parties), the Office cannot carry out its own factual research. It must base its decisions on the facts, evidence and arguments submitted by the parties. For example, if the owner of a registration files no evidence in non-use revocation proceedings, the Office cannot carry out its own research to assess whether the mark is in use: it must decide that use has not been proven, even if it is aware that the mark is in fact in use. However, the Office always assesses the relevant legal issues in such proceedings, whether or not the parties file any arguments relating to those legal issues or request that an assessment be carried out.

Before reaching a decision, the Office must give all relevant parties the opportunity to comment on the reasons or evidence on which the decision is to be based: in short, the parties have a 'right to be heard'. This 'right to be heard' does not, however, mean that parties are entitled to a hearing. Although oral proceedings are possible in theory, in practice all proceedings before the Office are conducted in writing.

The Office only hears oral evidence, either by experts or by witnesses on behalf of the parties, in very exceptional cases (the writers are not aware of any such hearings having been held during the past 15 years). If there are to be oral proceedings, the Office stipulates the hearing date, the facts to be proved at the hearing and the witnesses who are to be summoned to appear. In addition, the Office may decide to commission and appoint an expert witness.

In every case, all facts, evidence and arguments to be relied upon must be presented in writing. There is no requirement that evidence be filed in the form of a sworn statement or affidavit, although a sworn statement may be considered to be of greater credibility than an unsworn one in some circumstances. Further discussion on evidence in proceedings is contained in Chapter 13.

5. Communication with the Office

All documents relating to EUTM proceedings, of whatever nature, must be filed directly at the Office. Before 23 March 2016, EUTM applications could be filed at the national IPOs of the Member States, but this is no longer possible.

Where a party has appointed a representative, the Office sends all notifications and correspondence to that representative. All such notifications and correspondence are treated as if they had been sent to the relevant party personally. In the same way, all correspondence sent to the Office by an appointed representative is treated as if it had been sent by the relevant party directly. It is, however, still possible for a party which has appointed a representative to send correspondence to the Office directly. This correspondence is accepted by the Office unless that party is unable to act before the Office in the relevant proceedings and is required to appoint a representative (as to which, see section 10 below for further information).

The Office has an obligation to communicate all necessary information to parties in proceedings. This includes notifying parties of decisions reached, deadlines set and other necessary information. In addition, where a loss of rights arises, the Office is obliged to notify the person losing those rights. An example of this is where a potential opponent fails to pay the opposition fee, so that the opposition is deemed as never having been filed (as to which, see Chapter 11).

5.1 Sending correspondence to the Office

There are several different ways in which correspondence can be sent to the Office.

- *Electronically* – all communications with the Office can now be sent electronically, using the Office's online User Area. This allows correspondence to be uploaded directly and is generally the quickest and most efficient way of submitting documents to the Office. In addition, new EUTM applications and oppositions can be filed electronically using the online forms available on the Office's website (https://euipo.europa.eu). No original signatures are necessary if electronic communication is used, though the name of the individual sending the communication should be used.

- *By fax* – it is not necessary to send the original document after a fax has been sent. The only exception to this is where a document in colour is transmitted, in which case the original must be sent to the Office within a month if colour is an important feature, such as where an EUTM application is filed by fax. The faxed document must be signed. If it is not, the Office sends a deficiency notice and sets a deadline by which a signed version of the document must be submitted. The Office does not acknowledge receipt of faxes, except where a new EUTM application is filed. Having said that, where the Office receives a transmission that is not fully legible, or appears to be incomplete, it contacts the sender and requests that the relevant document be sent again.
- *In hard copy* – correspondence can be sent by post, whether by mail or by courier, or can be delivered to the Office by hand. Again, any document submitted this way must be signed and the Office sets a deadline by which signed versions of unsigned documents must be received.

5.2 Communications sent by the Office

The Office has the right to choose how it communicates with parties to proceedings. The options available to it are as follows.

- *Electronic communication* – for this option to be available, the relevant party must have an electronic account with the Office and must consent to communications being sent via the online User Area. The Office sends notifications to parties by placing the relevant documents in their inboxes, which are accessible through the User Area. Wherever possible, the Office sends documents electronically, except where there are a large number of pages to be transmitted. Correspondence transmitted this way is deemed to have been received on the fifth day after having been placed in the relevant inbox, whether or not it has been read before then.
- *By fax* – for this option to be available, the relevant party must of course have indicated a fax number to the Office. Correspondence sent this way is deemed to have been received on the date the fax is received by the recipient's fax machine.
- *By post* – this option is used where very large documents need to be sent, or where it is necessary for the original correspondence to be sent (eg, where evidence is filed that cannot be copied, scanned or faxed). In addition, some very important documents (eg, decisions that are subject to a time limit for appeal) are always sent by post. If a party is based in the Union, or has appointed a representative, these important documents are sent by registered letter and a record of delivery kept; if not, correspondence is sent by normal post. Correspondence sent this way is deemed to have been received on the date the registered letter is recorded as delivered or, where sent by normal post, on the tenth day following the posting of the document (whether or not it has actually been received by that date).
- *By deposit in a post box* – for this option to be available, the intended recipient

must maintain a post box at the Office. Correspondence delivered this way is deemed to have been received on the fifth day after it is placed in the relevant post box (again, whether or not it has been removed from the post box by that date).

- *By hand* – for this option to be available, the intended recipient must be present in the Office, so this means of communication is very rarely used. Correspondence delivered this way is deemed to have been received on the date of actual delivery.
- *By public notification* – this option is used where it is not possible to contact the intended recipient using any of the above means. The normal situation in which this occurs is where post is returned to the Office undelivered. Where this happens, the Office publishes a public notification on its website. Correspondence notified this way is deemed to have been received one month after it has been posted.

6. Time limits set by the Office in proceedings

There are two different categories of time limit:

- those set by the Regulation (the duration of which is thus predetermined); and
- those set by the Office (which can vary in length).

Time limits must be indicated in terms of years, months, weeks or days, although all time limits set by the Office must be between one month and six months in length. In practice, most such time limits are two months in length. When calculating a time limit, time starts to run on the day following the day on which the relevant event occurred. This means that a one-month time limit set in a notification deemed delivered on 12 January expires on 12 February.

Time limits expire at midnight on the last day of the relevant period. It should, however, always be remembered that time limits are governed by the local time in Spain, where the Office is based, not the time in the location of the party fulfilling the deadline. This means that the effective time limit will vary, depending on the time zone in which a party or its representative is based. Continuing with the example of 12 February given above, the effective deadline in the Ireland would be 23.00 on 12 February, whereas in Latvia it would be 01.00 on 13 February.

Where a time limit is due to expire on a day on which the Office is not open, or is not receiving postal deliveries, that time limit is automatically extended until the next working day on which the Office is open. This means that no time limits expire on Saturdays, Sundays or Spanish public holidays. Before the start of a new calendar year, the President publishes a list of all days on which the Office will be closed during that year. The Office is usually closed for 18 days each year and there are a further two days on which it does not receive post.

Where there is a period of interruption in the delivery of physical mail or electronic communications to or from the Office, the President is able to extend all time limits for a defined period. In addition, if there is a natural disaster, strike or other exceptional occurrence in one or more Member States, the President may issue a decision extending all time limits for parties or representatives located in those Member States. For example, when restrictions were placed on withdrawals from Greek banks during the summer of 2015, all time limits which required parties based in Greece to make payments between 24 July and 10 August 2015 were extended.

7. Extensions of time limits

It is possible for some, but not all, time limits to be extended. The basic rule is that any request to extend a time limit must be filed before the original time limit expires. It is not possible to apply for retrospective extensions of time. If a time limit is not met, it may be possible for the party involved to seek continuation of proceedings (see Chapter 27) or *restitutio in integrum* (see Chapter 26), but no extension of time will be granted.

Except in certain specific circumstances, a first request for an extension of a time limit set by the Office is always granted. No explanation needs to be given and all that is required is a simple request to extend the time limit. The extension is given for up to the same time period as the original time limit. For example, the time limit given to respond to absolute grounds objections (see Chapter 7) is two months. This time limit can be extended for a further two months, or a shorter period if requested, but no longer extension will be granted.

The Office only grants second extensions of time limits in very exceptional circumstances. The party requesting such an extension must explain and justify the exceptional circumstances that have prevented it carrying out the necessary action within the original time limit. Examples of acceptable reasons include:

- circumstances beyond the control of the party (such as natural disasters);
- death or serious illness; and
- difficulties in concluding large-scale evidence gathering (in which case a detailed account of the work that has been done to date must be provided).

Where a request to extend a time limit is refused, the Office always gives the requesting party one day to meet the former's deadline. This means that, in practice, if the extension of time request is filed before the deadline, and is not processed immediately by the Office, some additional time can be obtained simply by filing the extension request.

8. Languages

Language is an important issue when dealing with the Office and there are clear rules as to which language(s) can, or must, be used in proceedings as set out below. If these rules are not followed, the Office issues a deficiency notice and the relevant application or request is refused if the language deficiency is not remedied.

Most, but not all, proceedings before the Office are carried out in one of the five Languages of the Office. In some circumstances, however, it is possible to use any of the 24 Languages of the Union in proceedings before the Office.

Where a translation of a document is required in proceedings before the Office, the translation should clearly identify the document of which it is a translation. Translations do not need to be certified, although the Office has the right to require a certified translation if it has concerns about the accuracy of the translation.

8.1 EUTM applications

An EUTM application can be filed in any of the 24 Languages of the Union. However, a second language must be indicated, which must always be one of the Languages of the Office. The choice of languages cannot be changed once the application has been filed.

(a) *The 'correspondence language'*

The correspondence language is important because the Office sends all correspondence relating to the application in that language (subject to a different language being chosen in opposition proceedings – see Chapter 11).

In addition, all correspondence sent to the Office relating to an application made prior to 1 October 2017 must be in the correspondence language. From that date, it will become possible to send applications or declarations relating to an EUTM application in either the first or second language of that application. For example, if an application is filed in English with Italian as the second language:

- a restriction of the specification filed in Italian would not be actioned if filed prior to 1 October 2017 (because English is the correspondence language for the application); but
- from 1 October 2017, a restriction filed in Italian would be actioned in the same way as if it had been filed in English.

The correspondence language is chosen as follows:

- if the first language of the application is one of the Languages of the Office, this is automatically the correspondence language; and
- if the first language is not one of the Languages of the Office, the applicant can designate the second language of the application (which will always be one of the Languages of the Office) as the correspondence language.

In theory, the Office is entitled to send correspondence in the second language of the application if the first language is not one of the Languages of the Office. In practice, however, the Office sends all correspondence in the first language of an application unless the applicant specifically consents to use of the second language.

(b) *The 'reference language'*

One of the languages of an EUTM application is also designated as the reference language. This is the language from which all translations are made, and is important because most parts of an EUTM application are translated into 23 of the 24 Languages of the Union (no translation takes place into Irish).

The reference language is chosen as follows:

- where the first language of the application is one of the Languages of the Office, that language is the reference language;
- where the first language of the application is not one of the Languages of the Office but a translation of the goods and services into the second language of the application has been provided by the applicant, the second language of the application is the reference language; and

- where the first language of the application is not one of the Languages of the Office and no translation of the goods and services has been provided, the first language of the application is the reference language.

Ancillary requests (eg, a request to record an assignment or licence) relating to an EUTM application can be filed in either of the languages of that application. The language used in an ancillary request is the language used by the Office in dealing with the request.

8.2 EUTM oppositions

An opposition must be filed in one of the Languages of the Office. If both of the languages of an EUTM application are Languages of the Office, the opponent can choose which of these to use. Otherwise, the second language must be used.

It is technically possible for an opponent to file the initial Notice of Opposition in a Language of the Office that is not one of the languages of the application being opposed. If this is done, a translation into an acceptable language (ie, a Language of the Office that is one of the languages of the opposed application) must be filed within one month of the expiry of the opposition period.

The language in which the Notice of Opposition is filed (or into which it is translated) is normally the language in which the proceedings are then conducted. It is, however, possible for the parties to agree to conduct the proceedings in another language, which must be one of the Languages of the Union.

For a more detailed discussion on the use of languages in opposition proceedings, see Chapter 11, section 7.

8.3 EUTM registrations

All requests and correspondence relating to an EUTM registration must be submitted in one of the Languages of the Office.

The only exceptions to this are invalidity and revocation actions, which follow the same rules as set out above for oppositions (ie, the language used should be one of the two languages of the attacked EUTM registration and a Language of the Office). However, as there is no deadline for filing such actions, if a translation is required the one-month deadline for filing the translation runs from the date on which the action was originally submitted.

For a more detailed discussion on the use of languages in cancellation proceedings, see Chapter 17 (revocation proceedings) and 18 (invalidity proceedings).

In addition, from 1 October 2017 the rules for applications and requests made in relation to registrations filed using a form provided by the Office will be relaxed. In those circumstances, it will be possible to use a form in any of the languages of the Union, provided that the form is completed using one of the Languages of the Office. For example, a request to record the assignment of an EUTM registration for which the languages are French and Spanish could be filed on the Czech-language version of the Office form, provided that the relevant details are added to the form in, for example, German (being one of the Languages of the Office).

9. Fees

A number of different fees must be paid in relation to EUTM applications and registrations and other proceedings before the Office. These are set out in Annex I to the Regulation and can be found on the Office's website. The current fee levels are referred to at various points in this book, as relevant.

'Fees' (which are paid to the Office) should be differentiated from 'costs' (which are awarded to the successful party in *inter partes* proceedings before the Office) and 'charges' (which are fixed by the President and relate to payments not set out in the Regulation, eg, mediation fees).

All fees need to be paid directly to the Office and must be paid in Euros. Any attempt to pay fees in a different currency will be rejected.

Three different methods of paying fees to the Office are possible:

- *Office current account* – most representatives have established current accounts with the Office. Provided that sufficient funds are maintained within an account, this is the most convenient way of paying fees to the Office. If this method is used, a response can be filed on the day a time limit expires without having to worry about whether payment will be received by the Office in time. In addition, a request to debit a current account does not need to specify the size of the fee to be paid; the Office always debits the correct amount, meaning that it is not possible for a fee to be accidentally underpaid (or indeed overpaid). Issues only arise where there are insufficient funds in a current account to meet the payments that are due. If this happens, the Office contacts the holder of the current account and gives it an opportunity to replenish the account and pay an administration fee of 20% in respect of the fees that could not be paid. If this is done, any deadline for receipt of that payment is treated as satisfied.
- *Credit card* – where EUTM applications and renewals are filed online, the relevant fees can be paid by credit card. Currently, the Office only accepts payments made by Visa, MasterCard and EuroCard. Credit card payments are taken immediately, so this method cannot be used to make deferred payments. Credit cards can only be used to pay for online applications and renewals. They cannot be used to pay any other fees due to the Office. The Office never refunds credit cards; where a refund is due, it is paid either into an Office current account or by bank transfer.
- *Bank transfer* – it is possible to pay all fees by bank transfer. The Office has specified the information that must be included in a bank transfer form to ensure the payment is allocated to the correct fee (eg, when paying an opposition fee, there should be a reference to the payment being for an opposition fee, as well as the number and owner of the EUTM application being opposed). If the Office cannot identify the fee for which a payment is intended, a deficiency notice is issued. If the necessary information is not provided, the payment is rejected and sent back.

If a fee must be paid within a particular time limit, the Office must receive the payment prior to the expiry of that time limit. The only exception to this is where the applicant provides clear evidence showing that instructions to pay the relevant fee were given to a bank or other institution:

- more than 10 days before the expiry of the time limit; or
- less than 10 days before the expiry of the time limit and, at the same time, the applicant pays a surcharge of 10% of the total fee due.

If either of these is proved, the fee is deemed to have been paid in time. If the evidence filed is not sufficient to convince the Office that late payment should be allowed, the time limit for payment is deemed to have been missed.

Fees are refunded in certain circumstances. In particular:

- fees paid after the expiry of a time limit are always refunded, except where late payments sent by bank transfer are deemed to have been made in time, as referred to above;
- it is possible to obtain a refund of the application fee if an EUTM application is withdrawn on the same day as payment of the fee is made to the Office (see Chapter 5); and
- it is possible to obtain a refund of the opposition fee if an opposition is withdrawn either on the same day as it is filed or following a restriction of the specification of the opposed application in the cooling-off period (see Chapter 14).

Further, if a fee is overpaid, the excess paid is refunded, unless such excess is insignificant in amount (currently fixed at €15).

10. Representation

A representative must be appointed by all parties involved in proceedings before the Office who are not domiciled in, do not have their principal place of business in, or do not have a real and effective industrial or commercial establishment in, the European Economic Area ('EEA'). This means, for example, that a French national living in Australia with no current business activity in the Union would need to appoint a representative. Conversely, an Australian company operating mainly in Australia but with a small business presence in France would not need to appoint a representative.

Parties who are domiciled, have their principal place of business, or have a real and effective industrial or commercial establishment in the EEA are not required to appoint a representative. In practice, however, most parties involved in proceedings do instruct representatives to act on their behalf.

There are four categories of people who are entitled to be representatives in proceedings before the Office.

10.1 Legal practitioners

Any individual practitioner must satisfy all the following criteria in order to be entitled to act before the Office:

- he must be qualified in a Member State of the EEA – the means of qualification and the title given to a qualified lawyer varies between the Member States;

- he must have his place of business within the EEA – this does not need to be in the Member State in which the legal practitioner is qualified. Further, a legal practitioner may have more than one place of business, provided he has at least one within the EEA; and
- he must be entitled to act as a representative in trade mark matters within the Member State in which he is qualified.

It should be noted there is no requirement for a legal practitioner to be a national of a Member State.

10.2 Professional Representatives

Individuals named in the list of Professional Representatives maintained by the Office are entitled to act as representatives. To be entered on this list, a person must meet the following criteria:

- he must be a national of a Member State of the EEA;
- he must have his place of business or employment within the EEA; and
- he must provide a certificate from the national IPO of a Member State of the EEA confirming his entitlement to represent third parties in trade mark matters before that IPO. The conditions that must be met before such a certificate is provided vary between the Member States, but generally involve the individual having a specific professional qualification (such as being a registered trade mark agent in Ireland) or having acted before the national IPO for at least five years.

It is possible for the President of the Office to grant an exemption from these criteria in certain circumstances (eg, where a non-EEA national has practised within the EEA for a long period). Individuals must apply for entry on the list of Professional Representatives and, once admitted, will remain on the list unless they ask to be removed from it or no longer qualify to be a Professional Representative (eg, because they have changed nationality).

10.3 Employees

Parties who are domiciled, have their principal place of business, or have a real and effective industrial or commercial establishment in the EEA may be represented by their employees (usually in-house lawyers). Technically, this is not 'representation' as such, so that no costs award will be given in favour of an employee who represents an employer (on the basis that there is no external cost for the employer to pay). In addition, an employee may act for legal entities that have an economic connection with his employer (eg, where they are within the same group of companies), even where the connected legal entity is not based in the Union.

10.4 Legal representatives pursuant to national law

This category applies where an individual is entitled to act on behalf of a natural or legal person. For example, a minor may be represented by his parents or by a legal custodian, provided that the latter is based within the EEA. In addition, a company may be represented by a liquidator once it has been declared insolvent.

Most legal practitioners and persons who are entitled to be Professional Representatives work in firms rather than individually. As a result, it is normal for a party to appoint an 'association of representatives' to act on its behalf rather than a specific individual. Where an association of representatives is appointed, the appointment extends to all representatives at the relevant firm from time to time, so that leavers will no longer be entitled to act and joiners will automatically be entitled to act. It should be noted that only persons who are entitled to be representatives can act on behalf of the association of representatives.

As noted previously, the appointment of a representative is mandatory for parties from outside the EEA. Where this rule is not complied with, the party concerned is given an opportunity by the Office to remedy this by appointing a representative. If it fails to do so, the application or request filed by that party is refused (so, for example, an opposition filed by a party without the proper representation will automatically be rejected – see Chapter 11).

There is no requirement to provide a power of attorney or other written authorisation when appointing a representative. Instead, any representative who contacts the Office on behalf of a party is deemed to have been authorised to do so. Where this involves the replacement of an existing representative, the Office asks the new representative to confirm his appointment. It is entitled to ask a representative to provide written proof of his authorisation (and other parties involved in *inter partes* proceedings can also request that this be done). This happens very rarely, however.

Representation can be withdrawn at any time. This can be done by:

- the represented party contacting the Office;
- a new representative indicating to the Office that he is now instructed to act; or
- the representative specifically withdrawing his representation.

If a representative dies or becomes legally incapacitated, all proceedings before the Office for which he is responsible are interrupted. If a new representative is not appointed within three months, the Office resumes the proceedings and deals directly with the unrepresented party. If, however, it is mandatory for that party to appoint a representative, the Office requires it to do so, failing which the application or request filed by that party is refused.

11. Correction of errors made by the Office

It is possible for the Office to correct mistakes that it makes; the way this is done depends on the circumstances and on the effect of the mistake.

Procedural errors that lead to an incorrect entry being made in the Register or an incorrect decision being published are very serious. In these circumstances, the relevant entry is cancelled or the relevant decision revoked, subject to the following:

- the error must be noticed within six months (for errors made prior to 1 October 2017) or one year (for errors made on or after 1 October 2017) of the date of the error. If the error is noticed after this time period, it is not possible for the entry to be cancelled or the decision to be revoked;

- all parties to the relevant proceedings must be given an opportunity to comment on the proposed cancellation or revocation of the entry or decision. The only exception to this is where the cancellation or revocation has been requested by the sole party to proceedings. If a party to proceedings objects to the proposed cancellation or revocation, the operating division concerned makes a decision as to whether cancellation or revocation should occur; and
- prior to 1 October 2017, it is not possible to revoke a decision that is the subject of an ongoing appeal. On or after 1 October 2017, however, it will be possible for the Office to revoke decisions that have been appealed. If that happens, the appeal will become devoid of purpose and the appeal fee will be refunded.

Linguistic errors, errors of transcription or obvious mistakes in decisions that do not affect the outcome of the decision are not as serious as those considered above. As a result, it is easier and simpler to correct them and different considerations apply:

- there is no time limit for the correction of these types of error;
- the correction of the error does not affect the date of the original decision; and
- any deadlines (including appeal deadlines) running from the decision are not extended or reopened.

Mistakes in notifications other than decisions are very easy to correct. In these circumstances, the Office simply sends a replacement notification cancelling the original notification containing the error.

Mistakes on the Register, or when an application is published, that do not affect the validity of the Register entry are dealt with in different ways, depending on the nature of the mistake:

- if a mistake is made that affects the mark when an application is published for opposition purposes (eg, where a word mark is spelt incorrectly), the application is republished (and a new opposition period begins);
- if a mistake is made in the specification when an application is published for opposition purposes and correcting that mistake expands the goods and/or services published originally (eg, where a class is omitted in error), the application is republished (and a new opposition period begins); and
- in all other circumstances, the mistake is corrected and the correction is published but no further actions are taken (in particular, if a mistake is corrected after an application has been published, the application will not be republished).

Further reference

Regulation – Articles 75-80, 82a, 83, 92, 93, 115-144c

Implementing Regulation – Rules 27, 52-54, 61-72, 75-82, 95-96

Regulation (EU) No 386/2012 on entrusting the Office with tasks related to the enforcement of intellectual property rights, including the assembling of public and

private-sector representatives as a European Observatory on Infringements of Intellectual Property Rights
Directive 2012/28/EU on certain permitted uses of orphan works
Office Guidelines – Part A, Sections 1-7
TMDN website – https://www.tmdn.org
Observatory website – https://oami.europa.eu/ohimportal/en/web/observatory

Chapter 3: Before an application is filed

1. Introduction

There are many things a potential applicant should consider before filing an EUTM application. This chapter provides a high level overview of the key issues, which can be summarised very simplistically under two headings:

- *Use* – is the mark available for use in the Union? The issue here is whether using the mark in the Member State(s) of interest will infringe existing rights (which may be either national or Union-wide rights); and
- *Registration* – is the mark free for registration in the Union? This involves consideration of both whether the mark is inherently capable of protection and whether there are earlier rights that could be used to prevent registration of the mark (including, but not limited to, earlier rights that could prevent use of the mark). It is also necessary to consider the best way to obtain protection for the mark.

2. Why are these issues important?

Failure to consider and investigate properly whether a mark is available for use before use is started or an application is filed can lead to the potential applicant being sued. If the use of the mark does infringe existing rights, the potential applicant is likely to be prevented from using the mark. This will require a new mark to be chosen, which could be expensive and embarrassing. The earlier the potential applicant finds out whether a mark is available for use, the less wasted time, effort and expense there will be.

It is also worth finding out whether a mark is capable of registration before a decision is taken to use it, in terms of both whether the mark is inherently capable of protection and whether there are existing rights that could block its registration. This can prevent both application fees being wasted and time and money being spent on disputes (eg, oppositions) that could otherwise have been avoided.

If a mark is not capable of registration because of its inherent nature, an EUTM application filed for that mark will almost certainly be rejected. It is very likely that the potential applicant will be able to use the mark, on the basis that nobody else will have been able to obtain rights in it either (subject to the possibility of proving acquired distinctiveness, as discussed in Chapter 8). However, the potential applicant is unlikely to be able to prevent other traders using the mark, which would make it more difficult to protect its investment in the mark and protect its business. For discussion of the reasons why a mark may not be inherently capable of protection, see Chapter 7.

If a mark conflicts with earlier existing rights, those earlier rights could be used to prevent its registration. It is likely that the same earlier rights could be used as the basis of both an infringement action and an opposition. There are, however, circumstances in which the owner of an earlier right will decide not to bring an infringement action but will file an opposition. For example, the owner of an earlier right and an EUTM applicant may have different commercial interests, so that there is no overlap between them in the marketplace, but there is an overlap between the earlier rights and the EUTM application. Further, the costs of opposition proceedings (and EUTM opposition proceedings in particular) are a lot lower than the costs of an infringement action in most Member States, so that while the owner of an earlier right is not concerned enough about the potential applicant's use to justify the costs of an infringement action, it may decide to file an opposition to prevent the potential applicant obtaining a conflicting registered right. This is sometimes referred to as 'keeping the register clear'. In addition, the owner of earlier rights could bring an opposition action first and, if successful, then decide to bring an infringement action.

It is not a good idea simply to file an EUTM application and assume any potential infringement problems can be identified and sorted out as part of the application process. There are a number of reasons for this:

- *The Office does not examine EUTM applications on relative rights grounds or cite earlier rights as bars to registration.* In fact, earlier rights in most Member States are not identified or notified to the applicant as part of the EUTM application process. It is possible for an applicant to obtain certain search reports as part of the EUTM application process, but these cannot be relied on to discover potential infringement problems (for more information on these search reports, see Chapter 4).
- *Owning an EUTM registration is not a defence to an infringement action.* This means that owning an EUTM registration does not give the owner any positive right to use the mark that has been registered. It is perfectly possible for an EUTM applicant to obtain a registration for a mark that, if used, would infringe existing EUTM and/or national trade mark rights.
- *There is no obligation to oppose.* If the owner of an earlier right fails to oppose an EUTM application, for whatever reason, this does not prevent it relying on that earlier right to prevent use of the mark that has been registered and/or cancel the registration of the mark through invalidity proceedings (as discussed in Chapter 18).
- *There is no point at which an EUTM registration becomes 'incontestable'.* EUTM registrations can be cancelled many years after they have been registered, subject to the rules on acquiescence (discussed in Chapter 18), which only apply once a mark has been registered for five years.
- *Owning a trade mark registration giving rights in one Member State does not give any right to use the mark in question on a Union-wide basis.* For example, a potential EUTM applicant who owns a national registration in Denmark may be able to prevent anyone else obtaining an EUTM registration for that mark on the basis of its Danish rights. However, it will not necessarily be able to use (or register) the mark outside of Denmark: owners of national registrations in other Member States could prevent the use (and registration)

of the mark in their Member States – and could also use those rights to oppose an EUTM application.

- *Unregistered rights also need to be considered.* The use of the mark chosen by a potential applicant could be prevented by the owners of unregistered rights in the Union, both Union-wide and in individual Member States.

Taking into account all of the above, it is always sensible to carry out clearance searches before a potential applicant uses or applies to register a mark. This allows the potential applicant to try to ensure that the mark can be used in the Union without fear of an infringement action.

As part of, or alongside, clearance searches, consideration should also be given to whether the mark is capable of protection in the Union, as referred to above.

3. What needs to be searched and protected?

Before searches are carried out, or applications filed, the potential applicant needs to decide on the trade mark(s) it is going to use and what they are going to be used for.

Even if the chosen trade mark is a word, thought should be given to the trading style that is to be adopted. If the word is to be used alone, searching for that word will usually be sufficient. In most cases, however, the form of use will include some stylisation, logo element or product 'get-up'. Depending on the nature of the intended trading style, it could be as important, if not more so, for those elements to be searched as it is for searches to be carried out for the word mark.

When looking at protection, different considerations apply. Infringement rights are stronger when an infringer uses the exact mark that has been registered, rather than something similar (see Chapter 22). If a word is used with a logo element, it may therefore be better to register the word and logo elements separately rather than together. This should be considered before any applications are filed.

The other thing that needs to be decided on before searches are carried out is the goods and/or services for which the mark is going to be used. In addition, insofar as is possible, the potential applicant should consider whether the mark could be used for different goods and/or services in the future. Searches should look beyond the exact goods and/or services of interest, as infringement claims can be based on registrations covering goods and/or services that are similar (and in some cases completely different) to the goods and/or services of interest. For further discussion of infringement, see chapters 21-23.

When deciding on the protection to apply for, it should be remembered that there is no need for an EUTM applicant to have an 'intention to use' the mark applied for. As a result, it can often be a good idea to include a wider range of goods and/or services in an EUTM application than those for which the mark is definitely going to be used. For further discussion, see Chapter 6.

4. Searches

Detailed consideration of search options and the factors to consider in developing search strategies is outside the scope of this book. However, these are important matters that should be addressed before using or registering a trade mark.

Searching in the Union is not a simple exercise and can be very expensive. This is due in part to the fact that searching the Register is simply not enough. In addition to the Register, 26 national registers are maintained by the IPOs of the Member States (although there are currently 28 Member States, there are only 26 national registers as a single register covers the three Benelux countries). The use of a mark in any given Member State can be prevented on the basis of earlier EUTM rights, earlier national rights in that Member State, or both; this means that both the Register and the national registers of the Member States in which use is to take place need to be checked.

Further, searching the Register and the 26 national trade mark registers is not really enough. It is also necessary to consider other registers and databases containing information as to rights that can be used to prevent the use and/or registration of marks within the Union. These include the following:

- *Designs registers* – design registrations can prevent the use and continued registration of a trade mark. To complicate matters further, there are 26 different national design registers to consider in addition to the RCD register.
- *Company name and business name registers* – in some countries, a company name or business name can be used to prevent the use and/or registration of a trade mark, which means they can be used to prevent EUTM applications going through to registration in some circumstances.
- *Registers and databases relevant for particular types of mark* – eg, if the mark contains a flag or emblem, it is necessary to consider whether the use and/or registration of that flag or emblem can be prevented under the Paris Convention for the Protection of Industrial Property (the 'Paris Convention') (see Chapter 7).
- *Registers and databases relevant for particular types of goods and/or services* – eg, if an application covers food products, it is necessary to consider whether use and/or registration could be prevented on the basis that the mark contains a protected designation of origin ('PDO'), protected geographical indication ('PGI') or traditional speciality guaranteed ('TSG') (see Chapter 7).

It is also necessary to consider the unregistered trade mark rights that exist. The rights given to unregistered trade marks vary enormously between Member States, but it is possible for an infringement claim to be based on unregistered rights in every Member State. While most unregistered trade mark rights will give protection in one Member State or possibly a few Member States, it is possible for a very well-known unregistered mark to have Union-wide protection. For further discussion of unregistered rights, see Chapter 12.

Given the number of different registers and rights that can be relevant, it is impossible to suggest a single search strategy that is suitable for all, or indeed most, cases. The types of search that should be carried out vary, depending on the circumstances, and multiple options are always available, not least when deciding on which Member States to search in and how detailed the searches should be. For example, if a potential applicant has no interest in, or is contractually prevented from trading in, a particular Member State, the national rights that exist in that Member State will not affect the potential applicant's intended use. Those national rights could, however, still be used to prevent an EUTM registration being obtained, so it would be better to be aware of them in advance of filing an EUTM application.

5. What type of protection is needed?

It is possible to protect three different types of mark under the EUTM system: trade marks, collective marks and certification marks. The basic and fundamental differences between these types of mark can be briefly summarised as follows.

- *Trade marks* – these indicate the trade origin of goods and/or services. The vast majority of marks in use (and over 99% of Union-wide registrations filed before the Office) fall into this category. This is the type of trade mark referred to as an EUTM throughout this book.
- *Collective marks* – these indicate that goods and/or services come from a member of a particular organisation, rather than from the trade mark owner itself. For further information on registering EU collective marks, see Chapter 28.
- *Certification marks* – these indicate that goods and/or services possess certain characteristics. Such marks do not indicate the trade origin of the goods or services. For further information on registering EU certification marks, see Chapter 29. It should be noted that it will only be possible to register EU certification marks from 1 October 2017.

It is very important that an application should cover the right type of mark. If a mistake is made, this can only be corrected in limited circumstances and a new application is likely to be necessary.

6. The advantages of EUTM registrations over national marks

The term 'EUTM' is used in this section for simplicity. In most cases, however, the same considerations apply for EU collective marks and EU certification marks as for EUTM registrations.

Once a decision has been taken to register a mark in the Union, the next thing to consider is whether or not to file an EUTM application. There are many potential benefits of owning an EUTM registration as opposed to separate national registrations in individual Member States. These include the following:

- *Union-wide rights and remedies* – The unitary nature of an EUTM registration means that Union-wide remedies can be obtained in one infringement action. If relying on national rights, separate proceedings have to be brought in each Member State in which remedies are sought (in this regard, see Chapter 21).
- *Cost* – The cost of obtaining and renewing an EUTM registration is substantially less than the costs involved in applying for and renewing individual national registrations in Member States. As a rough guide, obtaining protection in two or more Member States is (assuming no objections or oppositions) generally more expensive than obtaining an EUTM registration. The same applies where registrations are renewed. Further, if any changes need to be recorded, the cost of amending an EUTM

registration is, of course, substantially less than amending multiple national registrations.

- *Administration* – With just one registration to maintain, rather than up to 26 separate national registrations, using the EUTM system can lead to substantial administrative savings. For example, if an assignment needs to be recorded, this can be done through a request to the Office rather than having to deal with the 26 different national IPOs. Quite apart from costs savings, this reduces the administrative burden substantially.
- *Seniority* – The possibility of claiming seniority means that existing national registrations do not necessarily have to be maintained once EUTM protection has been obtained. This allows for further cost and administrative savings to be made and a brand owner's rights in the Union to be streamlined and simplified (see Chapter 24).
- *Resisting non-use actions* – Use in just one Member State can be enough to maintain an EUTM registration and defeat a non-use revocation action (as to which, see Chapter 17). This means that an EUTM registration can result in registered rights being maintained in Member States in which the trade mark has never been used. Conversely, a national registration can only be maintained by proving use in the Member State in which the mark is registered.
- *Automatic extension on enlargement of the Union* – As more countries join the Union, an EUTM registration automatically gives rights in the new Member States, subject to transitional rules that protect the existing rights of brand owners within those Member States (see Chapter 1). This automatic extension does not require any action from EUTM owners or the payment of any further fees.
- *Conversion* – If there is a problem in obtaining or maintaining an EUTM registration, the possibility of conversion allows for the filing date of the EUTM application to be maintained for the converted national applications (see Chapter 25).

7. When should an EUTM application not be filed?

The advantages listed in section 6 above do not mean that filing an EUTM application will always be the most appropriate course of action. There are circumstances in which it may not be prudent to file an EUTM application. These include the following:

- *When protection is only required in one Member State* – if a potential applicant is only going to use a mark in one Member State, and there is no real prospect of it trading outside that Member State, it often makes sense to file a national application. For example, a government agency that is only permitted to carry out activities in the Member State in which it is established should consider obtaining national rather than Union-wide protection. This would save costs and also prevent any potential problems with non-use (see Chapter 17).
- *Where there is a serious problem with the mark in one or more Member States* – in

these circumstances, it may not be possible to obtain an EUTM registration. For example, if the mark is descriptive in one of the languages of the Union, that would be enough to prevent an EUTM registration being obtained. Further, if a potential applicant is aware that its biggest competitor owns rights in the mark in a particular Member State, those rights could be used to prevent an EUTM registration being obtained. When faced with this situation, a potential applicant should consider alternative filing strategies, though it may still be worth filing an EUTM application anyway in some cases.

- *Where protection is also required in countries outside the Union* – in these circumstances, it is worth considering the IR system, especially if the potential applicant already has a registration for the mark. It is possible to designate the Union within an IR, which gives equivalent protection to a stand-alone EUTM application (see Chapter 32). Consideration should also be given to filing an EUTM application and then filing an IR on the basis of the EUTM application (see Chapter 31).

Chapter 4: Overview of the EUTM application process

1. Introduction

This chapter contains an overview of the EUTM application process and the options available to an applicant when filing an EUTM application.

The next few chapters discuss the key issues arising in the application process:

- the basic requirements for filing and information that must be contained in EUTM applications are considered in Chapter 5;
- the classification of goods and services in EUTM applications is considered in Chapter 6;
- the objections that may be raised against EUTM applications are considered in Chapter 7;
- the options for overcoming objections raised against EUTM applications are considered in Chapter 8;
- the other stages in the EUTM application process are considered in Chapter 9; and
- oppositions filed against EUTM applications are considered in chapters 10–14.

2. Overview of the EUTM application process

The EUTM application process can be broken down into four basic stages: filing, examination, opposition and registration. What happens during each of these stages is summarised in the flowchart below and discussed in the paragraphs that follow.

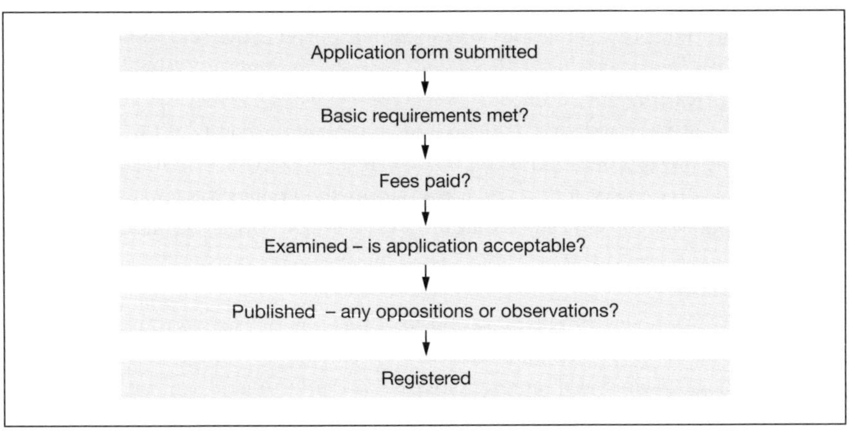

3. Filing an EUTM application

All EUTM applications are filed directly with the Office. Prior to 23 March 2016, an application could be filed at the national IPO of a Member State for onward transmission to the Office, but this is no longer possible.

There are three different ways in which an EUTM application can be filed:

- *electronically, via the Office's website* – applications filed electronically use one of the following systems:
  - *the Fast Track system*, which allows an application to be filed following a simple five-stage process if all the goods and/or services in the application are in the Office's approved list (see Chapter 6); or
  - *the normal e-filing system*, which is used if the application covers goods and/or services not in the Office's approved list (in which case the Fast Track system cannot be used);
- *by fax* – a hard copy must follow if there is detail in the trade mark (eg, colour) that will not be clear when sent by fax; or
- *on paper* – either by mail or by depositing the application form at the reception desk of the Office.

The vast majority of EUTM applications are filed electronically. This is usually the best way to file an application, not least because the fees are lower for electronic applications than they are for applications filed by fax or on paper.

Although it is not mandatory to use the official application form issued by the Office, it is highly advisable to do so. The form sets out all the information to be provided to enable an application to be validly filed and acts as a checklist to ensure nothing is missed.

The information that must be contained in an EUTM application is considered in chapters 5 (basic requirements and formalities) and 6 (classification).

4. Examination

Once an EUTM application has been filed, the Office checks to ensure the necessary information has been provided (as set out in Chapter 5). If it has, a filing date is awarded. The application is then examined by the Office. This stage of the application process involves consideration of the issues set out below.

4.1 Classification

If the Fast Track system is used, no examination of the goods and/or services is necessary, as only pre-approved terms can be used. If the Fast Track system is not used, the Office reviews the goods and/or services listed in the application to ensure the terms used comply with the Office's classification requirements (as set out in Chapter 6).

4.2 Formalities

The Office reviews the application to ensure the rules governing basic formalities in relation to issues that do not affect the award of a filing date (such as signature, languages, owner and representative details, priority and seniority claims) have been followed. These issues are considered in Chapter 5.

4.3 Absolute grounds examination

The Office reviews the application and assesses whether the mark applied for is inherently capable of registration in relation to the goods and/or services listed in the application. This process, and the reasons why a mark may not be capable of registration, are considered in Chapter 7. It should be noted that no examination takes place as to whether there is any conflict with earlier existing rights.

4.4 Acceptance and publication

If the application meets the necessary conditions for registration, it is accepted and published for opposition purposes. The Office informs the applicant that the application is accepted prior to publication taking place. Post-acceptance issues are considered in Chapter 9.

5. Other steps in the application process

There are three additional actions that run alongside the examination process, as set out below.

5.1 Translation

The Office prepares a translation of the information in the EUTM application, to enable details of the application to be published in all the official languages of the Union (although, at the time of writing, EUTM applications are only translated into 23 of the 24 official languages – no translation into Irish is prepared). The translation is prepared from the reference language of the application (for further information on the reference language see Chapter 2, at section 8.1(b)).

5.2 EUTM search

The Office carries out a search of the Register to identify existing EUTM registrations and applications that could conflict with the current application (that is, rights the Office believes could form the basis of an opposition). This search is carried out for information purposes only and the Office cannot raise an objection on the basis of rights identified by the search. The results of the search are sent to:

- *the applicant* – but only if it requests this at the time the EUTM application is filed. If this request is made, the results of the search are sent to the applicant before the EUTM application is published. Prior to 23 March 2016, the Office sent the results of its search report to the applicant automatically, but this now needs to be specifically requested at the time the application is filed; and
- *the owners of any earlier rights identified in the search* – this happens whether or not the applicant requests a copy of the search results. Details of the EUTM application are sent to the owners of earlier rights once it has been published. It is possible for the owners of EUTM applications and registrations to opt out of receiving notifications relating to their rights if they do not want to receive them.

5.3 National searches

It is also possible for an applicant to request that searches of the national registers of

Member States be carried out. Only seven Member States currently participate in this system (the Czech Republic, Denmark, Greece, Hungary, Lithuania, Romania and Slovakia). If a request for national searches is made, the Office contacts the national IPOs of the participating Member States and requests that searches be carried out. The results of the searches are forwarded to the Office and sent to the applicant along with the EUTM search results (if these have been requested). A fee is payable for the receipt of national search reports, currently €84 (€12 per participating Member State). It is not possible to pick and choose which Member States provide national search reports; if this option is chosen, a search report is provided by all seven participating Member States. Given the limited number of such Member States, this option is of limited practical benefit, especially given the additional fees payable.

6. Oppositions and observations

Once an EUTM application has been published, it remains open to opposition for three months. This period is normally referred to as the 'opposition period. During this period, any third party who believes the application should not be allowed to proceed to registration may raise an objection by filing an opposition and/or observations.

If a third party believes it owns an earlier right with which the application conflicts, it may file an opposition against that application on the basis of its earlier right. The opposition process is considered in detail in chapters 10-14.

Objections relating to earlier conflicting rights owned by third parties are often referred to as 'relative grounds' objections. It is not possible to oppose an application on the basis of 'absolute grounds' (so that an opponent cannot argue that the mark is not inherently capable of registration).

If a third party believes the mark applied for is not inherently capable of registration, it may file third party observations, which are considered in Chapter 9. A third party can also file observations if it believes the applicant is not capable of owning an EUTM registration (on the basis that it is not a natural or legal person).

7. Registration

If no oppositions or observations are filed, or if the Office believes the objections raised do not mean the application should be refused, the application proceeds to registration.

The registration of the application is published and an electronic certificate of registration is issued. This stage of the process is considered in Chapter 9.

8. Appeals

It is possible to file an appeal against decisions taken at most stages of the application process. The issues that can be appealed are dealt with in the chapters relating to the corresponding stages of the application process as indicated above. The appeals process, and how appeals are dealt with, are considered in detail in chapters 19-20.

9. Issues that are not considered in the application process

There are a number of issues which are not considered by the Office as part of the application process that are worth mentioning briefly.

9.1 Intention to use

It is not necessary for an EUTM applicant to have an intention to use the mark applied for in relation to the goods and/or services covered by its application. As a result, EUTM applications and registrations can never be attacked on this ground. This is in contrast to many national registration systems, including some within the Union.

9.2 Bad faith

An EUTM application cannot be refused registration on the basis that it was filed in bad faith. As a result, an application can never be attacked on this ground. Objections relating to bad faith can, however, be raised in invalidity proceedings against EUTM registrations (as discussed in Chapter 18).

9.3 Absolute grounds objections raised in oppositions

As noted in section 6 above, it is not possible to oppose an application on the basis that the mark for which protection is sought is not inherently capable of registration. A third party wishing to object to an application on this basis must either file observations or wait until the trade mark is registered and raise this issue in invalidity proceedings.

9.4 Relative grounds objections raised in observations

The Office cannot refuse an application on the basis that it conflicts with an earlier right referred to in observations. A third party wishing to object to an application on this basis must file an opposition.

10. Timeline – how long does all this take?

The length of time between filing an EUTM application and registration being granted varies greatly, depending on the circumstances. Relevant factors include whether the application is filed using the Fast Track system, whether objections are raised during examination and whether oppositions are filed against the application. In addition, if application fees are not paid at the time of filing (they can be deferred for up to one month), the process will take longer as the Office does not examine the application until the relevant fees have been paid.

The Office aims to publish applications between eight and eleven weeks after payment of the application fees, after which there is a fixed opposition period of three months before the mark can be registered. If there are no objections or oppositions, an EUTM application should therefore progress to registration somewhere between five and six months from the date when the application fees have been paid. In practice, however, EUTM applications are often processed more quickly than this and it is common for the application process to be completed, and registration granted, in around four months.

For Fast Track applications, the Office aims for publication to take place four or five weeks after payment of the application fees. This means that the application process should normally be completed, and registration granted, within four months. In practice, Fast Track applications are often completed in around three and a half months if there are no objections or oppositions.

If an objection is raised or an opposition is filed against an EUTM application, the additional time taken for the application process to be completed depends on the nature of the objections and oppositions and how the applicant decides to deal with them. A minor specification objection that can be overcome very quickly may only add a couple of weeks to the overall process. If, however, an opposition is filed and no settlement is possible, it can take several years for the application process to be completed, especially if appeals are filed.

Further reference

The Office's online summary of the registration process – https://oami.europa.eu/ohimportal/en/registration-process

Details of the Fast Track process – https://oami.europa.eu/ohimportal/en/fast-track-conditions

Chapter 5: Basic requirements and formalities

1. Introduction

This chapter discusses the information that needs to be provided when filing an EUTM application and what happens if any of it is missing. It does not consider issues relating to whether the mark applied for is capable of registration (this is discussed in Chapter 7) or whether the description of the goods and/or services contained in an EUTM application is acceptable (this is discussed in Chapter 6).

2. What information must an EUTM application contain?

Every EUTM application must contain certain information, some of which must be provided before the application is given a filing date. The filing date is the date from which all rights in the EUTM application run (subject to any priority and/or seniority claims). As a result, it is prudent to ensure that the earliest possible filing date is obtained.

In addition, there is information which needs to be provided in order for an application to proceed, though it does not need to be provided for a filing date to be awarded.

In order to obtain a filing date, an EUTM application must contain the following:

- a request for registration;
- information identifying the applicant;
- a list of the goods and/or services for which registration is requested; and
- a representation of the mark to be protected.

Each of these requirements is discussed in turn in the following sections.

If all of this information is included with the application, the filing date awarded will be the date the application was received by the Office. If an application is submitted that does not include some of this information, the Office issues a deficiency notice. If the missing information is provided within two months of the deficiency notice, the filing date awarded will be that on which the Office received the missing information. If the missing information is not provided by the deadline set, the application is deemed never to have been filed and any fees paid are refunded.

In addition to the basic requirements set out above, application fees must be paid within one month of the application being submitted. If this is not done, the filing date is lost. The only exception to this is where the application fees are paid late and the applicant provides evidence that instructions were given to a bank (or other financial institution) to pay them:

- more than 10 days before the expiry of the one-month period after the application was submitted; or
- within the last 10 days of that one-month period and, at the same time, the applicant pays a surcharge of 10% of the total fee due.

If either of these is proved, the filing date is maintained.

It should be noted that the filing date is maintained if the basic application fee is paid at the time of submitting the application or within one month of that date, even if the fees due for additional classes are not paid. What happens in these circumstances is discussed in more detail in section 8 of this chapter.

3. Request for registration

To be validly filed, an EUTM application must contain a clear request for registration. How to achieve this depends on the form and method of the application:

- *applications filed electronically using the Office's e-filing system* – satisfactory completion and transmission of the electronic form is sufficient;
- *applications filed on paper using the form issued by the Office* – the form must be signed by the applicant or its validly appointed representative; or
- *applications filed on paper that do not use the Office's form* – the request for registration must be clear and unequivocal. It must be signed by the applicant or its validly appointed representative.

The application form provided by the Office is very clear and there seems no sensible reason for not using it, especially as it is available in 23 of the 24 Languages of the Union (it is not available in Irish). Using the form should allow an applicant to ensure that nothing is missed when an application is submitted.

If the Office receives an unsigned paper form, or is in any doubt about whether registration is being requested, a deficiency notice is issued.

4. Identification of the applicant

There is no restriction on who may file an EUTM application (or own an EUTM registration), other than the requirement that the applicant must be a natural person (ie, an individual) or a legal person (including authorities established under public law) capable of holding property. The important thing is that the applicant is clearly identified in the application form.

All parties to proceedings before the Office, including both the owners of EUTM applications and registrations, and parties in opposition or cancellation proceedings, are given an ID number by the Office. If an applicant has an ID number, indicating its name and ID number when filing an application is sufficient identification.

Where no ID number is given, the Office requires an applicant to provide the following pieces of information for a filing date to be awarded:

- *name* – legal entities must state their name in full (although legal forms can be shortened in accordance with custom, for example 'Limited Company' becoming 'Ltd') and individuals must indicate both their family name and given name(s);

- *address* – this does not have to be the registered office address for legal entities and there is no restriction on the type of address that may be used (so that post office box numbers and 'care of' addresses are acceptable). This is the address to which any hard copy correspondence will be sent if no representative is appointed; and
- *nationality (individuals) or place of incorporation, establishment or domicile (legal persons).*

It is possible for EUTM applications (and registrations) to be co-owned by two or more individuals and/or legal persons. When an EUTM application is filed in joint names, each of the applicants must be properly identified as set out above. If more than one address is included in an application, the Office uses the first address listed (unless a different address is specifically designated as the one to be used).

5. Goods and services

An EUTM application is only awarded a filing date if the goods and/or services contained in the application are clearly identified.

However, goods and/or services do not have to be correctly classified for a filing date to be obtained. In addition, the inclusion of terms that are not deemed acceptable for classification purposes does not prevent a filing date being awarded. For a more detailed discussion of classification issues, see Chapter 6.

6. Representation of the mark

An acceptable representation of the mark applied for must be provided to obtain a filing date. For word marks (see section 7.1), this is not normally an issue. It can, however, be more difficult for figurative and more complicated marks (see sections 7.2-7.6).

This section looks only at whether a representation is sufficient for the Office to award a filing date. It does not consider whether the representation filed is acceptable for the purposes of registration, which is dealt with in Chapter 7.

The format of the representation required depends on the type of mark as well as on how the application is filed:

- *applications filed electronically* – the rules at the time of writing require the representation of the mark to be in JPEG format (unless it is a simple word mark or a sound mark) and less than 2MB in size. It is possible to include an image size of up to 2385 × 2010 pixels, although all images are automatically scaled to 250 × 250 pixels by the e-filing system; and
- *applications not filed electronically* – the representation must be filed on a sheet of paper that is no larger than A4 size (29.7 × 21cm). The representation itself must be no larger than 26.2 × 17cm, with a margin of 2.5cm on the left-hand side of the sheet. To ensure there is no uncertainty as to which way the mark appears, the Implementing Regulation recommends that the word 'top' is added to the reproduction of the mark.

A filing date will be awarded even if the representation of the mark provided is not clear enough for the Office to use. In these circumstances, the Office requests that a clearer representation be filed. The new representation will not be accepted if it is seen as an amendment to the mark (which in practice means that the original representation must be clear enough for all aspects of the mark to be visible). Where an application is filed electronically, it is unlikely that a clearer representation will be needed, or indeed allowed, as an electronic application cannot be submitted if the representation provided is not of satisfactory quality.

7. Types of mark

In addition to filing a representation of the mark, the Office requires that the 'type' of mark being applied for be indicated. Applicants must select one of six basic categories, the last of which is designated 'other', as there is no limit on the types of mark that can be applied for. The only requirement is that the mark must be represented in an acceptable way. What is seen as an acceptable representation for the purposes of obtaining a filing date varies, depending upon the type of mark applied for. The choices an applicant has are considered below.

7.1 Word marks

This term covers any combination of letters, words, numbers, keyboard symbols (such as '@' and '%') and punctuation marks (such as '!' and '&'). Word marks must be typewritten in a standard font presented on one line without any stylisation. A word mark may be written in any of the Languages of the Union. Words in other languages (even those widely understood in the Union, such as Mandarin (Putonghua)) are considered to be figurative marks (see section 7.2).

7.2 Figurative marks

This term covers logos and other marks containing graphical and figurative elements, both standing alone and in combination with text. Where an application is filed electronically, it is necessary to choose between two sub-categories of figurative mark: 'figurative mark' or 'figurative mark containing word elements'.

The figurative mark type also covers:

- marks that consist of or contain verbal elements presented in colour (or a combination of colours);
- words, letters and characters in non-Union alphabets;
- signs that cannot be reproduced on a keyboard; and
- text in non-standard fonts (eg, signatures).

In short, any mark containing a stylised element is categorised as a figurative mark.

7.3 Three-dimensional marks

This term covers all three-dimensional shapes, including containers, packaging and shapes of products. This is how all shapes are categorised, whether the mark applied for is a shape *per se* or a shape combined with other elements (such as text, logos and/or colours). Where an application is filed electronically, it is necessary to choose between two sub-categories of three-dimensional mark: 'three-dimensional mark' or 'three-dimensional mark containing word elements'.

It is possible to file either photographs or graphic representations of the mark. Up to six different perspectives of the mark may be included in an application, provided that the perspectives are submitted in a single JPEG file (for applications filed electronically) or on a single sheet of paper no larger than A4 size (for non-electronically filed applications).

7.4 Colour marks

This term covers applications for colours *per se*, whether individual colours or combinations of colours. It does not cover other types of mark that include colour. To be acceptable, the representation must include both a visual representation of the actual colour and a description of the colour in words. While it is possible to describe the colour using internationally accepted colour codes, the colour must also be described in ordinary words. For example, it is not acceptable to describe a colour as "Pantone 18-3949 TCX". Instead, the colour should be described as "Blue, Pantone 18-3949 TCX" – or simply as "Blue".

Where a combination of colours is applied for, the representation must indicate the proportions in which the colours are used. For example, EUTM registration number 10924918 includes both a visual representation and the description "The trademark consists of a combination of the colour orange ("Pantone 151") over 41% of the area and the colour blue ("Pantone 303") over 59% of the area, as viewed from left to right: orange, blue".

7.5 Sound marks

This term covers both music and other sounds. It is not possible to describe a sound in words. If the sound can be described in musical notation, this is acceptable by itself. If the sound cannot be described in musical notation, it is necessary to file both an electronic sound file (in MP3 format and no larger than 2MB) and a sonograph. For examples of sound marks that have been described in an acceptable manner using this combination see (or, more accurately, listen to) EUTM registration numbers 5170113 ("the roar of a lion") and 6534887 ("oh yes").

7.6 Other marks

This term covers all types of mark that do not fit within the categories described above. Types of mark that have been accepted as 'other marks' include:

- *holograms* – as there is currently no means of reproducing a hologram on the Office's application form (or indeed on the Register), it is acceptable to provide multiple representations of a hologram mark, provided that the representations are submitted in a single JPEG file (for applications filed electronically) or on a single sheet of paper no larger than A4 size (for non-electronically filed applications). For an example of a hologram mark, see EUTM registration number 1787456 ("BIO-ACTIVE hologram");
- *movement marks/animated marks* – again, as there is no way of reproducing a sequence of movements or an animation on the Office's application form,

multiple representations are acceptable. The representations must clearly show the sequence of movement that is being applied for and indicate any changes in colour or shading. The representations must be submitted in a single JPEG file or on a single sheet of paper no larger than A4 size. For an example of a movement mark, see EUTM registration number 9742974 ("toothbrush pressing onto a tomato");

- *position marks* – this type of mark indicates where a particular sign is to be placed on, or in relation to, a product. It is necessary to provide both a graphic representation of the mark showing the sign in place and a description in words. For an example of a position mark, see EUTM registration number 1027747 ("red stripe on sole and heel of shoe"); and
- *tracer marks* – this type of mark relates to coloured lines or threads applied to products, generally textiles. It is necessary to provide both a photograph/picture of the mark in use and a description in words. For an example of a tracer mark, see EUTM registration number 3001203 ("golden band incorporated into a light-coloured functional band…").

Where a representation of a mark contains colour (which is only possible for figurative, three-dimensional and 'other' marks), the colour automatically forms part of the mark (and the mark cannot be changed to a black and white mark).

Where an applicant indicates the wrong type of mark (eg, one claiming that a mark containing colour is a 'word mark' rather than a 'figurative mark'), a deficiency notice is issued and a two-month period set for the mistake to be corrected. If the applicant fails to respond, the Office changes the mark type. If the applicant refuses to accept the change suggested by the Office, the application will normally be rejected.

Where there is a clear contradiction between the description of the mark and the type of mark indicated on the application form, some positive action by the applicant is necessary. For example, if an applicant applies for a mark described as being three-dimensional, but indicates the mark type as 'figurative', it will be given a choice: either the mark type should be changed to 'three-dimensional', or the description of the mark should be deleted, in which case the application will proceed as an application for a two-dimensional 'figurative' mark.

8. Application fees

The application fees payable for an EUTM application depend on three factors:

- *whether the application is filed electronically or on paper* – as an encouragement to applicants to use the e-filing system, the application fees payable for electronically filed applications are lower than those for applications filed on paper;
- *the number of classes of goods and/or services included in the application* – the 'basic fee' covers one class and 'class fees' are payable for each additional class. Until 23 March 2016, the basic fee included up to three classes. This change is expected to deter applicants from filing in as many classes as previously and, in particular, from including three classes in every EUTM

application as a matter of course and thus cluttering the Register; and

- *whether the applicant chooses to obtain national search reports* – an additional fee is payable (currently €84, being €12 for each participating Member State) if this option is chosen. For more information on national search reports, see Chapter 4.

The current fees payable for an ordinary EUTM application are as follows:

Method of filing	Basic fee (one class)	Fee for second class	Fee for each class over two
E-filing	€850	€50	€150
Paper filing	€1000	€50	€150

It should be noted that applications for EU collective marks and, where available, EU certification marks, are higher than for ordinary EUTM applications (see chapters 28 and 29 for details of these fees).

All application fees are paid directly to the Office and must be paid in Euros. Any attempt to pay application fees in other currencies will be rejected.

Application fees may be paid by bank transfer, credit card or via a current account held with the Office. For further information on these options, see Chapter 2.

Where application fees are paid by bank transfer or credit card, they are treated as paid when the Office receives the funds. Where fees are paid via an Office current account, an applicant may request that payment be taken either immediately or one month after the date of submission of the application.

The Office does not examine EUTM applications until application fees are paid. As a result, if the application fees are not paid at the time an application is filed, the overall length of the application process is extended. This means that there is no advantage in delaying payment of application fees, provided of course that funds are available.

If an application is withdrawn, it is possible to obtain a refund of application fees in certain limited circumstances. Whether this is possible depends on the method of fee payment chosen:

- *fees paid from a current account at the time of filing* – the withdrawal request must be made on the day the application is filed;
- *fees to be paid from a current account one month after filing* – the withdrawal request may be made at any point within the one-month period;
- *fees paid by credit card* – the withdrawal request must be made on the day the application is filed; and
- *fees paid by bank transfer* – the withdrawal request must be made before funds are received in the Office's bank account.

As noted previously, in addition to the basic fee it is necessary to pay class fees if an application contains more than one class of goods and/or services. Failure to pay the correct class fees will not, however, result in the filing date being lost, provided that the basic fee is paid in full within one month of the application being filed. Where the amount paid is insufficient to cover all classes indicated on the application form, a deficiency notice is sent and the applicant is given two months to pay the balance. If it fails to do so, the application will only proceed for the classes covered by the fees paid; the remaining classes are deemed to have been withdrawn from the application. Classes are chosen in number order, lowest first. For example, if an application covers classes 9, 14, 18, 25 and 28 but the amount paid is only enough to cover three classes, the application will continue for classes 9, 14 and 18 only.

9. Representation

This section provides a brief overview of the requirements where an EUTM application is filed. The representation requirements in proceedings before the Office are set out in detail in Chapter 2.

There is no requirement for a representative to be appointed in order for a filing date to be obtained. As a result, it is possible for anyone to file an EUTM application and pay the necessary application fees to the Office.

If an applicant is domiciled, has its principal place of business or has a real and effective industrial or commercial establishment in the EEA, there is no requirement for a representative to be appointed at any stage of the application process.

If, however, an applicant cannot satisfy at least one of the above criteria, it must appoint a representative once its application has been filed, irrespective of its nationality. If a representative is not appointed in these circumstances, the Office issues a deficiency notice and will not correspond further with the applicant until a representative has been appointed. For further information on this, see Chapter 2.

10. Languages

The choice of languages in an EUTM application is a very important issue. The languages indicated impact upon not only the application process but also opposition proceedings, cancellation proceedings and everything else that is done in connection with the application (and the registration that results from it). Careful consideration should be given to language considerations at the time of filing, as it is not possible to change the languages in an application after it has been filed.

Full details of the language requirements in proceedings before the Office are set out in Chapter 2. This section summarises the language choices where an EUTM application is filed.

Every EUTM application must indicate two different languages:

- *first language* – this can be any of the 24 Languages of the Union; and
- *second language* – this must be one of the Languages of the Office (see Chapter 2, section 8), regardless of the language chosen as the first language of the application.

Where an applicant does not comply with the above requirements, a deficiency notice is issued. If the deficiency is not remedied within the time period set, the application is refused.

All information on the application form must be given in the first language of the application. If this is not done, a deficiency notice is issued and a period of two months set for the information to be translated.

11. Claiming priority

It is possible for EUTM applications to give effective rights from a date up to six months before the date the EUTM application is filed. This is possible in the limited circumstances described in this section by claiming what is known as 'priority'. It is possible to claim priority:

- when an EUTM application is filed; and
- for EUTM applications filed before 1 October 2017, within two months of the filing date. It will not be possible after 1 October 2017 to claim priority after an application has been filed.

There are two different kinds of priority that may be claimed, namely Convention Priority and Exhibition Priority. These are dealt with separately below. Exhibition Priority is rarely used and, as a result, Convention Priority is normally referred to as simply 'priority' (and where the term 'priority' is used in this book it is, unless stated otherwise, a reference to Convention Priority).

12. Convention Priority

Convention Priority is a right that arises under the Paris Convention. It allows applicants to claim backdated rights from earlier filed trade mark applications for up to six months. If priority is claimed, an EUTM application is treated as if it had been filed on, and rights run from, the filing date of the earlier application.

It is only possible to claim priority from the first filing of a trade mark for any particular good or service, although priority may be claimed from multiple applications covering different goods and/or services.

Priority may be either total (for all the goods and/or services contained in the EUTM application) or partial (for only some of those goods and/or services).

It is possible to claim priority from applications filed in countries that:

- are signatories to the Paris Convention and/or the Agreement on Trade-Related Aspects of Intellectual Property Rights ('TRIPS Agreement'),
- are members of the World Trade Organization ('WTO'), or
- have reciprocal agreements in place.

In practice, this means priority can be claimed from applications filed in most, but not all, countries.

12.1 Conditions for priority to be claimed

For priority to be successfully claimed, there must be identity of marks, goods and/or services and owner. This is known as the 'triple identity rule'. There is also a strict time limit within which priority can be claimed.

- *Identity of marks* – The mark in the EUTM application must be identical to that in the earlier application or registration from which priority is claimed.

It is also possible to claim priority where the differences between the two marks are 'insignificant'. An 'insignificant difference' in this context is taken to be one that would only be noticed by a reasonably observant consumer when comparing the two marks side by side. For example, a change in the typeface of word marks or a change from lower case to upper case (eg, from 'example' to 'EXAMPLE') is generally seen as insignificant.

The issue of identity often arises with differences in colour. The general rule is that differences in colour between the marks in the earlier application and the EUTM application mean that priority cannot be claimed, unless the difference in colours is insignificant. In this context a difference will be 'insignificant' if reasonably observant consumers would only perceive it if they saw the marks side by side.

As a result, if the earlier application shows the mark in black and white or greyscale and the EUTM application shows the mark in colour, it is unlikely that priority can be claimed. The same applies where the earlier application is filed in greyscale: priority cannot be claimed where the later application is filed either in colour or black and white, unless the differences in shading are insignificant.

- *Identity of goods and/or services* – The goods and/or services for which priority is claimed must be contained within the earlier application. It is not, however, necessary for the goods and/or services to be identical. It is possible for different terms to be used, provided that the goods and/or services for which priority is claimed are clearly within the scope of the earlier application or registration. An example of how this works is given in section 12.4 below.
- *Identity of owner* – The general position is that the applicant must be the same in the EUTM application and the earlier application or registration from which priority is claimed.

Neither the assignment of the earlier right nor the applicant changing name have any effect on the right to claim priority (although providing evidence to prove that the ownership is the same could be more complicated).

In addition, it is technically possible for the right to claim priority to be assigned independently from the earlier application. If this happens, then the owners of the two applications will be different.

12.2 Timing of a priority claim

For priority to be successfully claimed, the EUTM application must be filed within six months of the earlier application, during what is often referred to as the 'priority period'. This requirement is subject to the proviso that where the priority period expires on a day the Office is closed, the priority period is extended and expires on the next day the Office is open.

As noted above, priority must be claimed either when the application is filed or, for applications filed before 1 October 2017, within two months of the EUTM filing date. It is not possible to claim priority more than two months after an application is filed under any circumstances.

12.3 How to claim priority

When claiming priority, the applicant must indicate the country in which the earlier application was filed and the date on which it was filed.

The application number and a copy of the earlier application must also be provided, although these may be filed up to three months after the claim to priority has been made. In fact, if sufficient information is included with the claim to priority, the Office consults the relevant national IPO website and, where possible, obtains the necessary information directly. This means that, in many circumstances, the applicant does not have to file a copy of the earlier application. If the Office is unable to obtain the necessary information, the applicant is asked to provide it. If a copy of the earlier application is filed, it does not need to be a certified copy, though the documentation provided must contain all the information the Office needs to examine the priority claim. It is only necessary to translate the earlier documentation if the Office requests a translation.

If priority is claimed but the above requirements are not satisfied, the Office issues a deficiency notice and the applicant is given two months to respond. If the deficiency is not remedied, the claim to priority is lost (the sole effect of which will be that the rights obtained will only run from the filing date of the EUTM application).

12.4 How priority works: an example

In order to explain more fully how priority works, it is worth considering an example. Let us assume that an EUTM application was filed on 2 January 2016 covering "watches" in class 14, "clothing" in class 25 and "toys" in class 28.

The applicant also owns registrations for the same mark in Germany (covering "watches", filed on 30 April 2015) and the Benelux (for both "watches" and "clothing", filed on 30 October 2015).

The EUTM application could claim priority from the Benelux registration (as that was filed less than six months before the EUTM application) but not from the Germany registration (which was filed more than six months before the EUTM application).

Priority could, however, only be claimed for "clothing", as the Benelux application was not the first filing for "watches" (as the Germany application covered "watches"). Priority could not be claimed for "toys" as no earlier application or registration exists.

This means that the EUTM application is the first filed application for "toys", so that the applicant could claim priority from the EUTM application in respect of "toys" for any application filed on or before 2 July 2016. Priority could not be claimed from the EUTM application for "watches" or "clothing" as the EUTM was not the first filed application covering those goods.

13. Exhibition Priority

Exhibition Priority is a right that arises under the Convention relating to International Exhibitions. It operates in much the same way as Convention Priority, save that Exhibition Priority does not run from an earlier filed application. Instead, priority is claimed from the date on which goods and/or services were displayed under the mark at a qualifying exhibition.

To check whether an exhibition is a qualifying exhibition, an applicant should check the Paris Bureau International des Expositions website (www.bie-paris.org).

13.1 Conditions for claiming Exhibition Priority

The requirements to be met before Exhibition Priority can be claimed are very similar to those for Convention Priority, as considered in section 12 above (and the criteria are interpreted in the same way):

- *identity of marks* – the mark used at the exhibition must be the same as the mark applied for in the EUTM application;
- *identity of goods and/or services* – the mark must have been used at the exhibition on or in relation to all the goods and/or services for which priority is claimed; and
- *identity of owner* – the EUTM applicant must be the individual or entity that used the mark at the exhibition.

13.2 Timing of an Exhibition Priority claim

The EUTM application must be filed within six months of the date the goods and/or services were first displayed at the exhibition.

Exhibition Priority must be claimed either when the EUTM application is filed or, for applications filed before 1 October 2017, within two months of the EUTM filing date. For EUTM applications filed on or after 1 October 2017, it is not possible to claim Exhibition Priority after the application has been filed.

If Exhibition Priority is claimed but the above conditions are not satisfied, the Office issues a deficiency notice and the applicant is given two months to respond. If the deficiency is not remedied, the claim to Exhibition Priority will be lost (the sole effect of which will be that the rights obtained will only run from the filing date of the EUTM application).

Exhibition Priority works in the same way as Convention Priority, so that a priority claim may be total or partial (see the Convention Priority example at section 12.4 above).

13.3 Claiming Exhibition Priority

An applicant claiming Exhibition Priority must indicate the name of the exhibition and the date on which the mark was first displayed on or in relation to the relevant goods and/or services.

The applicant must also file evidence in support of the Exhibition Priority claim within three months of the filing date of the EUTM application. This evidence must include a certificate issued by the authority responsible for the protection of industrial property at the relevant exhibition. The certificate must state:

- the opening date of the exhibition;
- that the mark was used for the relevant goods and/or services at the exhibition; and
- if the first public use of the mark did not begin on the opening date of the exhibition, the date of first public use.

The applicant must also file proof of the actual use of the mark at the exhibition, certified by the authority issuing the certificate. If this certificate is not provided in one of the Languages of the Union, the Office requires a translation to be filed.

14. Seniority

Seniority involves the replacement of national registrations by EUTM registrations. It is considered in detail in Chapter 24.

If seniority is claimed at the time an EUTM application is filed, the following information must be provided:

- the Member State(s) in which the trade mark is registered;
- the filing date(s) of the relevant registration(s);
- the number(s) of the relevant registration(s); and
- the goods and/or services for which the trade mark is registered.

15. Transformation

Transformation is relevant where a Union designation of an IR is cancelled. In some circumstances, it is possible to 'transform' the Union designation into an EUTM application. Transformation is considered in detail in Chapter 32.

For transformation to be successfully claimed, the applicant must provide the number and date of the IR when the EUTM application is filed.

16. Requesting search reports/opting out of notifications

If an applicant wishes to receive search reports from the Office and/or the national IPOs participating in the national search system, this should be requested on the application form. For further information on search reports, see Chapter 4.

It is also possible for applicants to opt out of receiving notifications of later filed trade mark applications that the Office believes may conflict with their rights. This can be done at the time an EUTM application is filed.

17. Disclaimers

A disclaimer is an indication that the owner of an EUTM application or registration does not claim exclusive rights in a part or parts of the trade mark applied for. For example, if an EUTM application were to be filed for the mark 'EX WHY ZED', it would be possible to disclaim exclusive rights to the word 'EX'.

It is possible to add a disclaimer when filing an EUTM application. If this is done, the disclaimer cannot be removed after the application has been filed.

Including a disclaimer does not increase the chances of an application being accepted, which means that there is no real benefit to including one. The only reasons why a disclaimer should be added are if there is a contractual obligation to do so or if priority is being claimed from an application which includes a disclaimer.

If a disclaimer is included, it can only cover non-distinctive elements. If a disclaimer covers a distinctive element, the Office raises an objection as the scope of protection requested is unclear.

The inclusion of a disclaimer for a non-distinctive element or elements has no effect on the way the application is examined. If the mark is sufficiently distinctive to be accepted, it will be, whether a disclaimer is added or not; if the mark is not distinctive enough to be accepted, a disclaimer will not make the mark acceptable.

As a result of the above considerations, disclaimers are not recommended. They should be used with caution and very sparingly, if it all.

18. Correction of errors made when filing applications

If an applicant makes an error in the information contained in an EUTM application, that error may be corrected (no matter what the error may be) if a request for correction is sent to the Office on the day the application is filed. If, however, the request for correction is filed after this point, it will only be accepted in limited circumstances, as set out in Chapter 9.

Further reference

Regulation – Articles 25-27, 29-33, 41, 119, Annex I
Implementing Regulation – Rules 1, 3, 6-10
Office Guidelines – Part B, Section 2
Paris Convention for the Protection of Industrial Property (adopted 1883)
The Convention relating to International Exhibitions (adopted 1928)
TMDN, Common Communication on the Common Practice of the Scope of Protection of Black and White Marks

Chapter 6: Classification

1. Introduction

All EUTM applications must list the goods and/or services in respect of which registration is sought. This list of goods and/or services is referred to as the 'specification' of the application.

This chapter considers the rules relating to how specifications are presented and interpreted in EUTM applications. For ease of reference, the expression 'goods' is used to refer to both goods and services in the remainder of this chapter.

As with most trade mark registration systems around the world, the goods included in EUTM applications must be placed in 'classes' in accordance with the Nice Classification system, which was established by the Nice Agreement Concerning the International Classification of Goods and Services for the Purposes of the Registration of Marks in 1957. The 2016 version of the 10th edition of the Nice Classification system is currently used by the Office.

The Office has in recent years been heavily involved in attempts to harmonise the way in which terms are classified and harmonised within specifications. In particular, it has been instrumental in the creation, development and expansion of the TMClass database.

2. Specifications of goods: summary of requirements

As discussed in Chapter 5, listing the goods to be covered by an EUTM application is one of the preconditions for obtaining a filing date. The goods do not, however, need to be properly classified for a filing date to be awarded, either in terms of the class in which the terms are placed or whether the terms used are acceptable.

To be acceptable, the goods listed in a specification must be identified with sufficient clarity and precision, so that the extent of the protection conferred by a registration can be understood from looking at the words alone. This point is expanded upon below.

In addition, the goods must be placed in the correct class of the Nice Classification. If there is any doubt as to whether a term has been placed in the correct class, the term may need to be clarified. For example, the term 'clothing' is part of the class heading for class 25 and will be accepted in that class. If 'clothing' is applied for in class 28, the term will need some further clarification, for example by amending it to 'clothing for dolls' or 'clothing for toys', both of which are in class 28. The effect of placing a term in the wrong class is considered in more detail below.

3. Terms that are not accepted in specifications

It is possible to include broad terms in specifications, including the class headings of the Nice Classification, provided that the terms used are sufficiently clear and precise. When the suitability of class heading terms was first assessed by the TMDN in 2014, 11 class heading terms were identified as failing the 'clear and precise' test and so found to be unacceptable. Under the 2016 version of the Nice Classification, which made amendments to some of the class headings, five class heading terms are deemed insufficiently clear and precise. The terms are (in class number order):

- class 7 – Machines;
- class 37 – Repair;
- class 37 – Installation services;
- class 40 – Treatment of materials; and
- class 45 – Personal and social services rendered by others to meet the needs of individuals.

These terms are not acceptable and the Office raises an objection if they are included in EUTM specifications.

In line with the requirement for clarity and precision, the Office raises an objection against terms that are too vague to be properly understood. For example, terms such as 'internet services' and 'retail services' require further explanation.

The wording 'all goods in class X' is not acceptable. In fact, any EUTM application that contains only this wording will not be awarded a filing date as the wording does not comply with the requirement that the goods covered by the application are listed.

Specifications cannot contain references to other classes. For example, the term 'retail services connected with the sale of goods included in class 25' would be objected to if included in an EUTM application.

In addition, specifications cannot contain words that are themselves registered trade marks. The Office requests that any registered trade mark included in a specification be replaced by a suitable generic term. For example, a reference to 'sellotape' (which is a registered trade mark in the Union) in class 16 would be objected to and would need to be amended to 'adhesive tape' or something similar.

Imprecise terms that attempt to qualify the goods covered by an application are not accepted. This means that terms such as 'and related goods' and 'and the like' are not accepted. Conversely, it is possible to use a qualifier such as 'namely' or 'in particular', provided that the term following the qualifier is sufficiently precise. For example, the term 'musical instruments, namely violins' is acceptable.

4. Interpretation of terms in specifications

Terms used in specifications are taken to cover only the literal meaning of the words used. This applies no matter when the EUTM application was filed.

Prior to the Regulation coming into force on 23 March 2016, this was not necessarily the case. Before that date, the use of a full class heading in an EUTM application could lead to a different interpretation of the coverage granted, depending on when it was filed:

- *applications filed before 22 June 2012* – a full class heading was taken to cover both the literal meaning of the words in the class heading and all the terms in the Nice Classification alphabetical list for that class at the time the application was filed;
- *applications filed between 22 June 2012 and 1 December 2013* – a full class heading was taken to cover the literal meaning of the words in the class heading. In addition, the applicant could elect to cover all (or some) of the goods in the alphabetical list for that class. This was done by the applicant indicating, at the time of filing, whether its intention was to cover all (or some) terms in the alphabetical list. If it did not make such an indication, only the literal meaning of the class heading terms was covered; and
- *applications filed between 2 December 2013 and 22 March 2016* – a full class heading was taken to cover only the literal meaning of the words in the class heading. If the applicant wanted to cover the full alphabetical list for a class, it became necessary for those terms to be listed individually in the application.

The change in law on 23 March 2016 meant there was a change in the way that many existing EUTM specifications were interpreted. In many cases, this narrowed the scope of protection of existing EUTM applications and registrations. For example, a registration from 2010 covering 'musical instruments' (the class heading for class 15) was previously interpreted as covering everything in the alphabetical list in class 15, including terms such as 'conductors' batons'. Since 23 March 2016, the term 'musical instruments' is interpreted as covering everything that can be described as a musical instrument, but does not cover 'conductors' batons'.

To counter the effects of this change, the Regulation created a six-month period (from 23 March 2016 to 24 September 2016) in which the owners of EUTM applications or registrations with a filing date earlier than 22 June 2012 and which included a full class heading could file a declaration (referred to in this section as a 'clarifying declaration') indicating that its intention when filing the EUTM application was to cover more than the literal meaning of the class heading terms. Filing a clarifying declaration allowed the specification to be amended to include terms within the alphabetical list that were not covered by the literal meaning of the class heading terms.

The Office restricted the scope of these clarifying declarations so that only those terms in the alphabetical list that it deemed were clearly not covered by the literal meaning of the terms in the class headings could be added to the specification. The Office took a wide view of what was covered by the class headings, so that relatively few terms in the alphabetical list could be added.

The Regulation also limited the effect of these clarifying declarations in order to try and ensure they did not extend the rights given by pre-June 2012 registrations. The Regulation prohibits an EUTM registration for which a clarifying declaration has been filed from being used:

- *in an infringement action* – to prevent use that:
  - started before the Register was amended following the clarifying declaration; and

    - did not infringe the EUTM registration on the basis of the literal meaning of the terms in the specification before it was amended; or
- *in an opposition or cancellation action* – to oppose an application or invalidate a registration that:
    - was filed before the Register was amended following the clarifying declaration; and
    - did not infringe the rights given by the EUTM registration on the basis of the literal meaning of the terms in the specification before it was amended.

In some ways, this limitation is nonsensical, as a clarifying declaration should only have the effect of maintaining terms in the specification that were already covered under previous practice. It does, however, ensure the protection of intervening rights obtained between an EUTM registration being filed and the specification for it being amended following a clarifying declaration.

5. Creating a specification for an EUTM application

There is no requirement for an applicant to have an intention to use the mark applied for in relation to all, or in fact any, of the goods included in an EUTM application. As a result, it is possible to apply for a wider range of goods than will ever be used. Doing this can extend the infringement rights given by an EUTM registration and, as a result, many applicants include in applications goods they do not intend using the mark on or in relation to.

If an applicant is to include goods in an EUTM application that go beyond their range of intended use, it is worth nothing that:

- care should be taken to avoid the inclusion of terms that are likely to lead to an absolute grounds objection being raised (see Chapter 7). While a mark may be perfectly capable of registration for the goods of direct interest to the applicant, it may be objectionable for others;
- the more goods included in an application, the greater the likelihood the application will come into conflict with an earlier right and so be opposed; and
- once an EUTM registration has been in place for five years, it can be challenged for non-use – parts of the registration could therefore face a non-use action at some point for goods covered by it that are never used (see Chapter 17).

With these considerations in mind, applicants should be sensible about the range of goods included in EUTM applications. While it makes sense to use broader terms than the exact goods of interest, going too broad can invite additional problems and costs. It is not advisable to rely on class headings or other very broad terms alone, because of the literal way these terms are interpreted. As a result, a combination of general and specific terms is often the best approach and is always worth considering.

The Office has been heavily involved in the development of the TMClass search tool, which allows applicants to search a harmonised database for terms that are deemed acceptable in EUTM applications (and by the other IPOs participating in the harmonisation programme). This tool can be accessed via the Office's website or direct at http://tmclass.tmdn.org.

Where an application is filed electronically using the Fast Track system (see Chapter 4), the specification must consist entirely of terms in the Office's database of accepted terms for classification purposes, which includes (and is created from) the terms in the TMClass database.

It is not, however, compulsory for every term in a specification to be included within the Office's database of accepted terms. Indeed, applicants often want to include terms that are directly relevant to their business but are not in the Office's database of accepted terms. In addition, an applicant may want to include additional terms because of priority and/or seniority claims where earlier applications or registrations contain terms that are not in the Office's database. Where an applicant wishes to include such a term, the application can still be filed electronically but it is not possible for the Fast Track system to be used. In these circumstances, the applicant needs to create the specification and add it into the application.

Where an EUTM application is not filed electronically, the same applies: the applicant needs to create the specification and add it into the application.

It is, of course, possible to search and use terms from TMClass to create most of the specification and simply add in the additional terms that need to be protected. If there is any uncertainty about whether a term is acceptable or not, it is recommended that a search be carried out on the TMClass database to try and minimise the chances of an objection being raised.

6. Examination of specifications by the Office

As an application filed using the Fast Track system can only include terms taken from the Office's database of accepted terms, no examination of the specification takes place for Fast Track applications.

If the specification is not created using the Office's database (whether the application is filed electronically, by fax or on paper), the Office examines the specification as part of the normal examination process.

Where the Office believes a term is not acceptable, either because it is not sufficiently clear and precise or because it has been placed in the wrong class, a deficiency notice is issued. In these circumstances the Office generally suggests how the terms objected to could be amended, or indicates the class in which it is felt the terms should correctly be placed. It is not, however, compulsory to accept the Office's suggestions and the applicant can suggest wording it feels is more appropriate.

When amending a specification – whether to try to overcome an objection raised by the Office or otherwise – it is important to remember that the amendment will not be accepted if it has the effect of extending or expanding the goods covered by the application. For example:

- the term 'retail services' (which will be objected to as imprecise) cannot be replaced with the term 'retail and wholesale services connected with clothing' (as wholesale services are not covered by the initial term); and

- the term 'tea' applied for in class 30 (which is the correct class for this term) cannot be amended to 'herbal tea for medicinal use' (which falls within class 5). Conversely, if the term 'tea' is incorrectly applied for in class 33, it is possible either to transfer the term to class 30 or amend it to read 'herbal tea for medicinal use' and transfer it to class 5. This is because, in the first example, the amendment relates to goods correctly listed in the original specification whereas, in the second, it does not (as the term was not correctly classified and so could not have been retained in the original class).

Where an extra class needs to be added to an EUTM application as a result of a term being incorrectly classified, an additional class fee must be paid. Adding a second class to an application involves a class fee of €50 becoming payable. Each additional class added from the third onwards leads to a class fee of €150 per class becoming payable. If the applicant agrees to an extra class being added to the application, it must pay the relevant fee; if not, the term that has been incorrectly classified must be deleted.

7. Amendments to specifications

It is possible for the specification of an EUTM application to be amended at any time before registration. Specification amendments are accepted, provided that the requirements considered in this chapter are satisfied, in particular:

- the amendment must restrict rather than expand the range of goods covered by the application; and
- the new wording used must be sufficiently clear and precise.

The specification of an EUTM application can also be amended if it contains an error of wording, a copying error or an obvious mistake. For example, an EUTM application with the specification 'hats; but including baseball caps' with a priority claim from an application with the specification 'hats; but not including baseball caps' could be amended by adding the word 'not' in the appropriate place.

The specifications of EUTM registrations cannot be amended as such. Specifications can, however, be limited, which is done by making a partial surrender of the registration (see Chapter 15).

Further reference

Regulation – Article 28

Implementing Regulation – Rule 2

Office Guidelines – Part B, Section 3

Nice Classification – see www.wipo.int/classifications/nice

Chartered Institute of Patent Attorneys v Registrar of Trade Marks, CJEU decision in Case No C-307/10, judgment dated 19 June 2012 (the 'IP TRANSLATOR' case)

TMDN, *Common Communication on the Implementation of 'IP Translator'*, February 20 2014

TMDN, *Common Communication on the Common Practice on the General Indications of the Nice Class Headings*, 20 February 2014

TMDN, *Common Communication on the Common Practice on the Acceptability of Classification Terms*, 20 February 2014

Communication No 1/2016 of the President of the Office of 08/02/2016 concerning the implementation of Article 28 EUTMR and the Annex thereto

Chapter 7: Absolute grounds objections

1. Introduction

Once an EUTM application has passed the formalities checks, the Office carries out what is generally referred to as 'absolute grounds' examination. This involves the Office assessing whether the trade mark applied for is inherently capable of registration in relation to the goods and/or services covered by the application.

In addition, the Office carries out a separate assessment as to whether the classification is acceptable, which is considered in Chapter 6. This assessment is generally, but not always, completed before the 'absolute grounds' assessment.

The absolute grounds for refusal of EUTM applications are set out in Article 7 of the Regulation. Each of the grounds for refusal is independent of the others and can form the basis of a distinct objection, so that objections can be raised on multiple grounds against the same application. The grounds for refusal are considered separately below.

2. Principles of examination

The Office has a duty to carry out a "stringent and full examination, in order to prevent trade marks from being improperly registered ... [and] to ensure that trade marks whose use could successfully be challenged before the courts are not registered" (see the CJEU decision in *LIBERTEL*).

If the Office believes an absolute grounds objection is applicable, so that the application should not be accepted, it has a duty to inform the applicant and provide details of the basis of the objection. Further, the Office cannot finally refuse an application until the applicant has been given the opportunity to submit observations in response to the objection, amend the application or withdraw it.

Where the Office is of the view that a trade mark is not inherently registrable, it must clearly state each and every ground of objection that it thinks exists, providing clear reasoning as to why it has raised each ground as well as the extent of the objection (ie, whether it applies to all the goods and/or services covered by the application or only some of them).

It may be that the objection applies to every good and/or service contained in the specification; the Office must, however, consider each term in the specification separately before raising an objection.

One of the key features of the EUTM registration system is its unitary character. This means that, for an EUTM application to be accepted, the trade mark applied for must be capable of registration in each and every Member State. As a result, an objection relevant to only one Member State, or indeed to part of a single Member State, is enough for an EUTM application to be refused. For example, if a trade mark is descriptive in one of the Languages of the Union, an objection is raised. In addition, an objection is raised if the trade mark is descriptive in a significant non-official language of a Member State (eg, Catalan or Basque, which are widely spoken in Spain) or a non-Union language that is understood in a Member State (eg, Turkish, which is widely understood in Cyprus). When raising an objection, the Office must indicate whether it relates to the entire Union or only part of it, so that the applicant will fully understand the extent of the problem.

As noted in Chapter 1, section 8, objections can only be raised in relation to Member States in the Union at the filing date. If a new Member State joins the Union after an application has been filed, no objection can be raised in respect of that State. It is worth noting that it is the filing date of the EUTM application that is important, not the priority date. If an EUTM application is filed after a new Member State joins the Union, an objection can be raised in respect of that State, even if the EUTM application has a priority date that is earlier than the date on which that State joined the Union.

The Office examines applications and raises objections in a 'notice of grounds for refusal' as soon as possible. It is, however, possible for additional objections to be raised later. The Office can reopen examination at any time before a trade mark becomes registered if it believes a ground for objection exists that has not been considered previously. This is sometimes seen in response to third party observations filed during the opposition period (see Chapter 9).

Previously, the Office could invite applicants to disclaim non-distinctive parts of a trade mark if it was felt this would give clarity to the scope of protection sought. This is no longer possible, although it was very rarely used in any event. Disclaimers can now only be included at the time of filing an application. For further information on disclaimers, see Chapter 5.

As part of the examination process, examiners use a variety of reference materials to assess whether a mark should be accepted for registration. This is essential, given the number of different languages used in the Union, as well as the large cultural differences between the Member States. In an attempt to ensure consistency in approach, reduce examination time and improve the quality of decisions, the Office has developed the Common Examiner's Support Tool (CESTO). This produces a report to be used when applications are examined, which looks at relevant data sources. For example, if an application covers classes 31 (eg, 'fresh fruits and vegetables' or 'natural plants and flowers') and 33 (eg, 'alcoholic drinks'), searches are made in the Community Plant Variety Office database (see section 15 below) and on the E-BACCHUS database (see section 13 below). In addition, examiners can ask that the report includes searches in dictionaries. Online searches are also routinely carried out.

The various absolute grounds for refusal are considered separately below.

3. Signs that cannot be trade marks

This objection derives from Article 7(1)(a) of the Regulation: it is not possible to register "signs which do not conform to the requirements of [what can be a trade mark]".

To prevent an objection under this ground, a trade mark must satisfy three criteria.

- *It must be an acceptable sign* – this is defined in the Regulation as "any signs, in particular words, including personal names, designs, letters, numerals, the shape of goods or of their packaging". With effect from 1 October 2017, 'colours' and 'sounds' will be added to this definition. It is very rare for an objection to be raised on the basis that a mark is not a 'sign' (understandably, as there is no restriction on what can or cannot be a sign). However, this does happen occasionally. An example of an application refused on this basis is *Dyson's UK application*, which was for a mark described as consisting of "the transparent bin or collection chamber forming part of the external surface of a vacuum cleaner as shown in the representation", which the CJEU held was not a 'sign' but "a mere property of the product concerned".
- *It must be capable of distinguishing the goods and services of one undertaking from those of other undertakings* – this is not defined, but as virtually every sign is capable of distinguishing in some way, it is very rare for a mark to be found not to satisfy this requirement. The Office Guidelines give the example of the word TRADEMARK, which would give rise to an objection on this basis. The Office generally raises objections along these lines under Article 7(1)(b), on the basis that the trade mark is devoid of distinctive character (see section 4 below).
- *It must be applied for in an acceptable representation* – what this means depends on when the EUTM application was filed:
  - *applications filed before 1 October 2017* – the trade mark must be "capable of being represented graphically"; or
  - *applications filed on or after 1 October 2017* – the trade mark must be applied for "in a manner which enables the competent authorities and the public to determine the precise subject of the protection afforded to its proprietor".

Under the current definition, applicants are effectively prevented from applying for some types of mark simply because those marks are impossible to represent in graphic form. The definition is being changed on the basis that "a sign should be permitted to be represented in any appropriate form using generally available technology, and thus not necessarily by graphic means" (see the recitals to the Regulation). It will, however, remain necessary for the trade mark to be "clear, precise, self-contained, easily accessible, intelligible, durable and objective" (per the test laid down by the CJEU decision in *SIECKMANN*). The new definition could lead to a decrease in the number of marks objected to under this ground, although changes to other absolute grounds (in particular, the extension of the Article 7(1)(e) objection, considered in section 7 below) mean it is unlikely that there will be a large increase in the types of mark that will be accepted for registration.

Satisfying the 'acceptable representation' test is not an issue for the most common types of mark, namely words and logos. Potential issues do, however, arise with other types of mark.

- *Colours* – Although a specific reference to colours will only be added into the definition of a 'sign' from 1 October 2017, it has been possible to register colours as trade marks for many years. Simply filing a sample of the colour is not, however, sufficient. A written description must also be provided. Where possible, this should contain a reference to an "internationally recognised identification code" such as the Pantone matching system. Where an application is for a combination of two or more colours, it is necessary to provide a "systematic arrangement associating the colours concerned in a predetermined and uniform way", showing how they will be used in combination (see the CJEU decision in *HEIDELBERGER BAUCHEMIE*). For examples of EUTM registrations for colour marks, see numbers 212787 (Deutsche Telekom, magenta) and 475210 (Eurostar International, blue and yellow).
- *Shapes* – When applying to register a three-dimensional mark, a description of the shape is not sufficient. It is necessary to include a photograph or graphic representation. Up to six different perspectives of the mark can be included and it is advisable to include as many as necessary to ensure the mark is clearly identified (for most three-dimensional marks, front, back, side, top, bottom and perspective views should be considered). For examples of EUTM registrations for three-dimensional marks, see numbers 50450 (Lego, character) and 4670766 (Coca-Cola, bottle).
- *Sounds* – While describing a sound solely in words is not enough, there are two ways in which such a mark can be represented in an acceptable fashion. Firstly, if the sound can be clearly described using musical notation, this will be acceptable. Secondly, for non-musical sounds, it is possible to describe the sound using a sonogram or oscillogram in combination with a sound file submitted electronically: this option is therefore only possible for applications filed electronically. For examples of EUTM registrations for sound marks, see numbers 3481744 (Intel, jingle) and 5170113 (MGM, roaring lion).
- *Smells* – There have been many unsuccessful attempts to obtain EUTM registrations for smells. Such attempts have described smells using chemical formulae, by using words and by depositing odour samples with the Office, none of which (either separately or in combination) have been deemed acceptable. Under current practice, it appears there is no satisfactory way to represent a smell, so any attempt to register a smell will lead to an objection.
- *Tastes* – For the reasons applicable to smells, any attempt to obtain an EUTM registration for a taste will, under current practice, lead to an objection.
- *Movement marks* – A movement mark should be described by using a combination of a graphic representation and a textual description which clearly describes the movement being made. For an example of an EUTM registration for a movement mark, see number 5910831 (Microsoft, logo).

Where a description is included within an EUTM application, it should not be in any way ambiguous or contradictory, otherwise, an objection is raised, even if the other guidance set out above is followed. An example of an EUTM application refused on this basis is number 5650817 (Seven Towns, puzzle).

4. Lack of distinctiveness

This objection derives from Article 7(1)(b) of the Regulation: it is not possible to register "trade marks which are devoid of any distinctive character".

The word 'devoid' means that even a minimum degree of distinctiveness is enough to allow a mark to be accepted, provided that this minimum degree of distinctiveness applies across the entire Union.

Distinctiveness is assessed by reference to two factors:

- *the goods and/or services in respect of which registration is sought* – it is possible for an objection to relate to some but not all of the goods and/or services covered by an application. Any objection raised must specify the goods and/or services to which it relates; and
- *the perception of the relevant public* – this normally involves an assessment of the perception of the general public and ultimate consumers, though other people (eg, retailers and wholesalers) within the distribution chain may be relevant. Where a product is only relevant to a specialist market (or part of the market, eg, if the goods applied for relate solely to products sold at the wholesale level) then members of that specialist market make up the relevant public.

The way the relevant public perceives a mark is judged by what is sometimes referred to as the 'average consumer test', which presumes that:

- *consumers are reasonably well-informed and reasonably observant and circumspect* – they do not spend a lot of time analysing trade marks, but will notice their obvious and apparent features;
- *the level of attention given by consumers varies between products* – they pay more attention when choosing expensive, luxury items than when making less expensive, day-to-day purchases; and
- *consumers do not think in trade mark terms* – they see trade marks in practical terms, as giving them information that helps them to purchase the goods and services they need.

It has been emphasised in a number of cases that the assessment of distinctiveness is technically the same for all trade marks. As a result, it is not possible to apply stricter criteria to some types of mark than to others (so that, for example, a trade mark cannot be refused registration purely on the basis that it is a single letter: see below).

Having said that, it is acknowledged that consumers do not view all types of trade mark in the same way. For example, the CJEU has held that "consumers are not in the habit of making assumptions about the origin of products based on slogans" (see *DAS PRINZIP DER BEQUEMLICHKEIT* (*'The Principle of Comfort'*)).

As noted in section 1 above, each objection under Article 7(1) is independent of the others. Despite this, if a trade mark faces an objection under Article 7(1)(c) (see section 5 below) on the basis that it is descriptive of characteristics of the goods and/or services applied for, an objection will also always be raised on the basis that the mark in question is lacking in distinctiveness. This is because it is felt that descriptive marks cannot be inherently distinctive and so cannot indicate trade origin. The objections do, however, remain separate and each must be addressed separately: overcoming the descriptiveness objection does not necessarily lead to the lack of distinctiveness objection being waived.

It should be remembered that an objection that a mark lacks distinctiveness raised under Article 7(1)(b) can be overcome if the applicant demonstrates 'acquired distinctiveness' (see Chapter 8).

It is worth considering distinctiveness issues for the different key types of trade mark.

- *Words* – As noted above, descriptive word marks are always deemed to be non-distinctive. Words are also refused registration if they are so frequently used that it is felt they will not be perceived as an indication of origin. Examples of words refused on this basis include MEDI (not capable of distinguishing as it would be seen as relating to medical products), PREMIUM (not capable of distinguishing as it would be seen as a reference to high-quality) and domain name suffixes (.com, .org, etc). In the same way, words that are very well-known within a particular sphere are refused registration within that sphere. For example, STAR WARS would not be seen as inherently distinctive in relation to the 'showing of films' or 'rental of films', as the name would be seen as a reference to the film series rather than an indication of origin.
- *Single letters* – An objection cannot be raised simply on the basis that the trade mark consists of a single letter. However, most, if not all, applications for single letters face non-distinctiveness objections. For examples of registrations for single letters, see EUTM registration numbers 6474795 (Thomas Arndt, Y) and 13838198 (Verdes Innovations S.A., V).
- *Slogans* – Under current practice, most slogans face non-distinctiveness objections, usually on the basis that the relevant public would view them as mere promotional messages rather than as badges of origin.

  A slogan is likely to be seen as distinctive if it:
  - has a number of meanings;
  - constitutes a play on words;
  - is imaginative or surprising;
  - has some particular originality or resonance;
  - requires an interpretive effort before it is understood;
  - employs unusual syntactic structures; and/or
  - uses particular linguistic and stylistic devices, such as alliteration, metaphor and rhyme (see the CJEU decision in *VORSPRUNG DURCH TECHNIK*).

    An example of an EUTM registration for a slogan is UNMASKING THE

SOCIAL NETWORK OF FRAUD (Early Warning Services, number 10477941).

- *Common signs and symbols* – most common signs and symbols face non-distinctiveness objections on the basis that consumers do not view them as indications of origin. Examples of such marks include:
  - typographical symbols, such as '!' and ';'
  - mathematical symbols, such as '%' and '+'
  - currency symbols, such as '€' and '$'
  - pictograms, such as 🍴 (for restaurant services) and ♿ (for services intended for wheelchair users).
- *Single colours* – As colours are not generally seen as indications of trade origin in themselves, applications to register single colours *per se* always face an objection that the mark is not distinctive. If an applicant is able to prove a particular colour is very unusual or striking in relation to the products applied for, the objection can in theory be waived. In practice, however, this is only likely to happen where an application covers a narrow range of goods and/or services and the relevant market is very specific. In the Office Guidelines, the example is given of the colour black for milk, though the authors are not aware of any single colour EUTM application that has been accepted as inherently distinctive.
- *Colour combinations* – To avoid a lack of distinctiveness objection, an application to register a combination of colours must clearly indicate how they will be used in combination. If this requirement is satisfied, colour combinations are usually seen as distinctive unless there is some reason why a particular combination should not be accepted. Where one of the colours in a colour combination is not distinctive in relation to the goods or services in question, that colour is ignored in assessing distinctiveness and the other colour or colours are considered alone. For example, an application to register the colours red and orange for fire extinguishers would be objected to (as red is a common colour for fire extinguishers, so the application would be treated as if just for the single colour orange). There are also products for which colour combinations are almost always objected to, on the basis that colours are perceived as decorative rather than indicating origin, eg, clothing.
- *Basic two-dimensional shapes and figurative elements* – Basic shapes and figurative elements are often objected to on the basis that consumers do not view them as trade marks. Examples of marks that are objected to on this basis include:
  - basic geometric shapes, such as squares and circles, which do not have the inherent capacity to distinguish;
  - marks that are likely to be perceived by consumers as decorative elements (eg, refused EUTM application number 113843444 for one half of a smile);
  - commonplace elements relating to the particular products applied for, such as grapes for wine; and
  - marks that are likely to be perceived by consumers as product labels (eg,

refused EUTM application number 4373403, for a label shape applied for in respect of adhesive labels).

- *Patterns* – Marks consisting of patterns that are commonplace or typically used for the goods and/or services applied for, as well as patterns consisting of very simple or basic designs, usually encounter objections on the basis that they lack distinctiveness. Conversely, patterns that are unusual, fanciful and memorable are capable of protection. Particular care needs to be taken when the goods applied for include products that normally feature patterns on them as decorative elements (eg, clothing, wallpaper and textiles). An example of a mark refused on this basis is the tartan pattern in EUTM application number 8423841.
- *Three-dimensional marks* – The shapes of goods and their packaging are specifically mentioned in the Regulation as being capable of protection as trade marks. This does not mean, however, that consumers will view all product or packaging shapes as distinctive indications of origin. In addition, three-dimensional marks often face objections under Article 7(1)(e), which the Office tends to consider before looking at distinctiveness: see section 7. The inclusion of a further distinctive element within a mark, in addition to the shape, usually results in an objection being avoided. For example, see EUTM registration number 9844119 (Camper SRL, shape of shoe with brand name 'CAMPER' clearly visible).

Three-dimensional marks can be separated into three categories:

- *marks consisting of the shape of the goods applied for* – a mark which consists entirely of the shape of the goods in relation to which protection is sought will encounter an objection if the shape in question is a basic shape, a commonly used shape, or a shape that consumers would expect to see used for the products in question. There are a large number of examples of marks that have been refused on this basis, particularly for laundry and dishwasher tablets. To be seen as distinctive, a shape must be memorable. For an example of a product shape that was held to be inherently distinctive, see EUTM registration number 31237 (Toblerone, triangular chocolate bar);
- *marks consisting of the shape of product packaging* – the same basic rule applies as above, namely, that to be seen as distinctive the packaging shape must be memorable, must not be commonplace and must be different to the type of shape that a consumer would expect to see for the relevant products. For an example of product packaging that was held to be inherently distinctive, see EUTM registration number 12638896 (De Rigo, perfume bottle);
- *marks that have no relevance to the goods and/or services applied for* – normally this type of mark is seen as distinctive and so capable of registration. For example, see EUTM registration number 4222634 (UK Insurance, Churchill the dog);
- *Position marks* – A position mark is one that includes a description of the position in which the mark is used on, or in relation to, the relevant products. When assessing whether such a mark is capable or registration, the

Office considers whether consumers will view the mark as an indication of origin in terms of both the mark itself and the position in which it appears on the relevant product. For an example of a position mark that was found to be devoid of distinctive character, see refused EUTM application number 5658117 (X-Technology Swiss, orange colour used on toe of sock). For an example of a position mark that was found to be inherently distinctive, see EUTM registration number 9045907 (CNH Global, colours used on tractor).

5. Descriptive trade marks

This objection derives from Article 7(1)(c) of the Regulation: it is not possible to register "trade marks which consist exclusively of signs or indications which may serve, in trade, to designate the kind, quality, quantity, intended purpose, value, geographical origin or the time of production of the goods or of rendering of the service, or other characteristics of the goods or service".

The test for descriptiveness is very strict for EUTM applications. An objection will be raised against a mark "if at least one of its possible meanings designates a characteristic of the goods or services concerned" (see the CJEU decision in *POSTKANTOOR*).

A number of factors are deemed to be irrelevant in assessing whether a mark is descriptive, further demonstrating how strict the test is:

- *Whether or not there are synonyms capable of designating the same characteristics of the goods or services* – an objection will be raised even if there are lots of other names that could be used to describe the relevant characteristics.
- *Whether there are more usual signs or indications for designating the relevant characteristics* – an objection will be raised even if a different word or words are normally used to describe the relevant characteristics.
- *How many of the applicant's competitors may have an interest in using the mark* – an objection will be raised even if the applicant is the only trader likely to use the mark.
- *Whether the mark is being used descriptively at the time the application is filed* – an objection will still be raised on the basis that the mark could be used in a descriptive way in the future.

In addition, combining a number of descriptive elements to create a neologism (new word) does not necessarily prevent a descriptiveness objection being raised. Such a trade mark is likely to be deemed descriptive "unless there is a perceptible difference between the word and the mere sum of its parts". This requires some "unusual variation, in particular as to syntax or meaning," rather than "merely bringing those elements together", so the impression created by the mark is "sufficiently far removed" from the descriptive meaning of the combination (see the CJEU decisions in *POSTKANTOOR* and *BIOMILD*).

Having said that, an objection should not be raised if the meaning, or potential meaning, of a mark is not directly descriptive but instead only suggestive, allusive, vague or indirect. This can be a very fine distinction to draw and, under current practice, the Office tends to raise an objection if there is any possibility of a mark being seen as descriptive.

When assessing whether a mark is descriptive or not, an examiner takes account of his own understanding of the mark, as well as considering the dictionary meaning of the mark, which can include the meaning of individual elements within it. The examiner also carries out internet searches and considers examples of descriptive use found online (for information on the resources generally used by examiners, see section 2 above).

An objection should be raised if a mark is descriptive of the goods and/or services covered by the application in any language understood in a part of the Union. The dictionaries used when assessing descriptiveness depend on the mark, though the basic rule is that checks are carried out in all the languages of the Union. Further checks may be carried out if the examiner has some personal knowledge of the mark having relevance in a particular language or if a meaning in a particular language is found as a result of internet searches. In addition, any information provided to the Office through third party observations results in additional checks being carried out (see Chapter 9).

It should be remembered that an objection that a mark is descriptive can be overcome if the applicant demonstrates 'acquired distinctiveness' (see Chapter 8).

The inclusion of the wording "or other characteristics of the goods or service" means that the list of characteristics in Article 7(1)(c) is not exhaustive, as virtually all objections relate to one or more of the characteristics listed in that Article. However, it is worthwhile to consider each briefly:

- *Kind* – this excludes from registration references to the nature of the goods and/or services themselves. For example, it would not be possible to register ROSES for 'flowers'.
- *Quality* – this excludes from registration laudatory marks implying that a mark is of higher quality than the norm, as well as marks referencing specific qualities of the goods and/or services. It also prevents registration of marks that are references to the subject matter of the goods and/or services. For example, it would not be possible to register PREMIUM for 'lager' (or a large number of other goods and/or services), 1600 for 'motor vehicles' (as this is a common engine size) or NAPOLEON BONAPARTE for 'books' (as the books would be perceived as being about Napoleon).
- *Quantity* – this excludes from registration references to a measure of the quantity in which the goods and/or services are to be sold or provided. For example, it would not be possible to register LITRE for 'soft drinks'. Arbitrary numbers that are unlikely to be used as a measure should, however, be acceptable, eg, 7392 for 'soft drinks'.
- *Intended purpose* – this excludes from registration references to the reason for using the goods and/or services, as well as references to the way they could be used. For example, it would not be possible to register RELAX for 'massage services' or ROCKBASS for 'guitar accessories'.
- *Value* – this excludes from registration references to the price of the goods and/or services, as well as references to value in terms of quality. For example, it would not be possible to register either 10 EUROS or MORE FOR YOUR MONEY for most, if not all, goods and/or services.

- *Geographical origin* – this excludes from registration references to the place where goods are produced or where services are rendered, as well as references to the subject matter of a particular product. An objection is raised if a location is currently associated with a particular product or service, or if it could foreseeably be so associated in the future. For example, it would not be possible to register NORTH POLE for 'skis' but it would be possible to register this for 'pizza delivery services' (as nobody would expect their pizza to be produced in, or delivered from, that location). It should be noted that protected designations of origin (PDOs) and protected geographical indications (PGIs) are given specific protection in Article 7(1)(j) and are considered in section 12 below.
- *The time of production of the goods or of rendering of the service* – this excludes from registration references to when goods are produced and when services are available. For example, it would not be possible to register 2008 for 'wine' or 24/7 for most, if not all, services.

6. Customary (generic) signs or indications

This objection derives from Article 7(1)(d) of the Regulation: it is not possible to register "trade marks which consist exclusively of signs or indications which have become customary in the current language or in the *bona fide* and established practices of the trade".

The term 'the trade' has been defined as "all consumers and end users and, depending on the features of the market concerned, all those in the trade to deal with that product commercially" (see the CJEU decision in *BOSTONGURKHA*) where intermediaries such as wholesalers and retailers are involved in the distribution of products. It is not, however, necessary to show that the mark is used generically both by traders and consumers and end users; it can be enough for consumers and end users to use the mark in a generic sense. All of these groups must be considered when assessing whether a mark is generic.

Where the Office raises an objection under this Article, it provides the applicant with evidence showing use of the mark in a generic sense. Such evidence is almost always obtained as a result of the internet searches carried out as part of the examination process.

For an objection to be raised on this ground, it is not sufficient that the mark has been used generically by the applicant or just one other trader, although such evidence could lead to objections for lack of distinctiveness or descriptiveness. Instead, there must be evidence of more widespread use in the trade.

It is also important to note that the relevant date for assessing the mark is always the filing date of the application. As such, it is irrelevant whether a mark was distinctive when it was first used, or for a considerable period after that, if it had become generic by the time the application was filed.

It should be remembered that an objection raised under Article 7(1)(d) can be overcome if the applicant demonstrates 'acquired distinctiveness' (see Chapter 8).

No objection should be raised under Article 7(1)(d) against applications to register plant variety names in respect of the relevant products. This is because there is a specific ground of objection relating to plant variety names under Article 7(1)(l) (see section 14 below).

7. Characteristics which result from the nature of the goods, are necessarily technical or add substantial value

These objections derive from Article 7(1)(e) of the Regulation: it is not possible to register "trade marks which consist exclusively of: (i) the shape or another characteristic which results from the nature of the goods themselves; (ii) the shape or another characteristic of goods which is necessary to obtain a technical result; or (iii) the shape or another characteristic of goods which gives substantial value to the goods."

The Office generally considers Article 7(1)(e) as a preliminary objection where it thinks an objection on these grounds might be relevant, although there is no requirement for it to do so.

Previously, this Article only covered shapes (both two-dimensional and three-dimensional), but it was extended to cover all relevant characteristics on 23 March 2016. As a result, many non-traditional marks, such as smells, may now face objections under Article 7(1)(e). This change limits the potential effects of the change in representation requirements discussed in section 3 above.

Each of the parts of Article 7(1)(e) is separate and distinct and needs to be considered separately.

- *Characteristics which result from the nature of the goods themselves* – an objection should only be raised under this ground if the trade mark consists 'exclusively' of the natural shape or other characteristics of the goods covered by the application. If only part of the mark results from the nature of the goods, or there are alternative shapes for the goods, an objection should not be raised. In this context, the expression 'natural' covers both characteristics appearing naturally without any human intervention and characteristics of manufactured products. For example, it would not be possible to register the shape of an apple for 'apples'.
- *Characteristics which are necessary to obtain a technical result* – an objection should only be raised under this ground where a mark consists 'exclusively' of a shape that performs a technical function or where a mark consists 'exclusively' of other characteristics of the relevant products that perform a technical function. This means that all the essential elements of the characteristic in question must perform a technical function. If the shape or other characteristic is, or was previously, the subject of a patent or patent application, that would be taken by the Office as an indication that the shape or other characteristic is necessary to achieve a technical result: it is not possible to use the trade mark system to extend into perpetuity a monopoly obtained as a result of patent protection. The fact that there are other characteristics that could perform the same function is irrelevant. The inclusion of a non-functional element within the mark should, however, prevent an objection being raised, unless the non-functional element is minor or arbitrary in nature. For example, it was not possible for Lego to

maintain a registration for the shape of a red brick (see the CJEU decision in *Red Lego Brick*).

- *Characteristics which give substantial value to the goods* – the Office raises objections under this ground where it thinks a product is worth more as a result of the shape or other characteristic for which protection is sought. Again, it must be kept in mind that this objection is only relevant if the mark consists 'exclusively' of the shape or other characteristic of a product. If it also contains additional elements, an objection should not be raised, unless the objectionable shape or other characteristic is the main (or only) reason consumers would buy the relevant product. For example, it would not be possible to register the shape of the cut of a diamond for 'diamonds'. An application for the smell of a perfume is also likely to face an objection under this article.

As consumer perception is not the determining factor, objections raised under this Article are generally very difficult to overcome, unless the Office has made a clear error in assessing the mark.

It should be emphasised that being able to prove 'acquired distinctiveness' is of no help when facing an objection under Article 7(1)(e). No matter how high the level of distinctiveness or consumer recognition, this will not enable an objection to be overcome.

8. Public policy and morality

This objection derives from Article 7(1)(f) of the Regulation: it is not possible to register "trade marks which are contrary to public policy or to accepted principles of morality".

This ground for refusal is intended to prevent the registration of trade marks that have criminal or religious connotations, consist of explicit or taboo signs and/or offend against the basic moral norms of society. It is not, however, necessary for the use of the mark to be illegal for an objection under this ground to be raised: the objection relates to the mark applied for *per se*, not the use that has been or might be made.

Unusually, the relevant public when assessing this article is wider than the potential consumers of the goods or services applied for: it also extends to people who may encounter the mark, even if they are not targeted as potential consumers. For example, the Office Guidelines indicate that an application to register SCREW YOU for products sold in sex shops would not face an objection under this Article, as the potential consumers of such products (ie, consumers who choose to go inside sex shops) are not likely to be offended by the term. By contrast, an application to register SCREW YOU for products sold to the general public would be likely to face an objection.

The intentions of the applicant are not relevant, so an objection will be raised even if the applicant does not know the mark is potentially immoral or contrary to public policy. For example, there have been several rejections of the common English word CURVE, which translates as 'whores' in Romanian.

While public policy (see 8.1 below) and accepted principles of morality (see 8.2 below) often overlap, they are distinct concepts and need to be considered separately. Public policy can be assessed by reference to objective criteria, whereas accepted principles of morality are by their very nature subjective. It should be noted that examiners are supposed to consider morality at an objective level and not be guided by their personal views.

8.1 Public policy

The term 'public policy' is considered by reference to Union law, and the common understanding within the Union of basic principles and values, such as human rights. For example, objections would be raised against applications to register Nazi symbols (contrary to German law) or the names of terrorist organisations (contrary to a common position taken by the Council). The use of the mark does not have to be illegal for an objection to be raised on the basis that it is contrary to public policy.

8.2 Accepted principles of morality

As noted above, the term 'accepted principles of morality' has to be considered as objectively as possible. There is, however, no clear guidance on how this concept should be defined in any particular context. Marks consisting of offensive and/or vulgar words are normally refused registration, as are marks with potentially offensive religious connotations. In addition, terms with a particular significance are refused registration if their use in a banal context would be offensive. For example, an application to register ATATURK was rejected as the word has an important spiritual and political meaning for people of Turkish origin.

Conversely, an objection should not be raised simply because a mark is in bad taste or likely to upset particular individuals. Rather, a mark should only be deemed objectionable if it is likely to have a clearly offensive impact on people of normal sensitivity. However, it is of course often very difficult for examiners to assess accurately the impact a mark will have on the average consumer.

9. Deceptive trade marks

This objection derives from Article 7(1)(g) of the Regulation: it is not possible to register "trade marks which are of such a nature as to deceive the public, for instance as to the nature, quality or geographical origin of the goods or services".

This objection covers situations where there is evidence of "actual deceit or a sufficiently serious risk that the consumer will be deceived" (see the CJEU decision in *ELIZABETH EMANUEL*). It should be noted that the reference to "nature, quality or geographical origin" in the Article is non-exhaustive, so that if a trade mark is deceptive in relation to any characteristic of the goods and/or services applied for, an objection will be raised.

When assessing whether a mark is deceptive, it is necessary to take account of how relevant consumers will view the mark. If the public is likely to view it as fanciful or as advertising puffery, rather than truly indicating a characteristic of the goods, no objection should be raised under this Article. For example, no objection should be raised against an application for the mark CARLSBERG – PROBABLY THE

BEST BEER IN THE WORLD, even if (on which no comment is made) this statement is not correct.

The Office objects to a mark which cannot be used in a non-deceptive way in relation to the goods and/or services applied for, with each term in the specification being considered separately. For example, an application to register XX's CHOCOLATE SAUCE in relation to 'chocolate sauce; strawberry sauce' would only face an objection in relation to 'strawberry sauce'. Conversely, if the specification were for the wider term 'sauces', no objection would be raised, despite the fact that this term would include lots of sauces other than chocolate sauce. This is because it is not impossible for the mark to be used in a non-deceptive way in relation to those goods.

It should be noted that marks objected to on the basis that they are deceptive often face other objections as well. In particular, objections are commonly raised under Article 7(1)(c) relating to descriptive marks (see section 5 above) and Article 7(1)(j) relating to protected designations of origin and geographical indications (see section 12 below).

Applicants also need to be careful when attempting to overcome objections under other Articles to ensure they do not open themselves up to a 'deceptiveness' objection. For example, an application for MADE IN IRELAND for 'clothing' would face a descriptiveness objection; amending the specification to read 'clothing, none made in 'Ireland' would overcome this particular descriptiveness objection but lead to a new deceptiveness objection.

10. Flags and emblems protected under the Paris Convention

This objection derives from Article 7(1)(h) of the Regulation: it is not possible to register "trade marks which have not been authorised by the competent authorities and are to be refused pursuant to Article 6ter of the Paris Convention".

Article 6ter of the Paris Convention prevents the unauthorised use and/or registration of trade marks consisting of or containing any of the following:

- *armorial bearings, flags, and other State emblems, official signs and hallmarks indicating control and warranty and heraldic imitations of these things* – this protection extends to the armorial bearings, flags etc of all countries that are signatories to the Paris Convention and/or are members of the WTO; and
- *armorial bearings, flags, other emblems, abbreviations and names of international intergovernmental organisations of which a relevant country is a member, together with heraldic imitations of these things* – a 'relevant country' in this context again means countries that are signatories to the Paris Convention and/or are members of the WTO. Protection under Article 6ter does not, however, extend to armorial bearings, flags, etc that are protected separately under international agreements already in place when the Paris Convention was signed.

In the remainder of this section, things that are covered by Article 6ter are referred to simply as 'emblems' for ease of reference.

There is a caveat to the above: Article 6ter of the Paris Convention does not prevent any use or registration that does not suggest a connection between the organisation concerned and either the emblem used or the person using the emblem. In practice, examiners have a tendency to raise an objection and leave it for the applicant to show that this caveat applies.

The emblems protected by Article 6ter are contained in a searchable database that can be accessed through the World Intellectual Property Organisation ('WIPO') website (www.wipo.int/ipdl/en/6ter/search-struct.jsp). They are described by reference to the Vienna Classification, established by the Vienna Agreement (1973), which is an international classification system relating to the figurative elements of marks. The relevant classification under the Vienna Classification system can also be searched on the WIPO website.

In explaining the kinds of emblem covered by Article 6ter, it is worth considering some examples (the numbers referred to are those in the 6ter database).

- *Armorial bearings* – this term is generally defined as "heraldry consisting of a design or image depicted on a shield" and covers coats of arms. For example, the coat of arms of Belgium is protected under number BE10. It is possible for a country to have more than one set of armorial bearings protected (for example Germany has 28).
- *Flags* – this covers both national flags and other official flags. For example, Portugal has protection for its national flag (PT23), the flag of the President of the Portuguese Republic (PT24) and the flag of the Assembly of the Portuguese Republic (PT25). An example of a protected flag for an intergovernmental organisation is QO1529, the flag of the Organisation for the Prohibition of Chemical Weapons.
- *Other state emblems* – this covers state emblems other than flags and armorial bearings. For example, the Royal Cypher of Queen Elizabeth II of the UK is protected under number GB6.
- *Emblems of international intergovernmental organisations* – this covers logos and other emblems used by such organisations, often the same emblem translated into different languages. For example, the logo of the WHO Framework Convention on Tobacco Control is protected in English, French, Spanish, Arabic, Russian and Chinese (QO1357 to QO1362 inclusive).
- *Official signs and hallmarks indicating control and warranty* – this covers a very wide range of emblems, most of which certify that a particular good or service has a certain quality. This includes hallmarks indicating that products are made from a particular material (eg, LV32, a Latvian registration indicating platinum) and signs indicating that products come from a particular country (eg, AR9, indicating organic products produced and/or manufactured in Argentina). Other protected signs include the seal of the US Copyright Office (US117) and other governmental organisations. The protection given to these signs and hallmarks is limited to the relevant goods and/or services.
- *Abbreviations and names of international intergovernmental organisations* – there are registrations for a very wide range of different organisations from across the globe. The names of most of the protected organisations are unlikely to be used accidentally or out of context (eg, the United Nations Entity for

Gender Equality and the Empowerment of Women, QO1547). The same cannot, however, be said for many of the other abbreviations, which could be used accidentally (eg, initialisms and acronyms such as ERA, FIT, EVA, NIB and PAM are all protected). If an objection is raised, the applicant will need to demonstrate that there is no likelihood of consumers thinking there is a connection between it or its trade mark and the relevant organisation, which is generally possible unless the exact mark is being applied for in relation to directly relevant products.

Where a trade mark consists of or contains an identical reproduction of an emblem protected by Article 6ter, the situation is clear. An objection will be raised and the application will be refused, unless either authorisation from the competent authority is (or has been) obtained or the Office is persuaded that the public will not be misled or presume a connection between the mark and the protected emblem.

The situation is not as straightforward if a trade mark consists of or contains something that may or may not be a 'heraldic imitation' of an emblem protected by Article 6ter. When assessing whether something is a heraldic imitation, it is necessary to consider "the heraldic description of the emblem at issue" and the "heraldic connotations which distinguish the emblem from other signs" (see the CJEU decision in *AMERICAN CLOTHING*).

If the Office thinks a trade mark may contain a protected emblem, it will obtain an official reproduction of the relevant protected emblem and compare it with the mark applied for (and of course check whether authorisation has been given by the competent authority). This involves consideration of the way in which the protected emblem is described and classified on the Article 6ter database. For example, the Swedish flag (which has a relatively simple design) is classified as follows: one flag (Vienna Classification number 24.07.01); a cross within a square or rectangle (24.13.23); a cross without any figurative element (24.13.24); other crosses, that is, one of a type not specifically covered by a separate section (24.13.25); the colour yellow or gold (29.01.02); the colour blue (29.01.04); and two predominant colours (29.01.12).

If the characteristics of the protected emblem are contained in the mark applied for, it is considered to be a heraldic imitation and an objection is raised, unless there are sufficient differences to mean it will not be perceived as an imitation of the protected emblem. For example, see EUTM registration number 7087281, which was found not to be a misleading heraldic imitation of the Finnish flag, despite all the essential features of that flag being present.

It is possible for a trade mark to be deemed to be a heraldic imitation of a protected emblem even if all parts of that emblem are not present. This is the case where the elements that are reproduced are the most significant and unique heraldic features of the emblem. For example, see refused EUTM application number 4820213, found to be a heraldic imitation of the US Justice Department emblem (6ter number US40).

If a trade mark falls foul of Article 7(1)(h), the application will be refused for all goods and/or services covered by the application. The only exception to this is "official signs and hallmarks indicating control and warranty", which are specific to particular goods. If the objection is raised on this basis, the refusal will only relate to the protected goods and any similar goods.

11. Trade marks of particular public interest

This objection derives from Article 7(1)(i) of the Regulation: it is not possible to register "trade marks which include badges, emblems or escutcheons other than those covered by Article 6ter of the Paris Convention and which are of particular public interest, unless the consent of the competent authority to their registration has been given". (An 'escutcheon' is a shield or emblem (normally shaped like a shield) bearing a coat of arms.)

In the remainder of this section, things covered by this Article are referred to simply as 'emblems' for ease of reference.

Trade marks covered by Article 6ter of the Paris Convention are discussed in section 10: the present Article needs to be read alongside this as equivalent protection is given. In particular, 'heraldic imitations' of the emblems protected under Article 7(1)(i) are also covered.

There is no restriction on who can own the protected emblems – they can be owned by countries, international intergovernmental organisations (as with the emblems protected under Article 6ter) or any other body.

As there is no specific database or list of the emblems protected under this Article, it is very difficult for the Office to search for emblems that may be relevant. As a result, most objections are raised in relation to well-known emblems protected under international treaties (eg, the Olympic symbol of five interlocking rings, which is protected under the Nairobi Treaty on the Protection of the Olympic Symbol and in specific legislation in some of the Member States). In addition, this Article protects the symbols of the Union, such as the Euro sign (€).

An objection is only raised if it is felt that relevant consumers will be misled into thinking there is a connection between the mark applied for and the owner of the relevant emblem. This 'connection' can be quite wide: it includes consumers believing the products in question were produced by, warranted by, licensed by, approved by or otherwise linked to the owner of the relevant emblem.

An objection does not necessarily have to cover all the goods and/or services in the application. Rather, it should only relate to the goods and/or services that are deemed relevant (that is, goods and/or services in respect of which the public will make the necessary 'connection'). In practice, however, if the necessary 'connection' is made at all for many of the emblems protected under this Article, it is likely to extend to all goods and services.

12. Protected designations of origin and geographical indications

This objection derives from Article 7(1)(j) of the Regulation: it is not possible to register "trade marks which are excluded from registration pursuant to Union legislation or national law or to international agreements to which the Union or the Member State concerned is party, providing for protection of designations of origin and geographical indications".

- *Protected designations of origin (PDOs)* give protection to agricultural products

and foodstuffs that are produced, processed and prepared in a given geographical area using recognised know-how. Protection is only given if consumers expect that products bearing the PDO fulfil this criterion, so that a product name cannot be protected if it is generic. For example, 'Cheddar' has been found to be generic and so could not be protected (although 'West Country Farmhouse Cheddar Cheese' has been afforded protection). Conversely, cheeses such as 'Roquefort' and 'Feta' have been granted PDO status.
- *Protected geographical indications (PGIs)* give protection to agricultural products and foodstuffs that are closely linked to a particular geographical area, with at least some part of the production, processing or preparation of the product taking place in that area. As such, the link between the product and the area is not quite as strict for PGIs as it is for PDOs. Continuing the cheese theme, examples of PGIs include 'Gruyère' and 'Yorkshire Wensleydale'.

The Council considered that, under the previous version of the Regulation, PDOs and PGIs were not given the same level of protection as other instruments of Union law. As a result, Article 7(1)(j) was included in the Regulation with the intention of clarifying and ensuring consistency in the scope of protection of PDOs and PGIs.

The products given protection under the PDO and PGI schemes are listed on the searchable Database of Origin & Registration (DOOR), which can be found on the Commission website (http://ec.europa.eu/agriculture/quality/door/list.html). For a product to be granted PDO or PGI status, producers need to apply to the Commission (normally through the national authority dealing with the relevant products) and demonstrate that the product is worthy of protection. Further information about the PDO and PGI schemes can also be found on the Commission website (http://ec.europa.eu/agriculture/quality/schemes/index_en.htm).

Objections are only raised on this ground for refusal where an EUTM application covers either the exact goods for which the PDO or PGI is protected or goods that are comparable to those goods.

An objection should be raised where:

- *the mark applied for consists of an exact PDO or PGI* – here, it is clear that the mark cannot be registered. In addition, an objection should also be raised on the basis that the mark is descriptive;
- *an exact PDO or PGI is contained within the mark* – an objection should be raised even if there are additional elements in the mark that make it distinctive or if the PDO or PGI is used in a descriptive or indirect way (for example, on a mark consisting of a label containing generic references and materials);
- *the mark consists of or contains an imitation or evocation of a PDO or PGI* – for an objection to be raised, the mark must make consumers think of the PDO or PGI. This can be done in several ways, including (using the example of 'Gorgonzola'):
  - misspelling the PDO or PGI (eg, 'Gorganzole');

- using an adjectival form of the PDO or PGI (eg, 'Gorgonzolaful'); and
- using a translation of the PDO or PGI (eg, 'горгонзола', which is 'Gorgonzola' in Bulgarian);

or

- *the mark contains misleading elements that will be seen as a reference to a PDO or PGI* – This objection is only raised very rarely and is perhaps most commonly seen where the mark applied for includes images associated with the PDO or PGI region.

13. Protected traditional terms for wine

This objection derives from Article 7(1)(k) of the Regulation: it is not possible to register "trade marks which are excluded from registration pursuant to Union legislation or international agreements to which the Union is party, providing for protection of traditional terms for wine".

This objection prevents the registration of trade marks that consist of or contain traditional terms for wine which are protected in the Union. Examples of protected terms include: 'Claret', which can only be used for wine from Bordeaux in France; 'Crianza', which can only be used for wines from Spain with a minimum period of ageing; and 'Winzersekt', which can only be used for sparkling wines produced and processed in specified wine-growing zones in Germany. Details of the protected traditional terms can be found on the E-BACCHUS database (http://ec.europa.eu/agriculture/wine/e-bacchus).

The protection given to traditional terms for wine is similar to the protection given to PDOs and PGIs and most of the practice referred to in section 12 above applies equally here. There are, however, some differences that are worth noting.

- *Protection for traditional terms for wine only extends to the particular language of the term.* As such, a translation of the traditional term will not face an objection, unless it is thought that the mark is likely to mislead consumers as to the geographical origin of the product.
- *Where a mark contains a traditional term along with other elements, an objection will be raised if the mark seems likely to mislead consumers.* No objection should, however, be raised if the traditional term is being used in relation to wines that are qualified to use the traditional term in question. For example, it would be possible to register a mark consisting of a wine label on which the term 'Vin de Pays' appears in relation to French wine if the production zone of the wine is also apparent on the label and the application covers wine from the relevant production zone.

As traditional terms for wine are used alongside PDOs and PGIs, it is likely that many applications will face objections under both this Article and that protecting PDOs and PGIs (see section 12 above). In the example of the label given previously, the term 'Vin de Pays' would need to be used with an indication of where the wine comes from. The term 'Vin de Pays de Vaucluse' would be an acceptable use of the traditional term, but 'Vaucluse' is a PGI, so an objection could also be raised on that basis.

14. Protected traditional specialities

This objection derives from Article 7(1)(l) of the Regulation: it is not possible to register "trade marks which are excluded from registration pursuant to Union legislation or international agreements to which the Union is party, providing for protection of traditional specialities guaranteed".

The term 'traditional specialities guaranteed' (TSG) relates to protected terms which indicate that an agricultural product intended for human consumption or foodstuff has a traditional composition or has been produced according to a traditional production method. The list of protected TSGs can be found on the DOOR database alongside PGIs and PDOs (http://ec.europa.eu/agriculture/quality/door/list.html). There are not many registered TSGs, but examples include 'Mozzarella' and 'Jamon Serrano'.

The protection given to TSGs is comparable to that given to PDOs and PGIs and the practice referred to in section 12 above applies equally here.

15. Protected plant variety names

This objection derives from Article 7(1)(m) of the Regulation: it is not possible to register "trade marks which consist of, or reproduce in their essential elements, an earlier plant variety denomination registered in accordance with Union legislation or national law, or international agreements to which the Union or the Member State concerned is a party, providing for protection of plant variety rights, and which are in respect of plant varieties of the same or closely related species".

Plant variety rights protect new varieties of cultivated varieties or subspecies of live plants and agricultural seeds. Protection for plant varieties comes from two sources:

- *registration as a Community plant variety right (CPVR),* which gives the breeder the exclusive right to produce that variety within the Union; and
- *registration with the International Union for the Protection of New Varieties of Plants (normally known as UPOV),* which gives the breeder the exclusive right to produce that variety in countries that are UPOV members. UPOV members include both the Union and all the Member States individually.

The duration of CPVR and UPOV registrations varies between 20 and 30 years, depending on the products involved. One of the Union's obligations as part of the membership of UPOV is, however, to ensure that the use of a plant variety name cannot be hindered even after the registration has expired. As a result, plant variety names can never be registered as trade marks, whether or not they are still registered as plant varieties.

An objection is raised where a trade mark consists of or contains a protected plant variety name, or the essential elements of that name, and the EUTM application covers relevant products. 'Relevant products' include the exact species of plant or seed protected, similar species of plants or seeds and dried, preserved and/or frozen versions of those plants or seeds. For example, if a variety name were protected for 'seedless grapes', it would not be possible to obtain an EUTM registration for that name in respect of seedless grapes, seeded grapes, dried and preserved grapes or, potentially, grape juice.

Objections can be overcome by removing the objectionable products from the application. Where broad terms are used, this can be done by exclusion. For example, if an application covering 'fresh fruits and vegetables' were to face an objection because of a plant variety right covering 'raspberries', amending the specification to read 'fresh fruits and vegetables, none being raspberries' would allow the objection to be overcome.

Details of plant varieties protected in the Union (and elsewhere) can be found on the Community Plant Variety Office website (http://www.cpvo.europa.eu), though an account must be created before a search may be carried out.

Where a plant variety name is in use, but has not been registered as a CPVR or with UPOV, an objection should not be raised under this Article. EUTM applications for marks that are unregistered plant variety names can, however, still face objections on the basis that they are descriptive (see section 5 above).

Further reference

Regulation – Articles 4, 7

Implementing Regulation – Rule 11

Office Guidelines – Part B, Section 4

WIPO website – details of Article 6ter and searchable database – www.wipo.int

Commission website – details of PDOs, PGIs, TSGs and traditional terms for wine, with searchable databases – http://ec.europa.eu

Community Plant Variety Office (CPVO) website – http://www.cpvo.europa.eu

UPOV website – www.upov.int

Libertel Groep BV v Benelux-Merkenbureau (*'LIBERTEL'*) (Case C-104/01), CJEU decision dated 6 May 2003

Sieckmann v German Patent and Trademark Office (*'SIECKMANN'*) (Case C-273/00), CJEU decision dated 12 December 2002

Heidelberger Bauchemie GmbH v DPMA (*'HEIDELBERGER BAUCHEMIE'*) (Case C-49/02), CJEU decision dated 24 June 2004

Erpo Möbelwerk GmbH v OHIM (*'DAS PRINZIP DER BEQUEMLICHKEIT'*) (Case C-64/02), CJEU decision dated 21 October 2004

Audi AG v OHIM (*'VORSPRUNG DURCH TECHNIK'*) (Case C-398/08), CJEU decision dated 21 January 2010

Koninklijke KPN Nederland NV v Benelux-Merkenbureau (*'POSTKANTOOR'*) (Case C-363/99), CJEU decision dated 12 February 2004

Campina Melkunie BV v Benelux-Merkenbureau (*'BIOMILD'*) (Case C-265/00), CJEU decision dated 12 February 2004

Björnekulla Fruktindustrier AB v Procordia Food AB ('BOSTONGURKHA') (Case C-371/02), CJEU decision dated 29 April 2004

Lego Juris A/S v OHIM (*'Red Lego Brick'*) (Case C-48/09), CJEU decision dated 14 September 2010

Elizabeth Florence Emanuel v Continental Shelf 128 Ltd (*'ELIZABETH EMANUEL'*) (Case C-259/04), CJEU decision dated 30 March 2006

American Clothing Associates SA v OHIM (*'AMERICAN CLOTHING'*) (Joined Cases C-202/08 and C-208/08), CJEU decision dated 16 July 2009

Dyson Ltd v Registrar of Trade Marks (*'Dyson's UK application'*) (Case C-321/03), CJEU decision dated 25 January 2007

Chapter 8: Overcoming objections and amendments to applications

1. Introduction

This chapter looks at ways of overcoming the various 'absolute grounds' objections discussed in Chapter 7. It also considers certain actions and arguments that will not result in objections being waived, as well as the options available to an applicant if an objection cannot be overcome.

2. Overcoming absolute grounds objections – summary

There are usually a number of different ways in which an applicant can try to get around an absolute grounds objection. The options available in any given situation depend on both the nature of the objection and the scope of the application (ie, the mark at issue and the goods and/or services concerned).

When notification of an objection is received, the first thing an applicant should do is ensure that it properly understands the nature and scope of the objection. The Office has a duty to raise objections clearly and to provide separate reasons for each objection raised. However, the precise nature and scope of the objections raised is sometimes not entirely clear. If there is any uncertainty in this regard, the applicant should request clarification from the examiner before deciding how to try and overcome the objection

When an absolute grounds objection is raised, the applicant is given two months to respond. This deadline can be extended once, for another two months, with further extensions beyond this only being granted in exceptional circumstances. Applicants need to ensure they respond fully to all objections raised within the time allowed.

It may be possible to obtain more than one extension of time to overcome an objection if evidence of acquired distinctiveness is being compiled in multiple jurisdictions. Even then, in order to obtain more than one extension of time, the applicant needs to give detailed reasons why more time is necessary, as well as details of the evidence that has been compiled up to that point. In short, applicants should not rely on being able to obtain more than one extension of time. Continuation of proceedings (see Chapter 27) is, however, an option, so that it is possible to pay to obtain a further two months if absolutely necessary.

It is worth noting that overcoming most types of absolute grounds objections is not an easy task. Once an examiner has raised an objection, it is often very difficult to persuade him to change his mind. As a result, it is better to try to avoid objections being raised by obtaining advice on whether a mark is capable of registration prior to filing an EUTM application.

Responses to objections need to be filed in writing. While it is possible, and sometimes advisable, to discuss issues with examiners, there are no oral hearings in examination proceedings and a formal response in writing needs to be prepared. This response can be filed electronically, or by fax, meaning that it can be filed on the last day of the time period given if necessary.

3. Ways in which objections can be overcome

There are three main ways in which objections can be overcome.

- *Persuade the examiner to waive the objection* – this involves filing written submissions and, where relevant, evidence demonstrating that the objection should never have been raised and that the mark is inherently capable of registration for the goods and/or services applied for. If this option is available, it is generally the best option. It does not involve any limitation of the application and avoids the costs of filing evidence of acquired distinctiveness. The arguments that need to be filed depend on the nature of the objection raised, the mark, the goods and/or services applied for and who the relevant consumers of those goods and/or services are. The types of argument that can be raised in relation to particular types of mark are discussed in Chapter 7.
- *Amend the specification* – where an objection only relates to some of the goods and/or services in an application, the removal of those goods and/or services necessarily leads to the objection falling away. If the applicant wants to convert the goods and/or services that have been removed into national applications in one or more Member States (see Chapter 25), the goods and/or services being removed should technically be 'withdrawn' from the application and it makes sense to use this wording when restricting the specification. For further information, see Chapter 6.
- *File evidence of acquired distinctiveness* – this is only an option for overcoming objections that the mark is not distinctive, is descriptive and/or is a customary (generic) sign. Compiling evidence of acquired distinctiveness is an expensive and time-consuming process and the evidence needs to be compelling for it to be accepted. This matter is discussed further in section 4 below.

These three options can be used in combination, so that, for example, it is possible to file evidence of acquired distinctiveness for some goods and/or services, argue against the objection for some goods and/or services and withdraw the remainder of the goods and/or services.

4. Acquired distinctiveness

'Acquired distinctiveness' is a way of overcoming objections raised on the basis that a mark is non-distinctive, is descriptive and/or is a customary (generic) sign (that is, in respect of objections raised under Articles 7(1)(b), (c) and/or (d) of the Regulation). It cannot be used to overcome objections raised on any other ground.

To rely on acquired distinctiveness, an applicant needs to prove that the mark applied for "has become distinctive in relation to the goods or services for which registration is requested in consequence of the use which has been made of it".

The applicant must prove that a significant proportion of relevant consumers of the goods and/or services applied for recognise the mark as a trade mark. The burden of proof is high and detailed evidence needs to be filed: proving acquired distinctiveness is not an easy exercise. The evidence filed by the applicant must prove that the mark had acquired distinctiveness as of the filing date of the EUTM application. Where priority is claimed, the relevant date for assessing acquired distinctiveness is the priority date. For Union designations of IRs, the relevant date is the registration date of the IR (or the date on which a subsequent designation of the Union was filed).

It is necessary to prove the mark has acquired distinctiveness in every Member State in which the objection is relevant. Where the objection applies to the whole Union, that objection can in theory only be overcome by proving that the mark is distinctive in every Member State. This is very difficult to do for all but the very largest traders – and is always going to be very expensive, given the cost of compiling evidence relating to every Member State.

In practice, the Office does not generally require acquired distinctiveness to be proved in every Member State, provided that it is able to extrapolate from the evidence filed that the mark has acquired distinctiveness Union-wide. It is, however, necessary to file at least some evidence in relation to each Member State to which the objection relates. For example, the evidence filed in relation to EUTM registration number 63289 (John Deere, combination of the colours green and yellow) did not meet the necessary criteria to prove acquired distinctiveness in two of the (then 15) Member States, but sufficient evidence was filed for the Office to be able to extrapolate and conclude that the mark had acquired distinctiveness in those Member States.

Where an objection only relates to specific Member States, it is only necessary to prove acquired distinctiveness in those Member States. This almost always arises with word marks and relates to the meaning of a word or phrase, or the way it will be perceived, in a particular language. It is normally necessary to provide evidence covering more than one Member State, as the applicant will need to prove acquired distinctiveness in those Member States where:

- *the relevant language is an official language* – and many languages are official languages in more than one Member State. These include:
  - Croatian – an official language in Croatia and Austria;
  - Czech – an official language in the Czech Republic and Slovakia;
  - Danish – an official language in Denmark and Germany;
  - Dutch – an official language in Belgium and the Netherlands;
  - English – an official language in Ireland, Malta and the UK;
  - French – an official language in Belgium, France, Italy and Luxembourg;
  - German – an official language in Austria, Belgium, Germany and Luxembourg;
  - Greek – an official language in Greece and Cyprus;
  - Hungarian – an official language in Austria, Hungary, Romania, Slovakia and Slovenia;

- Irish – an official language in Ireland;
- Italian – an official language in Croatia, Italy and Slovenia;
- Slovakian – an official language in the Czech Republic and Slovakia;
- Slovenian – an official language in Austria, Hungary, Italy and Slovenia; and
- Swedish – an official language in Finland and Sweden;

and

- *the Office believes the mark would be understood* – and many languages are widely understood in more than one Member State. Some languages are always taken to be understood in Member States in which they are not official languages (for example, German is widely understood in some parts of Italy). It is not, however, possible to create a definitive list, as the Member States in which a mark will be understood vary depending on the nature of the mark and the goods and/or services applied for. For example, the General Court has held that English is understood throughout the Union by specialist consumers in the financial markets – for these goods and/or services, therefore, acquired distinctiveness would in theory need to be proved in every Member State. Conversely, if the same mark were applied for in respect of goods and/or services where the relevant consumers were the general public, it is very unlikely that acquired distinctiveness would need to be proved in every Member State in order to overcome an objection successfully.

  As a result of the above, it is, in the event of any doubt, worth discussing with the examiner the Member States in which acquired distinctiveness needs to be shown before any evidence gathering process is started. While it is possible for the Office to extrapolate from the evidence where an objection only relates to a few Member States, this is less likely to occur where an objection covers all, or a very large number of, Member States.

4.1 Preparing evidence of acquired distinctiveness

When assessing acquired distinctiveness, the Office considers four broad factors, each of which the applicant should address in the evidence filed for each relevant Member State:

- *the market share* – the larger the percentage of the market enjoyed by goods and/or services sold under or by reference to the mark, the better;
- *the intensity, geographic scope and length of use* – the wider and longer the mark has been used, the better;
- *the investment made* – the more the mark has been promoted in the relevant markets, the better; and
- *the proportion of the relevant public who recognise the mark as a trade mark* – the higher the percentage the better, but there is no fixed percentage that must recognise the mark. Instead the mark must be known to a 'significant part' of the relevant public.

It is very important to note that acquired distinctiveness cannot be proved simply by filing evidence of the applicant's use of the mark. What is important is consumer recognition, not use, so it is vital that independent evidence is obtained if possible. While a lot of the necessary evidence usually needs to be prepared by the applicant (turnover figures, for example), greater weight tends to be given to independent evidence of consumer recognition than to equivalent evidence prepared by the applicant.

For guidance on the preparation of evidence to be filed with the Office, see Chapter 13. Although that chapter relates to opposition proceedings, the same considerations apply equally when preparing evidence of acquired distinctiveness. Of particular note here are opinion polls and surveys, which (if done well) are often the most effective ways of demonstrating consumer recognition. Statements from the trade (from both the trade press and other traders) and independent bodies such as chambers of commerce can also be very useful in proving acquired distinctiveness, as can awards given to the applicant (assuming that an award is connected to the use of the mark in some way).

Although the relevant date for proving acquired distinctiveness is the filing date, it is possible for evidence relating to the period after the filing date to be taken into account if this indicates what the perception of the relevant public was, or was likely to have been, at the relevant date.

5. Things that will not overcome an objection

- *Amendment of the mark* – once an EUTM application has been filed, it is not possible to amend the mark covered by the application. As a result, it is not possible to overcome an objection by either removing an element (for example, a PDO that has been included accidentally in a composite mark) or adding a further distinctive element to the mark.
- *Existing EUTM registrations* – the Office is not bound by its own previous decisions. Therefore, the existence of EUTM registrations for the same mark (and covering the same goods and/or services) does not in itself enable an objection to be overcome. This is the same whether the pre-existing registrations are owned by the applicant or someone else. Of course, the Office considers whether the objection was validly raised in the light of the earlier EUTM registrations, but it may be that law and practice have changed since the earlier registrations were obtained.
- *Existing registrations in Member States* – an existing registration for the mark covered by the EUTM application in one Member State, or indeed in all Member States, does not in itself allow an objection to be overcome. This is because each national IPO carries out a national, rather than Union-wide, assessment that is different to the assessment carried out by the Office. In any event, the Office is not bound by the decisions of national IPOs. The only way earlier national registrations can really be of assistance is where an objection relates to specific Member States and there are decisions in those States permitting the registration of the mark, especially on the basis of acquired distinctiveness. Even in those circumstances, however, the Office is not bound to follow the earlier national decisions, although it will consider them and may find them persuasive.

- *Existing registrations outside the Union* – such registrations are considered to be of no relevance, given that the laws under which a mark was registered are always different to those in the Union. As a result, existing registrations outside the Union (whether owned by the applicant or someone else) will never allow an objection to be overcome.
- *Adding a disclaimer* – it is not possible to add a disclaimer to overcome an objection. If an applicant wants to disclaim exclusive rights to an element of a mark, this needs to be done at the time the application is filed. The existence of a disclaimer does not, however, prevent an objection being raised if the mark is not capable of registration: thus, there seems no real benefit to including one (see Chapter 5).
- *The applicant arguing that it is the only trader using the mark* – having a 'factual monopoly' in the use of the mark does not mean it is inherently capable of registration. The inherent nature of a mark cannot be affected by how many traders are using it. Being the only trader using a mark may make it easier to prove acquired distinctiveness, but it cannot make the mark more registrable in itself.

6. Division

Where an objection is raised against only some of the goods and/or services in an application, the applicant may decide to divide the application into two parts, to separate the goods and/or services in relation to which the objection applies from the remainder. The fee payable for dividing an EUTM application is currently €250.

An application that is divided becomes two separate applications. So long as the division clearly separates the goods and/or services to which the objection applies from the remainder, the divided application which covers goods and/or services that are not the subject of an objection is accepted and published.

The divided application that contains the goods and/or services to which the objection relates remains subject to the objection. As such, division does not overcome an objection: it merely allows the application to proceed immediately for goods and/or services that are not covered by the objection.

An EUTM application can be divided at any point before registration. This means it is possible to divide an application after it has been refused, for whatever reason, if there are ongoing appeal proceedings.

It is also possible to divide a registration. For further information see Chapter 15.

7. If an objection cannot be overcome

If an objection or objections raised against an application cannot be overcome through any of the means discussed above, the application is refused for all the goods and/or services to which the objection relates. If the objection does not relate to the full specification, the application is accepted and proceeds to publication as to the remainder.

If an applicant does not want its application to be deemed to have been finally refused, it has the option of withdrawing the application before a final refusal is issued. Unless the applicant is going to convert the EUTM application into national applications (see Chapter 25), however, there is no real difference (except perhaps psychologically) between an application being finally refused and an application being withdrawn because an objection cannot be overcome.

If the applicant is interested in conversion, the application should be withdrawn before a refusal is issued. This is because it not possible to convert into national applications in the Member States to which a refusal relates. For more information, see Chapter 25.

If the applicant believes the objection should not have been maintained, and that the mark in question is capable of registration, it is possible to appeal against the refusal of the application to the Boards of Appeal. For information on appeals, see chapters 19 and 20.

Where an objection definitely cannot be overcome, the applicant should consider whether it would be worthwhile filing a new application for a mark that would not face the same objections. For example, if a mark is refused on the basis that it is not distinctive, a new application for the mark combined with some other distinctive element (such as a logo) may well be capable of registration. It is generally preferable to have some rather than no registered protection in place.

There is nothing to prevent an applicant re-filing an application that has been refused. Generally, re-filing an identical application to one that has been refused will simply lead to another refusal. There are, however, circumstances in which re-filing an application could lead to a different outcome. Examples of situations in which the later application might be accepted include where there has been a change in law or practice or where the mark has acquired distinctiveness since the filing date of the earlier application.

Further reference

Regulation – Articles 7 and 44

Implementing Regulation – Rules 11 and 13a

Office Guidelines – Part A, Section 2; Part B, Sections 1 and 4

Chapter 9: After acceptance

1. Introduction

This chapter considers the steps in the EUTM application process other than absolute grounds examination (which is covered in chapters 6 and 7), as well as looking at the ways in which an EUTM application can be amended before it proceeds to registration. Finally, this chapter explains what happens at the end of the registration process.

2. Steps carried out alongside examination of the application

At the same time as examination on absolute grounds is taking place, the Office carries out two administrative tasks that are entirely independent of the examination of the application.

Translation: the Office translates the EUTM application into the Languages of the Union (save for Irish, for which no translation is prepared). This is done so that, if the EUTM application is accepted for publication, it can be published in all the Languages of the Union.

Searches: the Office carries out a search of the EUTM register for existing applications and registrations it feels could conflict with the mark applied for. If requested by the applicant, the Office also asks the IPOs of the Member States that participate in the national search system to prepare search reports. The relevant reports will be sent to the applicant before the EUTM application is published. For further information on these searches, see Chapter 4.

3. Publication and the opposition period

Once an EUTM application has been accepted, it is published in the *EUTM Bulletin*, which is available online. Following publication, the application remains open to challenge for a period of three months, generally referred to as the 'opposition period'.

During the opposition period, anyone who believes the application should not go through to registration can object. This can be done by filing an opposition and/or observations.

Over 10% of EUTM applications are opposed. Opposition proceedings are considered in detail in chapters 10-14. Oppositions can only be based on relative grounds (ie, earlier rights the owner feels should prevent registration of the application). It is not possible to base an opposition on absolute grounds and any such claims in oppositions are discounted.

Observations can only be based on absolute grounds (ie, a claim that the mark is not capable of registration for the goods and/or services applied for). It is not possible to base observations on relative grounds and any such claims in observations are discounted. Observations are considered further in section 5 below.

As they are based on mutually exclusive grounds, it is possible (though very rare) for the same party to file both an opposition and observations against the same application.

It is not possible to extend the opposition period under any circumstances. Oppositions filed after the expiry of the opposition period are discounted. If, however, an opposition is filed, observations can be filed at any point before a final decision is taken in the opposition proceedings.

Once the opposition period has expired, it is still possible to challenge the registration of the mark, on both absolute and relative grounds, through invalidity proceedings (see Chapter 18).

4. Errors in publication

If the Office makes an error when publishing an EUTM application, so that the information contained in the *EUTM Bulletin* is incorrect, it has an obligation to correct the error.

If the error relates to the mark (so that the wrong mark was published), or means that not all the relevant goods and/or services were included in the publication (eg, a term within the specification was omitted), the application must be re-published, resulting in a new opposition period.

In all other circumstances, the correction is published but the opposition period is not re-opened.

5. Observations

Observations can be filed by anyone who feels a mark applied for is not capable of registration on absolute grounds. This includes individuals, companies and any group or body that represents the interests of the manufacturers or producers of goods, the suppliers of services, retailers and other traders and consumers of goods and/or services.

Although often thought of as an alternative to an opposition, the filing of observations is not limited to the opposition period. Observations can be filed:

- *before publication* – in which case they are considered as part of the Office's examination of the application on absolute grounds;
- *during the opposition period* – in which case they are considered before a decision is taken on registration; and
- *after the expiry of the opposition period* – this is only possible where an opposition has been filed, in which case the observations must be received by the Office before a final decision is taken in the opposition proceedings.

If observations are filed out of time (ie, after the expiry of the opposition period or after a decision has been taken in all the oppostions filed against an application), they are not considered by the Office.

Observations can be filed in any of the Languages of the Office or in the language of the proceedings if an opposition has been filed. Observations filed in any other language are discounted.

Filing observations does not make the person filing them a party to any proceedings. That person will receive confirmation of receipt of the observations from the Office, but no further correspondence.

The Office takes the following steps when observations are received:

- *confirm receipt* – this receipt also confirms that the observations have been sent to the EUTM applicant;
- *send a copy to the EUTM applicant for its comments* – the EUTM applicant is given a deadline by which to file a response. However, there is no obligation on the applicant to do so and failure to respond has no impact on the application. Having said that, EUTM applicants generally take advantage of the opportunity to explain why they disagree with the points raised in observations; and
- *consider whether, as a result of the observations, an objection on absolute grounds should be raised* – for this to happen, serious doubts must have been raised as to whether the mark is inherently registrable.

If both observations and one or more oppositions are filed, the Office suspends the opposition(s) if it is felt that the observations raise serious doubts as to whether the mark is capable of registration. The opposition will stay suspended until the outcome of the observations is decided.

Where the Office believes that the mark is not capable of registration, it raises an absolute grounds objection. If this happens, the EUTM applicant is given a deadline to respond to the objection in the usual way (see Chapter 8).

If, having considered the observations, the Office decides not to raise an absolute grounds objection, that is the end of the matter. As the person filing the observations is not a party to any proceedings, no appeal is available if the Office decides not to act on the observations. Indeed, as the person filing the observations does not receive any correspondence from the Office other than an acknowledgement of receipt, that person will not be told that the observations have been unsuccessful.

6. Amendment of an application

Once an EUTM application has been filed, it is only possible to amend it in a limited number of ways. The amendments that can be made to an application are:

- *restrictions to the goods and/or services* – this can be done at any time before registration. For further information, see Chapter 6;
- *division* – this involves the application being separated into two or more separate applications. For further information, see Chapter 8;
- *withdrawal* – see section 7 below;
- *correction of errors* – see section 8 below; and
- *amendment of the name, address and/or nationality of the applicant* – this can be

done at any time before registration (and after registration too: see Chapter 15). This covers situations where, for example, a company changes its name and place of business after a takeover. However, it is not possible to amend applications in this way where the identity of the applicant has changed. If any transfer of ownership has taken place, this must be recorded in a different way, as set out in Chapter 16. The Regulation does not mention changing the nationality of the applicant, but the Office permits this to be amended where necessary.

7. Withdrawal

It is possible to withdraw an EUTM application at any time before registration, or before a decision refusing protection becomes final (ie, during the two-month appeal period). Applications can also be withdrawn during opposition proceedings, as discussed in Chapter 14.

A withdrawal can be either partial (so that it only relates to some, but not all, of the goods and/or services in the application) or total (in which case the entire application is withdrawn).

In order to withdraw an application, an unequivocal declaration of withdrawal, in one of the languages of the application, must be sent to the Office. Where there is any doubt about the scope of the declaration, the Office seeks clarification from the EUTM applicant. This can happen if the wording used is not clear, or if an alternative specification is proposed and the Office is not sure whether the intention of the applicant is to withdraw the remainder of the specification.

It is not possible to place any conditions on a withdrawal. For example, if absolute grounds objections have been raised against an application and the applicant indicates that it will withdraw part of the specification if the objections against the remainder are waived, the Office does not treat this as a request for partial withdrawal. Instead it will simply treat this as the applicant suggesting the objection should be waived for part of the specification.

The Office actions a withdrawal by marking the application as 'withdrawn' on the Register. If the application had been published, the withdrawal is also published, irrespective of whether it is a total or partial withdrawal.

Once a declaration of withdrawal is sent to the Office, it can only be rescinded by contacting the Office on the same day it is sent. If this is not done, the withdrawal cannot be rescinded and will become effective.

8. Correction of errors

This section relates to errors made by EUTM applicants. For the correction of errors made by the Office, rather than by the applicant, see Chapter 2.

It is possible to amend an application by correcting errors of wording or of copying, or obvious mistakes made by the applicant, subject to some restrictions as set out below. Amendment is possible whether the error was made when the application was filed or at some other point during the application process, although the timing of the error does impact on whether it can be corrected.

Errors of any nature can be corrected on the day an application is filed. However, if a request for correction is not sent on the day of filing, or if the error is made after filing, there are only limited circumstances in which correction is possible. This is because an error cannot be corrected if the effect of doing so would be:

- *to make a substantial change to the mark applied for* – most changes to a mark are considered substantial, meaning that there is only very limited scope to amend marks themselves. In addition, it is only possible to amend where there was clearly an obvious mistake in the way the mark was filed, restricting the applicability of this type of amendment even more. The Office Guidelines give EUTM registration number 546010 as an example of an amendment that was accepted. In that case, an application was filed for the mark TOPFLOW, claiming priority from an application for TOP FLOW. It was accepted that the omission of the space between the words was obviously a mistake and that amending from TOPFLOW to TOP FLOW did not substantially change the mark; or
- *to expand the goods and/or services covered by the application* – for further information, see Chapter 6.

As a result of these restrictions, it is rarely possible to correct errors relating either to the mark or to the goods and/or services applied for. However, if an amendment is allowed and the application had already been published, the amendment is also published.

9. Registration

If no oppositions or observations are filed, the mark will become registered at the expiry of the opposition period. It takes a little longer, however, for registration of Union designations of IRs to be confirmed (as to which, see Chapter 32).

In the same way, if an applicant successfully defeats any oppositions filed and/or overcomes any objections raised after publication (whether these objections are raised following the filing of observations or otherwise), the mark will become registered.

Where there has been an unsuccessful opposition, the opposed application only proceeds to registration after the expiry of the appeal period following the final decision in the opposition proceedings. Registration is automatic and no fee is payable. Historically, the Office did charge a registration fee, but this was removed in 2009 and it seems very unlikely that such a fee will be reintroduced in the foreseeable future.

All registrations are published in the *EUTM Bulletin* and a certificate of registration is issued. The Office does not, however, issue paper copies of registration certificates. Instead, registration certificates can be downloaded from the Office's website and are normally available two days after registration has been published.

If it is necessary to provide a tribunal or other IPO with a paper copy of a registration certificate, copies can be ordered from the Office. These copies may be either certified or uncertified (both of which can be downloaded from the Office's website).

Once the registration process is completed, an EUTM registration remains in place for 10 years from its filing date, unless it is either revoked (see Chapter 17) or invalidated (see Chapter 18). If a registration is still in place at the expiry of the initial 10-year period, it can be renewed for an unlimited number of further 10-year periods (for details of the renewal process, see Chapter 15).

10. Rejection

If an applicant cannot overcome either objections raised or an opposition filed against an application, the application will be rejected. If this happens, it is possible to appeal against the rejection. The appeals process is discussed in chapters 19 and 20.

Conversely, it may be possible for an applicant to convert its EUTM application into a national application in one or more Member States. Conversion is discussed in Chapter 25.

Further reference

Regulation – Articles 38–40 and 43-45
Implementing Regulation – Rules 10, 12–14, 23 and 24
Office Guidelines – Part B, Sections 1 and 2

Chapter 10: Overview of the EUTM opposition procedure

1. Introduction

This chapter contains a general overview of the EUTM opposition procedure, including basic details of the possible grounds on which an opposition can be based and the key stages in opposition proceedings.

Chapters 11-14 discuss various aspects of opposition proceedings in more detail:

- the basic requirements for filing, who can file and the information that must be contained in a Notice of Opposition (Chapter 11);
- the various grounds on which an opposition can be based are considered (Chapter 12);
- issues to be addressed in evidence and submissions both by opponents and applicants in opposition proceedings (Chapter 13); and
- the ways in which opposition proceedings come to an end (Chapter 14).

2. Overview of the EUTM opposition procedure

Opposition is a type of administrative proceeding that takes place before the Office. It enables the owners of pre-existing registered and unregistered rights to try to prevent an EUTM application proceeding to registration.

The latest available figures, as provided in the Office's *Annual Reports*, show that in 2014 around 12% of EUTM applications were opposed, with 15 662 oppositions being filed. This marks a slight decrease over previous years, during which the figures were closer to 20%, although the actual number of cases brought is broadly similar.

Opposition is only possible once an EUTM application has been accepted as inherently registrable and published for opposition purposes. Such publication triggers the start of a non-extendable three-month 'opposition period' and an opposition cannot be filed after this period ends.

As the Office does not consider prior rights when it examines EUTM applications, the opposition process is vital for the owners of such rights. It is designed to enable them to prevent the registration of marks that would infringe their rights if used in relation to the goods and/or services for which protection is sought.

Opposition proceedings consist of five key stages:

- filing;
- admissibility checks;
- cooling off period;
- adversarial stage; and
- decision.

What happens during each of these stages is summarised in the flowchart below and discussed in the sections that follow.

Summary of opposition proceedings

Application published (opposition period 3 months)

↓

Notice of Opposition filed

↓

Admissibility checks and opposition timetable set

↓

Cooling off period (2-24 months)

↓

Opponent's evidence & submissions

↓

Applicant's evidence & submissions

↓

Opponent's reply

↓

Decision

3. Filing an opposition

A Notice of Opposition must be filed at the Office within the opposition period and an official fee paid (€320 at the time of writing).

It is only possible to base an opposition on 'relative grounds'. There are a number of different relative grounds, which are set out in section 10 below and considered in detail in Chapter 12. All of these grounds require the opponent to own some form of right that pre-dates the opposed application. Absolute grounds cannot be used as a basis of opposition. Further, it is not possible to oppose an EUTM application on the basis that it was filed in bad faith.

The entitlement to file opposition varies slightly, depending upon the rights in question. In general, the opponent has to be the proprietor of these prior rights. However, in some circumstances it is possible for licensees to file oppositions. Where an opposition is based on unregistered rights, the opponent can be anyone authorised to exercise those rights under the laws of the relevant Member State. These points are explored further in Chapter 12.

4. Admissibility checks

Once an opposition is filed, the Office reviews it to ensure sufficient information has been provided and that it is therefore admissible. There are strict requirements as to the information that must be provided for an opposition to be deemed admissible, some of which must be provided within the opposition period. and some of which can be provided later. These requirements are discussed in detail in Chapter 11.

In particular, the opponent must ensure that it clearly identifies the grounds and rights on which the opposition is based. It ultimately needs to provide evidence to substantiate the rights relied upon. These matters are discussed in detail in chapters 11 and 13.

Once an opposition is deemed admissible, the Office sets the timetable. The timetable is set for the proceedings, rather than separately for each party.

5. Cooling off period

The first stage in all opposition proceedings is a 'cooling off' period of two months, which expires two months from the date the opposition timetable is notified to the parties. The precise dates are indicated in the correspondence received from the Office, as the calculation of the time periods depends on the means by which the Office corresponds with each party.

The cooling off period has the effect of delaying the adversarial stage of the proceedings and is intended to give the parties an opportunity to try and reach an amicable settlement of the opposition. This period can be extended for a further 22 months if requested by both parties (either jointly or separately). Any request to extend the cooling off period results in an automatic 22-month extension; a shorter period cannot be requested. However, this does not mean the parties are committed to a two-year cooling off period. It is possible for either party to opt out of the extended cooling off period at any time, other than in the final month before the adversarial stage of the proceedings is due to start. If either party opts out, the cooling off period expires two weeks after notification to the other party by the Office and a new opposition timetable (without a cooling off period) is notified to both parties.

If either the application (to the extent it has been opposed) or the opposition are withdrawn during the cooling off period, the opposition proceedings come to an end and, depending on the circumstances, the official fee may be refunded to the opponent (as discussed in Chapter 14).

6. Adversarial stage

Once the opposition enters the adversarial stage, each party is given an opportunity to file evidence and arguments in support of its case. This is considered in detail in Chapter 13.

The deadlines by which the parties must file their evidence and arguments are set out in the opposition timetable. The process is summarised below.

6.1 Opponent's deadline

The opponent has a deadline two months after the end of the cooling off period to:

- substantiate the rights relied upon and demonstrate its entitlement to oppose, insofar as it did not do so when filing the Notice of Opposition; and
- file any further facts, arguments or evidence it deems necessary to support its case.

The first step above is crucial, as failure to substantiate any particular rights results in them being removed from the opposition. If none of the rights relied upon are substantiated, the opposition is rejected. What should be provided at this stage of the proceedings is discussed further in Chapter 13.

The filing of further facts, arguments and evidence that go beyond substantiating the opposition is optional.

6.2 Applicant's deadline

The applicant has a deadline four months after the end of the cooling off period to file facts, arguments and evidence explaining why it thinks the opposition should fail. In practice, it is rare for this deadline to remain on the same date as initially set, for two reasons:

- it is very common for opponents to obtain an extension of their initial deadline. If an opponent obtains an extension of time, the applicant's deadline is automatically extended to become two months after the new deadline given to the opponent;
- if the opponent files evidence and arguments, the Office ensures the applicant always has a full two months to respond, from the date it is taken to have received these materials. As most opponents tend to file their evidence and arguments close to their deadline, it is often the case that the relevant materials are not sent to the applicant until after its original two-month period has started, hence a new deadline is set.

If an opposition is based wholly or in part on earlier trade mark registrations that had been registered for more than five years at the time the opposed application was filed, the applicant can satisfy its deadline by filing a request that the opponent provides 'proof of use' of these earlier marks. New deadlines are then set relating to the proof of use request (as discussed further in Chapter 13). The applicant can then file arguments on the opposition as a whole at the same time as it files arguments on the proof of use evidence (insofar as such evidence has been filed).

It is not mandatory for the applicant of an opposed EUTM application to file evidence and arguments, or indeed any response at all, in opposition proceedings (or to file a proof of use request). Silence on the part of an applicant during opposition proceedings does not mean the application is deemed abandoned and does not result in the drawing of any negative inferences when a decision is being taken. In virtually all circumstances, however, it is sensible for an applicant to file a response to an opposition, as this can increase its chances of success.

6.3 Opponent's reply and further evidence rounds

If the applicant does not file a response to the opposition, the adversarial stage of the proceedings is deemed complete at the expiry of the applicant's response deadline. The Office then takes a decision solely on the basis of the materials filed by the opponent.

If the applicant files evidence and/or arguments, the opponent is given a two-month period within which to file a reply.

The Office also has discretion to allow further rounds of evidence and arguments, but in practice it usually deems the evidence rounds complete once the opponent's reply (if any) has been filed.

7. Decision

Once the adversarial stage is complete, the Office notifies both parties to this effect. The Office then takes a decision. As discussed in Chapter 2, while there is theoretically provision for oral hearings at the Office, in practice such hearings do not take place and every opposition decision is based entirely on the arguments and evidence filed by the parties.

8. Timeline – how long does all this take?

The length of time between the filing of a Notice of Opposition and the issuance of a decision varies greatly, depending on the circumstances. In particular, it depends on whether:

- there are any deficiencies in the Notice of Opposition;
- the opponent is put to proof of use by the applicant (as discussed in Chapter 13);
- either party obtains extensions of the deadlines they have to meet during the adversarial stage of the proceedings;
- there are related proceedings at either national or Union level; and
- the parties engage in settlement negotiations and thus take steps to put the proceedings on hold while they attempt to settle the matter amicably.

At a minimum, opposition proceedings that run their course must last just over six months from the opposition deadline to consideration of the matter by the Opposition Divisions. The length of time it then takes for the issuance of a decision varies, depending on the workload of the Opposition Divisions.

As a general guide, if there are no deficiencies in the Notice of Opposition, no proof of use request and no steps are taken by the parties either to extend or to end the proceedings, a decision may be issued within 12 months of the original opposition deadline.

Opposition proceedings can, however, last much longer than this and in some cases have been prolonged for more than ten years. Prolonged opposition proceedings often occur where there are cross-proceedings between the same parties, or where the prior rights relied on in the opposition are themselves the subject of separate attacks.

9. Appeals

It is possible to file an appeal against the decision to deem an opposition admissible, as well as against the substantive decision in the opposition itself. As a decision to deem an opposition admissible does not terminate the opposition proceedings, it can only be appealed together with the final opposition decision. It is not possible to delay or avoid the substantive opposition proceedings by appealing the admissibility decision at the time it is issued. The appeals process is discussed in chapters 19 and 20.

10. Grounds of opposition

As opposition is a relative rights proceeding, any potential opponent must own (or be entitled to rely upon) rights that pre-date the opposed application. What the rights are affects the ground or grounds on which the opposition can be brought.

The key rights and the grounds that can be relied on in opposition are considered below. The rights and grounds are all discussed in detail in Chapter 12 and a discussion of who can rely on each of these grounds is contained in Chapter 11.

10.1 Earlier trade marks

Most oppositions are based on 'earlier trade marks', as defined in Article 8(2) of the Regulation. Earlier trade marks can form the basis of three different grounds of opposition, as summarised in the next section.

The term 'earlier trade mark' includes each of the following:

- EUTM applications or registrations with a filing date (taking into account any relevant priority or seniority claims) earlier than that of the opposed application;
- national trade mark applications or registrations in Member States with a filing date (taking into account any relevant priority claims) earlier than that of the opposed application;
- IRs designating the Union and/or Member States with a filing date (taking into account any relevant priority or seniority claims) earlier than that of the opposed application; and
- trade marks protected as 'well-known' in at least one Member State under Article 6bis of the Paris Convention. The relevant date for assessing whether a trade mark is 'well known' is the filing date (taking into account any relevant priority or seniority claims) of the opposed application.

10.2 The different grounds of opposition

The possible grounds of opposition can be split into six distinct categories, as set out below. The requirements relating to each of these are discussed in detail in the chapters that follow.

- Earlier trade marks (as defined in section 10.1 above) that are identical to the mark opposed and are protected in respect of identical goods and/or services to those being opposed. This ground is referred to in the chapters that follow as the ***'double identity ground'***.
- Earlier trade marks that are:
  - identical to the mark opposed and are protected in respect of similar goods and/or services to those being opposed;
  - similar to the mark opposed and are protected in respect of identical goods and/or services to those being opposed; or
  - similar to the mark opposed and are protected in respect of similar goods and/or services to those being opposed.

  Each of the above criteria involves some degree of similarity of marks and goods and/or services and, to be successful under this ground, the opponent must show that there is a 'likelihood of confusion' as a result of that similarity. This ground is referred to in the chapters that follow as the ***'confusion ground'***;
- Earlier trade marks that are identical or similar to the mark opposed where the following criteria are satisfied:
  - the earlier trade mark is registered (this ground cannot be used as the

basis of an opposition where the earlier trade mark is an application or well-known under the Paris Convention);
    - the earlier trade mark has a reputation in the territory in which it is protected (ie, in the Union if it is an EUTM registration, or in the relevant Member State if it is a national registration);
    - the use of the mark being opposed would take unfair advantage of, or be detrimental to, the distinctive character or repute of the earlier trade mark; and
    - the use of the mark being opposed is without due cause.

  This ground of opposition is based on the reputation of the earlier trade mark and so is referred to in the chapters that follow as the ***'reputation ground'***.
- The application is filed by an agent or representative in its own name without the consent of the 'true proprietor' of that mark. Being the true proprietor in this context can mean:
    - owning a trade mark application or registration anywhere in the world for the mark;
    - owning unregistered trade mark rights anywhere in the world in the mark; or
    - owning a mark that is a well-known mark.

  This ground of opposition is based on the relationship between the opponent and the agent or representative and so is referred to in the chapters that follow as the ***'agent/representative ground'***.
- The application conflicts with rights in an unregistered trade mark or other sign used in the course of trade giving protection in one or more Member States, provided that the rights in the relevant mark or sign:
    - are of more than mere local significance;
    - were acquired before the filing date of the opposed EUTM application (taking into account any relevant priority claims); and
    - enable those who hold them to prohibit the use of a subsequent trade mark.

  This ground of opposition is referred to in the chapters that follow as the ***'unregistered rights ground'***.
- The application conflicts with a protected designation of origin (PDO) or protected geographical indication (PGI), provided that:
    - an application for a PDO or PGI was filed before the filing date of the opposed application (taking into account any relevant priority claims);
    - the PDO or PGI is successfully protected on the relevant register; and
    - the PDO or PGI gives the right to prohibit the use of a subsequent trade mark.

  This ground of opposition is referred to in the chapters that follow as the ***'PDO/PGI ground'***.

Further reference

Regulation – Articles 8 and 41-42

Implementing Regulation – Rules 15-22

The Office's online summary of the opposition process – https://oami.europa.eu/ohimportal/en/opposition
Office Guidelines – Part C
The Office's *Annual Reports*: https://euipo.europa.eu/ohimportal/en/annual-report

Chapter 11: Basic requirements and formalities

1. Introduction

This chapter looks at:

- the information that needs to be provided when opposing an EUTM application, and
- the initial stages of opposition proceedings up to the point of notification of the opposition to the applicant.

2. How to file an opposition

Various requirements must be met for an opposition to be validly filed. An opposition must be filed in writing, in the form of a Notice of Opposition. The Office provides an official form for this purpose. Although use of this form is not mandatory, it includes fields for all the information required to file a valid opposition, so using it is highly advisable, particularly when the language considerations set out in section 7 of this chapter are taken into account.

A Notice of Opposition can be filed:

- *electronically* – via the Office's website;
- *by fax* – the Notice of Opposition must be signed by an identified individual; or
- *on paper* – either by mail or by depositing the Notice of Opposition at the reception desk of the Office.

3. When to file

The Notice of Opposition must be received by the Office before the end of the opposition period. It is not possible to extend this period under any circumstances.

Although the length of the opposition period is fixed at three months, when the opposition period starts varies depending on the nature of the application:

- *For EUTM applications*, the opposition period starts when the application is published, so the opposition deadline is three months from the date of publication of the application.
- *For Union designations of IRs*, the opposition period starts one month after the first re-publication of the application, so the opposition deadline is four months after the first re-publication by the Office (see Chapter 32 for further information).

Oppositions filed before the start of the opposition period are treated as filed on the first day of the opposition period. If an opposition is withdrawn before the opposition period begins, the official opposition fee is refunded. The fee is also refunded if the opposition period never actually begins because the application in question is either withdrawn or refused.

4. Who can file an opposition?

The table below briefly summarises who can rely on each of the different grounds on which an opposition can be based. Each ground is individually discussed in detail in Chapter 12.

Ground	Who can rely on it
Double identity ground	Owner of earlier trade mark or (authorised) licensee
Confusion ground	Owner of earlier trade mark or (authorised) licensee
Reputation ground	Owner of earlier trade mark or (authorised) licensee
Agent/representative ground	Owner of the trade mark
Unregistered rights ground	Persons entitled to exercise the relevant rights under national law
PDO/PGI ground	Persons entitled to exercise the rights arising from the PDO or PGI

An opposition can be jointly filed by two or more opponents, but only where the parties are all entitled to oppose on the basis of the same rights (ie, because they are co-owners of the rights in question, are all authorised licensees of those rights or together are a combination of the owner/co-owners and authorised licensees of the same rights).

5. Filing a valid opposition

This section discusses the information that must be provided for an opposition to be deemed validly filed. Some of this information must be filed before the opposition deadline (see sections 5.1, 5.2 and 5.3 below) and some can be provided after the opposition period has expired (see section 5.4 below).

5.1 Information that must be provided before expiry of the opposition period

Before the expiry of the opposition period, the opponent must clearly identify both the contested EUTM application and the earlier rights and grounds relied upon. Full details of what is required are set out below in sections 5.2 (identification of the opposed application) and 5.3 (identification of the earlier rights and grounds). If any of the mandatory information is missing, the opposition is deemed inadmissible.

It should be noted that, even if the opposition period is still running, the Office does not tell the opponent that it has not provided the mandatory information. Opponents are expected to be aware of these requirements and to remedy any deficiencies themselves, before the opposition period expires. If such deficiencies are not remedied, the opponent is informed of the inadmissibility after the end of the opposition period and given an opportunity to provide comments. If the Office remains of the view that the opposition is inadmissible (which in practice is always the case, unless the opponent can show that it filed a document or pieces of information that were overlooked by the Office), a decision to this effect is issued and a copy is sent to the applicant.

In addition to ensuring the Notice of Opposition is filed before the end of the opposition period and contains the required information, an opponent has to make sure certain formalities requirements are met for its opposition to be deemed validly filed. These are considered below in sections 6 (payment of the opposition fee), 7 (language to be used) and 8 (appointing a representative, where necessary).

5.2 Identification of the EUTM application being opposed

In order to identify the application that is being opposed, the application number and the name of the applicant must both be provided before the expiry of the opposition period. The date of publication can also be indicated, but is not strictly necessary.

If the application number and applicant name provided do not tally with each other, the Office decides whether it can be established without doubt which application is being opposed. Including the publication date in the Notice of Opposition can assist in this regard.

If the Office is unsure which application is being opposed, it does not ask the opponent to clarify. As the opponent does not get an opportunity to correct any mistakes, great care needs to be taken to ensure there can be no doubt about the application being opposed.

5.3 Identification of the earlier right(s) and ground(s)

It is necessary to provide a clear indication of the earlier right(s) and ground(s) on which the opposition is based before the expiry of the opposition period.

While the official opposition form includes sections for all the necessary information, in practice the Office checks through any documents provided along with the Notice of Opposition or otherwise filed by the opponent during the opposition period, to see if it can clearly ascertain the rights and grounds relied upon.

The easiest way to identify the rights and grounds is to use the opposition form provided by the Office and complete the relevant box or boxes. The information that must be provided depends on the exact rights involved.

Earlier trade mark application/registrations: The following information must be provided for each trade mark application or registration relied upon under the double identity ground, confusion ground, reputation ground or agent/representative ground:

- official number;
- status (ie, application or registration); and
- type of mark (ie, EUTM or national/regional trade mark, including Member State/region). Where the national application(s) relied upon exist as a result of the conversion of an EUTM right, but the national application numbers are not yet available, it is sufficient to provide the EUTM application number and a list of countries for which conversion has been requested.

If the reputation ground is relied upon, information as to where the reputation is claimed to exist, as well as the goods and/or services to which it extends, can be provided after the expiry of the opposition period.

Earlier well-known mark: The following information must be included where the opponent relies on a mark as well-known under the double identity ground, confusion ground or agent/representative ground:

- an indication of the Member State(s) in which the mark is well known;
- if it is registered, the official number and territory of registration must be provided;
- if it is not registered, an indication of the mark must be provided.

Earlier unregistered trade mark or other rights: The following information must be provided where an unregistered trade mark or other rights are relied upon under the unregistered rights ground or the agent/representative ground:

- a representation of the mark or an indication of the sign;
- the official number, if appropriate (eg, if the right is a registered right, such as a company name);
- an indication of the nature of the right relied on under national law, which should be as specific as possible. General indications, such as stating that 'common law' rights are relied upon, are not accepted; and
- an indication of the territory in which the right is claimed.

If the earlier right relied upon in the opposition is not a right that can be relied upon for opposition purposes (eg, a design registration), the opposition is deemed admissible if the right is clearly identified. However, the opposition is then rejected at the substantive stage to the extent that this right is relied upon.

PDO/PGI rights: The following information must be provided where an opposition is based on the PDO/PGI ground:

- a representation of the mark;
- the official number of the PDO or PGI application or registration;
- an indication of the nature of the right relied on; and
- an indication of the territory in which the right is claimed.

5.4 Information that must be provided but can be sent after the expiry of the opposition period

For an opposition to be validly filed, the information set out below must also be provided. All of this information can, however, be sent to the Office after the expiry of the opposition period:

- filing, registration and priority dates for any earlier trade mark applications and registrations relied on;
- a representation of each of the marks covered by any earlier trade mark applications and registrations relied on;
- details of the goods and/or services on which the opposition is based;
- where the opposition is based, in full or in part, on the reputation ground, information about the Member State(s) and the goods and/or services for which a reputation is claimed for each of the earlier trade mark registrations relied on; and
- details of the opponent, which must include:
  - the name and address of the opponent;
  - the name and business address of the opponent's representative (if any – see further discussion at section 8.2 below); and
  - information on authorisation or entitlement to file if the opposition is being filed by a licensee or a person who is entitled under a national law to exercise an earlier right (see further discussion in Chapter 12).

If any of this information is missing from the Notice of Opposition, the Office issues a deficiency notice and gives the opponent a non-extendable two-month period within which to provide the missing information. If the information is not provided within this period, the opposition is rejected as inadmissible, unless that information relates to only some of the earlier rights relied on, in which case the rights for which the necessary information has not been provided are excluded from the opposition and it proceeds for the remainder.

5.5 Additional information

The following information can also be provided with the Notice of Opposition but is not essential for the opposition to be valid:

- details of the goods and/or services that the opposition is directed against: if this information is not provided, the opposition is taken as being against the full specification; and
- a statement detailing the arguments relied on and evidence to support these arguments: in most cases, there is little benefit to including arguments and evidence with the Notice of Opposition, not least because the time and expense of preparing these can be saved if the opposition is settled.

6. Payment of the opposition fee

The full opposition fee, €320 at the time of writing, must be received by the Office before the expiry of the opposition period.

If the fee is paid late, or only part of the fee is received during the opposition period, the opposition is treated as not having been filed and any amount paid is returned.

The only occasion on which an opposition may be treated as validly filed if payment was not received until after the end of the opposition period is if the opponent can prove that payment instructions were given to a bank before the opposition period ended. If the instructions were given within the last ten days of the opposition period, a surcharge of 10% of the opposition fee must also be paid, but no surcharge is payable if the instructions were given more than ten days before the end of the opposition period.

If the fee is paid in time but the Notice of Opposition itself is received late, the opposition is deemed inadmissible and the fee is not returned.

7. Languages to be used

There are two issues to consider here:

- the language of the opposition proceedings, and
- the language in which the Notice of Opposition is filed, which is normally (but not necessarily) the same language as the language of the proceedings.

These issues are considered separately below.

7.1 Language of the proceedings

Every EUTM application has to indicate both a first and a second language; at least the second language has to be one of the Languages of the Office (see Chapter 5, section 10).

Where both the first and second languages of an application are Languages of the Office, the opponent has a choice over which to use as the language of the opposition proceedings. If the opponent fails to indicate which of the two possible languages is to be the language of the proceedings (which can be done by filing the Notice of Opposition in one of those languages), a deficiency notice is issued and it is asked to indicate the language of the proceedings.

Where only the second language of an application is a Language of the Office, the opposition proceedings must be in that language. Therefore, failure to indicate the language of the proceedings in the Notice of Opposition or indicating an incorrect language has no effect. No deficiency notice is issued as there is only one possible language for the proceedings.

All of the above is subject to the proviso that the parties to an opposition may agree that a different Language of the Union is to be the language of the proceedings. Any request to change the language of the proceedings to another Language of the Union must be received by the Office before the end of the cooling off period.

During the course of opposition proceedings, it is open to each of the parties to use any Language of the Office. However, where a language other than the language of the proceedings is used, a translation into the language of the proceedings must be provided. The deadline for filing translations varies according to the deadline at issue, but is generally one month from transmission of the original document (see Chapter 13, section 2).

7.2 Language of the Notice of Opposition

A Notice of Opposition must be filed in one of the Languages of the Office. However, the Office's official opposition form is available in 23 of the 24 Languages of the Union (it is not available in Irish). Where the Office's form is used, the opposition is deemed admissible if any of the 23 language versions is used, provided the form is completed in one of the Languages of the Office so far as textual elements are concerned.

The best way of proceeding is usually to use the official form in the language of the opposed application that is a Language of the Office. Where both languages of the application are Languages of the Office, the opponent can pick the language that suits it best (eg, the one with which it is most familiar).

It is possible to meet the opposition deadline by using any of the 23 language versions of the official form and ensuring that the mandatory information set out in section 5 above is provided (so long as any textual elements that happen to be required for the particular rights and grounds relied on are included in one of the Languages of the Office, with a translation into the language of the proceedings being provided within a month of the opposition deadline).

In practice, most of this information can usually be provided on the official opposition form by either entering numbers or ticking boxes. Where unregistered rights are relied upon, however, it is necessary to provide some information on the nature of the rights, which requires at least a little written information.

If there is only one possible language for the opposition proceedings, that language is the language of the proceedings irrespective of the language version of the official form that is used and irrespective of whether a language of the opposition is indicated on the form. In such an instance, when the Office notifies the applicant of the opposition, it attaches a blank official form in the language of the proceedings and indicates the language of the proceedings.

If the opposition is filed in one of the Languages of the Union (or indeed any other language) that is not one of the Languages of the Office, and the official opposition form is not used, the opposition is inadmissible (even if the parties have agreed to conduct the proceedings in the language in question).

Where information that is not required for an opposition to be deemed admissible is provided at the time of filing the opposition (eg, a statement detailing the arguments relied upon), it does not matter if this information is provided in the wrong language, as it is not mandatory information. If a translation is not provided later, the information is simply treated as if it were never included.

If the Notice of Opposition is filed in a Language of the Office which is not one of the languages of the opposed application, the opponent must provide a translation into the first language of the application (if it is a Language of the Office) or the second language of the application (which is always a Language of the Office). The translation must be provided within one month of the opposition deadline and the language into which the Notice of Opposition is translated becomes the language of the proceedings. The opponent is not notified of this deficiency by the Office and if the translation is not provided in time the opposition is deemed inadmissible. In reality, the need to file such a translation only arises if the official opposition form is not used, or if it is used but contains textual elements that are necessary for admissibility and which are in a Language of the Office but not one of the languages of the opposed application.

If the parties request that the language of the proceedings is changed to another Language of the Union, a translation of the Notice of Opposition into that language must be filed within one month of the end of the cooling off period. If no such translation is filed, the language of the proceedings does not change.

As set out in section 5.4 above, certain pieces of information that must be provided in order for an opposition to be deemed admissible can be provided after the end of the opposition period. Much of this information is non-textual in nature, so there are no real language considerations in practice. This is clearly the case for the dates that are to be provided and for the representation of the earlier mark(s) relied upon. The requisite details of the opposing party do not usually bring language considerations into play and, in the case of reliance on earlier trade mark applications or registrations, generally should match the details shown on the relevant trade mark register at the time of filing the opposition. Therefore, in practice, the main information for which language considerations are of relevance is that relating to the goods and/or services on which the opposition is based, to include details of the goods and/or services for which reputation is claimed if applicable.

An indication of the class numbers is accepted as a sufficient indication of the goods and/or services of the earlier rights on which the opposition is based, provided an official extract from the relevant trade mark register in the language of the proceedings, showing details of the goods and/or services relied upon, is provided.

If the opposition is based on only part of the specification covered, the specific goods and/or services relied upon should be listed in the language of the proceedings. Alternatively, it is sufficient simply to indicate the relevant class numbers and provide an official extract from the relevant trade mark register, in the language of the proceedings, showing details of the goods and/or services relied upon.

8. Representation

There are two issues to consider here – representation of the applicant for an opposed EUTM application and representation of the opponent.

8.1 Representation of the applicant

Where an EUTM applicant is domiciled in, has its principal place of business in, or has a real and effective industrial or commercial establishment in, the EEA, there is no requirement for a representative to be appointed (see Chapter 2, section 10 for more information).

However, where the above criteria are not met an applicant must be represented before the Office in all proceedings, other than the act of filing an EUTM application. This necessarily includes opposition proceedings.

Normally, the issue of representation of the applicant is dealt with before an opposition is filed. If there is no representative on record for an opposed EUTM application but the applicant is a party that must be represented, the Office contacts it and sets a deadline for the appointment of a representative. If no representative is appointed, the application is refused and the opposition proceedings end.

8.2 Representation of the opponent

As in the case of applicants, opponents are only required to appoint a representative where they are not domiciled in, or do not have their principal place of business in, or do not have a real and effective industrial or commercial establishment in, the EEA.

Where an opponent has a designated representative, the name and business address of that representative should be indicated in the Notice of Opposition. If the opponent falls within the category of parties that do not need to be represented before the Office, failure to provide the details of a representative simply results in the Office corresponding directly with the opponent.

If the opponent is a party that must be represented in opposition proceedings, failure to appoint a representative or to provide the name and business address of the representative, results in a deficiency notice. If the deficiency is not remedied within the two-month non-extendable deadline set by the Office, the opposition is rejected as inadmissible.

Where an opposition is filed jointly by more than one party, it is possible for each opponent to have a separate representative (or indeed multiple separate representatives). If there is no common representative between the opponents, the Office generally treats the representative that is named first in the Notice of Opposition as the common representative and only corresponds with that representative.

Where a party is represented in opposition proceedings but is not required to have a representative, it is still possible for it to file documents directly with the Office in the course of the proceedings. Any documents filed direct by a party that is not entitled to act without a representative are not taken into account. Whether documents filed directly are taken into account or not, the Office continues to correspond only with the appointed representative.

Where either party in opposition proceedings ceases to be represented, but falls within the category of parties who must be represented, the Office sets that party a two-month time limit within which to appoint a new representative. Failure to do so by the applicant results in the opposed application being refused, while failure to do so by the opponent results in the opposition being rejected.

9. Admissibility checks & deficiencies

Once a Notice of Opposition has been filed, the Office carries out admissibility checks. These include checking whether the Notice of Opposition was filed within the opposition period and whether the fee was paid within this period. If either of these things has not happened, the opposition is rejected as inadmissible.

If any of the mandatory information set out at sections 5.2 or 5.3 above has not been provided, the Office invites the opponent to comment on the admissibility of the opposition. If (as is usually the case) the Office remains of the view that the necessary information has not been provided within the opposition period, the opposition is rejected.

For the purposes of the admissibility checks, it is sufficient that at least one earlier right is clearly identified. Once the Office is satisfied that this is the case (usually by checking EUTM rights first, if these have been relied upon), it does not continue to check the other rights or grounds relied on by the opponent.

When notifying the parties that an opposition has been deemed admissible, the Office identifies the right in relation to which the opposition has been found admissible. As discussed in Chapter 13, if this right is not substantiated by the opponent by the relevant deadline, further admissibility checks are carried out (provided the opposition is based on at least one additional right).

Once the Office is satisfied that at least one earlier right has been clearly identified, it checks whether any of the information set out at section 5.4 above is missing (ie, information that is required in order for an opposition to be deemed admissible but which does not have to be provided within the opposition period). If any of this information is missing, or if there are any problems with the information provided, the Office writes to the opponent and sets it a two-month non-extendable deadline by which to remedy the deficiency.

The Office also makes checks on the other formalities matters discussed above, including the language of the Notice of Opposition and professional representation.

Where multiple opponents are named in the Notice of Opposition, a deficiency notice is issued if it is not possible for all the parties identified to file opposition on the basis of the same rights. In those circumstances, the opponents are asked to pick an acceptable combination of opponents and earlier rights. If no response is received within the two-month non-extendable time limit set by the Office, the opposition is rejected as inadmissible.

10. Notification of the opposition

Once the admissibility checks have been completed and the opposition has been found admissible, the Office sets the opposition timetable. The timetable is notified to both parties, but only after the opposition period has expired.

Further reference

Regulation – Articles 8, 41, 92, 93, 119, 144b and 156
Implementing Regulation – Rules 15-18, 75, 77, 80-83, 95, 114
Office Guidelines – Part C, Section 1

Chapter 12: Relative grounds

1. Introduction

This chapter looks at each of the relative grounds of opposition in detail. The legal tests to be applied in assessing each ground are set out, as well as who is entitled to rely on each ground in opposition proceedings.

2. 'Earlier' rights

For an EUTM opposition to be successful, there must be a right or rights that are 'earlier' than the opposed EUTM application. This section considers what the word 'earlier' means in this context.

A right is generally taken to be an earlier right if it was in existence in advance of the filing date or priority date of the opposed EUTM application. If none of the rights relied upon in an opposition predate the opposed application, it is rejected.

2.1 Comparison of filing and priority dates

In the case of earlier trade mark applications or registrations, their filing or priority dates are what determines whether they are indeed earlier. For example, an EUTM registration filed on 14 January 2012 is clearly earlier than an EUTM application filed on 8 February 2016 and so can be relied on in opposition proceedings. However, if priority has been successfully claimed, the priority date takes precedence. As a result, an opposition can be based on a trade mark application or registration filed after the opposed EUTM application if it has successfully claimed priority from another application or registration that was filed before the EUTM application. For example, an EUTM application filed on 31 August1 2015 that has successfully claimed priority from a US application filed on 1 March 2015 can be used to oppose an EUTM application filed on 28 April 2015.

If the opposed EUTM application has successfully claimed priority, this must also be taken into account in determining which of the rights at issue is earlier. Considering the above example further, if the EUTM application filed on 28 April 2015 has successfully claimed a priority date of 28 October 2014, it cannot be opposed on the basis of the EUTM application with the 1 March 2015 priority date.

It is also possible to base an opposition on an EUTM application or registration with a filing date that is later than the filing date (or priority date) of the opposed EUTM application where the opponent's EUTM right claims seniority from a national right with a filing date earlier than the opposed EUTM application. For example, an EUTM application with a filing date of 19 September 2015 could be opposed on the basis of an EUTM application with a filing date of 3 November 2015 which includes an effective seniority claim from a Spanish registration with a filing date of 27 July 1975. To rely on an earlier right obtained as the result of a seniority claim, the opponent must show, within the opposition period, that the seniority claim has been accepted, that the earlier national right in question is no longer live and that the seniority is thus effective. For a more detailed discussion of seniority, see Chapter 24.

Where an opposition is based on an EUTM right that includes a valid seniority claim, but the EUTM right itself was not filed before the opposed application, the EUTM right has the same effect as the national right from which seniority has been claimed for the purposes of the opposition proceedings. If the opposition succeeds on the basis of this earlier right, the position is the same as if the opposition had been based on the original national right from which seniority was claimed. The opposed EUTM application can therefore be converted into national applications in all Member States other than that to which the seniority claim relates. In the above example, the opposed EUTM application could therefore be converted into national applications in all Member States other than Spain. For a more detailed discussion of conversion, see Chapter 25.

An application or registration which has the same effective filing date as an EUTM application (including by virtue of a priority or seniority claim) cannot be used to oppose that EUTM application. This remains the case even if it can be shown that the application or registration in question was filed at an earlier point in the day than the EUTM application.

2.2 Oppositions based on pending applications

A pending application, whether an EUTM application or national application, is only a valid earlier right if and to the extent that it becomes registered. If an opposition is based in whole or in part on a pending application that does not go through to registration, for whatever reason, that application cannot be relied on in the opposition to the extent it is refused.

2.3 Enlargement of the Union

The general position is that, when new Member States join the Union, existing EUTM registrations and applications automatically extend to those territories as from the date they join the Union. (See Chapter 1 for further discussion.)

Any new EUTM applications filed after a new Member State joins the Union also provide protection in that Member State. It is therefore logical that they can be opposed on the basis of national rights in the new Member State, provided that those national rights predate the EUTM application. The situation is, however, a little more complicated than that, as there are some transitional provisions to cover the period before a new Member State joins the Union.

Where an EUTM application is filed in the six-month period before a new Member State joins the Union, national rights in that Member State can be used to oppose the EUTM application, provided that:

- they actually are earlier rights (in line with the discussion in section 2.1 above); and

- they were acquired in good faith (although this is assumed and it is for the EUTM applicant to prove bad faith if it thinks there is an issue in this regard). 'Bad faith' in this context generally means that the national right was acquired with the specific purpose of obtaining rights in the new Member State for a trade mark that someone else owns in the Union. In practice, this has not happened very often, and it has not been as big a problem as originally feared.

An EUTM application filed more than six months before a new Member State joins the Union cannot be opposed on the basis of national rights in that Member State, even if that State has joined the Union by the time the EUTM application is published for opposition purposes.

An EUTM application filed on or after the date on which a new Member State joins the Union can be opposed on the basis of national rights in that Member State, provided they are indeed earlier rights, as discussed above. There is no good faith requirement in this instance, even if the EUTM application claims priority back to a date within the six-month period before the joining date. For example, Croatia joined the Union on 1 July 2013. An EUTM application filed on 22 July 2013 (ie, when Croatia had become a Member State) with a priority claim back to 22 January 2013 (ie, in the six-month period before Croatia became a Member State) could be opposed on the basis of a national application in Croatia dating from 1 January 2013, even if the Croatian application was not filed in good faith. If, however, the EUTM application was actually filed on 22 January 2013, the good faith requirement would bite and the national application could not be used to oppose it if the national application was acquired in bad faith.

3. The double identity ground

This ground is set out in Article 8(1)(a) of the Regulation. It can be relied on where an earlier trade mark is identical to the mark being opposed and is protected in respect of goods and/or services identical to those covered by the application being opposed.

3.1 Who can rely on the double identity ground?

The opponent must be either the owner of the earlier trade mark rights or a licensee of those rights authorised by the owner to file opposition.

Owner: Where the earlier rights are EUTM rights and the opposition is filed by the owner, the opponent name and the proprietor name should be the same. If the EUTM rights in question were assigned prior to the filing of the Notice of Opposition, the opposition should be filed in the name of the new proprietor and an application to record the change in ownership must have been filed in advance of the filing of the Notice of Opposition. If the recordal request has not been processed by the time of filing of the Notice of Opposition, details of that request should be provided together with the Notice of Opposition. (See Chapter 16 for further information on recordal requests.)

Where the earlier rights are national trade marks, the Notice of Opposition can be filed in the name of the old owner where the assignment has not yet been recorded on the national register (either because no recordal application has been filed or because the recordal process has not been completed). Any such ownership issues must, however, be addressed during the evidence stage (as discussed in Chapter 13).

Where an opposition is based on a combination of EUTM and national rights, all of which have been assigned from one party to another, the assignment recordal request for the EUTM rights should be filed at the Office before the Notice of Opposition is filed and the opposition should be filed in the name of the new owner.

Where the earlier rights are in the joint ownership of more than one party, the opponent can be any or all of the co-owners.

Licensee: Where the earlier trade mark rights are EUTM rights, the licence does not have to be recorded for the licensee to file an opposition (as there is no general requirement for such licences to be recorded) (see Chapter 16). In the case of earlier rights that are national applications or registrations, whether the licence must be recorded before an opposition can be filed by the licensee is a matter of national law.

In any event, for either EUTM or national trade mark rights, simply demonstrating that the licence has been recorded is not sufficient to establish entitlement to file opposition. The licensee must also prove that is has been authorised to file an opposition by the owner(s) of the relevant trade mark rights, as discussed further in Chapter 13. If such proof is not provided together with the Notice of Opposition, a deficiency notice is sent by the Office and the opponent is set a two-month non-extendable time limit within which to file it.

3.2 When can the double identity ground be relied upon?

To rely on this ground, the earlier mark must be identical to the mark applied for and must cover goods and/or services that are identical to those covered by the application being opposed. Although this sounds clear-cut, it is necessary to consider further what 'identity' means in this context.

Identical marks: Marks are considered 'identical' where they contain differences that are so insignificant that they may not be noticed by an average consumer. In practice, this means only extremely minor differences between the marks are acceptable. As in the case of priority claims (discussed in Chapter 5) and seniority claims (discussed in Chapter 24) an 'insignificant difference' is taken to be one that would only be noticed by a reasonably observant consumer when comparing the two marks side by side.

In the case of word marks, differences between lower and upper case do not usually prevent marks being deemed identical. For example, the marks GLOBAL CAMPUS and Global Campus have been held to be identical by the Office. However, a difference of just one character between marks can be enough for a finding of non-identity. For example, the marks NOVALLOY and NOVALOY have been held not to be identical by the Office.

A word mark and a figurative mark can be deemed identical, but this is usually only the case where the figurative mark effectively consists of the word at issue in a fairly basic font or with minimal stylisation.

In the case of figurative marks, again the marks are only considered identical if the differences between them are insignificant. Where one of the marks is in black and white or greyscale and the other is in colour, they are generally not considered identical, unless the differences are barely noticeable.

In the case of uncertainty as to whether the marks are likely to be deemed identical, it is sensible to include this ground as the Office considers the case under the confusion ground discussed below if it decides the marks are not similar (irrespective of whether that ground is also claimed). In reality, marks which are arguably identical always meet the lower threshold for similarity.

The benefit of including the double identity ground is that there is no requirement to prove a likelihood of consumer confusion to be successful. As a result, this ground is usually easier to succeed upon as the only substantive questions to be considered are whether the marks are identical and whether the goods and/or services are identical.

Identical goods and/or services: Goods and services are identical where exactly the same wording is used in the specifications of both the earlier mark and the opposed EUTM application and the terms appear in the same class. Identical terms appearing in different classes are not usually deemed identical unless the difference in classification is clearly due to an administrative error or a revision of the Nice Classification – eg, "handheld computer games" falls in class 28 under the 10th Edition of the Nice Classification, having previously been in class 9. Where a registration granted under the 9th edition still shows this term in class 9, the coverage is deemed identical for the purposes of an opposition against an application covering the same term but in class 28.

Coverage can also be identical where one of the rights covers a broad term that encompasses the other. However, this again often depends on whether the terms fall within the same class. For example, the broad term "mats" falls within class 27. This encompasses "door mats; reed mats; non-slip mats; bath mats", all of which also fall within class 27, so an opposition against an application covering any of these terms could be based on identical goods coverage. However, identical coverage could not be claimed when opposing an application covering "baking mats" (class 21), "sleeping mats" (class 20), "desk mats" (class 16), "dart mats" (class 28), "place mats, not of paper" (class 24), "insulating mats" (class 17) or "mouse mats" (class 9).

Where the earlier mark relied on in an opposition is an EUTM registration filed before 22 June 2012 that includes a class heading, it should be checked whether a declaration has been filed to the effect that the proprietor's intention at the time of filing was to obtain protection beyond the literal meaning of the terms in the class heading (see Chapter 6 for further explanation). If this is the case, it should be checked what the actual coverage is. However, for any terms included in the coverage that go beyond the literal meaning of the class heading terms, this additional coverage cannot be relied on for opposition purposes if:

- the opposed application was filed before the Register was amended (or the mark covered by the opposed application was in use before the application to amend the Register was filed); and
- use in relation to those additional goods and/or services did not infringe (or would not have infringed) the earlier rights as they appeared on the Register at the filing of filing/use (ie, the use did not (or would not) amount to infringement of rights extending to the literal meaning of the class heading).

As with identity of marks, if there is any doubt as to whether the goods and/or services at issue are likely to be deemed identical, it is sensible to include this ground as the Office considers the case under the confusion ground discussed below if it concludes that the requirements for the double identity ground are not made out.

Again, the benefit of including the double identity ground is that there is no requirement for a likelihood of consumer confusion, meaning that it is usually easier to succeed on this ground, as the only substantive questions to be considered are whether the marks at issue and the goods/services at issue are identical.

4. The confusion ground

This ground is set out in Article 8(1)(b) of the Regulation. It can be relied upon where:

- the marks are identical but the goods and/or services are similar rather than identical;
- the goods and/or services are identical but the marks are similar rather than identical; and
- the marks are similar and the goods and/or services are similar.

This ground also requires a likelihood of consumer confusion. This section considers how similarity is assessed in this context.

4.1 Who can rely on the confusion ground?

The opponent must be either the owner of the earlier trade mark rights or a licensee of those rights authorised by the owner to file opposition. The same considerations apply as those considered in section 3.1 above.

4.2 When can the confusion ground be relied upon?

The confusion ground involves some similarity of marks and/or of coverage. It may also involve identity in one of these aspects. In either case, it is necessary for there to be a likelihood of confusion. These issues are considered separately below.

Marks: The considerations outlined in section 3.2 above as to whether the marks are identical apply equally to the present ground. If the marks are not identical, it needs to be determined whether they are similar. The threshold for similarity of marks is fairly low. Marks are compared visually, phonetically and conceptually, but only need to be similar on one of these three levels for a finding of similarity.

The general principle is that there should be some form of overlap between the marks, although overlap only in purely minor or non-distinctive elements is not enough. The marks should each be considered as a whole in considering whether they are similar. For example, GOOGLE and APPLE would not be deemed similar despite the fact that both end with 'LE'. However, GOOGLE and FRUGAL are likely to be considered similar due to their phonetic similarities.

The Office tends to take a fairly formulaic approach to the comparison of marks:

With regard to the visual comparison:

- where the marks are word marks, a comparison of the number and sequence of letters is carried out, as well as consideration of the positioning of coinciding letters and the structure of the marks;
- where one mark is a word mark and the other is a figurative mark with a word element, consideration is taken of the number of letters in common, as well as whether the figurative mark is highly stylised;
- where both marks are figurative marks with word elements, the figurative elements are compared, as are the word elements;
- where one mark is a figurative mark with a word element and the other is a purely figurative mark. the figurative elements are compared. If the figurative elements are very close, the marks may be found to be visually similar, despite the inclusion of a word element in one;
- where both marks are purely figurative, the figurative elements are compared.

With regard to the phonetic comparison: the syllables and their sequence and stress are all considered.

With regard to the conceptual comparison:

- the semantic content of the words is considered, as well as the semantic content of parts of words, misspelled words, figurative elements, shapes and colours;
- if none of the marks has any conceptual meaning, a conceptual comparison will not be possible. If only one of the marks has a conceptual meaning it will be deemed to be not conceptually similar;
- marks may be found conceptually similar where:
  - they share a common word or phrase;
  - they share a word or phrase with a common meaning;
  - they share a common meaning, even though one may be a visual representation and the other is a word.

Goods and/or services: The considerations outlined in section 3.2 above as to whether the goods and/or services are identical apply equally here. If they are not identical, or only some of them are identical, it needs to be determined whether they are similar.

The issue of similarity of goods and/or services has been considered in detail in case law. The key factors normally taken into account are:

- *their nature* – this includes a comparison of factors such as how they are described or categorised, their physical composition and how they work;
- *their intended purpose* – this does not include all possible uses of the goods,

only the purpose for which the goods and/or services are ordinarily purchased;

- *the average consumer* – a differentiation is generally made between goods and/or services targeted at the general public and those targeted at a specialist public (ie, business customers or those operating in a very specialist field);
- *whether they are complementary* – this includes a consideration of whether the goods and/or services are sold or provided together, or rely on each other (ie, one cannot function without the other);
- *whether they are in competition* – this includes consideration of whether one of the goods and/or services could be used as a replacement, alternative or substitute for the other;
- *their distribution channels* – this involves an assessment of whether the goods and/or services are likely to be purchased from the same or similar places, though this does not necessarily lead to a finding of similarity (eg, the fact that goods and/or services can be bought online does not in itself lead to a finding of similarity);
- *for self-service consumer goods, where they are likely to be found on the shelves in retail outlets* – this comparison can be very important for goods normally sold in supermarkets or other large retail stores. It is of no relevance to services; and
- *their origin* – this involves a consideration of whether the goods are likely to be produced by the same type of manufacture or the services are likely to be offered by the same type of trader.

The Office has been involved in the development of the Similarity database, which allows potential opponents to obtain information on whether specific terms are considered similar and, if so, to what degree (identical, high degree, similar, low degree, dissimilar). This database is used by the Office in assessing opposition cases and can be accessed via the Office's website at http://oami.europa.eu/sim/.

Likelihood of consumer confusion: Unlike the double identity ground, the confusion ground requires there to be a likelihood of consumer confusion for the opposition to succeed.

The Office carries out a global assessment of the likelihood of confusion, taking into account all relevant factors. These factors include:

- the degree of similarity between the marks at issue;
- the degree of similarity between the goods and/or services at issue;
- the relevant consumers of those goods and/or services and their level of attention when purchasing them; and
- the distinctiveness of the marks.

A detailed assessment of the law relating to the likelihood of confusion is beyond the scope of this book. A summary of the principles on which the Office bases its decisions can be found in the Office Guidelines at Part C, Section 2, Chapter 1. In essence, the Office decides whether consumers seeing the mark applied for being used in relation to the goods and/or services applied for would think those goods and/or services originated from the owner of the earlier rights relied on in the opposition or from an economically-linked undertaking. The opposition will succeed in relation to those goods and/or services for which the Office thinks this is likely to be the case.

It is possible for opponents relying on this ground to claim that their earlier trade mark rights enjoy an enhanced level of distinctiveness through the use that has been made of them. Evidence of such enhanced distinctiveness must be provided, as discussed in Chapter 13. If the requisite evidence is provided, the enhanced distinctiveness is a further factor that is considered in the global assessment of the likelihood of consumer confusion.

5. Reputation ground

This ground is set out in Article 8(5) of the Regulation. It can be used where:

- the marks are identical or similar;
- the earlier mark enjoys a reputation;
- use of the mark applied for would take unfair advantage of, or be detrimental to, the reputation and/or the distinctive character of the earlier mark; and
- the use of the mark applied for is without due cause.

It is only possible to rely on the reputation ground where the opponent owns (or is an authorised licensee of) a trade mark registration in the Union (either an EUTM registration or a national registration). It is not possible to rely on this ground where the earlier trade mark right is a pending application or a mark that is 'well-known' under the Paris Convention.

5.1 Who can rely on the reputation ground?

The opponent must be either the owner of the earlier trade mark rights or a licensee of those rights authorised by the owner to file opposition. The same considerations apply as those considered in section 3.1 above.

5.2 When can the reputation ground be relied upon?

Unlike the grounds discussed above, the reputation ground can be relied upon irrespective of the goods and/or services covered by the opposed application. It is equally applicable whether the goods and/or services at issue are identical, similar or dissimilar.

Marks: The same considerations as those detailed at section 3.2 above in the context of the double identity and confusion grounds apply to whether the marks at issue are identical or similar for the purposes of the reputation ground. In practice, this means that marks which are deemed dissimilar for the purposes of the confusion ground will also be deemed dissimilar for the purposes of the reputation ground. If an opposition fails under the confusion ground for this reason, it will fail under the reputation ground for the same reason.

Marks which are deemed similar for the purposes of the confusion ground will also be deemed similar for the purposes of the reputation ground. However, this does not mean that an opposition which succeeds under the confusion ground on the basis of a particular earlier mark will also succeed under the reputation ground, owing to the differing additional considerations at play for each ground.

Goods and/or services: For the reputation ground, it is irrelevant whether the goods and/or services at issue are identical, similar or dissimilar. However, reputation can only be claimed for goods and/or services covered by the earlier trade mark registration(s) relied upon.

In most instances, if the goods and/or services at issue are identical or closely similar, little is likely to be gained by including this ground in addition to the confusion ground. In such cases, if the opposition does not succeed on the basis of the confusion ground, it is rare that it will succeed under the reputation ground. As the reputation ground is generally much more difficult to make out than the confusion ground (due to the need to provide detailed evidence of reputation as discussed in Chapter 13), and as the Office does not necessarily consider each ground (as discussed in Chapter 14), including it can unnecessarily increase costs without improving chances of success.

The reputation ground may, however, be useful instead of or in addition to the confusion ground in cases involving identical or closely similar goods and/or services if the reputation enjoyed by the mark is so great that consumers are likely to make a link between that mark and the mark applied for, even though they may not actually be confused or think there is an economic link between the parties involved.

The reputation ground can be extremely useful where the goods and/or services at issue are dissimilar. However, the need to demonstrate a reputation and that the use of the mark applied for would damage the distinctive character or reputation of the earlier mark in some way, means it is not a straightforward ground to rely on, not least because it always requires strong evidence to support it.

Reputation: For a mark to have a reputation, it must be known by "a significant part of the public concerned by the products or services covered by that trade mark" (wording from the CJEU decision in the *YPLON* case).

No fixed percentage is taken to be a 'significant part' of the relevant public and the level of recognition required varies case by case. Reputation is not judged on the basis of fixed criteria, such as percentage market share, and the Office must take account of all the relevant facts of the case. However, key factors in assessing whether a trade mark enjoys a reputation include:

- the market share held by the trade mark;
- the intensity of the use of the trade mark;
- the geographical extent of the use of the trade mark;
- the duration of the use of the trade mark; and
- the size of the investment made by the trade mark owner in promoting it.

If the earlier mark in question is a national trade mark registration, the reputation must be in the territory in which it is protected. The reputation does not have to exist throughout the entire territory – a substantial part is sufficient.

Where the earlier mark is an EUTM registration, the reputation must extend to a substantial part of the Union. In practice, reputation in a single Member State can be sufficient to sustain an opposition under this ground. However, each case depends on its own facts.

Link and risk of injury: To succeed under the reputation ground, an opponent does not need to show any likelihood of confusion. Instead, the opponent needs to demonstrate that a 'link' would be made in the minds of relevant consumers between the marks at issue. If the mark applied for brings the mark with a reputation to mind, that is generally sufficient.

If it thinks that such a link would be made, the Office needs to consider whether unfair advantage or detriment is likely to occur because of the link made between the marks. Mere association alone is not enough.

To be successful under the reputation ground, an opponent needs to prove that use of the mark applied for would:

- *take unfair advantage of the distinctive character or repute of the earlier trade mark: this is often referred to as 'free riding'.* The CJEU summarised what this means in the *L'OREAL v BELLURE* case. To be successful, an opponent must show that the use of the mark applied for would "ride on the coat-tails of the mark with a reputation in order to benefit from the power of attraction, the reputation and the prestige of that mark and to exploit, without paying any financial compensation, the marketing effort expended by the proprietor of the mark in order to create and maintain the mark's image";
- *cause detriment to the distinctive character of the earlier trade mark: this is often referred to as 'dilution' or 'blurring'.* The CJEU summarised what this means in the *INTEL v CPM* case. To be successful, an opponent must show that the use of the mark applied for would lead to "a change in the economic behaviour of the average consumer of the goods or services for which the earlier mark was registered consequent on the use of the later mark, or a serious likelihood that such a change will occur in the future"; or
- *cause detriment to the repute of the earlier trade mark: this is often referred to as 'tarnishment' or 'degradation'.* The CJEU summarised what this means in the *L'OREAL v BELLURE* case. To be successful, an opponent must show that the use of the mark applied for "may be perceived by the public in such a way that the [earlier] trade mark's power of attraction is reduced". An example of where this might occur is where the reputation of the earlier trade mark relates to products promoting a healthy lifestyle and the application being opposed is for cigarettes or alcoholic drinks.

Without due cause: An EUTM application can only be refused on the basis of the reputation ground if the use of the mark applied for would be "without due cause". The burden is on the applicant to prove that it has due cause to use the mark applied for. An example of where this might be the case would be a pre-existing co-existence agreement in place between the parties that expressly allows the applicant to use the mark in relation to the goods and/or services applied for.

Where the applicant does not raise the due cause point, it is assumed that use of the mark in question would be without due cause. It should, however, be remembered that this factor is only relevant if the opponent can satisfy all the other requirements of the reputation ground: an opposition cannot succeed just because an applicant cannot prove it has due cause to use the mark applied for (ie, an EUTM application cannot be opposed on the basis of bad faith).

6. The unregistered rights ground

This ground is set out in Article 8(4) of the Regulation. It can be relied upon where an opponent has rights in an unregistered trade mark or other sign used in the course of trade, provided that the rights in the relevant mark or sign:

- are of more than mere local significance;
- were acquired before the filing date of the opposed EUTM application (taking into account any relevant priority claims); and
- would enable the opponent to prohibit the use of the mark applied for.

6.1 Who can rely on the unregistered rights ground?

The opponent must be a person entitled under the relevant law (ie, the law of the Member State in which the unregistered right exists) to exercise the rights relied upon.

6.2 When can the unregistered rights ground be relied upon?

To rely on the unregistered rights ground, an opponent must show three things:

The opponent must prove it owns a right that can be used to prevent the use of the mark applied for: The rights that can be relied upon under this ground are national rights. These can be unregistered trade mark rights (eg, where a mark is entitled to protection as a *marchio di fatto* in Italy) or rights given by a registration for something other than a trade mark (eg, a company name in Sweden or the name of a proprietary medicinal product in Estonia). The Office Guidelines (at Part C, Section 4) provide a non-exhaustive list of the types of national rights that may be relied upon under this ground.

It is for the opponent both to set out what the law is and prove it would be able to rely on that law to prevent use of the mark applied for within the relevant Member State(s). Further details of the evidence required when relying on this ground of opposition are set out in Chapter 13.

The unregistered trade mark or sign must be used in the course of trade and that use must be of more than mere local significance: Although the rights relied on under the unregistered rights ground are national rights, whether the use made of those rights is sufficient to allow an opposition to succeed is judged under Union law rather than national law. As a result, when considering whether the use made is of "more than more local significance" the word 'local' may require more widespread use than would be the case under the relevant national law. There are no set criteria for assessing the use made, although the Office considers such factors as the length of use, the geographic spread of use, the intensity of use (in terms of both sales made and consistency of use) and the advertising and marketing activities carried out.

The rights in question must have been acquired before the filing date (taking into account any relevant priority claims) of the opposed application: What it means to have 'acquired' a right varies depending on the right in question. Where a right comes into existence once a registration (eg, of a company name) has been granted, it is very easy for the Office to assess whether that right was acquired before the relevant date. Conversely, where a right comes into existence once use has started or once a reputation has been obtained, the situation is not as clear and the opponent needs to file substantial evidence proving when the right was acquired.

It can often be very difficult to oppose an EUTM application successfully relying solely on the unregistered rights ground. This ground is heavily reliant on evidence and often requires the Office to consider national laws with which it may not be familiar. As a result, if an opponent can rely on one of the other grounds discussed in this chapter, this should be included in the Notice of Opposition alongside (or potentially instead of) this ground.

Other IP rights, such as patents, copyright and design rights, cannot be relied upon under the unregistered rights ground. Such rights can, however, be used as the basis of an invalidity action against an EUTM registration (as discussed in Chapter 18).

7. The PDO/PGI ground

This ground is set out in Article 8(4)(a) of the Regulation. It can be relied upon where the application conflicts with a PDO or PGI, provided that:

- an application to protect the PDO or PGI was filed before the filing date of the opposed application (taking into account any relevant priority claims);
- the PDO or PGI is successfully protected on the relevant register; and
- the PDO or PGI gives the right to prohibit the use of the mark applied for.

7.1 Who can rely on the PDO/PGI ground?

The opponent must be a person entitled under the relevant law (ie, the law relating to the PDO or PGI on which the opposition is based) to exercise the rights given by the PDO or PGI registration. In practice this is normally the owner of the registration in question.

7.2 When can the PDO/PGI ground be relied upon?

To rely on this ground, an opponent needs to show the things set out at the first and third points in section 6.2 above. As the PDO/PGI ground is based on a registration, it is normally a simple process for an opponent to provide the Office with details of the registration relied on (or application, if the registration process has not been completed yet) and show that it is entitled to rely on that registration. More information needs to be provided to prove the registration entitles the opponent to prevent the use of the mark applied for. Further details of the evidence required for this ground of opposition are set out in Chapter 13.

PDOs and PGIs can be either Union-wide or national in scope and protected under Union law and/or international agreements. Where they are Union-wide rights established under Union law, the opponent does not need to set out what the law is. However, the opponent still needs to prove it would be able to rely on that law to prevent use of the mark applied for. Where the PDO or PGI is a national right, more information about the relevant law needs to be provided to the Office.

The scope of protection given to PDOs and PGIs varies with the nature of the relevant law relating to the registration relied on. As discussed in Chapter 7, an EUTM application can be refused on absolute grounds where it conflicts with a PDO or PGI. The same considerations as those set out in Chapter 7 apply when an opposition is based on this ground. Where the PDO or PGI is a national right and/or protected under an international agreement, different considerations may apply. A more detailed analysis is beyond the scope of this book.

The PDO/PGI ground was introduced on 23 March 2016. Prior to this, oppositions based on PDOs and PGIs had to be filed under the unregistered rights ground and the higher evidential burden of that ground had to be met (ie, the second point in section 6.2 above had to be proved – for the PDO/PGI, only the first and third points are required). It is no longer possible to rely on PDOs or PGIs when filing opposition under the unregistered rights ground and if this is mistakenly indicated in the Notice of Opposition when a PDO or PGI is relied on, the Office considers the case under the PDO/PGI ground instead.

8. The agent/representative ground

This ground is set out in Article 8(3) of the Regulation. It can be relied upon when an agent or representative files an EUTM application in its own name without the consent of the 'true proprietor' of the mark applied for.

8.1 Who can rely on the agent/representative ground?

The opponent must be the rightful owner of the trade mark applied for. Opposition cannot be brought under this ground by licensees or other parties. In this context, owning the trade mark applied for means:

- owning a trade mark application or registration anywhere in the world for the mark that has been applied for;
- owning unregistered trade mark rights anywhere in the world in the mark that has been applied for; or
- owning a mark that is a well-known mark.

8.2 When can the agent/representative ground be relied upon?

For an opposition to be successful under this ground, the following five conditions must all be satisfied.

The applicant for the opposed application is or was an agent or representative of the opponent: It is for the opponent to prove that the applicant is or was its agent or representative. These terms are interpreted broadly and the key requirement is that the parties had entered into some form of agreement resulting in a fiduciary relationship, so that the applicant was under a general duty of trust and loyalty to the opponent. There does not need to be a formal written agreement between the parties. That said, in practice it is easier to prove the existence of the necessary relationship where such an agreement does exist.

Whether the agreement is express or implied, written or unwritten, it must relate to at least part of the Union and the relationship must have been established before the opposed application was filed. It is not essential that the agreement was still in force at the time of filing, so long as the applicant was under an ongoing duty of trust and loyalty to the opponent at that time.

The applicant filed the application in its own name: The starting position is that the applicant name should be the same as the name of the agent or representative. However, this is not an absolute requirement. A link between the applicant and the agent or representative can suffice, if it is clear that the applicant was effectively acting on behalf of the agent or representative.

The application was filed without the opponent's consent: It is usually sufficient for the opponent simply to state that it did not consent to the filing of the application. It is then up to the applicant to prove that the opponent did consent to the filing, or otherwise to explain why it filed the application.

In these circumstances, the applicant needs to establish both that the opponent consented to the filing of the application for the mark at issue and that it consented to the filing being made in the applicant's name. While express consent is usually required, it is possible to rely on implied consent if there is clear evidence relating to the opponent's intentions. However, silence or ambiguity in this regard is interpreted in favour of the opponent.

The applicant is unable to justify its actions: If the applicant is able to establish that the opponent consented to the filing of the application in the applicant's name, there is no need for the applicant to justify its actions further. However, if the applicant cannot prove consent, it may still defeat the opposition by demonstrating some other justification for its actions. In practice, only very exceptional reasons are accepted.

The marks at issue are identical or very highly similar and the goods/services at issue are identical or very closely related: This ground is mostly used when the mark applied for is identical to the opponent's mark and covers goods and/or services that are identical to those in respect of which the opponent enjoys protection (the tests for identity are the same as those set out at section 3.2 above for the double identity ground).

However, the scope of the ground extends beyond the identity situation. It can also be used where the mark applied for is a slightly modified version of the opponent's mark, so long as the modifications in question do not substantially affect the distinctiveness of the mark.

Further, this ground can be relied upon where the goods and/or services covered by the opposed application are closely related to those for which the opponent's mark enjoys protection, such that the public may think they have been authorised by the opponent. The evidence required in support of an opposition based on this ground is considered in Chapter 13.

Further reference

Regulation – Articles 8 and 41
Office Guidelines – Part A, Section 9; Part C, Sections 2, 3, 4 and 5
L'Oréal SA v Bellure NV (Case C-487/07) (*'L'OREAL v BELLURE'*)
Intel Corporation Inc v CPM United Kingdom Ltd (Case C-252/07) (*'INTEL v CPM'*)
Génesis Seguros Generales Sociedad Anónima de Seguros y Reaseguros v Boys Toys SA (Case C-190/10)
LTJ Diffusion SA v Sadas Vertbaudet SA (Case C-291/00)
Canon Kabushiki Kaisha v Metro-Goldwyn-Mayer Inc (Case C-39/97)
SABEL BV v Puma AG (Case C-251/95)
PAGO International GmbH v Tirolmilch registrierte Genossenschaft mbH (Case C-301/07)
Safariland LLC v OHIM (*'FIRST DEFENCE'*) (Case T-262/09)
General Motors Corporation v Yplon SA (*'YPLON'*) (Case C-375/97)

Chapter 13: Submissions and evidence

1. Introduction

This chapter looks at evidence and other material that need to be submitted by both the opponent and the applicant during the adversarial stage of opposition proceedings.

The basic running order of this stage of opposition proceedings is as follows:

- opponent's deadline to substantiate the opposition and file further submissions and evidence in support of its case;
- applicant's deadline to file submissions and evidence in support of its case;
- proof of use evidence rounds; and
- opponent's reply evidence and submissions.

The Office has discretion to request or allow further rounds of evidence, although in most cases the above sequence is followed. As a result, there is generally only one round of reply evidence (filed by the opponent), unless the parties are able to justify the filing of additional evidence.

If the opponent is asked to file proof of use (as explained in section 6 below), new deadlines are set. These can run either alongside or after the deadlines referred to above, depending on when the proof of use request is made. The sequence of the proof of use deadlines mirrors that of the ordinary evidence deadlines:

- the opponent is set a deadline by which it must file proof of use evidence;
- the applicant is given an opportunity to file evidence and submissions in response to the proof of use evidence filed; and
- the opponent is given an opportunity to file evidence and submissions in reply relating specifically to the proof of use evidence.

2. Languages

The language of opposition proceedings is decided as described in Chapter 11, section 7. Wherever possible, all evidence and submissions filed in the proceedings should be filed in that language. There are, however, slightly different rules depending on the documents being filed.

2.1 Substantiation of the opposition

In order to meet the substantiation deadline, the opponent must ensure the necessary evidence (as discussed in section 3 below) is filed in the language of the proceedings (or is translated into the language of the proceedings) before the deadline.

This applies to both the evidence required to substantiate the rights relied upon and any submissions filed in support of the opposition. Anything that is not provided in the correct language is disregarded, which could result in the opposition being rejected as unfounded shortly after the substantiation deadline passes.

2.2 The applicant's response to the opposition

Where the response is not filed in the language of the proceedings, the applicant has a period of one month from the date on which the response is filed to submit a translation in that language. This one-month period runs from the date on which the response is filed, not from the original deadline – eg, if the opponent's deadline to respond was 27 July 2016 but it filed a response on 25 July 2016, the deadline to file a translation would be 25 August 2016.

The translation requirements relate to the applicant's submissions in response, not any evidence filed in support of the applicant's case. Documents other than observations can be filed in any Language of the Union and a translation is only required if requested by the Office. The opponent must, however, be able to understand the substantive content of any documents filed, so it is generally a good idea to provide translations of at least the substantive parts of the documents filed.

2.3 Reply and proof of use evidence

The same rules apply to reply evidence and proof of use evidence filed by the opponent, as set out in section 2.2 above.

3. The opponent's deadline to substantiate the opposition

The opponent's deadline to substantiate the opposition and file further submissions and evidence in support of its case falls two months from the end of the cooling off period. If the cooling off period is extended, this deadline is reset to be two months from the end of the extended cooling off period. If one of the parties opts out of the extended cooling off period, the deadline is re-calculated but always falls two months from the date the cooling off period ends.

This deadline can be extended once by a period of two months, without the need to give reasons, so long as the extension request is filed and received before the deadline expires. Further extensions are generally only granted in exceptional circumstances that are beyond the control of the opponent.

The opponent's deadline requires it to complete its case by doing the following:

- proving the existence of the rights relied on in the opposition;
- proving the validity of the rights relied on in the opposition;
- proving the scope of protection of the rights relied on in the opposition; and
- proving that it is entitled to file opposition on the basis of these rights.

In addition to the above, the opponent can file legal arguments or other submissions to support its case within this deadline. Although it is not mandatory to do so, this is generally a good idea. Bearing in mind the lack of oral hearings in EUTM oppositions, it is the opponent's only opportunity to explain its case fully (if it has not done so at the time of filing the opposition). As oppositions are decided 'on the papers', an opponent should ensure the papers show its case in the strongest possible light.

What is required to substantiate an opposition depends on the grounds and types of rights relied upon by the opponent, as set out in detail below. Simply expressed, there are two parts to this:

- proving the existence of the earlier rights relied on; and
- proving that those earlier rights can be used to prevent registration of the mark being opposed.

3.1 The double identity ground

An opponent can only rely on the double identity ground where it is the owner or authorised licensee of an 'earlier trade mark' (see Chapter 10, section 10.1 and Chapter 11, section 4). The evidence that must be provided to substantiate an earlier trade mark right depends on the nature of that right, as set out in the remainder of this section.

Once the opponent has proved that it owns an earlier trade mark, no further evidence or submissions need to be provided for the opposition to be successful. If there is an earlier trade mark right for the identical mark covering identical goods and/or services, the opposed application will be refused for those goods and/or services. However, if the opposed application also includes further goods and/or services that overlap with the coverage of the opponent's earlier trade mark rights, there may be scope for dealing with them under the confusion ground (in which case further submissions are recommended, as discussed in section 3.2 below).

Where the earlier trade mark is an EUTM application or registration: The Office verifies the existence of these rights by checking the Register. If the Office's online opposition form has been used, this process is very quick and the opposition is likely to be found admissible very swiftly, bearing in mind the need for only one right to be found admissible (as discussed in Chapter 11, section 9).

The key issue for the opponent is thus making sure the applicant or proprietor name as it appears on the Office's database tallies with the opponent's name. If there is a discrepancy (eg, because a request to record an assignment or name change has been filed but not yet processed by the Office), this should be explained when substantiating the opposition.

Where EUTM rights have been assigned and the Notice of Opposition is filed in the name of the new owner, but a request to record the assignment was not filed before the Notice of Opposition, the opposition will be rejected shortly after the substantiation deadline passes. This problem can easily be avoided by filing the assignment recordal request before the opposition is filed (see Chapter 16 for further information on assignment recordals).

An opponent who is a licensee needs to prove both that it is a licensee and that it is authorised to file an opposition. Where the licence has been recorded with the Office, and it is clear from the documents provided with the recordal application that the licensee is authorised to file oppositions, nothing further is required. If the licence is recorded but the authorisation to oppose is not clear, evidence needs to be provided in this regard.

Where the earlier trade mark is a national trade mark application or registration: The opponent must provide evidence of the existence of each registration relied on, including proof that it is still in force. Where an application is relied on, the opponent must provide evidence of the filing of that application.

Acceptable proof includes:

- official documents (ie, filing receipts, registration certificates and renewal certificates) issued by a national IPO or WIPO;
- extracts from official databases (ie, the online databases of the national IPOs or WIPO); and/or
- extracts from the official bulletins of national IPOs and WIPO.

Extracts from commercial databases are not acceptable.

If a registration is due to expire before the substantiation deadline, a renewal certificate or other proof that the registration has been renewed must be filed to prove that the right will still be in force after the substantiation period ends.

It is important that the documents filed include all the information required to substantiate the rights, namely:

- the official number;
- the mark;
- the specification;
- the name of the applicant or proprietor;
- the application and registration dates; and
- (if relevant) the priority date.

It may be necessary to file evidence from more than one source to ensure all this information is provided for any given right.

It is possible to rely on national rights that have been assigned to the opponent before the end of the opposition period, even if no steps have been taken to record this assignment before the end of the opposition period. However, where this is the case, it is necessary to provide evidence of the transfer to prove that the opponent is entitled to rely on the rights in question in opposition proceedings.

An opponent who is a licensee needs to prove both that it is a licensee and that it is authorised to file oppositions.

Where the earlier trade mark is a well-known mark: There is a much higher evidential burden in this regard. In some cases, a well-known mark is also registered in the Union (either Union-wide or at the national level). In these circumstances, it is always sensible to rely on the registration itself as an earlier right as it is much more straightforward to substantiate earlier registered rights than well-known marks. Where the registration is relied upon and a claim is also made that the mark is well-known in the territory of the registration, this is generally considered by the Office as a claim to enhanced distinctiveness – ie, an additional factor to support the earlier registration ground.

Where the mark at issue is both used and registered in the Union, an opponent should consider whether a reputation claim should be made instead of, or possibly as well as, a well-known mark claim. An unregistered rights claim may also be worth considering in the case of use in the Union.

An opposition should only be filed on the sole basis of a well-known mark claim where:

- the mark in question is not used or registered in the Union and the opponent owns no relevant unregistered or other rights in the Union, but
- despite the lack of use and registration, it can be shown that the relevant consumers are aware of, and familiar with, the mark.

For any well-known mark claim, the opponent needs to state where in the Union the mark is well-known. Such a claim must be backed up with evidence.

The threshold for well-known marks is very high and compelling evidence is required to substantiate this ground. The Office needs to be convinced the mark is indeed well-known to the relevant public in the territory concerned. In considering this, the Office takes account of the factors laid down by the Assembly of the Paris Union and WIPO in their joint recommendation as follows:

- the degree of knowledge or recognition of the mark in the relevant sector of the public;
- the duration, extent and geographical area of any use of the mark;
- the duration, extent and geographical area of any promotion of the mark;
- the duration and geographical area of any registrations, and/or any applications for registration, of the mark, to the extent that they reflect use or recognition of the mark;
- the record of successful enforcement of rights in the mark, in particular, the extent to which the mark was recognised as well known by competent authorities; and
- the value associated with the mark.

These factors are intended to be guidelines only, rather than an exhaustive or prescriptive list of what should be provided. It is, however, sensible to ensure that evidence addresses as many of these factors as possible.

In addition to showing that the mark is well-known, the opponent needs to provide evidence showing its entitlement to rely on the mark in an opposition (ie, showing that it either owns it or is an authorised licensee).

3.2 The confusion ground

An opponent can only rely on the confusion ground where it is the owner or authorised licensee of an 'earlier trade mark' (see Chapter 10, section 10.1). The evidence that must be provided to substantiate an earlier trade mark right is considered in section 3.1 above and those rules apply equally in this case.

Once the earlier trade mark right has been substantiated, to be successful the opponent also needs to prove that there is a likelihood of confusion between its earlier trade mark right and the mark applied for. The way that this is assessed by the Office is considered in Chapter 12, section 4.2.

An opponent relying on the confusion ground should ensure that it files sufficient evidence and submissions to prove there is a clear likelihood of confusion. If the mark applied for is already in use, and the opponent has evidence of actual confusion in the marketplace, this can be very persuasive evidence. However, the lack of actual confusion is not determinative, especially where the earlier trade mark is an application or registration that has not been in place for five years (as the rights given will extend to the whole specification covered by the application or registration, irrespective of the actual use made of the mark by the opponent).

The key for an opponent is explaining to the Office why consumers encountering both the mark applied for and the mark covered by the earlier trade mark rights in relation to the relevant goods and/or services are likely to be confused. 'Confusion' in this sense can either mean that consumers would mistake one mark for the other, or that they would make a connection and thus assume that the goods and/or services at issue come from the same undertaking or from economically linked undertakings.

The confusion ground is the most commonly used ground of opposition. It is often used alone, but is sometimes relied on together with other grounds, particularly the reputation ground. When relying on the confusion ground, it is a good idea to refer to supporting case law to help demonstrate why the opponent believes the requirements for this ground have been satisfied. As this ground is commonly used, there are a number of decisions of the Office that deal with it, as well as Board of Appeal decisions and decisions of the General Court and the CJEU. Ultimately, each case depends on its own facts, but it is a good idea to present as strong a case as possible, especially as there are no oral hearings in EUTM opposition proceedings.

3.3 The reputation ground

An opponent can only rely on the reputation ground where it is the owner or authorised licensee of an earlier trade mark registration (either an EUTM registration or a national registration). The evidence that must be provided to substantiate both EUTM registrations and national registrations is as set out in section 3.1 above.

Once the earlier registration has been substantiated, to be successful the opponent also needs to prove that it enjoys a reputation in the mark in question. The reputation should be in relation to goods and/or services that are covered by the registration. Where the earlier right is an EUTM registration, the reputation must exist in the Union. Where the earlier right is a national registration, the reputation must exist in the relevant Member State. The opponent also needs to demonstrate that the other requirements of this ground are made out, ie, that use without due cause of the mark applied for would take unfair advantage of, or be detrimental to, the distinctive character or reputation of the opponent's mark. The way these requirements are assessed by the Office is considered in Chapter 12, section 5.

In practice, where the reputation ground is relied upon, it is crucial to file both evidence (to demonstrate the existence and nature of the reputation) and legal submissions (to put the reputation evidence into context and demonstrate why the other elements of this ground are made out).

In terms of reputation evidence, the key is demonstrating to the Office that the mark enjoys a reputation in the relevant territory. Where the earlier right is an entire EUTM registration, it is not necessary to prove reputation throughout the Union. The reputation must extend to a substantial part of the Union, although in practice reputation in a single Member State can be (but will not necessarily be) sufficient to sustain an opposition under this ground.

Evidence of reputation should, where possible, address the following key factors:

- the market share held by the trade mark;
- the intensity of the use of the trade mark;
- the geographical extent of the use of the trade mark;
- the duration of the use of the trade mark; and
- the size of the investment made by the trade mark owner in promoting it.

This list is neither prescriptive nor exhaustive and reputation is not judged on the basis of fixed criteria, such as percentage market share. However, the list serves as a useful framework of the matters to address in reputation evidence. While many of these factors are similar to those relevant to proving use of a trade mark, either in the context of proof of use within opposition proceedings (as discussed in section 6 below) or in the context of non-use revocation proceedings (as discussed in Chapter 17), the evidential requirements are different in each of these contexts. It is never enough to succeed under the reputation ground to show simply that the mark has been used.

There is no set format in which reputation evidence must be presented and no set list of acceptable types of evidence. The evidence should be dated and so far as possible relate to the period before the filing or priority date of the opposed application. However, evidence that post-dates the opposed application may be given some weight if it can be inferred from such evidence that the reputation must have existed at the relevant date.

The Office can only base its assessment of reputation on the evidence presented by the opponent. Even if the individuals in the Office deciding the case know from their own personal knowledge that the mark does indeed enjoy a reputation, the Office cannot find that a mark has a reputation if weak evidence is filed.

The Office tends to place more weight on objective, independent evidence than on statements from the opponent (or persons and entities related to the opponent) that cannot be independently verified, or that are expressions of opinion rather than fact. Often, however, certain information that is not publicly available can only be provided by the opponent. Where statements from the opponent are filed, they should provide detailed and concrete information and facts.

Where the mark in question has previously been found by the Office to enjoy a reputation in the Union, a copy of the decision to this effect should be submitted. Although the Office is not bound by its own earlier decisions, an earlier finding of reputation by the Office can amount to compelling evidence of the existence of a reputation.

This is also the case with regard to earlier decisions of national courts and national IPOs, although again the Office is not obliged to conclude that reputation must exist purely on the basis of such decisions. Any earlier decisions will have been based on the evidence presented in those cases. Therefore, they need to be explained and put into context by the opponent.

Other types of evidence that may help support a reputation claim include:

- opinion polls and surveys;
- press articles;
- company reports;
- invoices and commercial documents; and
- promotional and advertising material.

Again, the more objective and focused such evidence is, the more weight it is given. It is also important to place any evidence in context, and explain why it demonstrates that the mark in question enjoys a reputation – eg, turnover figures alone are less persuasive than such figures accompanied by evidence of the size of the relevant market and thus an indication of the market share enjoyed by the opponent.

It is important for opponents to remember that proving the existence of a reputation in the Union is not enough in and of itself to succeed under this ground. The other elements of this ground also need to be made out – ie, demonstrating a link and risk of injury, as discussed in Chapter 12, section 5. For this reason, the opponent should also ensure that it characterises the nature of the reputation that its mark enjoys. It is much easier to explain the potential injury if the nature of the reputation is clear. For example, if the opponent demonstrates that it enjoys a reputation in the Union in relation to a particular type of goods and that they are perceived by consumers as promoting healthy living, this is likely to assist in demonstrating that use of the mark under opposition in relation to goods such as cigarettes or alcohol would cause damage to this reputation.

In many cases, there is no concrete evidence available to support the contention that consumers would make a link between the marks at issue, or indeed that use of the mark applied for in relation to the goods and/or services covered by the opposed application brings with it a risk of injury to the opponent's mark. In such cases, the opponent should file legal submissions setting out a logical case as to why the requirements of this ground have been satisfied.

Where there is evidence to support this view, it should be provided. For example, if the opposition relates to a mark that is already in use, and the opponent can demonstrate a clear decline in its own sales figures corresponding with the applicant's entry into the market, this is likely to be very persuasive evidence.

It is not necessary for all the evidence filed to be specific to the parties. In some contexts, it can be very useful to file more general evidence (eg, evidence showing that consumers tend to perceive a certain category of products in a negative light). This evidence can be used to support arguments that use of the mark applied for is likely to have a detrimental effect on the reputation that the opponent enjoys in its mark.

3.4 The unregistered rights ground

To rely on the unregistered rights ground, an opponent must demonstrate the existence of a relevant earlier right and that it is entitled to rely on that right to prevent the use of the mark applied for. The evidential burden can be very heavy under this ground, depending on the exact right relied on.

To substantiate an opposition based on this ground, the opponent must file evidence to demonstrate:

- that it has acquired the right relied on, and did so before the filing (or priority) date of the opposed EUTM application:
  - in the case of registered rights (eg, company or business name registrations), official documentation should be filed as evidence of acquisition of the right;
  - in the case of unregistered rights (eg, rights based on a *marchio di fatto* in Italy), more extensive evidence is required. The opponent should file the same evidence as would be required in national proceedings to enforce the right in question. Where the opponent has successfully relied upon the right in question in national proceedings, the national decision can serve as good evidence that the opponent has acquired the right at issue, but this is not in itself enough to prove that the right is still in existence.
- that the right enables the holder to prohibit the use of a subsequent trade mark;
- that the opponent uses the mark or sign at issue in the course of trade, and did so prior to the filing date of the opposed EUTM application;
- that the use is of more than mere local significance;
- what the relevant law is and how that applies to the current situation. The opponent must provide details of, and explain the provisions of, the law in question. It must also show why it thinks it would be successful in an action brought to prevent the use of the mark applied for in relation to the goods and/or services covered by the opposed EUTM application.

The last point is especially important. The Office may not be familiar with the relevant national or other law on which the opposition is based, so it is vital that the opponent files detailed submissions explaining why the case is made out under that law.

As the law varies so much between both the Member States and types of unregistered and other rights that can be relied on under this ground, detailed guidance on the evidence that must be filed in support of this ground cannot be provided here. However, it is important to ensure the evidence clearly addresses all of the points listed above and that as much as possible is done to explain clearly to the Office what the relevant national law is and why the opposition should therefore succeed.

It is generally difficult to oppose an EUTM application successfully solely on the basis of the unregistered rights ground, so if an opponent has an 'earlier trade mark' right that could be used as the basis of an opposition, additional grounds of opposition should be included.

3.5 The PDO/PGI ground

To rely on the PDO/PGI ground, an opponent must demonstrate the existence of a relevant earlier right and that it is entitled to rely on that right.

To substantiate an opposition based on this ground, the opponent must file evidence to demonstrate:

- that an application for the PDO or PGI was filed before the filing (or priority) date of the opposed EUTM application – this requirement should be easy to satisfy, by providing a copy of the application and a database/register extract. If the PDO or PGI has achieved registration, details of the registration can also be provided;
- that the right enables the holder to prohibit the use of a subsequent trade mark; and
- what the relevant law is and how that applies to the current situation. The opponent must provide details of, and explain the provisions of, the law in question. It must also show why it thinks it would be successful in an action brought to prevent the use of the mark applied for in relation to the goods and/or services covered by the opposed EUTM application.

For the opposition to be successful, the PDO or PGI must actually become registered. If the PDO or PGI application is refused, for whatever reasons, this ground cannot be relied upon. As a result, an opponent needs to prove that a PDO or PGI registration has been achieved before a decision under this ground can be taken.

As with the unregistered rights ground, the Office is unlikely to have very detailed knowledge of the laws protecting many PDOs or PGIs, so opponents should ensure that the legal effect of their rights, and why the existence of those rights means the opposition should be successful, are explained in great detail.

Having said that, an opposition based on the PDO/PGI ground is more likely to succeed now than was the case before this specific ground was introduced in March 2016, due to the fact that there is no longer a need to show use in the course of trade of more than mere local significance (which was the case prior to 23 March 2016, when PDOs and PGIs could only be relied on under the unregistered rights ground).

3.6 The agent/representative ground

As detailed in Chapter 12, section 8, this ground allows the owner of a trade mark to oppose an EUTM application for that mark that has been filed by its agent or representative without its consent.

To substantiate an opposition based on this ground, the opponent must file evidence establishing that:

- it is the owner of the trade mark applied for, and was the owner prior to the date on which the EUTM application was filed:
  - where the opponent owns a trade mark application or registration for the mark (anywhere in the world) that predates the opposed EUTM application, it should provide details of that application or registration, providing the information set out in section 3.1 above for oppositions based on earlier trade mark applications and registrations; and/or

    - where the opponent owns unregistered rights in the mark (anywhere in the world) that predate the opposed EUTM application, it should provide details of such rights, in line with the evidence to be provided for oppositions based on earlier unregistered trade mark rights, as set out in section 3.4 above;
- the applicant is or was its agent or representative prior to the filing of the EUTM application, and that it was under an ongoing duty of trust and loyalty to the opponent at the time the EUTM application was filed:
    - a copy of a formal written agreement between the parties is usually the most compelling evidence of both the existence and timing of such a relationship; but
    - there is no requirement for a formal or written agreement between the parties. Where the agreement is informal and/or unwritten, its existence and scope is usually much more difficult to prove. Evidence that can assist in this regard includes copies of correspondence between the parties, or documents such as invoices that demonstrate a course of dealing between the parties. However, it is important to explain how such evidence proves the applicant was the opponent's agent or representative.
- the agreement between the parties related to at least part of the Union; and
- the application was filed in the name of the agent or representative:
    - this is usually self-evident, particularly if there is a written agreement between the parties with the names of the parties to that agreement tallying with the names of the applicant and the opponent; and
    - this ground can be relied on where the agent or representative has filed the application in the name of a third party, provided that the opponent can demonstrate there is a clear link between the applicant and the agent or representative, such that the applicant was effectively acting on behalf of the agent or representative.

The opponent is not expected to file evidence to demonstrate that it did not consent to the filing of the application by the applicant. However, if such evidence exists and is available, it should be filed together with the evidence substantiating the opposition as this will assist in making out the case as a whole. Otherwise, it is for the applicant to show that the opponent did positively consent to the filing, as discussed further in section 5 below.

4. Failure to substantiate the opposition

Once the substantiation deadline has passed, the Office reviews the evidence filed to determine whether the rights relied upon have been properly substantiated. The opposition is refused as unfounded if none of the rights have been substantiated. The Office then issues a decision to this effect, without waiting for the applicant's reply to the opposition.

As detailed in Chapter 11, section 9, an opposition is deemed admissible at the admissibility stage if at least one right is clearly identified. If the right on the basis of which the opposition was deemed admissible is not substantiated, the Office carries out further checks to ensure that the absolute admissibility and substantiation requirements have been met for at least one other earlier right. Any rights that have not been substantiated are excluded from the opposition.

As it is much easier to check whether earlier trade mark applications or registrations have been substantiated than any of the other rights on which an opposition can be based, the Office looks at those first in deciding on whether to allow the opposition proceedings to continue.

5. The applicant's response to the opposition

The applicant is set a deadline of four months from the end of the cooling off period to file a reply to both the Notice of Opposition and any further material submitted by the opponent. As is the case with the substantiation deadline, this deadline can be extended once by a period of two months, without the need to give reasons, so long as the extension request is filed and received before the deadline expires. Further extensions are only granted in exceptional circumstances.

It is not mandatory for the applicant to file a response in opposition proceedings and, unlike under some national systems, the opposition does not automatically succeed if no response is filed. If, however, the applicant has any interest in maintaining the application, it is highly recommended that a response be filed. The only exception to this is where the opposition is based on grounds on which the opponent cannot possibly hope to succeed (eg, where the opposition is based on the confusion ground and the goods and/or services in question are clearly very different). Even then, most applicants want to file some kind of a response setting out their position.

The applicant's response often takes the form of written arguments, highlighting any flaws or weaknesses in the evidence and/or arguments presented by the opponent. If, however, there is evidence that can be used to rebut the case put forward by the opponent, the applicant should ensure that this is filed. As in the case of the evidence filed to support the opposition, any rebuttal evidence is given greater weight by the Office if it is independent in nature.

As a general rule, no negative inferences are drawn from an applicant's failure to file a response. Where, however, the opponent has filed an opposition on the ground that the application was filed by an agent or representative, it is for the applicant to prove that the opponent consented to the filing of the application. In relation to this ground, failure by the applicant to respond to the opposition is interpreted in the opponent's favour (ie, it is presumed that the opponent did not consent to the filing of the application).

Where the opposition is based on earlier rights with a reputation, failure by the applicant to demonstrate that it has due cause to make use of the mark applied for in relation to the goods and/or services covered by the opposed application is taken to mean that there is no such due cause. Thus, where the applicant does have due cause to use the mark, it should file evidence to prove positively that this is the case.

6. Proof of use

6.1 When is proof of use relevant?

Trade marks that have been registered in the Union for more than five years but have not been used for any continuous five-year period following registration can be revoked and removed from the relevant register, as discussed in detail in Chapter 17. This is the case for both EUTM registrations and national registrations in each of the Member States (the law across the Union is harmonised in this regard).

Where an opposition against an EUTM application is based on one or more EUTM registrations or national trade mark registrations that had been registered for five years or longer by the filing date of the opposed application (or the priority date for that application, if applicable), the applicant can request that the opponent files proof of use of the mark or marks at issue.

Without the proof of use provisions, applicants would have to file revocation proceedings against old (unused) registrations to prevent them being relied on in opposition proceedings. In practice, proof of use is a form of defence, so that applicants do not need to be concerned about registrations that could be removed from the relevant register. It is, however, worth noting that the effect of failing to file adequate proof of use evidence during opposition proceedings is simply that the right or rights at issue are excluded from the opposition. They remain on the relevant register and can only be removed through separate revocation proceedings.

Given the consequences if no proof of use is filed (as discussed in section 6.6 below), applicants are almost always advised to request proof of use where possible. This is the same even if the applicant knows the earlier marks on which the opposition is based are in use, as the burden of proving such use remains on the opponent.

6.2 Timing and effect of a proof of use request

At any time before the expiry of its deadline to file a response to the opposition, an applicant can request that proof of use be filed by the opponent. A proof of use request should be sent to the Office, rather than to the opponent, and must clearly identify each registration for which proof of use is requested. The Office then sets a two-month deadline (extendable once by a further two months) by which the opponent must file its proof of use evidence.

The effect of a proof of use request on the normal deadlines in opposition proceedings depends on when the request is sent to the opponent:

- *proof of use request sent during the cooling off period* – the opponent's deadlines both to substantiate the opposition and provide proof of use are two months after the expiry of the cooling off period;
- *proof of use request sent before the opponent's deadline to substantiate the opposition* – the opponent's deadline for substantiating the opposition is extended to coincide with the deadline for filing proof of use evidence (ie, two months after the proof of use request is sent to the opponent);
- *proof of use request sent after the opponent's deadline to substantiate the opposition* – the applicant's deadline to respond to the opposition is automatically

extended to be two months after the opponent's proof of use deadline (or two months after the proof of use is forwarded to the applicant by the Office, if later). This means the applicant can satisfy its response deadline by simply filing a proof of use request, even if the opposition includes additional rights or grounds to which the request does not apply.

6.3 What does 'use' mean in this context?

The evidence to be filed by the opponent in response to a proof of use request in opposition proceedings is essentially the same as that required in non-use revocation proceedings (see Chapter 17).

To be acceptable in this context, use must comply with the following criteria:

- *the use must be genuine* – there must be actual use of the mark as a trade mark. This means that mere token use, made with the intention of maintaining the relevant registration, is not sufficient. The use must be consistent with the essential function of a trade mark, to guarantee the origin of the goods and/or services in relation to which it is used;
- *the use must be in the course of trade* – there must be consumer-facing, not merely internal, use of the mark. This means that, for example, use of a mark as the name of a publication sent only to employees of a company or group of companies is not sufficient;
- *the use must be made with the intention of creating or maintaining a market share for the goods and/or services covered by the registration* – purely promotional use is not sufficient. This means that use in relation to gifts given away when a different good and/or service is purchased is not sufficient. Further, use of the mark on promotional items is usually not enough, especially where those items are used to promote a different sort of good and/or service, eg, use on T-shirts promoting a nightclub is not use in relation to clothing;
- *the level of use must be seen as acceptable in the relevant economic sector concerned for the purposes of creating or maintaining a market share* – what is seen as acceptable varies enormously between economic sectors. This assessment involves consideration of such factors as the nature of the relevant goods and/or services, the characteristics of the relevant market and the frequency of use of the relevant mark. It is important to note that it is the genuine nature of the use that is important, so that use does not necessarily need to be quantitatively significant to be genuine. There is no minimum level of use that must be made for it to be sufficient and each case has to be judged according to its own particular circumstances;
- *the mark must be used as registered* – though some flexibility is given. Use of the mark in a slightly different form is acceptable, so long as the distinctive character of the mark remains the same. The Office looks at the distinctive and dominant elements of the registered mark and assesses whether these elements are all present in the mark as used. It also considers any additions or omissions in determining whether the form of use is close enough to the registered mark to amount to evidence of use of that mark;
- *the use must be made by the proprietor, or with its consent* – use by licensees is

often relied on in in this regard. There is no requirement for the licence to be recorded in the relevant register for such use to be relied upon. The Office usually assumes that all evidence filed shows use by the proprietor or with its consent, though if this is questioned (either by the Office or, more usually, the other party) the proprietor can be asked to prove that this is the case. If that happens, the proprietor is set a deadline by which to file such proof;

- *the use must have been made in the relevant territory* – where the proof of use relates to a national registration, use must be shown in the relevant Member State. Where the proof of use relates to an EUTM registration, use must be shown in the Union. It is not necessary to show use in every Member State to prove use in the Union, and use in just one Member State can be, but is not necessarily, sufficient. This is because territorial borders are not relevant when use of an EUTM registration is assessed. What matters instead is whether the use made is seen as sufficient in the relevant market;
- *the use made must be in relation to the goods and/or services covered by the relevant registration* – each good and/or service is looked at individually, so that it is very common for use to be proved for some, but not all, of the goods and/or services covered by a registration. Where broad terms are used and the use shown relates only to an identifiable sub-category falling within that broad term, the registration can only be relied upon in relation to that sub-category. For example, if a registration covers "clothing" in class 25 but the evidence of use filed relates solely to 'skirts', the registration can only be relied on insofar as it covers 'skirts'; and
- *the use must have been made in the relevant time period* – the use must clearly relate to the relevant time period, which in oppositions is the five-year period immediately before the filing date (or priority date, if priority was claimed) of the opposed application.

6.4 Filing acceptable proof of use evidence

It is the responsibility of the opponent to ensure that proof of use evidence is presented in a structured and clear manner. Failure to do so runs the risk that certain pieces of evidence will not be taken into account or given the weight intended by the opponent. The considerations set out at section 8 below in terms of how evidence is presented and filed should also be taken into account.

As with reputation evidence, the Office can only base its assessment on the evidence presented by the opponent. It is therefore important to provide evidence that is as strong as possible. It is not necessary to present proof of use evidence in the form of annexes to a sworn statement or affidavit. All evidence should, however, be clearly identified and explained. This can be done in a sworn statement or in written submissions.

When filing proof of use evidence, it is necessary to ensure that the place, time, extent and nature of the use made are all clear from the evidence. Each of these matters is considered in turn below:

- **Place of use:**
  - The evidence must clearly show that the use was made in the relevant

territory. For EUTM registrations, use must be made in the Union. For national registrations, use must be made in the Member State covered by the relevant registration. Special care needs to be taken when proof of use of EUTM registrations is filed. While use in a single Member State can be enough, evidence should, wherever possible, be filed demonstrating use in several Member States.
  - Use solely for import or export purposes can amount to use in the relevant territory, so long as the mark in question is affixed to goods (or their packaging) within that territory. However, use in relation to goods that are merely in transit through, and are never put on the market in, a particular territory does not amount to use in that territory.
  - It is often a good idea to explain in supporting submissions why the use shown is sufficient, particularly if it relates to use in only a small geographical area. For example, if the Union market in the relevant goods and/or services is concentrated in just two Member States, proving use in those Member States should suffice.
- **Time of use:**
  - Opponents need to ensure that their evidence relates to the correct period for it to be taken into account (ie, the five-year period immediately before the filing date of the opposed application, or the priority date of the opposed application if there was a successful priority claim).
  - Wherever possible, evidence should be dated so that it is clear when the use was made.
  - It is also worth noting that, prior to 23 March 2016, the relevant time period was calculated from the publication date (not the application/priority date) of the opposed application.
- **Extent of use:**
  - As noted above, the evidence filed needs to demonstrate that the use made was with the intention of creating or maintaining a market share for the relevant goods and/or services. There is no financial or volume threshold that needs to be reached for use to be proved. However, the greater the extent of the use, the more likely it is to be deemed sufficient.
  - The evidence filed should show the scale of the commercial activity undertaken under the mark, with the number of sales and the value of those sales included, if possible. It is also worth including details of the advertising and promotional activities undertaken.
  - The duration of the use made should be indicated and, if possible, it should be demonstrated that the use made was continuous throughout the relevant five-year period. However, use that was made in only part of the relevant period can be enough, especially where there is a high frequency of use (and a high level of sales).
  - The evidence should, wherever possible, demonstrate use in relation to all the goods and/or services the opponent needs (or wants) to rely on in the opposition. If there has been no use in relation to some of the goods and/or services covered by the proof of use request, it is often a good idea

to draw this to the attention of the Office and confirm that no evidence has been filed in relation to those goods and/or services. That way, the Office can be directed to focus on the evidence relating to the goods and/or services for which use can be shown.
    - Where the registration contains broad terms and use can only be shown for some goods and/or services falling within the broad term, whether the use in question is sufficient to allow the broad term to be maintained depends on whether the goods and/or services for which use has been shown form an identifiable sub-category within the broader category: see the example of 'clothing' and 'skirts' given in section 6.3 above. If the opponent wants to argue that the broad term should be taken into account, despite the limited evidence filed, arguments on this point should be filed along with the relevant evidence.
- **Nature of use:**
    - The evidence filed should demonstrate that the type of use made satisfies the criteria set out in section 6.3 above.
    - If there is any doubt as to whether these criteria have been satisfied, the opponent should explain why it believes they have been satisfied. For example, where evidence of use shows use of a slightly different mark to that covered by the relevant registration, the evidence should be supplemented by legal arguments explaining why the use supports the registration in question.

In terms of content, acceptable evidence includes (but is not limited to):

- packages;
- labels;
- price lists;
- catalogues;
- invoices;
- photographs;
- newspaper advertisements; and
- written statements.

Where the mark in question has previously been found by the Office to have been used (either in proof of use proceedings within another opposition or in cancellation proceedings) the opponent can refer to such proceedings. Any material previously submitted does not have to be submitted again, so long as it is clearly identified. However, a simple reference to an earlier decision accepting that use was proven is unlikely to be sufficient to satisfy a proof of use request on its own as there will be different date ranges to consider. The opponent can also refer to earlier decisions of national courts and national IPOs, which the Office can take into account but does not have to follow.

6.5 Proper reasons for non-use

If the opponent has not used a mark for which proof of use has been requested, the relevant right is still taken into account in the opposition if the opponent can prove that it has justifiable reasons for not making use of the mark.

To be seen as justifiable in this context, the reasons must relate to something that is beyond the control of the opponent and must directly affect its ability to make use of the mark in question. In practice, there are very limited circumstances in which this can be proved, not least because those reasons must have been in place for at least five years (ie, the period during which use has to be shown). Examples of acceptable reasons include import restrictions and government requirements, such as regulatory procedures.

6.6 Outcome of proof of use requests

If the opponent does not file any proof of use evidence, or proper reasons for non-use, the relevant registrations are not taken into account in the opposition. The opposition continues where there are other rights that are not subject to the proof of use request. Where an opposition is based entirely on rights subject to a proof of use request, the opposition is rejected if no proof of use evidence, or proper reasons for non-use, are filed. As discussed above, such rights nonetheless remain on the relevant register.

If the opponent files some proof of use evidence, or submissions arguing that it has proper reasons for not using the mark, the applicant is given a two-month time period within which to file a response. This period can be extended once by a further two months. The applicant is given this opportunity to respond no matter when in the proceedings the proof of use is filed (see section 6.2 above for the options in this regard).

The Office assesses proof of use evidence, as well as any submissions related to that evidence, together with the rest of the arguments and evidence after the end of the adversarial stage of the opposition proceedings. It is only where no proof of use evidence is filed (and no proper reasons for non-use are given), and all the rights on which the opposition is based are reliant on such evidence, that the opposition ends after the proof of use stage. Even very limited proof of use evidence is enough to keep the proceedings going.

The evidence of use filed is assessed separately in relation to each registration covered by the proof of use request. As a result, it is possible (and is often the case) that the evidence filed allows some but not all of the earlier registrations to be maintained in the opposition. For example, if an opposition is based on national registrations in France, Germany, Hungary and Latvia, but the evidence of use filed only relates to Germany and Hungary, the French and Latvian registrations are effectively removed from the proceedings and the Office decides the opposition solely on the basis of the German and Hungarian registrations.

7. Reply by the opponent

If the applicant does not file anything to satisfy its deadline, the Office normally writes to the parties indicating that the adversarial stage of the proceedings is complete. It then considers the papers submitted and takes a decision.

Where the applicant files evidence and/or submissions within the period set for it to do so, a copy is sent to the opponent by the Office. The opponent is given a two-month time period within which to file a reply. The opponent's deadline can be extended once by a period of two months, without the need to give reasons, so long as the extension request is filed and received before the deadline expires. Further extensions are generally only granted in exceptional circumstances.

Where the opponent files a reply that is not in the language of the proceedings, a translation into that language must be filed within a period of one month. This one-month period runs from the date on which the response was filed with the Office, not from the original deadline (eg, if the opponent's deadline to respond was 27 July 2016 but it filed a response on 25 July 2016, the deadline to file a translation would be 25 August 2016).

The opponent should limit its reply to addressing only the points and evidence submitted by the applicant in its response. Evidence on new points not previously raised by either party, or additional evidence to support points already raised by the opponent but not addressed by the applicant, should not be filed at this stage. In practice, however, the Office does not automatically exclude such evidence. Thus, if useful evidence in support of the opposition becomes available at this stage, it is sensible to file it at this point. Indeed, additional proof of use evidence filed at this stage has been taken into account by the Office in the past.

8. Filing evidence with the Office

The Office specifically lists the following key points in its Guidelines, which are relevant to all forms of evidence presented to the Office, including proof of use evidence in opposition proceedings:

- the relevant file number should be included on all correspondence;
- a separate communication for documents with proof of use should be provided;
- annexes should include page numbers and the total number of pages of correspondence should be indicated;
- correspondence should not exceed a total number of 110 pages if possible (ie, the evidence and any observations together should not run to more than 110 pages);
- if documents are sent in multiple packages, an indication of the total number of packages should be given;
- if a large number of documents are submitted by fax, and across multiple faxes, an indication of the total number of fax communications, and overall total number of pages, should be given;
- plain DIN-A4 sheets should be used;
- physical specimens, containers and packaging should not be submitted as evidence. Rather, photographs of such items should be used;
- any original items or documents that are sent to the Office should not be stapled, bound or placed in folders;
- where evidence is sent to the Office in hard copy (rather than submitted by fax or electronically) a second copy should be provided, for forwarding to the other party, and this second copy should be clearly identified as such;

- where the original is submitted to the Office by fax or electronically, no second copy should be sent;
- the front page should clearly indicate whether the correspondence contains colour elements that are relevant to the file. If this is the case, a second set of colour elements should be provided for sending to the other party.

These points are aimed at making it as easy as possible for the Office properly to identify and assess the evidence presented and it is highly recommended that they are adhered to.

9. Oral proceedings

It is technically possible:

- for the parties to opposition proceedings to request an oral hearing at any stage during the proceedings, and
- for the Office to insist that an oral hearing takes place.

In reality, however, the Office never suggests such hearings and rejects any requests in this regard from parties to opposition proceedings.

Although hearings never happen in practice, there are rules surrounding the procedure for parties to appear before the Office. Where the Office summons parties to appear, it must give them a minimum of one month's notice, unless they have expressly agreed to a shorter period. The legal provisions relating to oral proceedings make clear that any such hearings in relation to opposition proceedings are not open to the public.

The lack of oral hearings in practice means that both parties should work on the assumption that their only chance to present their case will be in written form during the adversarial stage of the proceedings.

Further reference

Regulation – Articles 8, 15, 41, 42, 51 and 76-78
Implementing Regulation – Rules 19-22, 56-60, 79, 79a and 95-98
Office Guidelines – Part C, Sections 1-6
Joint Recommendation concerning Provision on the Protection of Well-Known Marks, issued by the Assembly of the Paris Union for the Protection of Intellectual Property and the General Assembly of the World Intellectual Property Organization (WIPO Publication 833), available at: www.wipo.int/edocs/pubdocs/en/marks/833/pub833.pdf
Leno Marken BV v Hagelkruis Beheer BV (Case C-149/11)
Ansul BV v Ajax Brandbeveilining BV (Case C-40/01)
La Mer Technology Inc v Laboratoires Goemar SA (Case C-259/02)

Chapter 14: Termination of proceedings

1. Introduction

This chapter looks at the various ways in which opposition proceedings can come to an end, including through amicable resolution by the parties and the issuance by the Office of a decision on the substance of the case.

The manner in which an opposition terminates can affect whether it is possible for the applicant to make use of the conversion process, which is discussed in Chapter 25.

2. Conclusion of proceedings other than through a decision on the substantive case

Although many opposition proceedings run their full course through to a decision on substance, opposition cases often come to an end through a variety of other means.

The most common ways for an opposition to end, each of which is discussed separately below, are as follows:

- the opposition is deemed inadmissible;
- the opposition is not properly substantiated;
- proof of use evidence is not provided when requested;
- the opposition is withdrawn;
- the opposed application is withdrawn;
- the specification of the opposed application is restricted, removing the goods and/or services against which the opposition was directed;
- the rights on which the opposition is based cease to exist;
- the opposed EUTM application is rejected for other reasons; and
- the parties reach an amicable settlement.

2.1 Opposition deemed inadmissible

Once a Notice of Opposition is filed, the Office carries out admissibility checks. If any of the absolute admissibility requirements are not satisfied by the end of the opposition period, the opposition is rejected as inadmissible.

If any of the relative admissibility requirements are not satisfied by the end of the opposition period, the Office notifies the opponent and sets a two-month non-extendable deadline by which the missing information must be provided. If this deadline is not satisfied, the opposition is rejected as inadmissible.

An opposition is also rejected as inadmissible if:

- the Notice of Opposition is not filed before the end of the opposition period;
- the opposition fee is not paid in time; or
- the language and representation requirements are not met.

These requirements are discussed in full in Chapter 11.

2.2 Opposition not properly substantiated

As discussed in Chapter 11, the opposition timetable is set once an opposition is deemed admissible. The opponent is given an extendable period of two months from the end of the cooling off period within which to substantiate the opposition.

Full details of the evidence required to substantiate an opposition are provided in Chapter 13, section 3. If this evidence is not provided, the Office rejects the opposition shortly after the expiry of the opponent's deadline without waiting for the applicant's reply on the substantive case.

2.3 Failure to file proof of use evidence

As discussed in Chapter 13, section 6, where an opposition is based on earlier trade mark registrations that were registered five or more years before the date on which the opposed application was filed, the applicant can request that the opponent files proof of use evidence for those registrations.

If the opponent fails to file such evidence within the time period set, and the opposition is not based on any other rights, the Office rejects the opposition shortly after the expiry of the proof of use deadline without waiting for the applicant's reply on the substantive case.

If proof of use evidence is not filed but the opposition is based on additional rights for which proof of use does not have to be filed, the opposition proceeds on the basis of those other rights, provided of course that they have been properly substantiated (as set out in Chapter 13, section 3).

2.4 Withdrawal of the opposition

It is possible for the opponent to withdraw an opposition at any time during the proceedings. Any such withdrawal should be made in writing and should be clear and unambiguous. The easiest way of achieving this is by making an electronic request through the Office's online platform. Alternatively, the withdrawal can take the form of a letter or fax.

The effect of a withdrawal is always to bring the proceedings to an end. However, the implications in terms of fees and costs depend on two factors:

- the stage the proceedings have reached when the withdrawal request is made; and
- whether the withdrawal is made as the result of a restriction to the opposed EUTM application.

A brief summary of the potential outcomes is set out in Table 1 below (and further details about decisions on costs are provided in section 4 below).

Table 1

Timing	Fees & costs
Opposition and withdrawal filed on the same day	• Official opposition fee refunded • No decision on costs
Opposition withdrawn before being deemed admissible	• Official opposition fee not refunded • No decision on costs
Opposition withdrawn during cooling off period and no restriction has been made to opposed application	• Official opposition fee not refunded • No decision on costs
Opposition withdrawn during cooling off period and restriction has been made to opposed application (or to part of the application that has been opposed, if not opposed in full)	• Official opposition fee refunded • No decision on costs
Opposition withdrawn during period between end of cooling off period and the Office taking a decision	• Official opposition fee not refunded • Decision on costs issued in favour of the applicant, unless the parties jointly submit an agreement on costs
Opposition withdrawn during appeal period after the Office has taken a decision	• Official opposition fee not refunded • Original opposition decision stands, as does original decision on costs • No further decision on costs issued

A request to withdraw an opposition cannot be reversed unless the original withdrawal request and a further communication indicating that the opposition is not in fact to be withdrawn are received by the Office on the same day.

2.5 Withdrawal of the opposed application

An EUTM applicant can withdraw its application at any stage before registration, irrespective of whether it has been opposed or not, and irrespective of the stage any opposition proceedings have reached.

The withdrawal must be filed in writing and should be clear and unambiguous. The easiest way of achieving this is by making an electronic request through the

Office's online platform. Alternatively, the withdrawal can take the form of a letter or fax.

Where an application that has been opposed is withdrawn, the opposition proceedings are terminated as they no longer have an object. The effect of such a withdrawal in terms of fees and costs in the opposition proceedings depends on the stage the opposition proceedings have reached when the application is withdrawn. A brief summary of the potential outcomes is set out in Table 2 below (and further details about decisions on costs are provided in section 4 below).

Table 2

Timing	Fees & costs
Application withdrawn before opposition deemed admissible	• Official opposition fee refunded • No decision on costs
Application withdrawn during cooling off period	• Official opposition fee refunded • No decision on costs
Application withdrawn during period between end of cooling off period and the Office taking a decision	• Official opposition fee not refunded • Decision on costs issued in favour of the opponent, unless the parties jointly submit an agreement on costs
Application withdrawn during appeal period after the Office has taken a decision	• Official opposition fee not refunded • Original opposition decision stands, as does original decision on costs • No further decision on costs issued

If a decision on the substance of the opposition has been issued and has become final (ie, the appeal period has ended without an appeal being filed), and if that decision has rejected the application in its entirety, the application can no longer be withdrawn as it ceased to exist on the date on which the decision became final.

2.6 Restriction of specification of opposed application

It is also open to an EUTM applicant to restrict the specification of its application at any point before registration, irrespective of whether or not the application has been opposed, and irrespective of the stage any opposition proceedings have reached.

Any restriction should be made in writing and should be clear and unambiguous. The effect of any such restriction on ongoing opposition proceedings depends on three factors:

- the stage the proceedings have reached;
- whether the opposition is directed against all or only some of the goods and/or services covered by the application; and
- whether the restriction relates to all or only some of the goods and/or services against which the opposition is directed.

Application opposed in full: effect of restriction: Where an opposition is directed against the full specification covered by the opposed application, any restriction to the specification (as opposed to a full withdrawal of the application) necessarily means the opposition proceedings remain live, as the opposition still has an object, albeit a narrower one.

If the restriction is made before the Office has completed the admissibility checks, the opponent is informed of the restriction at the same time as it is told about the outcome of the admissibility checks. If the opposition has been found admissible, the opponent is set a deadline by which to indicate whether the opposition is maintained following the restriction. If the opposition is deemed inadmissible (either on absolute grounds or on relative grounds that are not remedied) the opposition fee is refunded due to the restriction (and despite the inadmissibility).

If the restriction is made after the opposition has been deemed admissible, the opponent is informed of the restriction by the Office and is set a deadline by which to indicate whether the opposition is maintained. If it decides to maintain the opposition, the proceedings continue as normal.

This situation can arise repeatedly in the course of any one set of opposition proceedings if the applicant restricts the scope of its application, the opponent then maintains the opposition, the applicant then makes a further restriction and the opponent still maintains the opposition.

If the opponent decides to withdraw the opposition following a restriction by the applicant, the opposition proceedings end once the Office is informed of the withdrawal. The effect in terms of fees and costs is as set out in Table 2 above, namely:

- the opposition fee is refunded if the restriction and withdrawal are made during the cooling off period and no decision on costs is issued. In practice, if the restriction is requested by the applicant during the cooling off period and the opposition is not withdrawn until after this period has ended, the withdrawal is treated as being as a result of the restriction and thus treated as if it had been made during the cooling off period;
- the opposition fee is not refunded if the restriction and withdrawal are made after the cooling off period has ended and a decision on costs is issued (as discussed further in section 4 below).

Application opposed in part: effect of restriction: Where an opposition is directed against only part of the specification of the opposed application, the effect of any restriction to that application depends on whether it relates to some or all of the goods and/or services against which the opposition is directed.

If the restriction relates to goods and/or services not covered by the opposition, the restriction has no bearing on the opposition proceedings. Such a restriction may be made because of separate opposition proceedings directed against another part of the specification.

If the restriction clearly relates to all the goods and/or services that are subject of the opposition proceedings, the effect of the restriction is the same as the effect of withdrawal of the application, in that it ends the opposition proceedings. The effect in terms of fees and costs is as set out in Table 2 above, namely:

- the opposition fee is refunded if the restriction is made before the opposition has been deemed admissible or during the cooling off period and no decision on costs is issued;
- the opposition fee is not refunded if the restriction is made after the cooling off period has ended, but a decision on costs is issued. In these circumstances, costs are awarded to the opponent, which seems correct as the removal of all the goods and/or services against which the opposition was targeted means the opposition was (effectively) entirely successful.

If the restriction relates to only some of the goods and/or services that are the subject of the opposition proceedings, the restriction does not automatically end the opposition proceedings as they still have an object, albeit a narrower one. The opponent is set a deadline by which to indicate whether it wishes to maintain the opposition in light of the restriction.

If the opponent decides to withdraw the opposition following the restriction, the opposition proceedings end once the Office is informed of this fact. The effect in terms of fee and costs is as set out in Table 1 above, namely:

- the opposition fee is refunded if the restriction and withdrawal are made during the cooling off period and no decision on costs is issued. In practice, if the restriction is requested by the applicant during the cooling off period and the opposition is not withdrawn until after this period has ended the withdrawal is treated as being as a result of the restriction and thus treated as if it had been made during the cooling off period;
- the opposition fee is not refunded if the restriction and withdrawal are made after the cooling off period has ended and a decision on costs is issued.

2.7 Ceasing of existence of the earlier rights on which the opposition is based

Opposition proceedings can also end without a decision on the substantive case if all the earlier rights relied upon cease to exist. This could be because they are not renewed, or because they are cancelled or surrendered.

If any of these things happen before the deadline for the opponent to substantiate the opposition, it will be unable to meet the substantiation requirements and the opposition will be rejected so far as these rights are concerned, as discussed in Chapter 13, section 3.

If the rights cease to exist after they have been substantiated but before the Office takes a decision on the substance of the case, the Office should be informed. The Office can only base a substantive decision on rights that are live at the time of making that decision.

Before making a decision on the substance, the Office checks to see if any of the earlier trade mark rights relied on by the opponent were due to be renewed in the period between the opponent's substantiation deadline and the time of taking a decision. If this is the case, the Office asks the opponent to file evidence demonstrating that the rights in question have been renewed and are therefore still live.

In practice, the parties should inform the Office if the earlier rights in question are cancelled or surrendered. Where the rights in question are EUTM rights, the Office may become aware of the termination of rights of its own accord or may specifically ask the parties to keep it informed with regard to the continuing existence of the rights, particularly where the opposition proceedings have been suspended pending the outcome of cancellation proceedings against the rights relied upon.

Where the rights in question are national rights, the Office is not automatically informed by the relevant national IPO if the rights are cancelled or surrendered. Therefore, it will only become aware this has happened if informed by the parties. Where one of the parties informs the Office that the national rights in question no longer exist, the Office grants the other party to the proceedings a chance to respond to this information, after which the opposition is rejected to the extent that it is based on those rights.

2.8 Rejection of the opposed EUTM application for other reasons

In certain circumstances, an opposed EUTM application may cease to exist during the course of opposition proceedings for reasons other than withdrawal of the application by the applicant. The main situations in which this occurs are where:

- the Office raises post-publication inherent registrability objections and rejects the application on such grounds (this can be because of the filing of third party observations). In this case, the opposition proceedings end as they no longer have an object. The opposition fee is not refunded and no decision on costs is issued;
- the EUTM applicant is a party that must be represented before the Office (as discussed in chapters 2 and 11), but it did not have a representative when the opposition was filed against its application and failed to appoint one when required to, so that the Office refused the application. In this case the opposition proceedings end as they no longer have an object. The opposition fee is not refunded and no decision on costs is issued;
- the EUTM application was the subject of multiple oppositions, has been rejected in its entirety as a result of one of the other oppositions, and the present proceedings were suspended pending the outcome of the opposition for which a decision has been issued. In this case, the remaining opposition proceedings cease to have an object and 50% of the opposition fee is refunded to each of the other opponents.

2.9 Amicable settlement between the parties

While EUTM opposition proceedings are contentious proceedings between two (or sometimes more) parties, the EUTM opposition system has various features built into it to help encourage or assist parties to settle disputes amicably.

- *Cooling off period:* EUTM opposition proceedings include an automatic initial two-month cooling off period, which is designed to give the parties an opportunity to enter into settlement discussions. This period can be extended by a further 22 months at the joint request of the parties. If the matter is resolved during either the initial or extended cooling off period, the official fee may be refunded and no costs award is issued (as set out in Sections 2.4, 2.5 and 2.6 above).
- *Suspension:* All contentious EUTM proceedings, including opposition proceedings, can be suspended to allow the parties time to explore amicable settlement. Although suspension cannot be requested during the cooling off period, it can be requested at any time after this, irrespective of whether the cooling off period lasted the maximum 24 months possible. Where jointly requested by the parties, no reasons are required and the suspension is automatically granted for a period of one year. Further suspensions can be requested and are usually granted for a year at a time. After three years, the parties are expected to provide an explanation as to why the negotiations have not come to an end and the Office may refuse to grant further suspensions.
- *Mediation:* The Office offers a mediation service that is in principle available to the parties to opposition proceedings, although at present only if a decision has been issued and appealed. This is considered in detail in Chapter 20.

There is provision for the Office to invite the parties to enter into settlement discussions and to issue proposals for amicable settlement. In reality, however, it tends not to do so.

Where a dispute is resolved amicably, the parties can jointly ask the Office to close the opposition case without giving any reasons. In such a situation, the Office simply closes the proceedings. Unless both parties have informed the Office that they have reached an agreement on costs, a decision on costs is issued.

An agreement concluded between parties may require the applicant to restrict or withdraw the opposed application, or may require the opponent to withdraw the opposition. The rules discussed in sections 2.4, 2.5 and 2.6 above relating to refunds of the official opposition fees and decisions on costs in the case of restrictions and withdrawals are applied unless the parties jointly inform the Office otherwise.

Parties that explore the option of amicable settlement are not prevented from later fighting the case should the settlement negotiations break down. In this regard, it should be noted that the extended cooling off period can be opted out of unilaterally by either party at any time (other than during the final month of the period) and that a jointly requested suspension can be opted out of unilaterally by either party at any time. Mediation proceedings are closed as soon as one of the parties declares that it wishes to end those proceedings, in which case the opposition proceedings resume.

3. Conclusion of proceedings through a decision on the substantive case

Once the adversarial stage of the proceedings is complete, the Office informs the parties of this fact and then considers the materials submitted by both parties before taking a decision.

The length of time between the end of the adversarial period and the Office taking a decision depends on the amount of material submitted, the complexity of the case and the workload of the Office. In general, a decision is taken within three months of the end of the adversarial period, although it can take longer for complex, evidence-heavy oppositions.

Opposition decisions are always issued in writing and must include the date of the decision, as well as details of the parties. The date is a crucial piece of information as it is used to calculate the deadline for filing an appeal against the decision (as discussed further in Chapter 20).

The Office uses a template for opposition decisions, adjusting it as appropriate to the circumstances of the case at hand. A short summary of the decision is provided which indicates the extent to which the opposition is successful and the decision on costs. This is followed by detailed reasons, in which the rights and grounds at issue are identified and discussed together with the Office's conclusions.

Where an opposition is based on multiple grounds and/or multiple earlier rights, the Office usually considers the ground or right it thinks offers the strongest case. If the opposition succeeds in full on the basis of that ground or right, the other grounds and/or rights are not considered. The Office should always make clear in its decision whether this has happened.

If the opposition succeeds only in part on the basis of the first-selected ground or right, the Office goes on to consider relevant further rights and/or grounds to the extent it deems this worthwhile. Again, full reasoning should be provided for the approach adopted.

If an opposition does not succeed on the basis of the first-selected ground or right, it is often refused as regards the other grounds and/or rights identified, on the basis that, for example, the other rights are less similar. Once again, full reasoning should be provided for the approach adopted.

The Office approaches decisions in this manner for reasons of procedural economy. However, it can result in difficulties on appeal, as well as for conversion.

Where the opponent has been put to proof of use of any of the earlier marks relied on in the opposition, the Office only examines the proof of use evidence if it is relevant to the outcome of the decision. The same is true with regard to evidence filed to demonstrate that a mark is well-known or that it enjoys a reputation.

While these points all go to the existence, validity and scope of protection of the earlier trade mark rights at issue, in practice if at least some evidence has been filed by the relevant deadline (ie, the substantiation deadline for both well-known marks and reputation and the proof of use deadline for proof of use evidence), the Office generally allows proceedings to continue and only considers the evidence in detail if it is relevant to the outcome of the case. For example, if an opposition is based on both the confusion ground and the reputation ground and the Office can take a decision on the basis of the confusion ground only, it tends not to consider the reputation evidence. However, this ground would have fallen away if no reputation evidence had been filed.

An outline of the key issues considered in decisions for the various grounds of opposition is set out below. Each of these grounds is explored in more detail in Chapter 12.

3.1 The double identity ground

The Office normally begins by considering whether the goods and/or services at issue are identical. If it concludes that they are (or that at least some of them are) consideration is given to whether the marks are identical. The approach adopted by the Office in assessing whether marks are identical and whether goods and/or services are identical is set out in Chapter 12, section 3.2.

If an opposition is based on the double identity ground only but the Office decides that either the marks or the goods and/or services at issue are not identical, it proceeds to consider the case under the confusion ground.

3.2 The confusion ground

The Office normally begins by considering whether the goods and/or services at issue are either identical or similar. As discussed in Chapter 12, the Office has been involved in the development of the Similarity database, which it uses in assessing whether goods and/or services in opposition proceedings are similar. The database can be accessed via the Office's website at http://oami.europa.eu/sim/.

If the Office is of the view that all of the goods and/or services at issue are dissimilar, it does not comment on the similarity of the marks at issue in the context of the confusion ground. A statement of reasons should always be given in the decision regarding the outcome of the comparison of the goods and/or services.

If there is found to be at least some degree of similarity between the goods and/or services, the Office then considers whether the marks at issue are identical or similar. Again, reasons should be given for the outcome of this comparison. Assessments are made on the level of visual, phonetic and conceptual similarity between the marks, using the approach outlined in Chapter 12, section 4.2.

In the event that identity or similarity are found to exist with regard to the goods and/or services and the marks for at least one earlier right, the Office proceeds to carry out an assessment of the likelihood of consumer confusion, taking account of all the relevant factors, as discussed in Chapter 12, section 4.2.

In its decision, the Office should set out the factors and principles that it has taken into consideration in reaching a conclusion on the likelihood of confusion. This should include information on the weight it has accorded to each of the relevant factors.

3.3 The reputation ground

For an opposition to succeed under this ground, the following conditions all need to be satisfied:

- the marks at issue are identical or similar;
- the opponent's mark enjoys a reputation in the relevant territory; and
- use of the mark applied for without due cause would take unfair advantage of, or be detrimental to, the distinctive character or repute of the opponent's earlier trade mark.

If any one of these requirements has clearly not been satisfied, the Office rejects the opposition on that basis, without considering the other conditions. The assessment of whether the marks are identical or similar is the easiest one on which to make a quick assessment; it is therefore the one most likely to result in an opposition failing without consideration of the others.

However, even if the Office is satisfied that the opponent has made out the positive requirements needed to support the opposition case, it also needs to consider whether the applicant has shown that it would have due cause to use the mark. If the applicant has not provided any evidence or comment in this regard, it is assumed that there is no such due cause.

3.4 The unregistered rights ground

For an opposition to succeed under this ground, the following conditions must all be satisfied:

- the opponent owns an unregistered trade mark or other right;
- the rights in question were acquired before the filing date of the opposed application (taking into account any relevant priority claims);
- the rights enable the opponent to prohibit the use of the mark applied for;
- the mark or sign at issue is used in the course of trade; and
- the use is of more than mere local significance.

If one of these requirements clearly has not been satisfied, the Office rejects the opposition on that basis, without considering the other conditions. If an opposition succeeds under this ground, each of the above conditions should be considered in the opposition decision.

3.5 The PDO/PGI ground

For an opposition to succeed under this ground, the following conditions must be satisfied:

- the opponent owns a PDO or PGI registration;
- the PDO or PGI application was filed before the filing date of the opposed application (taking into account any relevant priority claims); and
- the registration enables the opponent to prohibit the use of the mark applied for.

If one of these requirements clearly has not been satisfied, the Office rejects the opposition on that basis, without considering the other conditions. If, however, an opposition succeeds under these grounds, each of the above conditions should be considered in the opposition decision.

3.6 The agent/representative ground

For an opposition to succeed under this ground, the following conditions all need to be met:

- the opponent owns the mark applied for;
- the applicant is or was the agent or representative of the opponent;

- the application was filed in the name of the agent or representative;
- the application was filed without the consent of the opponent;
- the applicant is unable to justify its actions;
- the mark applied for and the mark owned by the opponent are identical or only slightly different; and
- the goods and/or services covered by the application and those for which the opponent enjoys protection are identical or very closely related.

The Office does not necessarily consider or comment on each and every one of these elements if they are not all satisfied and the opposition is therefore rejected. Rather, it provides reasoning for those that have been determinative in reaching the conclusion that the opponent has not made out its case. If, however, the opposition succeeds, each of these points should be addressed in the decision.

4. Costs

A decision in opposition proceedings always includes a decision on the apportionment of costs. The costs in opposition proceedings are virtually always limited to the official opposition fee and the representation costs of the parties (if they are professionally represented). These costs are always expressed in Euros.

The basic principle is that the 'winning' party is awarded costs against the 'losing' party.

If the opposition is successful in full, the applicant has to pay the opponent both the amount of the official opposition fee and an amount towards the latter's representation costs. The level is the same for both parties, so that if the opposition is rejected in full, the opponent has to pay the applicant an amount towards the latter's representation costs.

Where an opposition succeeds in part and is rejected in part, both parties are deemed to be partially successful, in which case they each have to bear their own costs.

In practice, the representation costs are set at a very low level, irrespective of the actual costs incurred in engaging professional representatives. At the time of writing, the amount of costs awarded for representation is fixed at €300.

Further reference

Regulation – Articles 8, 41-43, 75, 79, 85
Implementing Regulation – Rules 20-22, 52, 55, 94
Office Guidelines – Part C, Section 1

Chapter 15: Maintenance and amendment

1. Introduction

Once an EUTM registration is granted, there are important issues to consider to ensure it remains both live and valid. This chapter looks at the maintenance of EUTM registrations and the limited circumstances in which they can be altered or amended.

The chapters that follow discuss various other issues that EUTM proprietors may have to deal with, in the form of:

- steps taken by the proprietor of an EUTM registration that affect its registered rights, including voluntary surrender, assignment and licensing (Chapter 16); and
- steps taken by third parties to cancel EUTM registrations, namely revocation actions (Chapter 17) and invalidity actions (Chapter 18).

2. Duration

An EUTM registration lasts for an initial period of 10 years. This date is calculated from the filing date accorded to the registration, irrespective of any priority or seniority claims (see Chapter 5; as to seniority claims, see Chapter 24).

It is possible for the registration to be renewed at the end of this 10-year period. The renewal date falls 10 years from the filing date. Therefore, the first renewal date for an EUTM registration with a filing date of 5 January 2015 would be 5 January 2025. The renewal date is not affected by priority or seniority claims, or the date on which the registration process was completed.

A new 10-year period of protection begins every time an EUTM registration is renewed. The 10-year periods are always calculated by reference to the original filing date, irrespective of when the renewal request is actually filed. For the example above, whether the first renewal request is filed on 19 September 2024 or on 5 January 2025, the next renewal date would be 5 January 2035.

It was previously the case that the renewal deadline fell on the last day of the month in which the renewal was due, rather than the actual anniversary of the filing date. For a registration with a filing date of 18 May 1997, the renewal deadline was therefore 31 May 2007. However, for EUTM registrations with renewal dates falling on or after 22 September 2016, the renewal deadline falls on the actual anniversary of the filing date. Continuing with the above example, the next renewal deadline for this registration would be 18 May 2017.

There is no limit on the number of times an EUTM registration can be renewed.

It is therefore theoretically possible for the rights granted by an EUTM registration to last forever – provided that renewal requests continue to be filed and the registration is not removed from the Register (either by the proprietor or as the result of a third party challenge).

If a renewal request is not filed for an EUTM registration, the registration expires. As discussed further in section 3 below, there is a six-month grace period following the renewal deadline, during which late renewal is possible. The Office takes no action in respect of a non-renewal until after this grace period has ended. If no renewal request is filed during that period, the Office informs the EUTM proprietor (and any person recorded in the Register as having rights in the registration) that it has expired and the EUTM registration is removed from the Register. If a request to renew the registration in relation to some classes only is filed before the renewal deadline, it is possible to renew the additional classes during the grace period for late renewal.

In certain very limited circumstances, the EUTM proprietor may have the registration reinstated after it has expired by making use of the process of *restitutio in integrum* (see Chapter 26).

3. Renewal

At least six months before an EUTM registration is due to expire, the Office sends a notification to the registered proprietor (or its representative, if it has one), and to any person recorded in the Register as having rights in the registration, informing them that the registration is shortly due for renewal. If the Office fails to send this notification for any reason, there is no effect on the renewal date or expiry of the registration – ie, a proprietor who misses a renewal deadline cannot rely on the failure of the Office to provide such a notification in order either to avoid late renewal fees or to make use of the process of *restitutio in integrum*. As a result, EUTM proprietors should ensure that they keep a note of the renewal dates for their registrations, and have in place a proper reminder system, to ensure registrations that remain of interest are renewed in time.

3.1 When can an EUTM registration be renewed?

An EUTM registration can be renewed up to six months before the date on which it is due to expire. It cannot be renewed any earlier than this. A renewal request should be accompanied by the appropriate renewal fees, as set out in section 3.2 below.

There is also a six-month grace period during which late renewal of an EUTM registration is possible. Where the grace period is used, additional fees must be paid, again as set out below.

There is no obligation to file a renewal request where an EUTM application is still pending at the ten-year anniversary of its filing date. If, however, the application subsequently proceeds to registration, the Office then asks the proprietor whether it wishes to renew the registration. The proprietor is set a two-month deadline (which can be extended by a further two months) to file the renewal request and pay the renewal fees. There is no grace period for late renewal in these circumstances.

3.2 Fees

The renewal of an EUTM registration is subject to the payment of official renewal fees. The request is not processed unless the fees are received in time – ie, by the renewal deadline or, in the case of late renewal, by the late renewal deadline. Any fees that are paid more than six months before the renewal is due are not taken into consideration and are returned.

The current fees payable for renewal of an ordinary EUTM registration are set out in Table 1 below.

Table 1: Fees payable for renewal of an ordinary EUTM registration

Method of filing	Basic fee (one class)	Fee for second class	Fee for each class over two
E-filing	€850	€50	€150
Paper filing	€1000	€50	€150

The fees payable for the renewal of an EU collective mark registration are higher than those for an ordinary EUTM registration, and are set out in Table 2 below.

Table 2: Fees payable for renewal of an EU collective mark registration

Method of filing	Basic fee (one class)	Fee for second class	Fee for each class over two
E-filing	€1500	€50	€150
Paper filing	€1800	€50	€150

Although not confirmed at the time of writing, it is expected that the renewal fees for EU certification mark registrations will be the same as those for EU collective mark registrations. (See Chapter 28 for further information on EU collective marks and Chapter 29 for further information on EU certification marks.)

Where renewal is requested during the six-month grace period following the original renewal deadline, both the original renewal fees and an additional late fee must be paid before the end of the grace period. The additional fee due is 25% of the original renewal fees, subject to a maximum of €1500.

If the total amount paid by the end of the grace period covers the basic renewal fee and the fee for late payment, but not all the class fees, the registration is renewed for some classes only. In the absence of any indication from the proprietor as to which classes it wants to renew, the Office renews the classes in numerical order, starting with the lowest, and only renews the number of classes for which the fees have been paid.

If the EUTM proprietor has a current account with the Office, it must still request renewal. In the absence of other instructions, the renewal fees are debited on the renewal deadline or, if this date has passed, on the last day of the grace period for late renewal.

3.3 What information must an EUTM renewal request contain?

A renewal request must include the following information:

- the name of the person making the request;
- the registration number of the EUTM registration to which the renewal request relates; and
- an indication of the goods and/or services for which renewal is requested. It is possible to renew a registration for part of the specification. However, the default position in the event this information is not provided is that the renewal covers all goods and/or services in the registration.

Payment of the appropriate fees can itself constitute a renewal request if the identification of the payment includes the above information.

A renewal request can be filed electronically via the Office's website, or by fax or on paper. The Office provides an official renewal form which can be used, but is not mandatory. It is usually best to file a renewal request electronically. The online form provided for these purposes is very simple and can only be submitted if all the necessary information is provided. In addition, the official fees are lower if the request is filed electronically.

A renewal request can be filed in any of the Languages of the Office. The form provided by the Office is available in 23 of the 24 Languages of the Union (the form is not available in Irish). Any one of these languages can be used, provided the form is completed in one of the Languages of the Office so far as textual elements are concerned (ie, the goods and/or services for which renewal is requested).

Multiple EUTM registrations can be renewed together if the registration numbers for each are indicated, the fees are paid for each and they are all eligible for renewal.

3.4 Who can renew an EUTM registration?

An EUTM registration can be renewed by the EUTM proprietor (or its representative), or by anyone who has been expressly authorised by the EUTM proprietor to do so. Proof of authorisation does not have to be provided to the Office unless specifically requested. Such proof is usually only requested if two separate sets of fees are received by the Office and neither has come from the proprietor or its representative.

The EUTM proprietor can file a renewal request directly with the Office without using a representative even if it falls within the category of parties who must be represented before the Office (see Chapter 2, section 10).

If an EUTM registration has been transferred, the new owner is entitled to file a renewal request once the request to record the transfer has been received by the Office. (See Chapter 16 for further information on transfers and recordal of transfers.)

3.5 Deficiencies in an EUTM renewal request

A renewal request is only examined for compliance with requirements as to formalities – ie, to check that the renewal fee has been paid and that the information listed at section 3.3. above has been provided.

Where a renewal request is filed during either the six-month period before the renewal deadline or the grace period for late renewal, but all the information listed at section 3.3. is not provided, the Office issues a deficiency notice and sets a deadline by which the missing information must be provided. The following should be noted.

- If the missing information relates to identification of the party requesting payment or identification of the registration to be renewed, and this information is not provided by the deadline set, the registration is not renewed and any fees that have been paid are returned.
- If the missing information relates to the extent of the renewal, a deficiency notice is only issued if the fees paid do not cover renewal for all classes covered by the registration. If no response to the deficiency notice is filed, the registration is renewed for the number of classes for which fees have been paid, in numerical order starting with the lowest class.

If multiple parties request renewal of the same registration and pay the necessary fees, and none of the parties is the owner or its listed representative, the Office contacts the EUTM proprietor for confirmation of which party it authorised to renew the registration. If no response is received, the first-filed request is accepted and processed. The Office's online renewal system does not allow for renewal of a registration that cannot be renewed. Using this system therefore helps avoid multiple renewal requests being filed for the same registration.

3.6 Reclassification

It should be noted that the Office does not check that the goods and/or services covered by the registration being renewed are properly classified. While this is usually not an issue, as classification issues will have been dealt with during the application process, it can be relevant for registrations covering terms that have been reclassified since the original filing date. For example, classes 43-45 were only introduced with the entry into force of the 8th edition of the Nice Classification in 2002. Prior to this, all services that now fall within one of classes 43-45 fell within class 42. This means that an EUTM registration filed in 1998 for "temporary accommodation" would have included this term within class 42. Such a registration could still be in force, and could still show these services within class 42, despite the fact that these services are now deemed to fall within class 43.

For registrations covering terms that now fall within a different class, it is good practice to update the registration so that the terms are listed in the current correct class. This means the registration will show up in searches carried out by other parties. However, the fact that it is not mandatory to update registrations in this regard means it is important to ensure that clearance searches carried out in relation to classes 43-45 always cover class 42. (See Chapter 3 for further discussion of clearance searches.)

A registration can be updated by filing a request with the Office. There is no fee for reclassifying terms in this manner. It can, however, affect renewal fees if the registration also covers some terms that have not been reclassified since filing. This means that it may be more sensible to file the reclassification request after the registration has been renewed rather than before. For example, an application filed in 1998 for "temporary accommodation; maintenance of computer software" would have only covered class 42. The first term is now proper to class 43, but the second is still proper to class 42. If the first term is not reclassified, the renewal fee for one class is payable upon renewal, and all terms will still show in class 42. If the first term is transferred to class 43, the renewal fees for two classes are payable upon renewal. (See Chapter 6 for further discussion of classification issues.)

3.7 Renewal of Union designations

IRs are renewed centrally at WIPO, irrespective of the contracting parties that have been designated. Where a Union designation is to be renewed, the WIPO renewals process should be followed. (See chapters 30-32 for further information on the IR system.)

4. Alteration

In principle, once a mark is registered under the EUTM system, it is not possible to change the mark covered by the registration. There is, however, one very limited exception to this. Alteration is possible where the mark itself includes the name and address of the proprietor and that name or address has changed. Even in these circumstances, the mark can only be altered if the change in question does not substantially affect the identity of the trade mark.

Where this is the case, an official request for alteration must be made. The request must be made in writing, in one of the Languages of the Office, and should contain the following information:

- the EUTM registration number;
- the proprietor's name and address;
- an indication of the element to be altered;
- the altered version of that element; and
- a representation of the mark as altered.

The alteration of multiple registrations can be requested in a single application, provided that they are all owned by the same proprietor and the element to be changed is the same for all. A fee is payable when an alteration request is made. At the time of writing, the fee is €200 per registration to be altered. If the change to be made appears in lots of registrations, the alteration process can become expensive. As the fees are per registration, it makes sense to request alteration for just one registration at the outset, and only proceed with the others if the first is accepted.

An alteration request is not treated as having been filed until the fees are paid. The request is examined once they have been paid. If any of the necessary information is missing, the Office issues a deficiency notice and sets a deadline for the EUTM proprietor to provide this information. The alteration request is rejected if the deadline is not satisfied, or if the Office is of the view that the alteration requested is not permissible (because either it relates to changes in an element other than the name or address of the proprietor, or it would substantially affect the identity of the trade mark).

Where an alteration request is accepted, it is registered and published. The publication shows the altered mark and there is a three-month period following publication during which third parties can challenge the alteration by filing an opposition. The usual opposition procedure is followed if such a challenge is filed. (See chapters 10-14 for information on the opposition process.)

5. Changes of name, address and/or nationality

Where an EUTM proprietor (or its representative) changes name, address and/or nationality, that change can be recorded in the Register. This covers situations where, for example, a company changes its name and place of business after a takeover. If, however, any transfer of ownership has taken place, this must be recorded in a different way, as set out in Chapter 16.

A request for a change of name, address and/or nationality should be filed in writing in one of the Languages of the Office. There is no fee and proof of the change is only required if specifically requested by the Office.

The request should include the following information:

- the EUTM registration number;
- the name and address and/or nationality as recorded in the Register; and
- the new name and address and/or nationality to be recorded.

6. Division

It is possible to divide an EUTM registration into two or more separate registrations. Where this happens, each registration maintains the filing and priority dates of the original registration, as well as any relevant seniority claims.

Division is usually used where there is a dispute or pending action relating to some but not all of the goods and/or services covered by an EUTM registration. In such a case it can be useful to separate out the part of the specification that has been challenged from the remainder. This enables the non-challenged part to be enforced without worrying about the pending challenge.

Where division is used, the resulting registrations are all held by the same party. This should be contrasted with the position where there is a partial transfer of an EUTM registration, in which case the resulting separate registrations are owned by different parties (see Chapter 16).

Division is not possible for Union designations of IRs and the Office does not have the authority to divide such designations. (See Chapter 32 for further information on Union designations.)

Any request for division must be made in writing, in one of the Languages of the Office, and should contain the following information:

- the EUTM registration number;
- the proprietor's name and address;
- the list of goods and/or services to be included in the new registration (or a

separate list for each new registration if the original registration is being divided into more than two registrations); and
- the list of goods and/or services to remain in the original registration.

There cannot be any overlap between the goods and/or services covered by the resulting separate registrations. For example, if the original registration covers "clothing; trousers", "trousers" can be divided out but the term "clothing" that remains in the original registration needs to be amended to exclude trousers (given that they are items of clothing). This can be achieved by amending the term "clothing" to read "clothing, except trousers". In any event, the specifications of the registrations taken together cannot be broader than the original specification covered by the registration before division.

A request for division must be accompanied by the official fee, which is €250 at the time of writing. The request is not considered to have been filed until the fee is paid. There are no further application fees or other fees to be paid when dividing a registration. The total renewal fees will, however, be greater if all the divided registrations are to be renewed (as the basic renewal fee will have to be paid for each, as well as any applicable additional class fees). Thus, if a registration is nearing renewal, it is sensible to delay requesting division until after renewal, if possible.

If there are any deficiencies in a division request, or problems with regard to the goods and/or services to be included in each registration, the Office notifies the EUTM proprietor and sets it a two-month deadline by which to remedy the problems. If the proprietor fails to do so, the request for division is refused.

Where there are pending cancellation proceedings (ie, invalidity and/or revocation proceedings) against an EUTM registration, division is only possible in relation to the goods and/or services not covered by the proceedings. The challenged goods and/or services must all remain together in a single registration: it is not possible for the challenged terms to be spread across multiple registrations as this would mean that the cancellation proceedings would have to be split. This is the case both where the cancellation proceedings are in the form of proceedings before the Office (see chapters 17 & 18) and where they are in the form of counterclaims in infringement proceedings (see Chapter 23). This rule also applies so long as proceedings are pending before the Boards of Appeal, the General Court or the CJEU.

Where a request for division is accepted, it takes effect from the date the request is accepted (not from when it was filed). One registration maintains the original EUTM registration number and the new registration(s) are each given new numbers. The division is published in the *EUTM Bulletin* and the Office sets up a new online file for each divisional registration, containing all the correspondence relating to the original EUTM registration as well as that relating to the division.

If a request for division is rejected, for whatever reason, the original registration remains unchanged. If the official fee for division has been paid, it is not returned. Where a request for division is rejected, it is open to the proprietor to file a fresh request in the future; where it does so, however, the fee has to be paid again.

7. Surrender

The proprietor of an EUTM registration may surrender that registration at any time. There is no fee for doing so and the surrender can relate to the full registration or to only some of the goods and/or services covered.

Surrendering a registration is an irrevocable act that cannot be undone. The only exception to this is where both a declaration of surrender and a revocation of that declaration are filed at the Office on the same day. In all other circumstances, a declaration of surrender cannot be reversed.

As it amounts to a renunciation of rights, a declaration of surrender must be clear and unequivocal. A declaration of surrender cannot contain conditions or time limitations. It should be made in writing, in one of the Languages of the Office, and must contain the following information:

- the EUTM registration number;
- the proprietor's name and address;
- an indication of the goods and/or services in relation to which the registration is being surrendered or an indication of the goods and/or services for which the registration is not being surrendered (if the surrender is not a full surrender); and
- where applicable, proof of consent or notification to licensees or others with a registered interest in the registration.

A declaration of surrender must be signed by the proprietor or its appointed representative (which can be done by indicating the sender's name in the case of electronic filing). Where the surrender is partial, the remaining specification should be no broader than the pre-surrender coverage and the terms used must constitute a valid description of the coverage (in line with the considerations discussed in Chapter 6).

Where a licence or other right is recorded in the Register, the proprietor should provide proof that the licensee (or other party with a recorded interest) has consented to the surrender. A declaration signed by the party in question, or its appointed representative, constitutes proof of consent. (See Chapter 16 for further discussion.)

In the absence of proof of consent, the proprietor should provide proof that the other party has been notified of the intention to surrender. In the latter case, if no explicit consent is provided, the surrender is registered three months from the date on which the proof of notification is provided to the Office (so long as the other party does not in the meantime indicate that it does not consent to the surrender).

Where a levy of execution is entered in the Register for a registration that is to be surrendered, the declaration of surrender must enclose a declaration of consent signed by the authority that is competent for the levy of execution. In the case of a registration that is the subject of insolvency proceedings, the surrender should be requested by the liquidator, administrator or other practitioner appointed in the insolvency proceedings. (See Chapter 16 for further information on levies of execution and insolvency proceedings.)

If the declaration of surrender does not contain all the necessary information, the Office issues a deficiency notice and gives the proprietor two months to remedy the situation. If it fails to do so, the surrender request is rejected. If, however, all the necessary information is provided, the surrender is recorded in the Register. A surrender only becomes effective from the date it is entered in the Register. It has no retroactive effect.

As a general rule, any proceedings involving the surrendered registration terminate when the surrender is entered in the Register. Where a declaration of surrender is filed in relation to a registration that is the subject of ongoing cancellation proceedings (either revocation proceedings or invalidity proceedings), the Office asks the applicant for cancellation if it wants to continue with the cancellation proceedings. If the applicant for cancellation does not respond, the proceedings are closed and no decision on the substance is taken. If the applicant for cancellation states that it wants the proceedings to continue, they will continue.

Once a final decision is handed down in ongoing cancellation proceedings, the surrender is then processed if any part of the registration still remains. In practice, an applicant for cancellation will usually be happy for the cancellation proceedings to end once a declaration of surrender has been filed. If, however, there are concerns about the dates during which the rights validly existed, it may opt for the cancellation proceedings to continue.

8. Replacement

The holder of an IR designating the Union who also owns a separate earlier EUTM registration for the same mark covering the same specification can request that the Office notes in the Register that the Union designation replaces the EUTM registration. (Replacement is considered further in Chapter 30.)

Further reference

Regulation – Articles 26-27, 46-50, 81, 87, 157
Implementing Regulation – Rules 9, 25-27, 36, 107
Office Guidelines – Part E, Sections 1 & 4
Communication No 5/05 of the President of the Office
Communication No 8/05 of the President of the Office
Communication No 2/2016 of the President of the Office

Chapter 16: Transactions involving EUTM rights

1. Introduction

By virtue of being objects of property, EUTM rights can be the subject of a variety of transactions. They can be bought and sold, as well as being licensed and used as security for debts.

This chapter looks at these matters, with a particular focus on transactions that can be entered in the Register, how recordals are made and the benefits of making them. The transactions considered are transfers, licences, rights *in rem* (security interests), levies of execution and insolvency proceedings. They are referred to collectively as 'transactions' for ease of reference.

Although this chapter is in the 'post-registration' section of this book, the transactions discussed relate equally to both applications and registrations, with some exceptions as noted below.

2. Dealing with EUTM rights as objects of property

Both EUTM applications and registrations are objects of property. As they are unitary rights, the ownership of these assets must remain the same Union-wide. This means, for example, that an EUTM registration cannot be transferred only insofar as it provides protection in Germany and France. In the same way, the rights afforded in Portugal by an EUTM registration cannot be used as security against a debt; the security attaches to the entire EUTM registration and so must relate to the whole Union. It is, however, possible for a licence of EUTM rights to be granted for part of the Union.

Where an issue is not specifically dealt with by the Regulation, and despite the unitary nature of EUTM rights, the law that applies is that relating to the treatment of such rights under national law. This means that, in some circumstances, EUTM rights are treated in the same way as national trade mark registrations in the Member State whose law applies to the particular issue in question. The national law that applies in any given instance (such as where there is a dispute relating to the treatment of EUTM rights as objects of property) is determined by applying the following cascade:

- the law of the Member State in which the EUTM applicant or proprietor has its seat or domicile applies;
- if the EUTM applicant or proprietor does not have its seat or domicile in the Union, the law of any Member State in which the applicant or proprietor has an establishment applies; and
- if the EUTM applicant or proprietor does not have an establishment in the

Union, and therefore neither of the above apply, the law of Spain applies (ie, the Member State in which the Office is located).

As discussed in Chapter 5, it is possible for EUTM applications and registrations to be co-owned by two or more individuals and/or legal persons. Where this is the case, the first step in the cascade is applied to each co-owner in turn in the order in which it appears in the Register until a Member State is identified. If none of the co-owners meet the criteria in this step, the second step in the cascade is then applied to each co-owner, again in the order in which it appears in the Register, until a Member State is identified. Spain becomes the default position if none of the co-owners has its seat or domicile in the Union or an establishment in the Union.

3. Recording transactions

Any of the various transactions that can involve EUTM rights can be entered in the Register if a request to record the transaction is made. Although there is no general requirement to record transactions, there are benefits associated with doing so (and there can be problems if a transaction is not entered in the Register). These are considered below.

The Office has an official recordal form that can be used. Although it is not mandatory to use this form, it is recommended. Any recordal request must be signed by the party or parties filing it (which can be done by indicating the sender's name if the request is filed electronically). In the case of co-owned rights, any request to record a transaction must be signed by all of the co-owners. Some, but not all, types of recordal request require the payment of fees and/or proof of the transaction to support the request, as set out in the sections below.

Although recording transactions helps ensure that the Register is accurate, which is often important if third parties acquire a conflicting interest, recordal requests are not always filed (particularly with regard to licences and rights *in rem*, where fees are involved).

A recordal request should be filed in one of the Languages of the Office (where it relates to an EUTM registration) or in the first or second language of the EUTM application (where it relates to a right that is not yet registered). Where additional documents are required as proof to support the request, they can be filed in any Language of the Union. If they are not in the language of the recordal proceedings, the Office may request a translation into a Language of the Office.

The Office examines the recordal request and sets the applicant for recordal a deadline of two months to remedy any problems. The examination includes checks to ensure the request includes all the necessary information and has been signed, as well as checks on whether the applicant is a party that must be represented before the Office.

Once any issues are resolved (or if there are no issues in the first place), the applicant for recordal (and the EUTM owner, if it is not that applicant) are notified and:

- *where the transaction relates to an EUTM registration* – the transaction is entered in the Register and published in the *EUTM Bulletin*; or

- *where the transaction relates to an EUTM application* – the transaction is noted in the application file.

4. Transfer

The ownership of EUTM applications and registrations can be transferred. Any such transfer can relate to all or to only some of the goods and/or services covered. As noted in section 2 above, however, it cannot relate to only part of the Union.

Where an EUTM registration was obtained by the agent or representative of the true proprietor without the latter's consent or authorisation, and the agent or representative is unable to justify its actions, the true proprietor can demand that the registration in question is assigned to it.

It is possible for EUTM rights to be transferred independently of the business or undertaking that owns those rights. However, where the whole of an undertaking is transferred, all EUTM rights owned by that undertaking are automatically transferred, unless there is a clear agreement to the contrary or the circumstances dictate otherwise.

There are several different ways in which EUTM rights can be transferred. The most common type of transfer is by way of assignment. To be effective, an assignment must be made in writing and signed by both parties (assignor and assignee). The only exception to this is where the assignment is the result of a court judgment.

In addition to assignment, EUTM rights can be transferred on death (in which case the heir of the deceased owner becomes the new owner) or by operation of law. Examples of where ownership of EUTM rights can be transferred by operation of law include where two companies merge to create a single company or where a company incorporated in England & Wales is dissolved without the EUTM rights being transferred (in which case the ownership of those rights passes to the Crown).

4.1 Recordal of transfers

Although a transfer does not have to be recorded at the Office to be legally valid, it is almost always a good idea to ensure that transfers are recorded. The legality of the transfer itself is a matter for the national law under which the transfer took place – eg, the law under which the contact of assignment was concluded.

Where a transfer is not recorded, the Office treats the EUTM rights in question as still owned by the applicant or proprietor whose name appears on record (referred to in this section as the 'listed owner'), and sends all correspondence relating to those rights to that party (or its listed representative). A transfer only has effect *vis-à-vis* third parties who do not otherwise know about it after it is entered in the Register. This can include third parties who innocently license or purchase the EUTM rights in question from the listed owner after they have been assigned to the new owner. In addition, EUTM rights can only be relied on in infringement and opposition proceedings by the listed owner.

4.2 Procedure for recording transfers

A request to record a transfer of EUTM rights can be made by the new owner, the listed owner or jointly by both parties. The request must include the following information:

- *the EUTM application or registration number(s)* – a single request can relate to multiple rights where both the listed owner and the new owner are the same for all of them;
- *details of the new proprietor* – these should include its name, address and nationality and the state in which it is domiciled or has its seat or an establishment;
- *details of the goods and/or services to which the transfer relates (in the case of partial transfers only)* – as in the case of division (see Chapter 15), there cannot be any overlap between the goods and/or services covered by the resulting separate registrations. For example, if the original registration covers "clothing; trousers" and it is transferred insofar as "trousers" are concerned, the term "clothing" that remains in the original registration needs to be amended to exclude trousers (given that they are items of clothing). This can be achieved by amending the term "clothing" to read "clothing, except trousers". In any event, the specifications of the registrations taken together cannot be broader than the original specification covered by the registration before division; and
- *proof of the transfer* – if the recordal form is signed by both the listed owner and the new owner (or their respective representatives), no further proof of the transfer is required. Otherwise, some form of written document signed by both parties and confirming the transfer must be filed. The assignment document itself can be submitted, but parties often do not want to place this on public record where it contains sensitive information (although the document can be redacted to hide any information the parties do not want to be visible in the Register).

In addition, the recordal request can include details of the new owner's representative, if it has appointed one. The normal requirements on representation apply, so it may be the case that the new owner is obliged to appoint a representative (see Chapter 2, section 10): this requirement applies to both the recordal of the transfer (if, as is usually the case, the new owner is the party applying to record the transfer) and to the EUTM application or registration itself. The representative appointed by the new owner for the recordal proceedings is recorded as the representative for the EUTM rights to which the recordal relates. Where the listed owner's representative is also appointed as the new owner's representative, he can sign the recordal form on behalf of both parties (which means that no further proof of the transfer is required).

There is no fee for recording a transfer of ownership of EUTM rights. This applies both to applications and registrations.

Until 1 October 2017, the Office can refuse to record a transfer where it is clear from the transfer documents that, because of the transfer, the trade mark in question is likely to mislead the public concerning the nature, quality or geographical origin of the goods and/or services covered by the EUTM application or registration. In such a situation, the Office gives the new owner the opportunity to amend the specification so that only goods and/or services for which the mark is not likely to mislead are covered.

Although technically a transfer relating to a pending EUTM application is noted in the individual application file, rather than entered in the Register, in practice the owner details on the Office's database (which is the same database both for applications and registrations) are updated. As a result, the effect of recording a transfer of an EUTM application is in real terms no different to recording the transfer of an EUTM registration.

When a transfer is entered in the Register, the entry indicates the date on which the transfer was registered, the new owner's name and address and details of the new owner's representative (if one has been appointed). In the case of a partial transfer, what remains of the original EUTM application or registration maintains the original application or registration number and the new application(s) or registration(s) are each given new numbers. The Register entry therefore indicates the official number and remaining specification of the original registration, as well as the official number(s) and specification(s) of the new registration(s).

4.3 Effect of transfer recordal on pending proceedings

Where some or all of the EUTM rights that have been transferred are involved in *inter partes* proceedings before the Office (whether opposition or cancellation proceedings), the basic principle is that the new owner simply replaces the listed owner in those proceedings. The replacement is effective from the time the Office receives a valid request to record the transfer and there is no effect on any pending deadlines. In the period between the filing of the recordal request and the request being actioned, it is possible for the new owner to make statements to the Office. This means that it can take steps to satisfy any outstanding deadlines that were the responsibility of the listed owner. However, a decision cannot be taken in the proceedings until the recordal of the transfer is complete.

In the case of opposition proceedings against an EUTM application that is transferred, the new owner simply becomes a party to the opposition proceedings. However, if there is a partial transfer of the opposed application, and both the old application and the new application include goods and/or services that were opposed, the Office opens a second opposition file. The opponent does not have to pay a new opposition fee, as the general rule is that any fees paid for the original application before the transfer request was filed are also deemed to have been paid for the new application.

In the case of oppositions based on EUTM rights that are then transferred, the new owner simply becomes the new opponent if the rights are all transferred to the same party. If, however, the result of the transfer is that some of the rights in question are owned by one party and some are owned by another, the listed owner remains as an opponent and the new owner becomes a second opponent. The parties are, however, treated as joint opponents and a second set of opposition proceedings is not opened.

If the result of the transfer is that the applicant and the opponent are the same party, the opposition proceedings are closed.

5. Licences

A licence is a type of contract under which the owner of a trade mark application or registration specifically authorises another party to use the mark covered by the application or registration, usually in return for a fee or royalty payment. However, the rights are still owned by the listed owner. Licensing can be a useful way of generating direct revenue from a trade mark. Use made by a licensee can be taken into account to prove use in the context of a non-use revocation action (see Chapter 17), a counterclaim in infringement proceedings for revocation on the basis of non-use (see Chapter 23) or a proof of use request in opposition, invalidity or infringement proceedings (see chapters 13, 18 and 23).

There are three categories of licence:

- *exclusive* – where this type of licence is granted, only the licensee can use the trade mark. It cannot be licensed to any other parties and the proprietor cannot use it;
- *sole* – where this type of licence is granted, there is one licensee but the owner remains free to use a mark. No further licences can be granted (so that use can only be made by one licensee and the owner); and
- *non-exclusive* – this type of licence allows both the licensee and the trade mark owner to make use of the mark. In addition, it is possible for the proprietor to grant non-exclusive licences of the same right to multiple parties.

Both EUTM registrations and EUTM applications can be licensed and any such licence can be for either the whole territory of the Union or only part of it. A licence can also relate to all the goods and/or services covered by an EUTM application or registration, or to only some of them.

It is possible in some circumstances (depending on the terms of the licence agreement) for a licensee itself to grant a licence of all or some of the rights licensed to it. Where this is done, the licence granted by the licensee is called a sub-licence. It is possible for both licences and sub-licences to be entered in the Register.

As a licence is a contractual arrangement, the specific requirements are a matter for the national law under which the contract is concluded. Any issues relating to the effect of a licence as an object of property should be determined in accordance with the cascade set out at section 2 above. Where a licensee breaches certain terms of the licensing contract, the EUTM proprietor can bring infringement proceedings against it (see Chapter 22, section 2). This is in addition to any breach of contract claim it may have under the applicable national law.

A licensee can file opposition against a later application on the basis of the rights it has licensed, provided the owner authorises it to do so (see Chapter 11, section 4; Chapter 12, section 3). In addition, a licensee can bring infringement proceedings in its own name if authorised to do so by the owner of the licensed rights. An exclusive licensee can bring infringement proceedings if it notifies the EUTM owner of allegedly infringing activity and the owner does not bring proceedings within an appropriate period, subject to this right being excluded by the licence agreement (see Chapter 22, section 2). A licensee who has suffered damage as the result of an infringement can intervene in infringement proceedings brought by the EUTM owner for the purposes of obtaining compensation for such damage.

5.1 Recordal of licences

There is no requirement to record a licence, and non-recordal does not prevent use made by the licensee being taken into consideration in a non-use revocation or proof of use situation.

There are, however, a number of benefits for licensees if licences are recorded:

- a licence only has effect *vis-à-vis* third parties who acquire conflicting rights in the same EUTM application or registration if either the licence is entered in the Register or the conflicting rights were acquired by a party who knew about the licence;
- a proprietor can only surrender an EUTM registration against which a licence is recorded if it proves that it has informed the licensee of its intention to surrender (see Chapter 15, section 7 for further information on surrender of EUTM registrations); and
- the Office notifies the licensee of upcoming renewals and of any loss of rights.

As a result, a licensee can protect its position by ensuring its interest appears in the Register. There is little benefit for a licensor in entering a licence in the Register, hence most recordals are requested by licensees.

5.2 Procedure for recording licences

A request to record a licence can be made either by the listed owner of the EUTM rights or the licensee, or jointly by both parties. The request must include the following information:

- *the EUTM application or registration number(s)* – a single request can relate to multiple rights where both the listed owner and the licensee are the same for all of them, and the contractual terms are the same for all of them;
- *details of the licensee* – these should include its name, address and nationality, and the state in which it is domiciled or has its seat or an establishment; and
- *proof of the licence* – if the recordal request is either signed by both the owner and the licensee (or their respective representatives), or is filed by the owner alone, no further proof of the licence is required. Otherwise, some form of written document signed by both parties and confirming the existence of the licence must be filed. The licence itself can be submitted, but parties often do not want to place this on public record where it contains sensitive information (although the document can be redacted to hide any information the parties do not want to be visible in the Register).

In addition, the recordal request can include details of the licensee's representative, if it has appointed one. The normal requirements on representation apply, so it may be the case that the licensee is obliged to appoint a representative (see Chapter 2, section 10).

Depending on the type of licence, it is also possible to have the following pieces of information recorded, in the form of an indication that:

- it is an exclusive licence;

- it is a sub-licence (provided that the head licence from which the sub-licence has been granted is itself recorded);
- the licence relates to only some goods and/or services (in which case the goods and/or services involved should be indicated in the recordal request);
- the licence relates to only part of the Union (in which case the territory to which the licence relates should be indicated in the recordal request); and
- the licence is granted for a limited period of time (in which case the time period for which the licence is granted should be indicated in the recordal request).

There is a fee for the recordal of a licence and the recordal application is not considered to have been filed until the fee has been paid. At the time of writing, the fee is €200 per EUTM application or registration to which the recordal request relates, up to a maximum total of €1000. The fee is not refunded if the recordal application is later withdrawn or refused.

5.3 Procedure for recording transfer of licences

It is possible for licences to be transferred from one party to another. Where this happens, the change can be entered in the Register. The requirements for recording the transfer of the licence are the same as those for the initial recordal, and the same fees apply (see section 5.2 above).

5.4 Procedure for modifying or cancelling recordal of licences

Any request to modify or cancel the recordal of a licence may be submitted by the EUTM owner or the registered licensee, or both parties together.

There is no official form for requesting modification or cancellation and fees are only payable in the case of cancellation, at the same level as those for recording a licence (ie, €200 per EUTM application or registration, up to a maximum total of €1000).

If the cancellation request is filed by the licensee or jointly by both parties, no further proof of the cancellation is required. If, however, it is filed by the owner of the EUTM rights alone, the request should be accompanied by evidence that the licence no longer exists, or that the licensee consents to the cancellation of the recordal.

In the case of a modification request, no further evidence is required if the request is jointly filed by both parties. If, however, it is filed by the EUTM owner alone, proof of the modification is required where that modification would diminish the rights of the registered licensee. If the modification request is filed by the registered licensee alone, proof of the modification is required where that modification would extend the rights of the registered licensee. Any proof that is submitted in these circumstances should bear the signature of the other party.

6. Rights *in rem*

'Rights *in rem*' are rights that attach to property, rather than to persons. Such rights enable their owners to take some form of legal action under certain conditions. The most common type of rights *in rem* are security interests. Both EUTM applications and EUTM registrations can be the subject of security interests, where the trade mark rights act as security for some form of loan or other debt. If the owner of the EUTM rights is unable to repay the debt, the creditor is entitled to take ownership of the relevant applications and registrations. The terms of a security interest are a matter of contract law and are therefore governed by the relevant national law under which the contract is concluded.

6.1 Recordal of rights *in rem*

As with licences, it is not compulsory for rights *in rem* to be recorded and there is little benefit for the owner of EUTM rights in requesting the recordal of such a right.

There are, however, benefits for the owner of the right *in rem* (the 'pledgee') in having that right entered in the Register:

- rights *in rem* only have effect *vis-à-vis* third parties who acquire conflicting rights in the same EUTM application or registration if either the rights *in rem* are entered in the Register or the conflicting rights were acquired by a party who knew about them;
- a proprietor can only surrender an EUTM registration against which rights *in rem* are recorded if it proves it has informed the pledgee of its intention to surrender (see Chapter 15, section 7 for further information on surrender of EUTM registrations); and
- the Office notifies the pledgee of upcoming renewals and of any loss of rights.

Contracts that grant rights *in rem* often include provisions relating to the recordal of such rights in the Register, including an indication of whether the rights are to be recorded for all applications and/or registrations involved, and who must pay the fees associated with the recordal.

6.2 Procedure for recording rights *in rem*

A request to record rights *in rem* in the Register can only be made by the listed owner of the EUTM applications or registrations or the pledgee. Either party can file a separate request, or the parties can together file a joint request. The request must include the following information:

- *the EUTM application or registration number(s)* – a single request can relate to multiple rights where both the listed owner and the pledgee are the same for all of them;
- *details of the pledgee* – these should include its name, address and nationality, and the state in which it is domiciled or has its seat or an establishment; and
- *proof of the rights in rem* – if the recordal request is filed by the owner of the EUTM rights, or is a joint request signed by that party, no further proof of the existence of the rights *in rem* is required. If the request is filed by the pledgee alone, it must be accompanied by proof of the existence of the rights *in rem*, which is usually some form of document that has been signed by the EUTM proprietor, such as the rights *in rem* contract or a declaration relating to the

existence of those rights (it is possible for this document to be redacted to hide any information the parties do not want to be visible in the Register).

In addition, the recordal request can include details of the pledgee's representative, if it has appointed one. The normal requirements on representation apply, so it may be the case that the pledgee is obliged to appoint a representative (see Chapter 2, section 10).

There is a fee for the recordal of rights *in rem* and the recordal application is not considered to have been filed until the fee has been paid. At the time of writing, the fee is €200 per EUTM application or registration to which the recordal request relates, up to a maximum total of €1000. The fee is not refunded if the recordal application is later withdrawn or refused.

6.3 Procedure for recording transfer of rights *in rem*

It is possible for rights *in rem* to be transferred from one party to another. Where this happens, the change can be entered in the Register. The requirements for recording the transfer of rights *in rem* are the same as those for the initial recordal and the same fees apply (see section 6.2 above).

6.4 Procedure for modifying or cancelling recordal of rights *in rem*

Any request to modify or cancel the registration of rights *in rem* may be submitted by the EUTM owner or the registered pledgee, or both parties together.

There is no official form for requesting modification or cancellation and fees are only payable in the case of cancellation, at the same level as the fees for recording rights *in rem* (ie, €200 per EUTM application or registration, up to a maximum total of €1000).

If the cancellation request is filed by the pledgee or jointly by both parties, no further proof is required. If, however, it is filed by the owner of the EUTM rights alone, it should be accompanied by evidence that the rights *in rem* no longer exist, or that the pledgee consents to the cancellation of the recordal.

In the case of a modification request, no further evidence is required if the request is jointly filed by both parties. If, however, it is filed by the EUTM owner alone, proof of the modification is required where that modification would diminish the rights of the registered pledgee. If the modification request is filed by the registered pledgee alone, proof of the modification is required where that modification would extend the rights of the registered pledgee. Any proof that is submitted in these circumstances should bear the signature of the other party.

7. Levy of execution

Where a creditor is owed money by a debtor, it can go to court and ask for a judgment for possession to enable it to recover what it is owed from the property of the debtor. Such property can include IP and therefore trade marks. Where such a judgment is obtained, the act by which the court seizes the property is known as a levy of execution.

The effect of a levy of execution *vis-à-vis* third parties who acquire conflicting rights in the same EUTM application or registration is a matter for the applicable national law (as determined in accordance with the cascade set out at section 2 above). However, entering the levy in the Register helps ensure that third parties are aware of it.

As with other transactions, there are other good reasons why the beneficiary of a levy of execution would want to have it entered in the Register:

- a proprietor can only surrender an EUTM registration against which a levy of execution is recorded if it proves that it has informed the beneficiary of the levy of execution of its intention to surrender (see Chapter 15, section 7 for further information on surrender of EUTM registrations); and
- the Office notifies the beneficiary of upcoming renewals and of any loss of rights.

7.1 Procedure for recording levies of execution

A request to record a levy of execution in the Register can only be made by:

- the EUTM applicant/proprietor;
- the beneficiary of the levy of execution; or
- the court that handed down the relevant judgment.

The request must include the following information:

- *the EUTM application or registration number(s)* – a single request can only relate to multiple rights where both the listed owner and the beneficiary are the same for all of them;
- *details of the beneficiary* – these should include its name, address and nationality and the state in which it is domiciled or has its seat or an establishment; and
- *proof of the levy of execution* – if the recordal request is filed by the EUTM applicant or proprietor, no further proof of the existence of the levy of execution is required. If the request is filed by the beneficiary or the court, it must be accompanied by proof of the existence of the levy of execution, usually the court judgment.

In addition, the recordal request can include details of the beneficiary's representative, if it has appointed one. The normal requirements on representation apply, so it may be the case that the beneficiary is obliged to appoint a representative (see Chapter 2, section 10).

There is a fee for the recordal of a levy of execution, unless the recordal request is filed by the court. Where the recordal application is filed either by the beneficiary or the owner of the EUTM rights, it is not considered to have been filed until the fee has been paid. At the time of writing, the fee is €200 per EUTM application or registration to which the recordal request relates, up to a maximum total of €1000. The fee is not refunded if the recordal application is later withdrawn or refused.

7.2 Procedure for modifying or cancelling recordal of levy of execution

A request to modify or cancel the registration of a levy of execution can be filed by the EUTM applicant/proprietor or the registered beneficiary. Either party can file such a request alone, or the parties can jointly file a request. Any such request must be accompanied by proof of the modification or cancellation, usually in the form of the corresponding court judgment.

There is no official form for requesting modification or cancellation, and fees are only payable in the case of cancellation, at the same level as those for recording a levy of execution (ie, €200 per EUTM application or registration, up to a maximum total of €1000).

8. Insolvency proceedings

Where a person or company is unable to pay the money that it owes to others in time, it is said to be insolvent. In such circumstances, insolvency proceedings can be commenced with a view to making the best use of the debtor's assets for the benefit of its creditors. There are a number of different types of insolvency proceedings and the options available vary between Member States. For convenience, the person managing the insolvency proceeding is referred to in this section as the 'liquidator', but the rules relate to all forms of insolvency proceedings, not only liquidations.

Both EUTM applications and EUTM registrations constitute assets that can be involved in insolvency proceedings and the opening, modification and closing of such proceedings can all be entered in the Register. However, such rights can only be involved in insolvency proceedings that are opened in the Member State in which the debtor has its centre of main interests – ie, where it regularly conducts the administration of its interests (usually where it has its administrative headquarters). The only exception to this is where the debtor is an insurance undertaking or credit institution, in which case EUTM rights can be involved in insolvency proceedings opened in any Member States in which the undertaking or institution has been authorised to practise.

The effects of insolvency *vis-à-vis* third parties who acquire a conflicting interest in the same EUTM application or registration is a matter for the applicable national law (as determined in accordance with the cascade set out at section 2 above). However, recording the insolvency proceedings in the Register helps ensure that third parties are aware of them.

In addition, recording insolvency proceedings brings other benefits for the liquidator:

- where the proceedings are entered in the Register, the EUTM applicant/proprietor loses its right to act and cannot perform any actions before the Office (including transfer, withdrawal and surrender of the right). Instead, the liquidator acts in place of the applicant/proprietor; and
- the Office notifies the liquidator of upcoming renewals and of any loss of rights.

8.1 Procedure for recording insolvency proceedings

A request to record insolvency proceedings in the Register can only be made by:

- the liquidator;
- a court involved in the insolvency proceedings; or
- the EUTM applicant/proprietor.

The request must include the following information:

- *the EUTM application or registration number(s)* – where multiple EUTM applications and/or registrations are owned by the same debtor, the Office registers the insolvency proceedings against the rights linked to the listed owner's ID number, irrespective of which rights are listed in the recordal request;
- *details of the liquidator* – these should include its name, address and nationality and the state in which it is domiciled or has its seat or an establishment; and
- *proof of the appointment of a liquidator and of the insolvency proceedings* – a copy of the insolvency judgment is usually the most suitable proof in this regard and can be submitted in part or in a redacted form, so long as the parties to the proceedings are clearly identified.

In addition, the recordal request can include details of the liquidator's representative, if it has appointed one. The normal requirements on representation apply, so it may be the case that the liquidator is obliged to appoint a representative (see Chapter 2, section 10).

There is no fee for recording insolvency proceedings in the Register.

8.2 Procedure for modifying or cancelling recordal of insolvency proceedings

A request to modify or cancel the registration of insolvency proceedings can be made by:

- the liquidator;
- a court; or
- the EUTM applicant/proprietor.

Any such request must be accompanied by proof of the modification or cancellation. There is no fee for requesting such a change.

Further reference

Regulation – Articles 16-24a

Implementing Regulation – Rules 31-35

Office Guidelines – Part E, Section 3 and Part C, Section 1

Directive 2001/17/EC of the European Parliament and of the Council of 19 March 2001 on the reorganisation and winding-up of insurance undertakings

Directive 2001/24/EC of the European Parliament and of the Council of 4 April 2001 on the reorganisation and winding up of credit institutions

Chapter 17: Revocation actions

1. Introduction

There are two different ways in which third parties can apply to cancel EUTM registrations, generally referred to collectively as 'cancellation actions':

- *revocation* – this is relevant in situations in which, although the mark might have been validly registered, something has happened post-registration such that the registration should not be allowed to remain in place. Revocation actions are considered in this chapter; and
- *invalidity* – this is relevant in situations in which the mark should not have been registered in the first place. Invalidity actions are considered in Chapter 18.

Third parties wishing to cancel EUTM registrations should file a cancellation action with the Office. Such actions are handled by the Cancellation Divisions. The only alternative to this is where the EUTM registration in question has been used to bring infringement proceedings, in which case a defendant should apply for revocation or invalidity by way of a counterclaim in those proceedings (see Chapter 23).

The latest available figures provided in the Office's *Annual Reports* show that 1405 cancellation actions were filed with the Office in 2014.

This chapter examines the process of cancelling an EUTM registration through revocation proceedings at the Office. This includes a review of the grounds on which a revocation action can be based, how to file an action and the process through to a first instance decision by the Cancellation Divisions.

2. Grounds for revocation

A revocation action is known as an 'application for revocation', and the party who files the action is the 'revocation applicant'. Revocation proceedings consider whether a registered mark should remain on the Register as a result of post-registration acts, or lack thereof, by the EUTM proprietor. No assessment of whether a mark was validly registered is made in revocation proceedings. If a mark should never have been registered, the appropriate way to attack that registration is through an invalidity action, not a revocation action.

An EUTM registration removed from the Register following a successful revocation action is considered to have legally existed between its original filing date and the effective date of the revocation.

There are three grounds on which EUTM registrations can be revoked:

- the EUTM registration has been on the Register for more than five years and there has been a continuous period of five years without genuine use of the mark in the Union, without good reason (the ***'non-use ground'***);
- the mark has become generic, either because of the proprietor's actions or because of its inactivity (the ***'generic ground'***); and
- the mark has become misleading because of how the EUTM proprietor has used it, or how others have used it with the proprietor's consent (the ***'misleading ground'***).

Additional grounds for revocation apply in the cases of both EU collective marks (see Chapter 28) and EU certification marks (see Chapter 29).

2.1 Non-use ground

An EUTM registration can only be attacked on the basis of non-use once it has been on the Register for at least five years. After this time, any interested party can rely on this ground as a basis for the removal of the EUTM registration from the Register. This is the most commonly used revocation ground.

Unlike the other revocation grounds, in the case of the non-use ground the burden of proof is on the EUTM proprietor to show that the mark should remain on the Register, not on the revocation applicant to show that it should be removed. This means that no evidence needs to be filed by the revocation applicant at the time of filing the application for revocation. Rather, it is for the EUTM proprietor to file evidence in defence of its registration.

The Office can only assess a non-use action on the basis of the evidence presented by the EUTM proprietor, irrespective of how widespread and prominent the use of the relevant mark may be in the marketplace. Thus, when defending a non-use action, it is important that detailed evidence of use is provided. The evidential requirements are discussed further in section 9.2 below.

Use must be shown for the five-year period counted back from the date the revocation action is filed. If there has been a continuous period of five years without genuine use of the mark at issue, but the EUTM proprietor can show genuine use after this period but before the non-use action was filed, the revocation action will not succeed (unless the use only occurred because the proprietor was notified that the action was to be brought, as discussed in the next paragraph). For example, consider an EUTM registration that was granted on 20 November 2002, but the proprietor made no use of the mark until December 2014. A non-use action was filed against this registration on 13 April 2016. For the purposes of the non-use action, the EUTM proprietor is required to show use of the mark between 13 April 2011 and 13 April 2016. If it does so, the revocation action fails and the EUTM registration remains on the Register with rights dating back to the original filing date, even though there was a period of 12 years without any use of the mark. It is therefore always a good idea to bring a non-use cancellation action as soon as possible if there is a real interest in removing a registration from the Register.

If an EUTM proprietor is notified by a third party that it is planning to file a non-use action against that proprietor's registration, and such an action is then filed within three months of this notification, any use (or preparatory acts) during the period between the notification and the date the revocation action is filed are not taken into account for the purposes of assessing the non-use action. In such a situation, it is for party who filed the revocation action to prove it made the approach.

In any event, an absence of use does not necessarily result in a non-use action succeeding. An EUTM proprietor who is able to demonstrate proper reasons for not using the mark in question can maintain its registration. However, the threshold for what constitutes proper reasons for non-use is extremely high, as discussed in Chapter 13, section 6.5.

2.2 Generic ground

An EUTM registration can be revoked under this ground by showing that:

- the mark in question has become the common name in trade for the goods and/or services for which it is registered; and
- this is because of either positive acts or inactivity on the part of the EUTM proprietor.

It is for the revocation applicant to prove that both of these requirements are met. The mark must have become generic during the period after registration and before the filing of the revocation action. If the mark was generic at the time the application for registration was filed, an invalidity action should be brought (see Chapter 18), as the application should have been refused on that basis (see Chapter 7, section 6).

When assessing whether a mark has become the common name in trade, an applicant for revocation needs to consider what the 'relevant public' is for this purpose. The term 'in trade' does not mean that this assessment is restricted to businesses trading in the relevant goods and/or services. It is necessary to consider "all consumers and end users and, depending on the features of the market concerned, all those in the trade who deal with that product commercially" (wording taken from the CJEU decision in *BOSTONGHURKA*) where intermediaries such as wholesalers and retailers are involved in the distribution of products. It is not, however, necessary to show that the mark is used generically both by traders and consumers and end users; it can be enough for consumers and end users to use the mark in a generic sense.

There is a high threshold for showing that a mark has become generic. It is not enough to show that some people use the mark in a generic sense. Rather, it must be clearly demonstrated that the mark in question is commonly used by the vast majority of the relevant public to refer to the goods and/or services covered by the EUTM registration.

As discussed at section 4.5 below, evidence showing that the above requirements are met must be filed together with the application for revocation. Relevant evidence can include examples of the mark being used in a generic manner on websites (including online marketplaces, in the case of goods), on social media, in catalogues, magazines and advertising material and in dictionaries. Survey evidence can also be useful under this ground. However, as with all evidence presented to the Office, the more independent in nature it is, the more weight it is likely to be given. Evidence from multiple sources helps present a strong overall case.

It is also important to show that the mark has become generic because of the acts or inactivity of the EUTM proprietor. If the revocation applicant does not have positive proof that this is the case, it is important to file written submissions to explain why this must have been the case – eg, by inferring from the nature and volume of examples of generic use provided in evidence that the proprietor clearly did not have in place a system for policing use of its mark to make sure it did not become generic.

The key consideration under this ground of revocation is whether the mark has stopped being able to function as a trade mark. The EUTM proprietor may, however, have a defence if it can show that it has taken steps to prevent the mark becoming generic, as discussed in section 9.4 below.

2.3 Misleading ground

An EUTM registration can be removed from the Register on the ground that the mark protected is liable to mislead the public with regard to characteristics of the goods and/or services for which it is registered. To succeed under this ground, the revocation applicant must positively prove that:

- the mark is liable to mislead; and
- this is because of the use that has been made of the mark by the EUTM proprietor (or with its consent).

Although not an exhaustive list, this ground is generally used where the characteristics at issue are the nature, quality, or geographical origin of the goods and/or services covered by the registration.

The mark should have become misleading after registration, but before the revocation action was filed. If it is felt that the mark was misleading at the time the EUTM application was originally filed, an invalidity action is the most appropriate course of action (see Chapter 18) as the application should have been refused on that basis. This is most likely to be on the basis that the mark was deceptive (see Chapter 7, section 9), although it could also be on the basis that it is descriptive (see Chapter 7, section 5) or that it consists of, contains or evokes a PDO or PGI (see Chapter 7, section 12).

As with the generic ground, evidence showing that the above requirements are met must be filed together with the application for revocation. Evidence for this ground is usually in the form of examples of how the mark has been used by the proprietor (or with its consent). This ground can be used where the mark includes descriptive terms together with additional distinctive material but the goods and/or services in relation to which the mark is actually used do not have those characteristics. For example, a registration containing the element 'Made in Ireland' registered in relation to clothing but used in relation to clothing that is made outside of Ireland could be revoked under this ground.

3. Overview of the Office's revocation procedure

Despite being contentious proceedings, a revocation action is a type of application. As a result, some of the principles relating to EUTM applications apply. As with EUTM applications, there is no deadline by which to file a revocation action.

Revocation proceedings consist of four key stages:

- filing;
- admissibility checks;
- the adversarial stage, and
- decision.

What happens during each of these stages is summarised in the following flowchart and discussed in the paragraphs that follow it. Unlike in opposition proceedings, there is no 'cooling off' period in revocation proceedings.

Summary of revocation proceedings

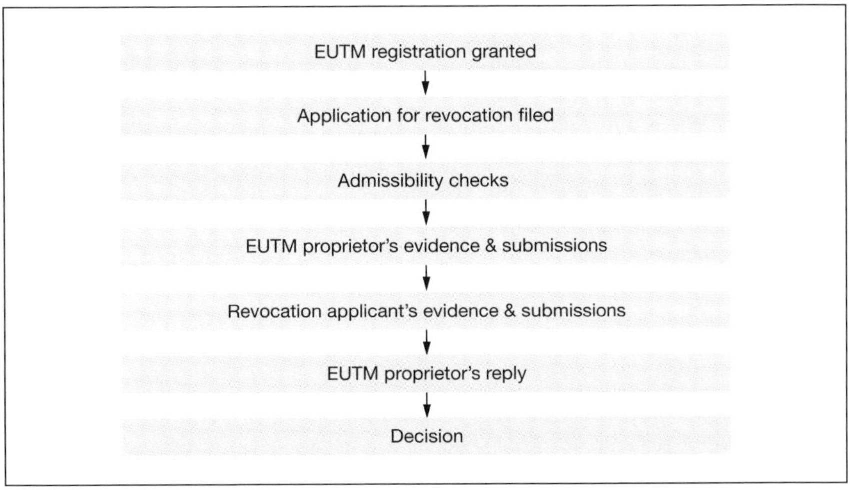

4. Filing a revocation action

The section examines the filing stage of revocation proceedings with the Office.

4.1 How to file a revocation action

Various requirements must be met for an application for revocation to be validly filed. The application for revocation must be filed in writing and an official fee paid (€630 at the time of writing). The Office provides an official form that may be used. Although the form does not have to be used, it includes fields for all the information required to file a valid revocation action, so using it is highly advisable, particularly when the language considerations set out in section 5 of this chapter are taken into account.

An application for revocation must be submitted directly to the Office, by post, by hand or by fax. The completed form should be signed and the name of the signatory must be indicated. It is not yet possible to file revocation actions electronically.

4.2 Payment of the official fee

The first thing the Office checks upon receipt of an application for revocation is that the official fee has been paid. If it has not, the Office sets the revocation applicant a deadline (usually one month) by which to pay it. If the money is not received within this timeframe, the application is treated as never having been filed. If the fees are paid late, or if the action is later withdrawn as a result of amicable settlement by the parties, the fees are not refunded. This contrasts with opposition proceedings that are resolved during the cooling off period (see Chapter 14).

The only time an application for revocation may be treated as validly filed despite payment not having reached the Office until after the deadline set is where the revocation applicant can prove that payment instructions were given to a bank before the deadline. If the instructions were given within the last 10 days before the deadline, a surcharge of 10% of the official fee must also be paid, but not if the instructions were given more than 10 days before the deadline.

The filing date of a validly filed revocation application is the date on which the written statement is received by the Office, not the date on which the fee is paid. The filing date is particularly important in the case of revocation actions filed under the non-use ground. While there is no deadline as such for the revocation applicant to meet in terms of filing the action, if it has notified the EUTM proprietor of its intention to file, this must occur within three months of the notification to take advantage of the provision enabling use between the notification and filing dates to be disregarded (see sections 2.1 above and 4.3 below). In any event, for all non-use actions the period for which the EUTM proprietor must show use of the mark at issue is calculated by reference to the date on which the action is filed.

4.3 When can a revocation action be filed?

A revocation action can only be filed against an EUTM registration; it cannot be filed against a pending application. In the case of the non-use ground, the EUTM right must have been on the Register for at least five years before the revocation action can be filed. If the revocation applicant tells the EUTM proprietor it is considering filing a non-use action, any use of the mark in question made by the proprietor after being notified but before the action is filed is not taken into account in the proceedings, so long as the revocation action is filed within three months of the notification.

Where an applicant for revocation has contacted the EUTM proprietor in advance of filing a revocation action, it is sensible to ensure the non-use action is filed within this three-month period, particularly where there are real concerns that the EUTM proprietor is making plans to commence use solely to avoid a non-use action.

It should, however, be noted that there is no requirement to notify the EUTM proprietor of any plans to file a non-use attack. It is perfectly acceptable simply to file the action once the registration in question is five years old. Despite this, if a potential revocation applicant knows that a mark has not been used for at least five years, contacting the EUTM proprietor and asking it to surrender the registration voluntarily can, if the proprietor knows that it will not be able to defend a non-use action, lead to the EUTM registration being removed from the Register without the need for a revocation action to be filed.

For revocation actions based on either the generic ground or the misleading ground, there is no requirement that the EUTM has been registered for a specific amount of time before the action can be filed. However, it must be the case that the mark has become generic or misleading since registration, which usually takes at least a few years. If the concern is that the mark was generic or misleading at the time of its filing or priority date, and that it should therefore not have been allowed on the Register in the first place, invalidity proceedings are more appropriate (see Chapter 18).

4.4 Who can file a revocation action?

A revocation action can be filed by any natural or legal person or by any group or body set up for the purpose of representing the interests of manufacturers, producers, suppliers of services, traders or consumers, which under the terms of the law governing it has the capacity in its own name to sue and be sued. Such actions are usually filed because the revocation applicant has a particular reason for wanting the registration in question removed from the Register. This is often because it wants to use and/or register the same mark (or something similar) and wishes to remove a potential obstacle. There is, however, no requirement to explain the motivation behind filing an action.

4.5 Filing a valid revocation action

In order to be deemed validly filed, an application for revocation must include the following information:

- the registration number of the EUTM registration in respect of which revocation is sought;
- the name and address of the proprietor of the attacked EUTM registration;
- a clear indication of the goods and/or services in respect of which revocation is sought;
- a clear indication of the ground(s) on which the application for revocation is based;
- the name and address of the revocation applicant; and
- the name and business address of the revocation applicant's representative if one has been appointed (or is required, as discussed in section 6.1 below).

Where the application for revocation is based on the non-use ground, nothing further is required at this stage. For this ground, it is for the EUTM proprietor to prove that the mark in question has been used and that the registration should remain on the Register. It is not for the revocation applicant to demonstrate that the mark has not been used.

Where the application for revocation is based on either the generic ground or the misleading ground, it should be accompanied by supporting evidence, as well as any legal arguments on which the revocation applicant wishes to rely. For these grounds, it is not enough simply to complete the official form. Rather, the case being made needs to be clear from the outset, as the burden is on the revocation applicant to prove that the registration in question should be removed from the Register. As there is no deadline for the revocation applicant to meet when filing an application for revocation, it is for that applicant to ensure that it has assembled all necessary materials and evidence in support of the action to be filed. The points set out in section 8 of Chapter 13 should be taken into consideration when filing evidence in support of a revocation action.

In terms of the content of the evidence, the points considered at sections 2.2 (generic ground) and 2.3 (misleading ground) of this chapter should be taken into account. The revocation applicant should also ensure that it files any supporting legal arguments or other submissions on which it wishes to rely in support of its case.

If any of the information set out above is missing, the Office issues a deficiency notice and sets the revocation applicant a deadline by which to provide it (as discussed further at section 7 below).

It is possible to include more than one ground in the same revocation action. However, if non-use is one of the possible grounds of attack, it is usually more prudent for a revocation applicant to rely solely on this ground, as it is then for the EUTM proprietor to show that it has made use of the mark.

5. Languages to be used

As with opposition proceedings, there are important considerations when filing an application for revocation in relation to both the language of the proceedings and the language in which the application for revocation is filed.

5.1 Language of the proceedings

Every EUTM application has to indicate both a first and a second language; and at least the second language has to be one of the Languages of the Office (see Chapter 5, section 10). The language of revocation proceedings is dictated by the languages indicated in the application for the EUTM registration that is being attacked.

The starting position is that the language of the revocation proceedings must be both one of the languages of the attacked EUTM registration and one of the Languages of the Office. It is, however, open to the parties to agree otherwise, in which case the language must be one of the Languages of the Union.

Where both the first and second languages of an EUTM registration are Languages of the Office, the revocation applicant has a choice over which to use as the language of the revocation proceedings. If the revocation applicant fails to indicate which of the two possible languages is to be the language of the proceedings (which can be done by filing the application for revocation in one of those languages), a deficiency notice is issued and the applicant for revocation is asked to indicate the language of the proceedings.

Where only the second language of an EUTM registration is a Language of the Office, the revocation proceedings must take place in that language (unless the parties agree otherwise). Thus, failure to indicate the language of the proceedings in the application for revocation or indicating an incorrect language has no effect. No deficiency notice is issued as there is only one possible language for the proceedings.

All of the above is subject to the proviso that the parties to revocation proceedings may agree that a different Language of the Union is to be the language of the proceedings. Any such agreement should be communicated to the Office within two months of the date the EUTM proprietor is notified of the revocation action by the Office. The revocation applicant has a further month from this date to file a translation of the revocation application into that language if it was initially filed in another language. If either of these deadlines is missed, the language remains unchanged. In certain circumstances, missing either of these deadlines can result in the application being deemed inadmissible (see section 7 below).

Although it is generally preferable to file all observations and evidence in the language of the proceedings, it is technically open to each of the parties to use any Language of the Office during the course of proceedings, provided that appropriate translations are provided. What needs to be translated, and the deadlines for providing such translations, is affected by the grounds relied upon, the stage the proceedings have reached and which party is filing the relevant documents.

Key considerations in this regard are as follows:

- *Application for revocation:* The language requirements of the application for revocation itself, and the associated translation requirements, are discussed at section 5.2 of this chapter;
- *Revocation applicant's evidence:* Any evidence filed by the revocation applicant that is not in the language of the proceedings must be translated into that language within two months of being filed. This includes evidence filed together with the revocation application (as required for the generic and misleading grounds), as well as evidence filed in response to documents filed by the EUTM proprietor.

  The Office does not notify the revocation applicant of this two-month deadline – the applicant is expected to be aware of it and to satisfy the deadline on its own initiative. Failure to provide the translations generally results in the evidence not being taken into account. In the case of applications under the generic ground or the misleading ground, the evidence may be necessary to assess the admissibility of the revocation action in the first place. Where this is the case, the Office issues a deficiency notice and sets a deadline by which the revocation applicant must file the necessary translations. Failure to provide the translations in these circumstances can result in the application for revocation being deemed inadmissible.
- *EUTM proprietor's evidence:* In the case of revocation proceedings based on either the generic ground or the misleading ground, the EUTM proprietor may submit evidence in any Language of the Union. A translation of such documents only has to be provided if the Office specifically requests it, in which case a deadline is set for the EUTM proprietor. If such a request is made but not satisfied, the documents in question are not taken into account in the proceedings.

  Where revocation proceedings are based on the non-use ground, it is for the EUTM proprietor to provide evidence of use of the attacked mark. The general principle in this regard is that it should be possible for the revocation applicant (and the Office) to determine from the evidence what is being shown. Where evidence is filed in a language other than the language of the proceedings, there is no automatic requirement to file a translation. Rather, the Office exercises discretion and sets a deadline for filing translations of any particular pieces of evidence for which it deems this to be necessary (which can be in response to comments from the revocation applicant). Failure to satisfy this deadline results in the pieces of evidence in question being excluded from the proceedings.

- *Observations:* Any observations filed by either party during the course of proceedings can be filed in any Language of the Office. If the language in question is not the language of the proceedings, the observations should be translated into the language of the proceedings within one month of their initial submission.

  The one-month deadline is the same irrespective of the initial deadline to file the observations. For example, an EUTM proprietor may be set a deadline of 16 February 2017 to file observations in response to a revocation action based on the generic ground. If it files observations in a Language of the Office that is not the language of the proceedings on 10 February 2017, the translation of those observations must be filed by 10 March 2017.

  The Office does not notify the parties of this one-month deadline for filing the translation – they are expected to be aware of it and to satisfy it on their own initiative. Failure to provide a translation results in the observations being deemed never to have been filed and therefore not taken into account in the proceedings.

5.2 Language of the application for revocation

The application for revocation must be filed in one of the Languages of the Office. However, the Office's official revocation form is available in 23 of the 24 Languages of the Union (it is not available in Irish). Where the Office's form is used, the revocation action is deemed admissible if any of the 23 language versions is used, provided that the form is completed in one of the Languages of the Office so far as textual elements are concerned.

Where the revocation action is filed in one of the Languages of the Office but not the language of the proceedings (and the parties have not entered into an agreement regarding the language of the proceedings), the revocation applicant must file a translation into the language of the proceedings within one month of filing the application. The revocation applicant is expected to satisfy this deadline on its own initiative and is not notified of this by the Office.

If the application for revocation is filed in a Language of the Union other than one of the Languages of the Office, it is deemed inadmissible unless the parties notify the Office within two months of the filing that they have agreed upon the language in which it was filed as the language of the proceedings.

6. Representation

There are two issues to consider here:

- representation of the revocation applicant, and
- representation of the EUTM proprietor.

6.1 Representation of the revocation applicant

As with the filing of EUTM applications, where a revocation applicant is domiciled in, has its principal place of business in, or has a real and effective industrial or commercial establishment in the EEA, there is no requirement for a representative to be appointed (see Chapter 2, section 10 for more information).

Where, however, the above criteria are not met, a revocation applicant must be represented before the Office. If this is the case but no representative has been appointed at the time of filing the revocation action (or if any such representative withdraws during the course of the proceedings), the Office issues a deficiency notice and sets the revocation applicant a deadline by which it must appoint a suitable representative.

6.2 Representation of the EUTM proprietor

An EUTM proprietor who is not domiciled in the EEA and does not have a place of business or real and effective industrial or commercial establishment in the EEA should be represented before the Office. In practice, a representative will almost always have been appointed during the initial application procedure.

Where the EUTM proprietor is not represented (but needs to be), the Office invites it to appoint a representative. If it fails to do so, procedural statements made by the proprietor are not taken into account, and the case is dealt with on the basis of the evidence before the Office (including evidence filed directly by the EUTM proprietor). The EUTM registration is not cancelled simply because the EUTM proprietor is not represented after registration.

7. Admissibility checks and deficiencies

Once the Office is satisfied the official fee has been duly paid (see section 4.2 above), it proceeds by completing admissibility checks.

A revocation action is automatically deemed inadmissible if, at the time of filing the action:

- the right against which the application was filed was not yet registered;
- the right against which the application was filed no longer existed, as it had already been surrendered, cancelled or allowed to lapse;
- the non-use ground is relied upon but the EUTM right had not yet been registered for five years;
- there is *res judicata*, ie, the matter to be decided had already been the subject of a final decision issued either by the Office or an EUTM Court in proceedings between the same parties (see Chapter 18, section 10.6); or
- the application is filed in an incorrect language and no translation has been provided within the timeframe for doing so (as discussed in section 5 above).

Where any of these issues apply, the Office simply provides the applicant with an opportunity to comment on the admissibility of the application. If the Office maintains its view (which it almost always does), the application for revocation is deemed inadmissible and a decision to that effect is issued. The revocation applicant cannot remedy these deficiencies.

Where any of the information set out at section 4.5 above is not provided at the time of filing, the Office issues a deficiency notice and sets the revocation applicant a deadline by which to provide it. This is usually a two-month non-extendable deadline. If the information is not provided within this period, the application for revocation is rejected as inadmissible, unless the application includes multiple grounds and the missing information does not relate to all the grounds. If this is the case, the application can continue for those grounds for which the necessary information has been provided.

If both revocation and invalidity grounds are included in a single application, the Office issues a deficiency notice and sets the cancellation applicant a deadline by which to choose between revocation proceedings and invalidity proceedings. If it fails to do so, the application is rejected as inadmissible and does not proceed as either a revocation or an invalidity application. If a choice is made, the applicant can file a separate application for the type of action that has not been chosen, subject to payment of the relevant fee.

8. Notification of the revocation action

Once the admissibility checks have been carried out, the Office notifies the EUTM proprietor that the revocation action has been filed. If no relative admissibility issues have been raised, the notification includes an indication of the deadline by which the EUTM proprietor can file a response to the action. In the case of an action based on the non-use ground, this first deadline is the EUTM proprietor's deadline to file evidence of use of the mark in question, or proper reasons for non-use.

The Office normally gives the EUTM proprietor three months to file its response. This deadline can be extended once by a further two months. Additional extensions are only granted in exceptional circumstances. However, this deadline is one for which continuation of proceedings can be utilised, as indeed are all the deadlines in the adversarial stage of revocation proceedings (see Chapter 27), so that it is possible for the EUTM proprietor to obtain more time to respond if necessary.

If relative admissibility deficiencies are raised during the admissibility checks, the EUTM proprietor is still notified of the revocation application after the initial admissibility checks are completed. It is also informed of the deficiencies, although the EUTM proprietor's deadline to respond is not set until after these deficiencies are remedied.

Further deadlines are not set down at the notification stage as they ultimately depend on whether the EUTM proprietor files anything. This is unlike opposition proceedings, primarily because the revocation applicant has to file all supporting evidence up front (other than for the non-use ground, where the burden of proof is on the EUTM proprietor). In opposition proceedings, the opponent is given time after the filing of the opposition to substantiate its case. However, there is a non-extendable deadline by which an opposition must be filed, whereas the timing of the filing of an application for revocation is at the discretion of the revocation applicant. (See chapters 10-14 for more information on opposition proceedings.)

9. Adversarial stage of proceedings

Once an application for revocation has been deemed admissible, the proceedings enter the adversarial stage. The Office has discretion as to the number of rounds of evidence and observations that are permitted. However, the usual running order is as follows:

- EUTM proprietor's deadline to file submissions and evidence in support of its case, as discussed in section 8 above (this is particularly important in the case of proceedings based on the non-use ground);
- revocation applicant's deadline to respond; and
- EUTM proprietor's deadline to respond to anything further filed by the revocation applicant.

The adversarial stage of proceedings is closed earlier if either party fails to meet one of its deadlines (as there is nothing to which the other party can respond).

The content of observations and evidence depends on the revocation grounds as well as on the facts of the case. Given the differing requirements, it is useful to look at each ground individually.

The points set out at section 5.1 regarding the language to be used for both observations and evidence should be noted, as well as those regarding translations.

9.1 EUTM proprietor's response to the revocation action

As detailed in sections 2.1 and 4.5 above, where a revocation action is based on the non-use ground alone, the revocation applicant only needs to file the basic revocation form and the burden is on the EUTM proprietor to file evidence of use or give proper reasons for not using the mark. If the proprietor fails to meet its deadline, the adversarial stage of proceedings is closed and the Office takes a decision. As the Office can only base a decision on the facts and evidence presented by the parties, in practice failure by the EUTM proprietor to file a response to a revocation action based on the non-use ground always results in the registration being revoked in relation to the goods and/or services referred to in the application for revocation. Where it is clear (or strongly suspected) that a mark has not been used for five or more years, a revocation action under the non-use ground can be a relatively quick and inexpensive way of removing a right from the Register.

9.2 Evidence of use

The legal principles to be taken into account when considering the use that needs to be made to defeat a revocation action based on the non-use ground, and the evidence that needs to be filed to prove that use, are equivalent to the rules relating to proof of use. This is discussed in detail in Chapter 13, section 6 in the context of oppositions and that section should be consulted if further information is required.

Put simply, in order, to maintain its rights, the EUTM proprietor must show that genuine use of the mark has been made (by it or with its consent) in the Union in relation to the goods and/or services covered by its registration, or that it has proper reasons for not using the mark. It is crucial to ensure that the evidence is clearly dated and shows that the mark was used in the five-year period before the revocation action was filed.

When filing evidence of use, the EUTM proprietor should ensure that all terms in its specification that are the subject of the revocation action are accounted for in its evidence of use (and supporting submissions). If not, the registration will be revoked in respect of those goods and/or services for which no evidence of use (and no proper reasons for non-use) was filed, as each term in a specification is considered individually. Where the specification includes broad terms, but the mark has only been used in relation to a fairly narrow category of goods falling within a broad term, whether the use in question is sufficient to allow the broad term to be maintained depends on whether the goods and/or services for which use has been shown form an identifiable sub-category within the broader category. For example, if a registration covers "clothing" in class 25 but the evidence of use filed relates solely to skirts, the registration is likely to be partially revoked, so that the specification is reduced down from the broad term "clothing" to the narrower category of "skirts".

When notifying an EUTM proprietor that a non-use revocation action has been filed against its registration, the Office encloses an information sheet on providing evidence of use in a structured and timely manner. In particular, it asks proprietors to enclose a numbered list of all the pieces of evidence submitted, with each item of evidence identified with the numbers corresponding to the list. The list should include a brief description of each piece of evidence, along with an indication of its purpose. If the Office's guidelines are not followed, the EUTM proprietor runs the risk that its evidence will not be taken into account, or not given the weight intended. The comments set out in section 8 of Chapter 13 also apply to evidence of use in revocation proceedings.

9.3 Reply evidence

If the proprietor does not file anything to satisfy its deadline, the Office writes to the parties indicating that the adversarial stage of the proceedings is complete. It then takes a decision. As indicated above, if the action is based on the non-use ground alone, failure by the proprietor to file evidence results in the registration being revoked to the extent it was attacked. In the case of other grounds of revocation, failure by the proprietor to file a response results in the Office taking a decision on the substance of the case, as discussed further in Sections 9.4 and 9.5.

Where the proprietor files evidence within the period set for it to do so, a copy is sent to the revocation applicant by the Office. The revocation applicant is given a two-month time period within which to file a reply. This deadline can be extended once, by two months, without the need to give reasons (so long as the extension request is filed and received before the deadline expires). Further extensions are generally only granted in exceptional circumstances. The revocation applicant does not have to file anything and, if it does not do so, the adversarial stage of proceedings is closed and the Office takes a decision on the basis of the evidence filed.

Where limited or weak evidence of use is filed by a proprietor, a revocation applicant may wish to file submissions highlighting the weaknesses or problems with the evidence (eg, if appropriate translations have not been filed, or the evidence is not dated). Care should, however, be taken when doing so as this can result in the proprietor being given an opportunity to supplement or amend its evidence.

If the revocation applicant files anything, the EUTM proprietor is usually given a chance to file a reply. Again, it is normally set a two-month deadline (which can be extended once by a further two months).

Any reply evidence (filed by either party) should, in theory, be limited to addressing only the points and evidence submitted by the other party. Evidence on new points not previously raised by either party, or additional evidence to support points already raised but not previously addressed, should not be filed at this stage. In practice, however, the Office does not automatically exclude such evidence. Thus, if useful evidence becomes available at this stage, it is sensible to file it.

Once the proprietor's reply deadline has passed, the Office usually considers the adversarial stage of proceedings complete and takes a decision.

9.4 Generic ground

As set out in sections 2.2 and 4.5 above, where this ground is relied on, the revocation applicant must file evidence in support of its case at the time of filing the application for revocation.

The first deadline in such proceedings is therefore the proprietor's deadline to respond to the case. Unlike with the non-use ground, failure by the proprietor to file anything to satisfy this deadline does not mean its rights will be revoked. Rather, it simply means that the Office considers the adversarial stage of proceedings complete and takes a decision based solely on the information and evidence filed by the revocation applicant.

If a proprietor can demonstrate that it has actively taken reasonable steps to prevent its mark becoming generic, it may be able to maintain its registration. Such steps can include requesting the removal of the mark from dictionaries, encyclopaedias and other reference works where it is used in a generic manner or in a way that suggests it is a generic term. Where an EUTM proprietor asks a publisher to remove any such uses, the latter is obliged to make sure the next edition includes a clear reference to the mark being a registered trade mark. This will not in itself be sufficient to defeat a revocation action, however.

If the proprietor has taken steps to try and prevent its mark being used generically, it should use its deadline to file evidence showing this, as well as any supporting submissions it deems useful. If the proprietor does file evidence, the revocation applicant is given an opportunity to file a reply. The proprietor gets a chance to make a further reply to anything further filed by the revocation applicant. The comments on such reply evidence set out in section 9.3 above apply equally here.

9.5 Misleading ground

As set out in sections 2.3 and 4.5 above, where this ground is relied on, the revocation applicant must file evidence in support of its case at the time of filing the application for revocation.

The first deadline in such proceedings is therefore the proprietor's deadline to respond to the case. Unlike with the non-use ground, failure by the proprietor to file anything to satisfy this deadline does not mean its rights will be revoked. Rather, it simply means the Office considers the adversarial stage of proceedings complete and takes a decision based solely on the information and evidence filed by the revocation applicant.

If the proprietor does file a response, the revocation applicant is given a chance to reply, after which the proprietor is given an opportunity to file its reply. The comments on such reply evidence set out in section 9.3 above apply equally here.

10. Oral proceedings

It is technically possible for the parties to revocation proceedings to request an oral hearing at any stage during the proceedings (and also technically possible for the Office to insist that an oral hearing takes place). In reality, however, the Office never suggests such hearings and rejects any requests in this regard from the parties to revocation proceedings.

Although hearings never happen in practice, there are rules surrounding the procedure for parties to appear before the Office. Where the Office summons parties to appear, it must give them a minimum of one month's notice, unless they have expressly agreed to a shorter period. The legal provisions relating to oral proceedings make clear that any such hearings in relation to revocation proceedings are open to the public, unless it is felt that admission of the public could seriously disadvantage one of the parties or otherwise cause serious problems.

The lack of oral hearings in practice means that both parties should work on the assumption that their only chance to present their case will be in written form.

11. Decision

Once the adversarial stage is complete, the Office notifies the parties that this is the case and takes a decision on the basis of the evidence and arguments that have been filed.

Revocation decisions are always issued in writing, and must include the date of the decision as well as details of the parties. The date is a crucial piece of information as it is used to calculate the deadline for filing an appeal against the decision (as discussed further in Chapter 20).

In the case of actions based on the non-use ground for which no evidence of use or reasons for non-use have been filed, the Office issues a short decision revoking the registration from the date on which the revocation application was filed.

Where evidence of use is filed, the Office assesses this evidence and reaches a conclusion on whether it is sufficient to maintain the registration, in whole or in part (ie, for the full specification or for only part of it). As discussed at section 9.2, where the specification covers general terms but the use shown only relates to specific sub-categories within those broad terms, the Office can decide to maintain the registration only in respect of such sub-categories.

Where proof of use evidence has been filed for some, but not all, of the goods and/or services covered by the registration, the registration is revoked in respect of the goods and/or services for which no evidence is filed and maintained for those for which sufficient evidence has been filed.

A decision in revocation proceedings always includes a decision on the apportionment of costs. The costs in revocation proceedings are limited to the official cancellation fee and the representation costs of the parties (if they are professionally represented). These costs are always expressed in Euros.

The basic principle is that the 'winning' party is awarded costs from the 'losing' party. If the revocation action is successful in full, the EUTM proprietor has to pay the revocation applicant both the amount of the official fee and an amount towards the latter's representation costs. The level is the same for both parties, so that if the revocation fails in full, the revocation applicant has to pay the EUTM proprietor an amount towards the latter's representation costs.

Where a revocation action succeeds in part and is rejected in part, both parties are deemed to be partially successful, in which case each has to bear its own costs.

In practice, the representation costs are set at a very low level, irrespective of the actual costs incurred in engaging professional representatives. At the time of writing, the amount of costs awarded for representation is fixed at €450.

12. Appeals

It is possible to file an appeal against the decision to deem a revocation action admissible, as well as against the substantive decision in the revocation action itself. As a decision to deem a revocation action admissible does not terminate the revocation proceedings, it can only be appealed together with the final revocation decision. It is not possible to delay or avoid the substantive revocation proceedings by appealing the admissibility decision at the time it is issued. The appeals process is discussed in chapters 19 and 20.

13. Multiple actions against the same EUTM registration

It is possible for both invalidity and revocation actions to be filed against the same EUTM registration. This might happen, for example, where the invalidity applicant has an earlier right that can be relied on in an invalidity action (as discussed in Chapter 18) and believes that the registration it is seeking to invalidate has not been used, so that a revocation action based on the non-use ground is also possible.

It is also possible for different parties to file invalidity and/or revocation actions against the same EUTM registration, whether deliberately or entirely coincidentally. The same rules apply whether there are multiple invalidity actions, multiple revocation actions or a combination of the two.

Where there are multiple invalidity and/or revocation actions against the same EUTM registration, the Office has discretion as to the order in which these actions are decided. In most circumstances, the Office decides to go forward with one action and suspends the rest, although it does not have to do so.

Given the different effects of a successful application for a declaration of invalidity (ie, the EUTM registration is deemed to have never existed) and revocation (ie, the EUTM registration is deemed to have been valid until a certain date), it is normal for invalidity actions to be dealt with before revocation actions. This is because a successful invalidity action necessarily means the revocation action has no purpose.

If the Office decides to deal with a revocation action first, and that action is successful, the applicant for invalidity is asked whether it wishes to proceed with its invalidity action. The action continues if it chooses to pursue it. The same rules apply where there are multiple revocation actions relating to the same EUTM registration claiming different effective dates of revocation.

Further reference

Regulation – Articles 15, 51, 56, 76, 78
Implementing Regulation – Rules 37-40, 55, 79
Office Guidelines – Part C, Section 6 and Part D
The Office's online summary of revocation and invalidity proceedings: https://euipo.europa.eu/ohimportal/en/invalidity-and-revocation
The Office's *Annual Reports*: https://euipo.europa.eu/ohimportal/en/annual-report
La Mer Technology Inc v Laboratoires Goemar SA ('LA MER') (Case C-259/02)
Ansul BV v Ajax Brandbeveilining BV ('MINIMAX') (Case C-40/01)
Leno Marken BV v Hagelkruis Beheer BV (Case C-149/11)
Reckitt Benckiser (España), SL v OHIM (Case T-126/03)
Björnekulla Fruktindustrier AB v Procordia Food AB (Case C-371/02) (*'BOSTONGHURKA'*)
Backaldrin Österreich The Kornspitz Company GmbH v Pfahnl Backmittel GmbH (Case C-409/12)

Chapter 18: Invalidity actions

1. Introduction

This chapter examines the process of cancelling an EUTM registration through invalidity proceedings at the Office. This includes a review of the grounds on which an invalidity action can be based, how to file an action and the process through to a first instance decision by the Cancellation Divisions.

Where multiple actions are filed against the same EUTM registration, the rules in Chapter 17, section 13 apply.

2. Grounds for invalidity

An invalidity action is known as an application for a 'declaration of invalidity', and the party who files the action is the 'invalidity applicant'. Invalidity proceedings are used when it is felt that a mark that is on the Register should never have been allowed to proceed to registration in the first place. A registration that is removed from the Register as a result of a successful invalidity action is considered never to have existed.

The potential grounds on which an application for a declaration of invalidity can be brought can be split into four categories, each of which is considered separately in this section. An invalidity action can be based on more than one ground, and both absolute and relative grounds can be relied on in the same action. The four categories are:

- the EUTM registration was granted incorrectly, as the mark was not inherently capable of registration (***'absolute grounds'***);
- the original EUTM applicant was acting in bad faith when it filed the application (***'bad faith ground'***);
- the EUTM was registered despite the existence of earlier rights that could have been relied on in an opposition (***'opposition rights grounds'***); and
- use of the registered mark may be prohibited pursuant to another earlier right under Union law or national law that could not have been used as the basis of an opposition (***'other IP rights ground'***).

Additional grounds for invalidity apply in the cases of both EU collective marks (see Chapter 28) and EU certification marks (see Chapter 29).

2.1 Absolute grounds

This category of grounds should be relied on in invalidity proceedings where it is felt that the attacked registration should never have proceeded through the examination stage, as one of the absolute grounds on which an application can be refused registration was applicable when the application was filed.

The absolute grounds are listed below and discussed in detail in Chapter 7 (the points set out there apply equally where these grounds are raised in invalidity proceedings rather than during examination):

- signs that cannot be trade marks;
- lack of distinctiveness;
- descriptive trade marks;
- customary (generic) signs or indications;
- characteristics which result from the nature of the goods, are necessarily technical or add substantial value;
- public policy and morality;
- deceptive trade marks;
- flags and emblems protected under the Paris Convention;
- trade marks of particular public interest;
- protected designations of origin and geographical indications;
- protected traditional terms for wine;
- protected traditional specialities; and
- protected plant variety names.

As discussed in section 4 of Chapter 8, 'acquired distinctiveness' is a way of overcoming objections raised on the basis that a mark is non-distinctive, is descriptive and/or is a customary (generic) sign. This is also the case in invalidity proceedings involving one or more of these grounds. In the case of invalidity proceedings, however, it is sufficient that the mark in question acquired distinctiveness after registration. This is different to the situation during examination, where it must be shown that the mark had acquired distinctiveness before the filing date of the application. This means that in some limited circumstances it is possible to defend against an invalidity application even though the mark in question should not have been registered as it was not capable of registration on the filing date.

2.2 Bad faith ground

This ground should be used where it is felt that the original EUTM applicant was acting in bad faith when the application was filed. The meaning of 'bad faith' in this context is considered below.

Bad faith issues cannot be raised by the Office during the examination process, or by third parties in opposition proceedings. The only way to deal with a bad faith issue is therefore through invalidity proceedings.

As there is a presumption that EUTM registrations are valid, it is for the invalidity applicant to prove positively that the application that resulted in the EUTM registration under attack was filed in bad faith. The threshold for proving bad faith is high and the Office can only base its decision on information and arguments presented by the parties. The evidence filed to support this ground should aim to establish the EUTM proprietor's intention at the time of filing the application.

'Bad faith' is not defined in the Regulation, but case law has provided the following guidance on how it is to be assessed:

- bad faith has to be assessed on the day the relevant application was filed – although evidence relating to the position after the filing date of an application can be taken into account if it helps assess the position on the filing date;
- the definition of 'bad faith' cannot be limited to "specific circumstances such as the existence of a particular kind of prior right, a lack of intention to use the mark or actual or constructive knowledge of the existing use of a similar mark", although these are relevant factors to be taken into account (wording taken from the Advocate General's opinion in the *Lindt* case);
- the assessment of bad faith requires a consideration of both objective and subjective factors. The Advocate General summarised this in the *Lindt* case as meaning that bad faith "relates to a subjective motivation on the part of the trade mark applicant – a dishonest intention or other 'sinister motive' – which will none the less normally be established by reference to objective criteria" and "involves conduct which departs from accepted principles of ethical behaviour or honest commercial and business practices, which can be identified by assessing the objective facts of each case against such standards". It is important to note that the applicant's view of what constitutes honesty (or acceptable commercial behaviour) is irrelevant;
- an EUTM proprietor can be found to have acted in bad faith against the Office where it deliberately lied to or misled the Office when filing its application. However, as there is no 'intention to use' requirement when filing EUTM applications, an argument that the application covers a very broad specification that goes beyond the applicant's legitimate interests will usually fail. Also, filing a new application for a mark and goods and/or services already covered by an earlier registration, where the earlier registration is vulnerable to cancellation for non-use, is not normally proof in itself of bad faith; and
- an EUTM proprietor can also be found to have acted in bad faith against a third party where the former attempted to appropriate someone else's trade mark. Bad faith can, for example, be found where the EUTM registration under attack is identical or similar to rights owned by another party (usually the invalidity applicant) and it is felt that the EUTM proprietor was acting either to free-ride on the other party's rights or prevent that party (or others) from entering the market. As with all bad faith arguments, whether this kind of bad faith can be shown depends on the evidence presented. In the example above, for an invalidity action to be successful, it would normally be necessary to demonstrate that the EUTM applicant clearly knew of the rights of the other party and had a clear dishonest intention when the application was filed.

The bad faith ground is often relied upon where there was some form of earlier relationship between the parties – eg, where the invalidity applicant was a supplier for the EUTM proprietor. This mere fact alone is insufficient for the Office to conclude that the EUTM application was filed in bad faith; it is for the invalidity applicant to provide clear and convincing evidence that the EUTM proprietor acted in bad faith and that it should therefore lose its registration. Where there was some form of pre-existing arrangement, it may be the case that it is more appropriate to rely on the opposition rights grounds in invalidity proceedings, specifically the agent/representative ground. (See section 2.3 below.)

Ultimately, when deciding a case under the bad faith ground, the Office makes an overall assessment of the facts and evidence presented by the parties and each case depends largely on its own particular facts.

2.3 Opposition rights grounds

All of the grounds available in opposition proceedings are also available in invalidity proceedings. These grounds are listed below and are discussed in detail in chapters 10-14. The first three rely on "earlier trade marks" (as defined in section 10.1 of Chapter 10).

- Earlier trade marks that are identical to the attacked mark and are protected in respect of identical goods and/or services to those covered by the attacked registration (the ***'double identity ground'***).
- Earlier trade marks that are:
  - identical to the attacked mark and are protected in respect of similar goods and/or services to those covered by the attacked registration;
  - similar to the attacked mark and are protected in respect of identical goods and/or services to those covered by the attacked registration; or
  - similar to the attacked mark and are protected in respect of similar goods and/or services to those covered by the attacked registration,

  and there is a "likelihood of consumer confusion" as a result of the similarity between the marks and/or the coverage (the ***'confusion ground'***).
- Earlier trade marks that are identical or similar to the attacked mark where the following criteria are satisfied:
  - the earlier trade mark was registered at the filing date of the attacked mark;
  - the earlier trade mark had a reputation in the territory in which it was protected (ie, in the Union for an EUTM registration or in the relevant Member State for a national registration);
  - the use of the attacked mark would take unfair advantage of, or be detrimental to, the distinctive character or repute of the earlier trade mark; and
  - the use of the attacked mark is without due cause (the ***'reputation ground'***).
- The application was filed by an agent or representative in its own name without the consent of the 'true proprietor' of that mark (the ***'agent/representative ground'***).
- At the time of filing, the application conflicted with rights in an unregistered trade mark or other sign used in the course of trade giving protection in one or more Member States, provided that the rights in the relevant mark or sign:
  - were of more than mere local significance;
  - were acquired before the filing date of the attacked registration (taking

  - into account any relevant priority claims); and
  - enabled those who hold them to prohibit the use of a subsequent trade mark (the ***'unregistered rights ground'***).
- The application conflicted with a protected designation of origin ('PDO') or protected geographical indication ('PGI'), provided that:
  - an application for a PDO or PGI was filed before the filing date of the attacked registration (taking into account any relevant priority claims);
  - the PDO or PGI was successfully protected on the relevant register; and
  - the PDO or PGI gave the right to prohibit the use of a subsequent trade mark (the ***'PDO/PGI ground'***).

The fact that the opposition grounds are all available in invalidity proceedings means that if an opposition deadline is missed (or for whatever reason the owner of relevant earlier rights decides not to oppose an EUTM application) there is another chance to attack a problematic right.

If an opposition against an EUTM application was unsuccessful, it is possible for the unsuccessful opponent to file an invalidity action against that application once it proceeds to registration. If, however, the same rights, grounds and evidence are relied on, a different outcome is unlikely.

2.4 Other IP rights ground

This ground involves the invalidity applicant relying on an IP right that cannot be used as the basis of an opposition. Like the bad faith ground discussed above, it can only be relied on in invalidity proceedings.

This ground allows an EUTM registration to be declared invalid where the use of the registered mark is prohibited pursuant to an earlier right under Union law or national law in a Member State. The Regulation lists the following specific examples of rights that may be relied on under this ground:

- *a right to a name* – eg, Spanish law prevents the titles of nobles (such as 'Marquesado de Del Bosque') being used without their permission;
- *a right of personal portrayal* – eg, French law prevents the reproduction of use of a person's image without his consent;
- *a copyright* – in all Member States, the reproduction of a copyright work without the consent of the copyright holder can be prevented; and
- *an industrial property right* – the most common right relied on here is some form of design right, giving protection either Union-wide or at the national level within one or more Member States.

It is for the invalidity applicant to provide details of the right in question, as well as the applicable law under which use of the registered mark is therefore prohibited. Most of the rights relied on under this ground are national rights in Member States. However, it also includes both registered and unregistered Union-wide design rights. In the case of reliance on Union-wide registered design rights (ie, RCD rights), the applicable law does not have to be explained to the Office as it is the body that deals with RCDs.

3. Overview of the Office's invalidity procedure

Despite being contentious proceedings, an invalidity action is a type of application. As a result, some of the principles relating to EUTM applications apply. As with EUTM applications, there is no deadline by which to file an invalidity action.

Invalidity proceedings consist of four key stages:

- filing;
- admissibility checks;
- the adversarial stage; and
- decision.

What happens during each of these stages is summarised in the flowchart below and discussed in the paragraphs that follow. Unlike opposition proceedings, there is no 'cooling off' period in invalidity proceedings.

Summary of invalidity proceedings

EUTM registration granted

↓

Application for a declaration of invalidity filed

↓

Admissibility checks

↓

EUTM proprietor's evidence & submissions

↓

Invalidity applicant's evidence & submissions

↓

EUTM proprietor's reply

↓

Decision

4. Filing an invalidity action

This section examines the filing stage of invalidity proceedings at the Office.

4.1 How to file an invalidity action

Various requirements must be met for an application for a declaration of invalidity to be validly filed. The application must be filed in writing and an official fee paid (€630 at the time of writing). The Office provides an official form that may be used. Although the form does not have to be used, it includes fields for all the information required to file a valid invalidity action, so using it is highly advisable, particularly when the language considerations set out in section 5 of this chapter are taken into account.

An application for a declaration of invalidity must be submitted directly to the Office, by post, by hand or by fax. The completed form should be signed and the name of the signatory must be indicated. It is not yet possible to file invalidity actions electronically.

4.2 Payment of the official fee

The first thing the Office checks upon receipt of an application for a declaration of invalidity is that the official fee has been paid. If it has not, the Office sets the invalidity applicant a deadline (usually one month) by which to pay it. If the money is not received within this timeframe, the application is treated as never having been filed. If the fees are paid late, or if the action is later withdrawn as a result of amicable settlement by the parties, the fees are not refunded. This contrasts with opposition proceedings that are resolved during the cooling off period (see Chapter 14).

The only time an application for a declaration of invalidity may be treated as validly filed despite payment not having reached the Office until after the deadline set is where the invalidity applicant can prove that payment instructions were given to a bank before the deadline. If the instructions were given within the last 10 days before the deadline, a surcharge of 10% of the official fee must also be paid, but not if the instructions were given more than 10 days before the deadline.

The filing date of a validly filed application for a declaration of invalidity is the date on which the written statement is received by the Office, not the date on which the fee is paid. While a successful invalidity action results in the attacked registration being deemed never to have existed, the date of filing of the application for a declaration of invalidity can be important where the action is based on relative rights. As discussed further at section 10.2 below, if the earlier trade mark rights relied on under the relative opposition grounds had themselves been on the Register for five years or more at the date of filing of the application for a declaration of invalidity, the EUTM proprietor can request that the invalidity applicant files proof of use evidence.

4.3 When can an invalidity action be filed?

An invalidity action can only be filed against an EUTM registration; it cannot be filed against a pending application. There is no requirement for the attacked registration to have been on the Register for a minimum amount of time before an invalidity action can be filed.

If, however, there is a delay between registration and the bringing of an invalidity action, the invalidity applicant may have to deal with *res judicata* issues (see section 10.6), acquiescence issues (see section 10.7) and/or proof of use issues (see section 10.2). It is therefore usually a good idea to file an application for a declaration of invalidity as early as possible.

4.4 Who can file an invalidity action?

An invalidity action based on absolute grounds can be filed by any natural or legal person, or by any group or body set up for the purpose of representing the interests of manufacturers, producers, suppliers of services, traders or consumers, which under the terms of the law governing it has the capacity in its own name to sue and be sued. An invalidity applicant does not have to explain why it decided to file the action.

An invalidity action based on relative grounds can only be filed by the natural or legal persons entitled to rely on those grounds. Details of who can rely on each of the opposition rights grounds are set out at section 4 of Chapter 11. With regard to the other IP rights ground discussed at section 2.4 above, this can be relied on by those who own the rights in question or those entitled under the law concerned to exercise those rights.

4.5 Filing a valid invalidity action

In order to be deemed validly filed, an application for a declaration of invalidity must include the following information:

- the registration number of the EUTM registration in respect of which invalidation is sought;
- the name and address of the proprietor of the attacked EUTM registration;
- a clear indication of the goods and/or services in respect of which invalidation is sought;
- a clear indication of the ground(s) on which the application for a declaration of invalidity is based;
- the name and address of the invalidity applicant; and
- the name and business address of the invalidity applicant's representative if one has been appointed (or is required, as discussed in section 6.1 below).

The application should be accompanied by supporting evidence, as well as any legal arguments upon which the invalidity applicant wishes to rely. It is not enough simply to complete the official form. Rather, the case being made needs to be clear from the outset, as the burden is on the invalidity applicant to prove that the registration in question should never have been allowed on the Register. As there is no deadline for the invalidity applicant to meet when filing an application for a declaration of invalidity, it is for that applicant to ensure that it has assembled all necessary materials and evidence before the action is filed. The points set out in section 8 of Chapter 13 should be taken into consideration when filing evidence in support of an invalidity action.

Where the invalidity action is based on relative grounds, the individual rights relied on should each be identified, in line with the requirements set out in sections 5.3 and 5.4 of Chapter 11. In addition, the application for a declaration of invalidity should be accompanied by evidence demonstrating the existence and validity of the earlier rights relied on, as well as the entitlement of the invalidity applicant to rely on them. In this regard, the substantiation requirements set out at section 3 of Chapter 13 apply for the opposition rights grounds. In the case of the other IP rights ground, the invalidity applicant should identify the right in question, as well as the relevant law, and should provide a detailed explanation of why the case is made out under that law.

Irrespective of the ground(s) relied on, the invalidity applicant should also ensure that it files any supporting legal arguments or other submissions on which it wishes to rely in support of its case.

If any of the information set out above is missing, the Office issues a deficiency notice and sets the invalidity applicant a deadline by which to provide it (as discussed further at section 7 below). It should, however, be noted that the Office does not inform the invalidity applicant of any deficiencies in the evidence substantiating its case (or demonstrating its entitlement to rely on the rights in question). There is no substantiation deadline as such in invalidity proceedings. Rather, the invalidity applicant can substantiate the earlier rights relied on at any time before the adversarial stage of the case ends. However, bearing in mind that this can happen just after the EUTM proprietor's first deadline (if it does not file anything), it is always sensible to include all such evidence at the time of filing the invalidity action.

5. Languages to be used

As with opposition proceedings, there are important considerations when filing an invalidity action in relation to both the language of the proceedings and the language in which the application for a declaration of invalidity is filed.

5.1 Language of the proceedings

Every EUTM application has to indicate both a first and a second language; and at least the second language has to be one of the Languages of the Office (see Chapter 5, section 10). The language of invalidity proceedings is dictated by the languages indicated in the application for the EUTM registration that is being attacked.

The starting position is that the language of the invalidity proceedings must be both one of the languages of the attacked EUTM registration and one of the Languages of the Office. It is, however, open to the parties to agree otherwise, in which case the language must be one of the Languages of the Union.

Where both the first and second languages of an EUTM registration are Languages of the Office, the invalidity applicant has a choice over which to use as the language of the invalidity proceedings. If the invalidity applicant fails to indicate which of the two possible languages is to be the language of the proceedings (which can be done by filing the application for a declaration of invalidity in one of those languages), a deficiency notice is issued and the invalidity applicant is asked to indicate the language of the proceedings.

Where only the second language of an EUTM registration is a Language of the Office, the invalidity proceedings must take place in that language (unless the parties agree otherwise). Thus, failure to indicate the language of the proceedings in the application for a declaration of invalidity or indicating an incorrect language has no effect. No deficiency notice is issued as there is only one possible language for the proceedings.

All of the above is subject to the proviso that the parties to invalidity proceedings may agree that a different Language of the Union is to be the language of the proceedings. Any such agreement should be communicated to the Office within two months of the date the EUTM proprietor is notified of the invalidity action by the Office. The invalidity applicant has a further month from this date to file a translation of the application for a declaration of invalidity into that language if it was initially filed in another language. If either of these deadlines is missed, the language remains unchanged. In certain circumstances, missing either of these deadlines can result in the application being deemed inadmissible (see section 7 below).

Although it is generally preferable to file all observations and evidence in the language of the proceedings, it is technically open to the parties to each use any

Language of the Office during the course of proceedings, provided that appropriate translations are provided. What needs to be translated, and the deadlines for providing such translations, is affected by the grounds relied upon, the stage the proceedings have reached and which party is filing the relevant documents. In addition, a distinction is drawn between evidence and observations (ie, arguments/ submissions filed in support of a party's position).

Key considerations in this regard are as follows:

- *Application for a declaration of invalidity:* The language requirements of the application for a declaration of invalidity itself, and the associated translation requirements, are discussed at section 5.2 of this chapter.
- *Invalidity applicant's evidence:* The general principle is that any evidence filed by the invalidity applicant that is not in the language of the proceedings must be translated into that language within two months of being filed. This includes evidence filed together with the invalidity application as well as evidence filed in response to documents filed by the EUTM proprietor.

  The Office does not notify the invalidity applicant of this two-month deadline – the invalidity applicant is expected to be aware of it and to satisfy the deadline on its own initiative. Failure to provide the translations generally results in the evidence not being taken into account. However, where the translations are required to assess the admissibility of the invalidity action in the first place, the Office issues a deficiency notice and sets a deadline by which the invalidity applicant must file them. Failure to provide the translations in these circumstances can result in the application for a declaration of invalidity being deemed inadmissible.

  If the invalidity action includes relative rights grounds and the invalidity applicant is put to proof of use of some or all of the rights relied on, the proof of use evidence can be filed in any Language of the Union. If this is a language other than the language of the proceedings, there is no automatic requirement to file a translation. Rather, the Office exercises discretion and sets a deadline for filing translations of any particular pieces of evidence for which it deems this to be necessary (which can be in response to comments from the invalidity applicant). The general principle in this regard is that it should be possible for the invalidity applicant (and the Office) to determine from the evidence what is being shown. Failure to satisfy this deadline results in the pieces of evidence in question being excluded from the proceedings.
- *EUTM proprietor's evidence:* The EUTM proprietor may submit evidence in any Language of the Union. A translation of such documents only has to be provided if the Office specifically requests it, in which case a deadline is set for the EUTM proprietor. If such a request is made but not satisfied, the documents in question are not taken into account in the proceedings.
- *Observations:* Any observations filed by either party during the course of proceedings can be filed in any Language of the Office. If the language in question is not the language of the proceedings, the observations should be translated into the language of the proceedings within one month of their initial submission.

The one-month deadline is the same irrespective of the initial deadline for filing the observations. For example, an EUTM proprietor may be set a deadline of 16 February 2017 to file observations in response to an invalidity action. If it files observations in a Language of the Office that is not the language of the proceedings on 10 February 2017, the translation of those observations must be filed by 10 March 2017.

The Office does not notify the parties of this one-month deadline for filing the translation – they are expected to be aware of it and to satisfy it on their own initiative. Failure to provide a translation results in the observations being deemed never to have been filed and therefore not taken into account in the proceedings.

5.2 Language of the application for a declaration of invalidity

The application for a declaration of invalidity must be filed in one of the Languages of the Office. However, the Office's official invalidity form is available in 23 of the 24 Languages of the Union (it is not available in Irish). Where the Office's form is used, the invalidity action is deemed admissible if any of the 23 language versions is used, provided the form is completed in one of the Languages of the Office so far as textual elements are concerned.

Where the invalidity action is filed in one of the Languages of the Office but not the language of the proceedings (and the parties have not entered into an agreement regarding the language of the proceedings), the invalidity applicant must file a translation into the language of the proceedings within one month of filing the application. The invalidity applicant is expected to satisfy this deadline on its own initiative and is not notified of it by the Office.

If the application for a declaration of invalidity is filed in a Language of the Union other than one of the Languages of the Office, it is deemed inadmissible unless the parties notify the Office within two months of the filing that they have agreed upon the language in which it was filed as the language of the proceedings.

6. Representation

There are two issues to consider here:

- representation of the invalidity applicant, and
- representation of the EUTM proprietor.

6.1 Representation of the invalidity applicant

As with the filing of EUTM applications, where an invalidity applicant is domiciled in, has its principal place of business in, or has a real and effective industrial or commercial establishment in the EEA, there is no requirement for a representative to be appointed (see Chapter 2, section 10 for more information).

Where, however, the above criteria are not met, an invalidity applicant must be represented before the Office. If this is the case but no representative has been appointed at the time of filing the invalidity action (or if any such representative withdraws during the course of the proceedings), the Office issues a deficiency notice and sets the invalidity applicant a deadline by which it must appoint a suitable representative.

6.2 Representation of the EUTM proprietor

An EUTM proprietor who is not domiciled in the EEA and does not have a place of business or a real and effective industrial or commercial establishment in the EEA should be represented before the Office. In practice, a representative will almost always have been appointed during the initial application procedure.

Where the EUTM proprietor is not represented (but needs to be), the Office invites it to appoint a representative. If it fails to do so, procedural statements made by the proprietor are not taken into account and the case is dealt with on the basis of the evidence before the Office (including evidence filed directly by the EUTM proprietor). The EUTM registration is not cancelled simply because the EUTM proprietor is not represented after registration.

7. Admissibility checks and deficiencies

Once the Office is satisfied that the official fee has been duly paid (see section 4.2 above), it proceeds by completing admissibility checks.

An invalidity action is automatically deemed inadmissible if, at the time of filing the action:

- the right against which the application was filed was not yet registered;
- the right against which the application was filed no longer existed, as it had already been surrendered, cancelled or allowed to lapse;
- there is *res judicata*, ie, the matter to be decided had already been the subject of a final decision issued either by the Office or an EUTM Court in proceedings between the same parties (see section 10.6 below);
- it is not the first relative grounds invalidity application filed against the EUTM registration in question by the invalidity applicant and is based on rights that could have been relied on in an earlier unsuccessful attack (see section 10.5 below); or
- the application is filed in an incorrect language and no translation has been provided within the timeframe for doing so (as set out in section 5 above).

Where any of these issues apply, the Office simply provides the applicant with an opportunity to comment on the admissibility of the application. If the Office maintains its view (which it almost always does), the application for a declaration of invalidity is deemed inadmissible and a decision to that effect is issued. The invalidity applicant cannot remedy these deficiencies.

Where any of the information set out at section 4.5 above is not provided at the time of filing, the Office issues a deficiency notice and sets the invalidity applicant a deadline by which to provide it. This is usually a two-month non-extendable deadline. If the information is not provided within this period, the application for a declaration of invalidity is rejected as inadmissible, unless the application includes multiple grounds and the missing information does not relate to all the grounds. If this is the case, the application can continue for those grounds for which the necessary information has been provided.

If both invalidity and revocation grounds are included in a single application, the Office issues a deficiency notice and sets the cancellation applicant a deadline by which to choose between invalidity proceedings and revocation proceedings. If it fails to do so, the application is rejected as inadmissible and does not proceed, either as an invalidity or as a revocation application. If a choice is made, the applicant can file a separate application for the type of action that has not been chosen, subject to payment of the relevant fee.

8. Notification of the invalidity action

Once the admissibility checks have been carried out, the Office notifies the EUTM proprietor that the invalidity action has been filed. If no relative admissibility issues have been raised, the notification includes an indication of the deadline by which the EUTM proprietor can file a response to the action.

The Office normally gives the EUTM proprietor three months to file its response. This deadline can be extended once by a further two months. Additional extensions are only granted in exceptional circumstances. However, this deadline is one for which continuation of proceedings can be utilised, as indeed are all the deadlines in the adversarial stage of invalidity proceedings (see Chapter 27), so that it is possible for the EUTM proprietor to obtain more time to respond if necessary.

If relative admissibility deficiencies are raised during the admissibility checks, the EUTM proprietor is still notified of the application for a declaration of invalidity after the initial admissibility checks are completed. It is also informed of the deficiencies, although the EUTM proprietor's deadline to respond is not set until after these deficiencies are remedied.

Further deadlines are not set down at the notification stage, as they ultimately depend on whether the EUTM proprietor files anything. This is unlike opposition proceedings, primarily because the invalidity applicant has to file all supporting evidence up front. In opposition proceedings, the opponent is given time after the filing of the opposition to substantiate its case. However, there is a non-extendable deadline by which an opposition must be filed, whereas the timing of the filing of an application for a declaration of invalidity is at the discretion of the invalidity applicant. (See chapters 10-14 for more information on opposition proceedings.)

9. Adversarial stage of proceedings

Once an application for a declaration of invalidity has been deemed admissible, the proceedings enter the adversarial stage. The Office has discretion as to the number of rounds of evidence and observations that are permitted. The usual running order is, however, as follows:

- EUTM proprietor's deadline to file submissions and evidence in support of its case, as discussed in section 8 above;
- invalidity applicant's deadline to respond; and
- EUTM proprietor's deadline to respond to anything further filed by the invalidity applicant.

The adversarial stage of proceedings is closed earlier if either party fails to meet one of its deadlines (as there is nothing to which the other party can respond). Indeed, it is not mandatory for the EUTM proprietor to file a response in invalidity proceedings and, unlike under some national systems, the invalidity action does not automatically succeed if no response is filed. However, if the proprietor has any interest in maintaining the registration, it is highly recommended that a response be filed.

The content of observations and evidence depends on the invalidity grounds as well as on the facts of the case. Although they can be combined in a single invalidity action, it is useful to consider absolute grounds and relative grounds separately.

The points set out at section 5.1 regarding the language to be used for both observations and evidence should be noted, as well as those regarding translations.

9.1 EUTM proprietor's response to the invalidity action

The EUTM proprietor's response often takes the form of written arguments, highlighting any flaws or weaknesses in the evidence and/or arguments presented by the invalidity applicant. If, however, there is evidence that can be used to rebut the case put forward by the invalidity applicant, the EUTM proprietor should ensure that this is filed. As with all evidence filed at the Office, the more independent in nature it is, the greater the weight it is likely to be given.

Some of the specific issues that can be raised by an EUTM proprietor when responding to an invalidity action are considered below in section 10.

9.2 Reply evidence

If the proprietor does not file anything to satisfy its deadline, the Office writes to the parties indicating that the adversarial stage of the proceedings is complete. It then takes a decision on the substance of the case.

Where the proprietor files evidence (or a proof of use request) within its deadline, a copy is sent to the invalidity applicant by the Office. The invalidity applicant is given a two-month time period within which to file a reply. This deadline can be extended once, by two months, without the need to give reasons (so long as the extension request is filed and received before the deadline expires). Further extensions are generally only granted in exceptional circumstances. Other than where a proof of use request is filed, the invalidity applicant does not have to file anything and, if it does not do so, the adversarial stage of proceedings is closed and the Office takes a decision on the basis of the evidence and arguments filed.

If a proof of use request is filed, the invalidity applicant must file evidence of use of the rights to which the request relates, or proper reasons for non-use. See Chapter 13, section 6 for discussion of proof of use evidence. If no proof of use evidence or reasons for non-use is filed, the invalidity application is rejected to the extent that it relies on the rights covered by the request.

Where proof of use evidence or reasons for non-use (or indeed any further evidence or submissions) is filed by the invalidity applicant, the EUTM proprietor is given a chance to file a reply. Where limited or weak evidence of use is filed, the EUTM proprietor may wish to file submissions highlighting the weaknesses or problems with the evidence (eg, if appropriate translations have not been filed, or the evidence is not dated). Care should, however, be taken when doing so as this can result in the invalidity applicant being given an opportunity to supplement or amend its evidence.

Any reply evidence (filed by either party) should, in theory, be limited to addressing only the points and evidence submitted by the other party. Evidence on new points not previously raised by either party, or additional evidence to support points already raised but not previously addressed, should not be filed at this stage. In practice, however, the Office does not automatically exclude such evidence. Thus, if useful evidence becomes available at this stage, it is sensible to file it.

Once the proprietor's reply deadline has passed, the Office usually considers the adversarial stage of proceedings complete and takes a decision.

10. Issues the EUTM proprietor may raise in response to an invalidity action

The EUTM proprietor's response to an invalidity action will vary depending on the grounds relied on in the action. Some of the issues that may be relevant are considered in this section.

10.1 Acquired distinctiveness

This is relevant where any of the following absolute grounds are relied on by the invalidity applicant:

- lack of distinctiveness;
- descriptive trade marks; or
- customary (generic) signs or indications.

The EUTM proprietor can prevent an invalidity action succeeding by showing that the mark in question had acquired distinctiveness either before the filing or priority date of the original application or after registration in relation to the goods and/or services covered. Evidence that the mark acquired distinctiveness between filing and registration is also sufficient to defeat an invalidity action based on the three grounds listed above. More information is provided on acquired distinctiveness in section 4 of Chapter 8.

10.2 Proof of use

In the case of an invalidity application based on earlier EUTM registrations and/or earlier national trade mark registrations that had been registered for five years or longer by the filing date of the invalidity action, the EUTM proprietor can request that the invalidity applicant files proof of use of the mark or marks at issue (or proper reasons for non-use). For a detailed discussion of proof of use see Chapter 13, section 6.

Two time periods need to be considered for proof of use in invalidity actions:

- the five-year period immediately before the date the invalidity action was filed; and
- the five-year period immediately before the filing date (or the priority date if priority was claimed) of the attacked EUTM registration, if the rights in question had been registered for five years at the filing date of the attacked registration.

Proof of use evidence should cover both of these periods for any rights to which they both apply.

Where the invalidity action is not based solely on rights that are subject to a proof of use request (ie, where other rights and/or grounds have also been relied on) the EUTM proprietor should not simply request that proof of use is filed. In addition, it is sensible for it to file observations and evidence in response to those other rights and/or grounds, together with the proof of use request. The reason for this is that there will not be a further opportunity for it to file observations or evidence if no proof of use evidence is filed.

10.3 Reputation and due cause

Where the invalidity action is based on earlier rights with a reputation, failure by the EUTM proprietor to demonstrate that it has due cause to make use of the mark applied for in relation to the goods and/or services covered by the attacked registration is taken to mean that there is no such due cause. Thus, where the proprietor does have due cause to use the mark, it should file evidence to prove positively that this is the case.

10.4 Consent

Another possible response that may be filed by the EUTM proprietor is that the invalidity applicant consented to the registration that is now being attacked. In these circumstances, the proprietor should file clear evidence of express consent. The consent should have been given before the date on which the invalidity application was filed. It does not have to have been given before the filing date of the attacked right.

10.5 Prohibition on multiple invalidity actions

As set out at section 7 above, an invalidity application is inadmissible if it is not the first relative grounds invalidity application filed against the EUTM in question by the invalidity applicant and is based on rights that could have been relied on in an earlier unsuccessful attack. Where the Office is not aware that this is the case when carrying out admissibility checks, the EUTM proprietor should provide evidence to this effect in advance of its first deadline. This provision overlaps with *res judicata*, which is considered in section 10.6 below.

10.6 *Res judicata*

The term '*res judicata*' translates into English as 'a matter judged'. This principle prohibits the filing of an invalidity action (or, in some circumstances, a revocation action) where either the Office or an EUTM Court has issued a final decision in an earlier action that related to:

- *the same subject-matter as the current invalidity action* – there will only be *res judicata* where the previous action related to the same EUTM right. Where the invalidity action is based on different grounds or rights to those in the first action, the invalidity action is admissible (subject to the rules prohibiting multiple invalidity actions considered in section 10.5 above);
- *the same cause of action as the current invalidity action* – an unsuccessful opposition against an EUTM application does not prevent an invalidity

action being filed against the resulting EUTM registration. If, however, the same rights, grounds and evidence are relied on, a different outcome is unlikely; and

- *the same parties* – where a different party to that involved in the earlier proceedings files the invalidity action, the action is admissible.

Res judicata is only applicable where the Office or an EUTM Court takes a final decision in the earlier proceedings. If the previous action was withdrawn or declared inadmissible, this does not prevent the same party filing an invalidity action on exactly the same grounds as the previous action.

10.7 Acquiescence

The EUTM proprietor may also seek to prove that the invalidity applicant acquiesced in the EUTM proprietor's use of the attacked mark. Where this is the case, the EUTM right in question cannot be declared invalid, unless it was applied for in bad faith.

Acquiescence can only be relied on where:

- the mark in question was used within the Union for a continuous period of five years;
- the invalidity applicant was aware of this use (or can reasonably be assumed to have been aware of it); and
- the invalidity applicant did not take any action to stop the use.

It is for the EUTM proprietor to prove that these requirements are all made out. The acquiescence should have been for five years or more – ie, there must have been five years of use without action by the invalidity applicant after the date on which the invalidity applicant became aware of the use. Acquiescence does not apply where the relative ground relied on is the PGO/PGI ground.

Where the requirements for acquiescence are proved, the invalidity action will fail in relation to those goods and/or services in relation to which there was use. Despite maintaining its EUTM rights, however, the EUTM proprietor cannot rely on those rights to prevent use of the earlier rights by the invalidity applicant.

11. Oral proceedings

It is technically possible for the parties to invalidity proceedings to request an oral hearing at any stage during the proceedings (and also technically possible for the Office to insist that an oral hearing takes place). In reality, however, the Office never suggests such hearings, and rejects any requests in this regard from the parties to invalidity proceedings.

Although hearings never happen in practice, there are rules surrounding the procedure for parties to appear before the Office. Where the Office summons parties to appear, it must give them a minimum of one month's notice, unless they have expressly agreed to a shorter period. The legal provisions relating to oral proceedings make clear that any such hearings in relation to invalidity proceedings are open to the public, unless it is felt that admission of the public could seriously disadvantage one of the parties or otherwise cause serious problems.

The lack of oral hearings in practice means that both parties should work on the assumption that their only chance to present their case will be in written form.

12. Decision

Once the adversarial stage is complete, the Office notifies the parties that this is the case and takes a decision on the basis of the evidence and arguments that have been filed.

Invalidity decisions are always issued in writing, and must include the date of the decision, as well as details of the parties. The date is a crucial piece of information, as it is used for calculating the deadline to file an appeal against the decision (as discussed further in Chapter 20).

A decision in invalidity proceedings always includes a decision on the apportionment of costs. The costs in invalidity proceedings are limited to the official cancellation fee and the representation costs of the parties (if they are professionally represented). These costs are always expressed in Euros.

The basic principle is that the 'winning' party is awarded costs from the 'losing party. If the invalidity action succeeds in full, the EUTM proprietor has to pay the invalidity applicant both the amount of the official fee and an amount towards the latter's representation costs. The level is the same for both parties, so that if the invalidity action fails in full, the invalidity applicant has to pay the EUTM proprietor an amount towards the latter's representation costs.

Where an invalidity action succeeds in part and is rejected in part, both parties are deemed to be partially successful, in which case they each have to bear their own costs.

In practice, the representation costs are set at a very low level, irrespective of the actual costs incurred in engaging professional representatives. At the time of writing. the amount of costs awarded for representation are fixed at €450.

13. Appeals

It is possible to file an appeal against the decision to deem an invalidity action admissible, as well as against the substantive decision in the invalidity action itself. As a decision to deem an invalidity action admissible does not terminate the invalidity proceedings, it can only be appealed together with the final invalidity decision. It is not possible to delay or avoid the substantive invalidity proceedings by appealing the admissibility decision at the time it is issued. The appeals process is discussed in chapters 19 and 20.

Further reference

Regulation – Articles 7, 8, 52-57, 77
Implementing Regulation – Rules 22, 37-40, 55, 79
Office Guidelines – Part C, Section 6 and Part D
The Office's online summary of invalidity and invalidity proceedings: https://euipo.europa.eu/ohimportal/en/invalidity-and-invalidity
Chocoladefabriken Lindt & Sprüngli AG v Franz Hauswirth GmbH (Case No C-529/07) ('*Lindt*') – both CJEU judgment and Advocate General's opinion

pelicantravel.com sro v OHIM, intervener Pelikan Vertriebsgesellschaft mbH & Co KG (*'Pelikan'*) (Case No T-136/11)

Chapter 19: Overview and the Boards of Appeal

1. Introduction

This chapter contains an overview of the EUTM appeals process, together with details of the structure and operation of the Boards of Appeal, which is the division of the Office responsible for deciding appeals against decisions of the Office.

Chapter 20 discusses the appeals process in more detail, as well as the Office's mediation service and possible further appeals that can be filed after a Board of Appeal has taken a decision.

The EUTM appeals process is relatively straightforward and inexpensive. The arguments and evidence filed before the Office as part of the proceedings to which the appeal relates can be referred to in the appeal. As with oppositions and cancellation actions, only very limited costs awards are given in appeal proceedings. As a result, a large number of appeals are filed. The most recent *Annual Report* of the Office (for 2014) shows that 3284 appeals were filed in 2014 and that the Boards of Appeal issued 2783 decisions. These figures continue to rise every year. The success rate for appeals is not very high: the Boards of Appeal refuse over 80% of appeals relating to absolute grounds refusals and over 65% of appeals relating to oppositions and cancellation actions.

2. What can be appealed?

It is possible to appeal every decision made by Examiners, the Opposition Divisions, the Cancellation Divisions and the department in charge of the Register.

There are, however, two caveats to this:

- *It is only possible to appeal 'decisions', as opposed to other communications received from the Office.* This is not ordinarily a problem, as most communications lead to a decision that can be appealed. For example, it is not possible to appeal against objections raised by the Office that a mark is not capable of registration: when, however, that objection becomes final, the Office issues a decision that can be appealed. Further, the Office informs parties to proceedings when an appeal can be filed, either in the decision itself or in a letter accompanying that decision, and gives details of the appeal deadline.
- *It is only possible to file an appeal after a 'final', as opposed to an 'interlocutory', decision has been taken.* Interlocutory decisions can be appealed, but it is not possible to appeal such a decision until a final decision has been issued in those proceedings. For example, if an opponent requests an extension of time to file evidence but its request is refused, it cannot immediately appeal

against that decision. When, however, the final decision in the opposition has been taken, the opponent can at that point appeal against both the refusal to grant the extension of time and any aspect of the final decision against which it wants to appeal.

It is also worth noting that a decision is 'final' if it ends proceedings for a particular party. For example, if an opposition is filed in joint names against an EUTM application, a decision that one of the opponents cannot continue in the proceedings can be appealed by that party, even though the opposition proceedings remain ongoing.

3. Who can file an appeal?

An appeal can be filed by any party to proceedings who is adversely affected by a decision taken by the Office.

It is rare that a person or entity who is not a party to proceedings is adversely affected by a decision, so this is not generally a problem. However, it means that, for example, it is not possible for a person or entity submitting observations (see Chapter 9, section 5) to file an appeal if those observations are ignored.

It is not necessary to obtain permission before an appeal is filed: the right to appeal is automatic whenever the Office issues a decision.

When an appeal is filed, any other parties to the relevant proceedings automatically become parties (technically, respondents) to the appeal. All respondents are entitled to file submissions and evidence in response to the appeal – and it is possible for a respondent to file submissions requesting that any part of the decision being appealed be annulled or amended, even if those parts of the decision are not challenged by the appellant. This means that, if an appeal is filed in *inter partes* proceedings, an appellant cannot limit the scope of the appeal: all parts of the original decision can be challenged by the respondent. The respondent cannot, however, continue to challenge the original decision if the appeal is withdrawn – if this happens, the respondent's challenge falls away (unless of course the respondent has also filed an appeal).

4. Overview of the appeal process

A detailed description of the appeal process is contained in Chapter 20. The following flowchart gives a basic overview of the steps in the appeal process.

The EUTM appeal process

Notice of Appeal (within two months of decision)

↓

Statement of Grounds (within four months of decision)

↓

If only one party in proceedings – revision considered

↓

If two or more parties – respondent's submissions and evidence, then possibly reply

↓

Decision

5. The Boards of Appeal

All EUTM (and RCD) appeal decisions are taken by the Boards of Appeal, which technically form part of the Office but function independently of the other divisions. A number of different bodies make up the Boards of Appeal:

- *the ordinary Boards of Appeal* – there are five different Boards of Appeal, each of which has a Chairperson and contains between four and eight members;
- *the Grand Board* – this sits alongside the ordinary Boards of Appeal and takes decisions in the most difficult and/or important appeals. It consists of nine people: a Chairperson; the Chairpersons of the other Boards of Appeal; and members taken from the Boards of Appeal on a rotational basis. Currently, the Chairperson of the Grand Board is also the Chairperson of the First and Third Boards of Appeal, hence the need for five rotating members;
- *the Presidium* – this is responsible for putting in place the rules under which the Boards of Appeal operate, as well as how appeals (and members) are allocated to the Boards of Appeal; and
- *the Registry* – this is responsible for the administration of all EUTM (and RCD) appeals, including the allocation of appeals between Boards of Appeal. As a consequence, the Registry deals with all correspondence relating to appeals sent to or by the Boards of Appeal, ensures deadlines are complied with and maintains the relevant files.

There is a President of the Boards of Appeal, appointed by the Council (which also appoints the Chairpersons of the individual Boards of Appeal). The President of the Boards of Appeal has a number of functions and chairs both the Presidium and the Grand Board.

The members of the Boards of Appeal are independent of any of the other activities of the Office. As such, they cannot be Examiners or members of the Opposition Divisions, Cancellation Divisions or the department in charge of the Register.

6. The allocation of cases between Boards of Appeal

The Registry allocates every appeal to a specific Board of Appeal. Currently the Third Board of Appeal only considers RCD appeals, so appeals relating to EUTM applications and registrations are allocated in rotation between the First, Second, Fourth and Fifth Boards of Appeal. There are, however, some exceptions, so that cases are not necessarily allocated in strict rotation. For example, appeals in German are currently never allocated to the Second Board of Appeal.

When a case is allocated to one of the Boards of Appeal, there are three options as to how the appeal is handled.

Decision taken by the Board of Appeal: In most cases, the appeal is considered and a decision taken by three members of the Board of Appeal to which it is allocated, at least two of whom must be legally qualified.

The Chairman of the relevant Board of Appeal designates one of the three members allocated to the appeal as rapporteur. The rapporteur is responsible for reviewing the content of the appeal, including all arguments and evidence filed by the parties, and preparing a draft decision for consideration by the other two members of the Board of Appeal allocated to the appeal. A time period is set for those two members to indicate if they disagree with the draft decision, or think that it should be amended in any way.

If all three members of the Board of Appeal agree with the content of the decision, it is issued as set out in Chapter 20.

If there is any disagreement as to the content of a draft decision, the relevant Board of Appeal meets to discuss the case. The rapporteur speaks first in these discussions and the Chairman of the Board of Appeal speaks last (unless he is also the rapporteur). A vote is then taken and the decision follows the view of the majority.

This is the process followed for most appeals relating to proceedings involving more than one party. There are, however, circumstances in which the allocated Board of Appeal decides that a different approach (one of the two discussed in the paragraphs that follow) is more appropriate.

Decision taken by the Grand Board: The allocated Board of Appeal normally refers an appeal to the Grand Board if it involves an issue of great legal difficulty or importance, or there are other special circumstances (eg, where previous Board of Appeal decisions conflict as to a point of law raised in the appeal).

The Presidium is also empowered to refer appeals to the Grand Board for cases relating to a very difficult or important point of law.

Very few cases are referred to the Grand Board, as the ordinary Boards of Appeal can deal with most issues. This means that referrals are limited to cases in which the outcome is likely to have a very significant impact on Union law or practice or on the parties to the appeal.

If an appeal is referred to the Grand Board after a rapporteur has been appointed (see above), that rapporteur forms part of the Grand Board for the appeal in question. If no rapporteur has already been appointed, the Chairman of the Grand Board designates one.

The rapporteur reviews the appeal and prepares a draft decision in the same way as with most other appeals. The Grand Board then meets to discuss the case and, if there is any disagreement as to the content of a decision, a vote is taken and the majority view followed. The Grand Board cannot meet unless at least seven of its members are present. If there are eight members of the Grand Board present at a meeting and a vote is required, the most junior member of the Grand Board is not able to vote.

Decision taken by a single member of the Board of Appeal: The Chairperson of the Board of Appeal that is allocated a case can devolve the responsibility to decide that case to a single member of that Board of Appeal if three conditions are met:

- the member to whom responsibility is devolved is legally qualified;
- the decision to be taken relates to one of the following:
    - the closure of appeal proceedings following an agreement between the parties;
    - the fixing of the amount of costs payable following an appeal decision;
    - a review of the amount of costs awarded following an appeal decision;
    - the admissibility of the appeal, where the necessary criteria and deadlines do not appear to have been met;
    - appeals against decisions by Examiners to refuse EUTM applications on absolute grounds (see Chapter 7);
- the decision does not relate to difficult factual or legal issues, is not of great importance and there are no other circumstances that mean it would be inappropriate for a decision to be taken by only a single member of a Board of Appeal.

If the above conditions are satisfied, the single member can take a decision without the substantive involvement of any other members of the Board of Appeal. However, this is not done where:

- the member does not believe that the third condition above is met; or
- the decision being appealed relates to a refusal on absolute grounds and the member believes the Examiner's decision should be annulled entirely or in part.

If either of these situations is relevant, the member to whom the decision was devolved refers that decision back to the Board of Appeal for it to consider in the usual way as set out above. In these circumstances, the member normally acts as rapporteur and prepares a draft decision for the Board of Appeal to consider.

Further reference

Regulation – Articles 58-60, 64-65a, 135-137

Commission Regulation (EC) No 216/96 of 5 February 1996, as amended by Regulation (EC) No 2082/2004, laying down the rules of procedure of the Boards of Appeal

The Office's *Annual Reports*: https://euipo.europa.eu/ohimportal/en/annual-report

Chapter 20: The appeals process

1. Introduction

This chapter discusses the appeals process, the Office's mediation service and possible further appeals that can be filed after a Board of Appeal decision has been taken.

2. Time limits for filing an appeal

The time limits for filing an appeal are calculated from the date on which the decision being appealed is deemed to have been notified to the parties in the relevant proceedings (see Chapter 2, section 6 for details of how this date is calculated).

Two different time limits are relevant, both of which must be satisfied for an appeal to be validly filed:

- a Notice of Appeal must be filed, and the appeal fee paid, within two months of the date of notification of the decision; and
- a Statement of Grounds must be filed within four months of the date of notification of the decision.

The contents of both the Notice of Appeal and Statement of Grounds are considered separately below.

The time limits for filing the Notice of Appeal and Statement of Grounds cannot be extended. In addition, it is not possible to apply for continuation of proceedings for either of these time limits (see Chapter 27). It is, however, possible to apply for *restitutio in integrum* in respect of these time limits (see Chapter 26).

3. Notice of Appeal

A Notice of Appeal must contain the following information for it to be validly filed:

- the name and address of the appellant;
- details of the appellant's representative, if one has been appointed;
- an indication of the decision being appealed; and
- an indication of the extent to which the decision is being appealed – it is possible to appeal either the whole of a decision or part of it. If a decision is not appealed in full, it is necessary to indicate very clearly which parts of the decision are being appealed.

The Office has produced a Notice of Appeal form. To ensure that all necessary information is given, appellants are advised to use this form. It is possible to file appeals online and it is recommended that appellants use the online filing portal to file Notices of Appeal, if possible.

Beyond the above information, no further detail needs to be given at the time the Notice of Appeal is filed, due to the additional two months given for the filing of the Statement of Grounds.

4. Language of appeal proceedings

The Notice of Appeal must be filed in the language of the proceedings in which the decision being appealed was taken. If an appeal is filed in a different language, it is rejected as inadmissible, unless a translation is filed (ie, a new Notice of Appeal is filed) before the two-month appeal deadline.

Despite this general rule, there are occasions on which it may not be possible to file an appeal in the language of the proceedings. An obvious example of this is where an opposition was refused because it was filed in the wrong language. In these circumstances, the safest course of action is to file the appeal in the language in which the opposition was filed and also file a translation into a language in which the opposition could definitely have been filed.

5. Appeal fee

The appeal fee must be filed within the same deadline as the Notice of Appeal. At the time of writing, the fee is €720.

As noted above, the deadline for paying the appeal fee cannot be extended and if it is not paid in time, the appeal is deemed never to have been filed. If the appeal fee is paid after the two-month deadline, the fee is refunded.

It is rare for an appeal fee to be refunded at the conclusion of an appeal (assuming the fee is paid within the relevant deadline). A refund is only possible in two circumstances:

- where there is only one party to the appeal and the decision is revised in favour of the appellant, as discussed in section 8 below; and
- where the appeal is entirely successful and the Board of Appeal considers that the appellant was the victim of a substantial procedural violation justifying the reimbursement of the fee.

6. Statement of Grounds

The Statement of Grounds must clearly set out the reasons why the appellant believes the contested decision was wrong and should be cancelled or amended, together with any evidence on which the appellant wishes to rely in the appeal.

An appellant is not given any further opportunity to file arguments or evidence in support of its case, except for evidence in reply where a respondent to the appeal files arguments and/or evidence. As a result, it is important that everything the appellant wants to rely on in the appeal is filed together with the Statement of Grounds.

It is not necessary to re-file documents that were already filed with the Office before the decision being appealed was taken. However, any such documents that the appellant wants to be taken into account should be very clearly identified in the Statement of Grounds. Simply telling the Boards of Appeal that an appellant is relying on everything filed at first instance is not acceptable and is likely to lead to the evidence not being considered in the way intended.

Ordinarily, it is not possible to file additional evidence on appeal, as the appeal decision should be taken on the basis of the evidence on which the contested decision was based. However, the Boards of Appeal have discretion to accept new evidence on appeal, and do so if three criteria are satisfied:

- the additional evidence seems likely to be relevant to the outcome of the proceedings (ie, the evidence may lead to the contested decision being changed);
- the additional evidence strengthens and clarifies evidence submitted within the time limits at first instance (ie, the evidence cannot be unrelated to the evidence filed previously and cannot be used to raise new arguments); and
- the stage of the proceedings at which the additional evidence is filed, and the circumstances surrounding the filing of the evidence, do not lead the Board of Appeal to believe it would be wrong to take the evidence into account (ie, the Board of Appeal does not believe that the party filing the additional evidence is acting in abuse of process, employing deliberate delaying tactics or acting negligently).

Given the above requirements, if an appellant wants to introduce additional evidence, it should be filed with the Statement of Grounds and a clear explanation provided as to why the evidence should be permitted.

Evidence in support of an appeal must be filed in the same format and contain the same information as discussed in Chapter 13, section 8 in the context of opposition proceedings.

7. Admissibility checks and allocation to a Board of Appeal

If a Notice of Appeal does not contain the information set out in section 3 above, or the appeal fee is not paid, the appeal is rejected as inadmissible.

The only exception to this is if the Notice of Appeal does not adequately identify the appellant and/or its representative, in which case the Office issues a deficiency notice and the appellant is given an opportunity to remedy the deficiency.

If the appeal is validly filed, the Registry allocates it to a Board of Appeal. The next steps in the appeal process then differ, depending on the number of parties to the appeal.

8. Procedure in proceedings involving one party

Appeals in proceedings involving only one party generally relate to refusals of applications by Examiners on absolute grounds (see Chapter 7). In addition, such appeals may relate to decisions made by the department in charge of the Register (eg, those relating to the failure to renew an EUTM registration).

The first step in proceedings involving only one party is for the Registry to refer the appeal back to the department which made the contested decision. That department then reconsiders its original decision and, if it is considered that the appeal is well founded, the original decision is rectified. This does not happen very often, except in the case of obvious errors or procedural mistakes, but can be a useful tool to shortcut the need to go through the full appeal process.

If the original decision is not revised within one month, the Registry remits the appeal to the allocated Board of Appeal, which then takes a decision on the appeal. There is no further opportunity for the appellant to provide information or file arguments or evidence.

9. Procedure in proceedings involving two or more parties

As noted above, all parties to the original proceedings that an appeal relates to automatically become parties to the appeal. Where more than one appeal is filed against the same decision, each party that files an appeal becomes both an appellant and a respondent. Where a party does not file an appeal, it is a respondent only.

Appeals in proceedings involving more than one party almost always relate to opposition or cancellation proceedings. It is possible for such appeals to relate to decisions made by the department in charge of the Register (eg, those relating to a refusal to record a change of ownership), but this is rare.

Where there are multiple parties to an appeal, the Registry remits the appeal straight to the Board of Appeal that has been allocated the case. Unlike proceedings involving only one party, the appeal is not sent back to the department that took the contested decision, so there is no potential for the original decision to be revised outside of the appeal process.

Each respondent to an appeal is sent a copy of the Notice of Appeal and the Statement of Grounds and is given two months to file submissions and evidence. This period can be extended once, up to a maximum of four months, but only where all parties to the proceedings consent to the extension (no automatic extension of time is available for a respondent). No further extensions are allowed unless there are very exceptional circumstances.

As noted in Chapter 19, respondents do not need to restrict their submissions and evidence to the parts of the original decision that have been appealed. In addition, respondents can challenge any part of the contested decision that they believe should be annulled or amended. This means that the appellant cannot limit the scope of the appeal to the parts of the decision it is not happy with.

All submissions and evidence filed by respondents are sent to the appellant and a two-month period is set during which submissions and evidence in reply can be filed. It may be possible for this period to be extended once, for a further two months, but all parties to the proceedings need to agree to the extension, so this cannot be relied upon. No further extensions are allowed unless there are very exceptional circumstances. The submissions and evidence must be strictly in reply to the respondent's submissions and evidence, so that it is not possible for new issues or grounds of appeal to be raised at this stage. Appellants do, however, regularly have to file submissions and evidence in reply to challenges made by respondents to aspects of the decision that the appellant did not challenge. This means that evidence in reply quite often expands well beyond the scope of the initial appeal and can be much costlier to put together than would ordinarily be the case.

Once the evidence stages are complete, the Board of Appeal takes a decision.

10. Joinder of proceedings

Where more than one party to proceedings files an appeal against the same decision, the appeals are combined and considered in a single appeal proceeding. As noted above, each party that files an appeal will be both an appellant and a respondent. The periods given to the parties to file their responses run in parallel.

Given that respondents can raise issues not contained in the appeal they are responding to, the fact that the other (or another) party also files an appeal has little practical effect on an appellant. Usually this only means that they file their arguments and evidence relating to issues raised by the other party in response to the other party's appeal, rather than in reply as part of their own appeal. The only real difference for an appellant is that it is able to raise challenges to parts of the decision against which it did not appeal if the other party also appeals, though it is rare that an appellant would want to do this.

It is also possible for appeals relating to decisions in more than one set of proceedings (and/or relating to different EUTM applications or registrations) to be combined in certain circumstances. This can happen where:

- *the appeals relate to the same or an equivalent issue* – as to which, see below;
- *the appeals are designated to the same Board of Appeal* – which is normally the case if it is apparent that they relate to the same or an equivalent issue; and
- *the parties consent* – this situation is likely to apply where the same party or parties are involved in all the appeals, though this is not necessarily the case.

An obvious example of where appeals are consolidated is where two oppositions filed against the same EUTM application are refused on the same basis. In these circumstances, if both opponents appeal it may be appropriate for the appeals to be consolidated.

There are also numerous examples of appeals relating to different EUTM applications or registrations being joined where the applications or registrations relate to variants of the same trade mark (eg, alternative spellings of the same word mark, the same figurative mark applied for in both colour and black and white or different three-dimensional marks applied for in respect of the same goods and for which the same objections are raised). Further, appeals have been combined where the same issue arose, even though the trade marks were very different (eg, where the same term in the specification was refused as being unacceptable in multiple applications).

11. Mediation

The Office offers a mediation service to parties involved in appeal proceedings. This service is not used very often, which is perhaps unsurprising given that by the time an appeal has been filed, the Office has already taken a decision one way or the other. It is, however, an option that should be considered. It is also worth noting that the Regulation empowers the Office to create a Mediation Centre. If mediation becomes an option at first instance, not only on appeal, this service is likely to be more widely used.

A request for mediation must be made jointly by all parties to the appeal proceedings and can be made at any time after an appeal has been filed. The joint request must contain:

- the number of the appeal to which the request relates;
- the name of the mediator the parties have agreed upon, if possible (as to which, see below);
- a request that the appeal proceedings be suspended;
- full contact details for the parties; and
- a signature for or on behalf of each of the parties.

The Office has prepared a mediation request form. It is suggested that parties use this form to ensure all relevant information is provided.

Before mediation can start, the parties must sign an agreement that includes, at a minimum:

- an authorisation to negotiate a friendly settlement;
- confirmation that all information provided as part of the mediation will be kept confidential; and
- confirmation that the outcome of the mediation will be kept confidential.

Again, the Office has produced a sample mediation agreement. It is suggested that parties use this sample as the basis of their agreement, or that they at least refer to it when drafting their agreement.

Mediation takes place in the Office's premises in Alicante or in Brussels. Where a mediation is held in Alicante, no fee is payable. Where parties choose to hold a mediation in Brussels, they must pay an administration fee, which is €750 at the time of writing. The fee is normally split equally between the parties, but this is not necessarily the case and the parties can agree to split this fee in a different way. The administrative fee is not refunded if the mediation fails.

The parties must also choose a mediator from a list provided by the Office. The mediators in the list are members of the Opposition Divisions, the Cancellation Divisions and the Boards of Appeal. At the time of writing, there are 23 people on the list. If the parties cannot agree on a mediator, the Registry of the Boards of Appeal assists in the choice of a mediator. Mediators do not receive payment for acting as mediators, hence using this service is more cost effective than the parties entering into mediation independently of the Office during appeal proceedings (although they are of course free to do so).

The language of the appeal proceedings is automatically the language of the mediation, though a different language can be used if the parties and the mediator all agree on this.

Once a request for mediation is filed, the appeal is suspended, provided that the Statement of Grounds is filed in time and the administrative fee (if the mediation is to be held in Brussels) has been paid. The appeal proceedings only resume if the mediation fails.

Mediation can end in one of three ways:

- *the parties are able to reach an agreement* – in which case the appeal also ends, as it will be of no purpose (assuming that the agreement does not involve the continuation of the appeal, which is very unlikely);
- *the mediator issues a decision that he does not believe a settlement is possible* – in

which case the appeal proceedings resume; or

- *one of the parties opts out of the mediation* – this could be because one party unilaterally decides not to continue with the mediation, or the parties agree between themselves that the mediation is not going to be successful.

12. Decisions

When taking a decision, the Boards of Appeal are entitled to exercise any of the powers of the department that took the contested decision (ie, the decision under appeal). This means the appeal decision is not restricted to the parts of the contested decision challenged by the parties to the appeal. As such, an appeal is effectively a re-examination of the case rather than simply a review of the contested decision. One of the consequences of this is that the appellant may find itself in a worse position than if it had never filed an appeal.

Alternatively, rather than taking a decision that (subject to any further appeals) ends the proceedings, a Board of Appeal may decide to remit the case back to the department that took the contested decision for further consideration.

The result of the above is that an appeal decision can:

- *confirm the contested decision* – either on the same basis (where it is considered that the original decision was entirely correct) or on a different basis (where it is considered that the outcome was correct but the reasons were not). An example of where a decision will be upheld on a different basis is where an opposition was successful on one ground that the Board of Appeal considers should have been refused, but another ground is claimed in the opposition (and was relied on by the opponent) under which the Board of Appeal considers the opponent should have succeeded;
- *overturn the contested decision* – either wholly (where it is considered that the original decision was incorrect) or in part (where it is considered that part of the decision was correct but other parts were not). The most common example of a decision being partly upheld is where a mark is refused registration (either on absolute grounds or as the result of an opposition) in relation to some but not all of the goods and/or services applied for and the Board of Appeal considers the mark is entitled to registration in respect of different goods and/or services;
- *remit the decision back for further consideration* – in these circumstances, the Board of Appeal effectively passes the decision back down to the department that took the original decision and asks it to look at the case again. The department then takes a new decision following the guidance of the Board of Appeal. When taking its decision, the department is bound by the Board of Appeal decision. For example, in an appeal against an opposition decision in which the Board of Appeal considers that the Opposition Divisions did not take into account evidence that it should have considered, if the Board of Appeal remits the decision back to the Opposition Division, that department must take the evidence in question into account when taking a new decision in the opposition.

The Board of Appeal's written decision is sent to all parties to the proceedings. The decision must contain certain information, namely:

- a statement that the decision is delivered by the relevant Board of Appeal;
- the date of the decision;
- the names of the Chairman and other members of the Board of Appeal responsible for taking the decision;
- the name of the competent employee of the Registry responsible for the appeal;
- the names of the parties and their representatives;
- a statement of the issues to be decided;
- a summary of the facts;
- the reasons behind the decision taken;
- the order of the Board of Appeal; and
- a decision on costs (where this is necessary).

As with oppositions, the level of costs that can be recovered in appeal proceedings is very low. At the time of writing, the costs that can be recovered in relation to professional representation are fixed at €550. It is also very rare for appeal fees to be refunded (see section 5 above).

13. Further appeals

Once a decision has been issued, the appeal proceedings end. This is not, however, necessarily the end of the case. There are two ways in which proceedings can continue:

- *if the case is remitted back to the department that took the contested decision* – the department will issue a new decision that can be (and often is) the subject of a new appeal to the Board of Appeal.
- *if the Board of Appeal decision is appealed to the General Court* – the parties to an appeal decision can file an appeal before the General Court within two months of the date of the decision of the Board of Appeal. The decision of the General Court can then itself be the subject of a further appeal to the CJEU.

13.1 Grounds for appeal to the General Court

While an appeal can be filed before the General Court as of right, such an appeal can only be brought on a point of law on one or more of the following grounds:

- *lack of competence* – ie, the person or body making the decision was not competent to do so;
- *infringement of an essential procedural requirement* – eg, the Office did not follow its own rules or procedures properly;
- *infringement of the Union Treaty, the Regulation or other any rule of law relating to the EUTM application or registration to which the appeal relates* – eg, the Office did not follow or interpret the Regulation correctly; or
- *misuse of power* – this is claimed very rarely in appeals from the Office as it involves a claim that the relevant Board of Appeal used its powers for a purpose other than that for which they were intended.

13.2 Basic summary of proceedings before the General Court

A detailed account of proceedings before the General Court is outside the scope of this book.

It is, however, worth briefly noting a number of important differences between proceedings before the Office, including Board of Appeal proceedings, and those before the General Court.

- *Parties* – the party filing an appeal before the General Court is of course the appellant in those proceedings. The respondent to the proceedings is the Office, even where there are other parties to the proceedings to which the appeal relates. Those other parties automatically become 'interveners' in the General Court proceedings, but are not given exactly the same rights in the proceedings as the appellant and the Office. There is no requirement for interveners to be involved in a General Court appeal and so, if such parties decide to take no action, they can simply ignore the appeal.
- *Representation* – parties must be represented before the General Court by a lawyer authorised to practise before a court of a country that is part of the EEA. This means that parties may need to appoint a different representative to the person who represented them before the Office (eg, where a non-legally qualified employee of a company has represented that company before the Office).
- *Procedural rules* – the rules of the General Court are very strict and the procedures to be followed are, in many cases, very different to the procedures of the Office (and indeed most courts and national IPOs). Great care must be taken to ensure these rules are followed, not least in relation to the preparation and service of documents and time limits. There are two parts to an appeal to the General Court: the written procedure and, once the written procedure has concluded, the oral procedure.

Approximately 10% of Board of Appeal decisions are appealed to the General Court, which amounted to 281 appeals in 2014 (the last official figures published at the time of writing). Between 15% and 20% of General Court decisions tend to be appealed to the CJEU.

It is also worth noting that the General Court and CJEU are of relevance to EUTM applications and registrations beyond appeals from Board of Appeal decisions. This is because EUTM Courts regularly refer infringement actions to the General Court to obtain guidance on how Union law should be interpreted.

Further reference

Regulation – Art 58-65a, 135-137a

Implementing Regulation – Rules 48-51

Office Guidelines – Part A, Section 7

Commission Regulation (EC) No 216/96 of 5 February 1996, as amended by Regulation (EC) No 2082/2004, laying down the rules of procedure of the Boards of Appeal

Decision No 2014-3 of the Presidium of the Boards of Appeal of 26 May 2014 on the

devolution to a single member of cases on appeal against decisions of the Examiners taken according to Article 7 CTMR
Decision No 2013-3 of the Presidium of the Boards of Appeal of 5 July 2013 on the amicable settlement of disputes

Chapter 21: Basic principles

---

1. Introduction

This chapter looks at the basic principles of enforcement of EUTM rights, including consideration of where proceedings can be brought and when Union-wide relief can be sought.

Details of the types of act that constitute infringement of an EUTM registration are set out in Chapter 22 and defences to infringement are discussed in Chapter 23.

2. Terminology

The following terms are used as indicated below in chapters 21-23 inclusive (these terms are those used in the Regulation in the given contexts):

- *Plaintiff* – the proprietor (or in some circumstances a licensee) of an EUTM registration that is alleging its rights have been infringed and, if infringement proceedings are issued, the party that issues those proceedings;
- *Defendant* – the party that is being accused of infringement and, if infringement proceedings are issued, the party defending those proceedings;
- *Mark* – the plaintiff's trade mark (ie, a trade mark protected by an EUTM registration that the plaintiff alleges has been infringed); and
- *Sign* – the trade mark used by the defendant (ie, a trade mark that the plaintiff alleges is being used in a way that infringes its EUTM registration).

3. EUTM Courts

When the EUTM system was first introduced, it was decided that each Member State would designate specific national courts to deal with disputes relating to the infringement and validity of EUTM registrations. This was instead of setting up new courts to carry out these functions. These courts are known as EUTM Courts, and any actions alleging infringement of an EUTM registration must be issued in and heard by an EUTM Court.

Each Member State has nominated courts of both first instance (ie, the court in which the action is brought) and second instance (ie, the court to which appeals from first instance decisions are made) to act as EUTM Courts. A list of such courts can be found at: http://euipo.europa.eu/pdf/mark/ctmcourts.pdf. An updated version of this list is published in the *Official Journal of the European Union* each time a Member State informs the Commission of a change to the designated courts in its territory. At the time of writing, the list on the Office's website is not up to date and the latest list can be found at: http://eur-lex.europa.eu/legal-content/DE/TXT/?uri=uriserv:OJ.C_.2014.332.01.0004.01.ENG.

Where no EUTM Court has been designated for any given Member State, jurisdiction lies with the national courts that have jurisdiction in respect of national trade mark matters. At the time of writing, each of the 28 Member States has designated EUTM Courts, so this rule is currently inapplicable.

One of the key benefits of obtaining EUTM protection is the ability to seek Union-wide relief, even where an infringing act has occurred in only one Member State. Where such relief is sought, there is a jurisdictional cascade that determines the Member State in which the action should be brought. The cascade is set out and explained in section 5 below. There are occasions when applying the cascade results in more than one option with regard to where to bring an action. However, the manner in which the system is set up theoretically minimises the possibility of forum shopping.

If, as is sometimes the case, a plaintiff does not want to seek Union-wide relief, the action still has to be dealt with by an EUTM Court. The EUTM Court in question is, however, only able to provide the remedies available under national law. By virtue of other Union-wide legislation, including the so-called 'Enforcement Directive', there is a level of harmonisation with regard to the relief and remedies available under the national laws of Member States.

Irrespective of which EUTM Court deals with a particular action, the Union rules on jurisdiction and the recognition and enforcement of judgments in civil and commercial matters apply (under the Recast Brussels Regulation). This ensures the decision of a court in one Member State is recognised by the courts of the other Member States (unless recognition is contested). As a result, it is possible for a successful plaintiff to take the judgment of an EUTM Court in Germany to an EUTM Court in Greece and ask the Greek court to enforce the German judgment in Greece.

4. Jurisdiction

The types of action discussed below can only be decided upon by EUTM Courts. Any such action brought before a court that is not an EUTM Court is dismissed for lack of jurisdiction.

For matters that do not have to be decided by an EUTM Court, the rules of the Brussels I Regulation and the national rules of the Member States determine which court or courts have jurisdiction. If no court appears to have jurisdiction, the fallback position is that the courts of Spain have jurisdiction.

4.1 EUTM infringement actions

These are actions in which a plaintiff alleges its EUTM registration has been infringed by the activities of the defendant. Such actions are discussed in detail in Chapter 22.

4.2 Actions in respect of threatened infringement of an EUTM registration

These are actions in which a plaintiff alleges that, although its EUTM registration is not currently being infringed, the defendant is threatening to do something that will infringe the registration. Such actions can only be brought before a given EUTM Court if they are permitted under the national law of the Member State in which that EUTM Court is located. This is the case even if the threatened infringement takes place in a Member State whose national law provides for such actions.

4.3 Actions for declarations of non-infringement of an EUTM

These are actions in which a potential defendant asks an EUTM Court to confirm that its activities or planned activities do not (or will not) infringe a particular EUTM registration. Such actions can only be brought before a given EUTM Court if they are permitted under the national law of the Member State in which that court is located.

4.4 Actions requesting compensation for acts after the publication date of an EUTM application

These are actions brought by plaintiffs on the basis of EUTM applications that have been published but not yet registered. The Regulation allows such a plaintiff to obtain compensation for acts taking place in the period between publication of an EUTM application and publication of the registration of that application, where the acts in question would amount to infringement of the EUTM registration once granted. The merits of any such compensation request cannot be decided upon until after publication of the EUTM registration (ie, an EUTM Court cannot issue a decision until after the EUTM application on which the action is based has either been registered or refused). If the application is refused, there can of course be no infringement and the action will also be refused.

4.5 Counterclaims for revocation of an EUTM registration

A revocation action can only be heard by an EUTM Court by way of a counterclaim in proceedings for infringement or threatened infringement, as discussed further in Chapter 23. Revocation actions are discussed in detail in Chapter 17.

4.6 Counterclaims for a declaration of invalidity of an EUTM registration

An invalidity action can only be heard by an EUTM Court by way of a counterclaim in proceedings for infringement or threatened infringement, as discussed further in Chapter 23. Invalidity actions are discussed in detail in Chapter 18.

5. Where to bring an action

There are many EUTM Courts spread across the Union. The question for a plaintiff seeking to bring an action thus becomes the individual EUTM Court to which it should go.

The most important variable in deciding where to bring an action is usually whether Union-wide relief is of interest. Where a plaintiff wishes to obtain such relief, which is of course one of the reasons why an EUTM registration is so desirable in the first place, there is a jurisdictional cascade to follow in determining in which Member State the action should be brought.

If Union-wide relief is sought, the cascade must be followed, unless:

- the parties expressly and jointly agree that an EUTM Court in a particular Member State is to have jurisdiction; or
- the defendant appears before a different EUTM Court, other than to contest jurisdiction. This means, in effect, that if a plaintiff begins an action in an EUTM Court that is not the EUTM Court the cascade says should be used, Union-wide remedies are still available if the defendant appears before that court.

As both these exceptions require some input or action on behalf of the defendant, in practice plaintiffs who want Union-wide relief usually have to follow the cascade, which is as follows:

- the action should be brought in the Member State in which the defendant is domiciled;
- if the defendant is not domiciled in the Union, the action should be brought in a Member State in which the defendant has an establishment;
- if the defendant is neither domiciled nor has an establishment in the Union, the action should be brought in the Member State in which the plaintiff is domiciled;
- if the plaintiff is not domiciled in the Union, the action should be brought in a Member State in which the plaintiff has an establishment; or
- if the plaintiff does not have an establishment in the Union, and thus none of the above apply, the action must be brought in Spain (ie, the Member State in which the Office is located).

It is possible for defendants (particularly non-physical persons, ie, companies) to be domiciled in or to have an establishment in more than one Member State. This means that, in any given situation, there may be more than one Member State in which a plaintiff can bring an action seeking Union-wide relief.

Even where there is only one possible Member State within which an action seeking Union-wide relief can be brought, a plaintiff may still have a choice of courts, as a number of Member States have designated multiple courts as EUTM Courts.

Where a plaintiff has a choice of more than one possible EUTM Court with jurisdiction to provide Union-wide relief, factors such as cost and speed of proceedings often feature in decisions as to which particular EUTM Court to choose.

Where the cascade is followed, the chosen EUTM Court has jurisdiction with regard to infringing acts committed or threatened in any Member State, even where no infringing acts have been committed or threatened in the Member State in which that EUTM Court is located.

A plaintiff can, however, always bring proceedings in the Member State in which the activity complained of took place. Where this happens, the EUTM Court in question only has jurisdiction in relation to infringing acts that took place in that Member State, unless it also happens to be the EUTM Court with Union-wide jurisdiction under the jurisdictional cascade. Where an EUTM Court does not have Union-wide jurisdiction, it can only give national remedies (ie, the remedies it may provide in dealing with matters relating to national trade marks). It is not able to give Union-wide remedies or remedies not provided for under its national law.

Where the same defendant is engaged in infringing acts in more than one Member State, the plaintiff again has a choice of EUTM Courts with jurisdiction at the national level. In such instances, it is usually more sensible to bring proceedings in an EUTM Court with Union-wide jurisdiction, which can deal with all the infringing acts by a single defendant in one action. Otherwise, separate actions are required in each Member State in which infringing acts are taking place; this is likely to increase overall costs and brings with it the potential for different remedies to be granted in different jurisdictions.

Courts with Union-wide jurisdiction are able to grant injunctions preventing use in the entire Union, avoiding the need for multiple actions where the same infringer is operating in multiple Member States. A Union-wide injunction can be granted on the basis of infringing acts in only one Member State, so a plaintiff does not need to wait until infringing acts start in further Member States before it can stop the infringer.

6. Simultaneous and successive actions

It is possible for a plaintiff to have both an EUTM registration and separate national registrations that would enable an infringement action to be brought against an infringer. As a result, more than one set of proceedings is sometimes issued.

If a proprietor brings an infringement action in an EUTM Court in one Member State on the basis of a particular EUTM registration, and also brings proceedings in another Member State against the same party for infringement of a national trade mark registration for the same mark, the court first seized has jurisdiction. If the marks and coverage are both identical, the court first seized has jurisdiction over both cases. If the marks are identical but the goods and/or services are similar, the second-seized court may stay its proceedings pending the outcome of the case in the first-seized court.

The provisions in the Regulation on this point are intended to avoid conflicting decisions being handed down by different courts dealing with the same issue. They do not, however, address what happens if actions are brought in different Member States on the basis of the same EUTM registration. This situation can arise where a proprietor decides to bring actions in multiple Member States in which infringing activity is occurring but none of the EUTM Courts hearing the actions has Union-wide jurisdiction under the jurisdictional cascade. If the defendant appears before the first-seized court and the plaintiff requests Union-wide relief, that court has Union-wide jurisdiction. If, however, only national relief is sought in each court, it is possible for each court to decide the merits of the same issue differently.

The Regulation provides that, where a national court has issued a final decision on the infringement of a national trade mark registration and proceedings are brought against the same defendant on the basis of an EUTM registration for the identical mark covering identical goods and/or services, the court to which the EUTM infringement action has been brought must reject the action. The same is true in reverse, so that it is not possible to bring infringement proceedings based on a national registration if a final decision has already been handed down on the basis of an EUTM registration for the identical mark covering identical goods and/or services. It should, however, be noted that these provisions do not apply to requests for interim measures, such as preliminary or temporary injunctions.

7. Jurisdiction on appeal

As noted in section 3 above, all Member States have designated courts of both first instance and second instance to act as EUTM Courts. The decision of an EUTM Court of first instance in any given Member State can be appealed to the EUTM Court of second instance in that Member State.

The conditions under which such an appeal can be made, as well as the rules relating to appeals from the EUTM Court of second instance, are governed entirely by the national law of the Member State in question.

8. Applicable law and sanctions

Although EUTM Courts are primarily concerned with applying the provisions of the Regulation, in practice they apply a mixture of laws and also follow their usual national rules of procedure. Where more than one EUTM Court theoretically has jurisdiction, there may be an element of forum shopping. Issues such as the relevant national rules of procedure are often considered by plaintiffs in deciding which court to use.

8.1 Applicable law

The starting point is that EUTM Courts must apply the provisions of the Regulation in deciding actions based on or relating to EUTM registrations.

The Regulation does not, however, set out the rules to be followed in infringement actions. For all matters not covered by the Regulation, an EUTM Court must apply the applicable national law of the Member State in which that court is located, as well as the rules of procedure relating to national trade marks in that Member State.

8.2 Sanctions

Where an EUTM Court finds that an EUTM registration has been infringed, it is obliged to issue an order prohibiting the defendant from continuing to carry out the infringing acts, unless there are special reasons why such an order should not be issued. This is also the case for actions for threatened infringement, where they can be brought.

An EUTM Court is able to make use of any measures available under its national law that are aimed at ensuring a prohibition on carrying out infringing acts is complied with. In addition, it can apply any measures or orders available under the applicable national law that it deems appropriate.

The Regulation also provides for the possibility of plaintiffs seeking interim relief. The most common type of interim relief applied for is a temporary injunction preventing the defendant from carrying out allegedly infringing acts, which if granted remains in place until a final decision is given in the action (unless the defendant is able to have the injunction set aside). Additional types of interim relief include applications that allegedly infringing goods be seized or financial assets frozen pending the outcome of the action.

A plaintiff can apply to any court in a Member State, including but not limited to EUTM Courts, for such interim relief as is available in actions relating to the infringement of national trade mark registrations in that Member State. Interim relief can be requested even where another court has jurisdiction over the substance of the dispute. Where the request for interim relief is made to an EUTM Court with Union-wide jurisdiction, following the jurisdictional cascade, the interim relief can be granted Union-wide. This allows a Union-wide injunction to be put in place pending the outcome of the infringement action if the court considers this to be justified in the circumstances.

9. Validity and counterclaims

The starting position in any infringement action is that the allegedly infringed EUTM registration is considered to be valid. The defendant can, however, contest the validity of an EUTM registration by bringing a counterclaim for revocation and/or invalidity of the EUTM registration as part of the infringement proceedings. The principle of *res judicata* applies, so that no counterclaim can be brought if the Office has already made a decision on the same issue. With regard to invalidity, other issues are also relevant, including consent, acquiescence and earlier invalidity proceedings in which the rights now relied upon could have been raised but were not. (See Chapter 18 for further information about invalidity actions and *res judicata*, Chapter 17 for further information about revocation actions and Chapter 23 for further information about counterclaims.)

Where an invalidity or revocation action is filed at the Office before a counterclaim for the same action is brought before a court, the court proceedings are suspended pending the outcome of the action at the Office, unless there are special reasons why this should not be the case. The filing of such a cancellation action at the Office in these circumstances is referred to as an 'EUIPO torpedo'. Where any EUTM Court proceedings are stayed pending the outcome of an action at the Office, the EUTM Court can grant interim relief during the period of the stay.

It is also possible for an EUTM Court faced with a counterclaim for revocation or invalidity to stay the court proceedings at the request of the EUTM proprietor and ask the defendant to file a revocation or invalidity action at the Office within a specific time limit. If the defendant does not file the action at the Office within the time limit set, the counterclaim is treated as withdrawn. If no such request is made by the plaintiff, the EUTM Court must decide on the merits of the counterclaim. Where it does so, the court informs the Office of the outcome and the Office updates the Register accordingly.

Finally, it should be noted that counterclaims can be raised in proceedings to which the plaintiff is not a party – eg, actions brought by exclusive licensees. If this happens, the plaintiff is contacted and may be added as a party to the proceedings.

Further reference

Regulation – Articles 14, 94-107

Directive 2004/48/EC on the enforcement of intellectual property rights ('the Enforcement Directive')

Regulation (EU) No 1215/2012 on jurisdiction and the recognition and enforcement of judgments in civil and commercial matters ('the Recast Brussels Regulation')

DHL Express France SA v Chronopost SA (Case C-235/09)

The owners of the cargo lately laden on board the ship 'Tatry' v The owners of the ship 'Maciej Rataj' (Case C-406/92)

The *'Rodeo'* case, decisions of the Higher District Court of Düsseldorf (8 November 2005, Az I-20 U 110/04) and the Paris Court of Appeal (2 December 2005, Az 04/22 431)

Chapter 22: Infringement

1. Introduction

This chapter looks at the key aspects of EUTM infringement, including the acts that amount to infringement and who can bring infringement proceedings.

The defences and counterclaims that can be raised in response to an infringement claim are discussed in Chapter 23.

2. Overview of EUTM infringement actions

2.1 Who can bring infringement proceedings?

The general rule is that infringement proceedings should be brought by the proprietor of an EUTM registration, as the rights conferred by an EUTM registration are exclusive rights conferred on the proprietor.

Where an EUTM registration has been transferred to a new owner, that new owner cannot rely on the EUTM registration in infringement proceedings, or indeed otherwise, until the transfer has been entered in the Register. See Chapter 16 for further information on recording transfers.

Where an EUTM registration has been licensed, in practice the licensee will often be based in the Member State in which the infringement occurs and become aware of that infringement before the EUTM proprietor. See Chapter 16 for further information on licences and the recordal of licences in the Register.

It is possible for a licensee to bring infringement proceedings in certain circumstances:

- non-exclusive and sole licensees are only entitled to bring infringement proceedings if they have obtained the consent of the EUTM proprietor, or if they are entitled to do so under the terms of their licence agreement; and
- exclusive licensees are entitled to bring infringement proceedings if they notify the EUTM proprietor of the allegedly infringing activity and the EUTM proprietor fails to bring such proceedings itself within an appropriate time. This right is again subject to the terms of the licence agreement and it is generally advisable for an EUTM proprietor to ensure the licence prevents an exclusive licensee bringing actions (not least to prevent actions being brought that might lead to a counterclaim for revocation or a declaration of invalidity, which could result in the EUTM registration being lost).

Where infringement proceedings are brought by an EUTM proprietor, a licensee can intervene in the infringement proceedings for the purpose of obtaining compensation for damage it has suffered as a result of the infringement.

If the licensee of an EUTM registration breaches the terms of its licence, the EUTM proprietor can bring infringement proceedings against the licensee if the breach relates to any of the following:

- the duration of the licence (ie, the licensee continues to use the registered mark after the licence has expired);
- the form of use of the mark (ie, the licensee uses it in a way that is prohibited by, or goes beyond the forms of use permitted by, the licence);
- the goods and/or services covered by the licence (ie, the licensee uses the mark on or in relation to goods and/or services that are not covered by the licence;
- the territory covered by the licence (ie, the licensee operates outside the geographical scope of the licence); and
- the quality of the goods and/or services provided by the licensee (ie, the licensee is in breach of any quality control provisions in the licence or has not met the criteria set out in the licence relating to the quality of goods and/or services it must provide).

The ability of the EUTM proprietor to bring such proceedings helps it maintain control over its EUTM registration. Where any one of the above provisions of a licence agreement has been breached, the EUTM proprietor is usually able to bring contractual proceedings for breach of the licence agreement. However, in light of the remedies available for EUTM infringement, including the possibility of Union-wide injunctions, and bearing in mind that a licence agreement is a contract concluded under the law of a single country (which may or may not be a Member State), there are circumstances in which it is prudent to bring EUTM infringement proceedings against a wayward licensee instead of or in addition to proceedings for breach of the licence.

2.2 When can action be taken against infringers?

EUTM rights are only effective against third parties once registration has been obtained. It is, however, possible for a plaintiff to obtain compensation for infringing acts that took place in the period between publication of its EUTM application and publication of the EUTM registration. As a result, plaintiffs can begin infringement proceedings before registration has been obtained.

If an infringement action is based on an EUTM application, the EUTM Court hearing the action cannot decide on the merits of the infringement claim until the EUTM application has either gone through to registration or been refused. If the application is refused, then there can of course be no infringement and the action will also be refused.

Infringement proceedings can be brought by the EUTM proprietor and, in certain circumstances, by licensees (as discussed in section 2.1 above). The grounds of infringement effectively mirror the relative grounds of opposition set out in Chapter 10, section 10 (and discussed in detail in Chapter 12).

It is usually a good idea to bring infringement proceedings as soon as possible after becoming aware of infringing activity. There are, however, often reasons why it is not appropriate to issue proceedings immediately. For example, if an action is brought during the opposition period for an EUTM application, the defendant may file an opposition and so delay the infringement proceedings. Also, in many Member States there can be costs consequences if a plaintiff brings proceedings without notifying the defendant of its intention to do so and giving the defendant an opportunity to stop the infringing use.

2.3 Where should action be taken?

By virtue of being a Union-wide right, an EUTM registration can be infringed by use anywhere in the Union. Further, one of the key advantages of an EUTM registration (as opposed to national registrations in the Member States) is that Union-wide remedies can be obtained in a single set of proceedings.

If a plaintiff wants to obtain Union-wide remedies, it must ensure that proceedings are brought in an EUTM Court in the correct Member State. This is discussed in detail in Chapter 21.

If a plaintiff is not concerned about obtaining Union-wide remedies, proceedings can instead be brought in an EUTM Court in any Member State in which the alleged infringing activity is taking place. In these circumstances, the EUTM Court only has jurisdiction in relation to infringements taking place in the Member State in which it is based, and it is only able to provide remedies that are available in that Member State. Again, this is discussed in more detail in Chapter 21.

3. The most common types of infringement

Virtually all infringement actions based on EUTM registrations relate to three types of infringement, which are equivalent to the 'double identity', 'confusion' and 'reputation' grounds of opposition set out in Chapter 10, section 10 and discussed in detail in Chapter 12. These are considered below in this section.

In addition, the owners of EUTM registrations are entitled to take action in certain other circumstances, as discussed in section 5 below. The restricted acts discussed in section 5 have not to date been widely used by plaintiffs, either because they relate to situations that do not occur very often or because the restricted act in question was only introduced into the Regulation very recently.

The three main types of infringement are as follows.

Use, in the course of trade, of a sign that is identical to the mark in the EUTM registration in relation to goods and/or services that are identical to those covered by the EUTM registration: For this type of infringement to be proved, three things must be shown:

- *use without consent in the course of trad*e – this is discussed in section 4.1 below;
- *the mark and the sign must be identical* – whether a mark and sign are identical for the purposes of infringement is assessed in the same way as when two marks are compared in opposition proceedings. This is discussed in Chapter 12, section 3.2; and
- *identical goods and/or services* – whether goods and/or services are identical for

the purposes of infringement is assessed in the same way as in opposition proceedings. This is discussed in Chapter 12, section 3.2.

Use, in the course of trade, of a sign that is identical or similar to the mark in the EUTM registration in relation to goods and/or services that are identical or similar to those covered by the EUTM registration, where there is a likelihood of consumer confusion: For this type of infringement to be proved, four things must be shown:

- *use without consent in the course of trade* – this is discussed in section 4.1 below;
- *the mark and the sign must be identical or similar* – whether a mark and sign are identical or similar for the purposes of infringement is assessed in the same way as in opposition proceedings. This is discussed in Chapter 12,sections 3.2 and 4.2;
- *identical or similar goods and/or services* – whether goods and/or services are identical or similar for the purposes of infringement is assessed in the same way as in opposition proceedings. This is discussed in Chapter 12, sections 3.2 and 4.2; and
- *likelihood of consumer confusion* – this is also assessed in the same way for the purposes of infringement as in opposition proceedings, as discussed in Chapter 12, section 4.2. The key difference between opposition proceedings and infringement proceedings is that in infringement proceedings there necessarily has been use in the marketplace at least by the defendant, and in many instances also by the plaintiff. This means there may be evidence of actual confusion. Although such evidence is not required to succeed in infringement proceedings, it can be highly persuasive.

Use, in the course of trade, of a sign that is identical or similar to the mark in the EUTM registration where that mark has a reputation in the Union and use of the sign in question without due cause takes unfair advantage of, or is detrimental to, the distinctive character or repute of the mark: For this type of infringement to be proved, four things must be shown:

- *use without consent and in the course of trade* – this is discussed in section 4.1 below;
- *the mark and the sign must be identical or similar* – whether a mark and sign are identical or similar for the purposes of infringement is assessed in the same way as in opposition proceedings. This is discussed in Chapter 12, section 5.2;
- *the mark must have a reputation in the Union* – this is also assessed in the same way for the purposes of infringement as in opposition proceedings, as discussed in Chapter 12, section 5.2; and
- *use without due cause that takes advantage of, or is detrimental to, the distinctive character or repute of the EUTM* – again, this is assessed in the same way for the purposes of infringement as in opposition proceedings, as discussed in Chapter 12, section 5.2.

4. Key requirements of an infringement action

4.1 The sign must be used in the course of trade

Unlike opposition proceedings, EUTM infringement proceedings require the contested sign actually to be in use for there to be an infringement. The only exception to this is where a third party is threatening to do something that, if done, would infringe an EUTM registration. In some Member States, it is possible to bring an action to prevent this threatened infringement, as discussed in Chapter 21, section 4.2.

Not all use of a sign amounts to infringing use. Only use that is in the course of trade can be infringing use. The term 'in the course of trade' is generally described as use "in the context of commercial activity with a view to economic advantage and not as a private matter" (wording taken from the CJEU decision in the *ARSENAL* case).

In addition, use only amounts to infringing use if it affects, or is liable to affect, the 'functions' of a mark. There are a number of different functions that, if affected, mean use is infringing use, the most important of which is the ability of the mark to indicate the unique origin of the goods and/or services in respect of which it is registered (normally referred to as the 'origin function'). Other functions include the function of guaranteeing quality, as well as advertising and investment functions. Most infringing use is capable of affecting the origin function, so that it is rare for this point to become an issue.

4.2 The kind of acts that amount to infringement

The Regulation details a number of specific acts that amount to use for the purposes of infringement. The list is not exhaustive and other acts can also constitute infringing use.

The acts that are laid down as being prohibited are as follows:

- affixing a sign to goods or to packaging for goods;
- offering goods for sale under a sign, including stocking them so that they can be put on the market;
- offering or supplying services under a sign;
- importing goods under a sign;
- exporting goods under a sign;
- using a sign as a trade name or a company name or as part of a trade name or company name;
- using a sign on business papers or in advertising; and
- using a sign in comparative advertising in a manner that is contrary to the rules laid down in the Comparative Advertising Directive (as to which, see below).

In addition to the above, transportation of goods through the Union, even if those goods are not released for sale in the Union, is a prohibited act in some circumstances, as discussed in section 5.1 below.

Further, use of a sign on packaging, labels, tags, security or authenticity features or devices or any other means to which the sign is affixed which are not themselves attached to goods is a restricted act in some circumstances. This is considered in section 5.2 below.

The majority of the acts in the above list are fairly self-explanatory and involve using the sign at issue in a consumer-facing manner to sell, promote or advertise goods and/or services or taking steps that will help others to do so.

The only act on the list that warrants further discussion at this point is the use of a sign in comparative advertising. In simple terms, comparative advertising involves a defendant using someone else's mark in advertising for the purpose of showing that the defendant's goods and/or services are superior to those of the other party. For obvious reasons, trade mark owners are often not very happy about their marks being used in this way.

The Comparative Advertising Directive sets out a list of conditions that a comparative advertisement must meet to be permissible. If any of these conditions are not met, the advertisement both breaches the Comparative Advertising Directive and amounts to trade mark infringement (which means the use of the relevant mark can be prevented by the EUTM proprietor).

According to the Comparative Advertising Directive, a comparative advertisement is permissible where all of the following conditions are met:

- the advertisement is not misleading;
- it compares goods and/or services that are intended for the same purpose or meet the same needs;
- it objectively compares one or more or more objective features of the goods and/or services, which can include price;
- it does not discredit or denigrate the trade marks or goods and/or services or activities of a competitor;
- for goods with designation of origin, it relates to goods with the same designation;
- it does not take unfair advantage of the reputation of a trade mark or of the designation of origin of competing products;
- it does not present goods and/or services as imitations or replicas of goods and/or services bearing a protected trade mark or trade name; and
- it does not create confusion among traders between the advertiser and a competitor or between the advertiser's trade marks or the advertiser's goods and/or services and those of a competitor.

4.3 Without consent

For use to constitute an infringement, it must be without the consent of the EUTM proprietor. As discussed in Chapter 23, section 3.1, a defendant wishing to argue that its actions were undertaken with the consent of the EUTM proprietor must show evidence of such consent, which can be either express or implied.

5. Other restricted acts

As noted above, the proprietors of EUTM registrations can in some circumstances take action in relation to use falling outside the three most common types of infringement considered in section 3 above. These other restricted acts are considered in this section.

5.1 Stopping goods in transit through the Union

The proprietor of an EUTM registration can prevent third parties from transporting goods through the Union, even where such goods are not destined to be put on the market in the Union.

For a plaintiff to prevent the transportation of goods through the Union on the basis of an EUTM registration, the following conditions must be met:

- the goods must be brought into the Union from outside the Union. If the goods originate within the Union, it is not necessary to rely on this provision as one or more of the prohibited acts listed in section 4.2 above will be relevant;
- the sign used on the goods (or their packaging) must be identical to the mark protected by the EUTM registration, or must be so similar that it cannot be distinguished in its essential aspects from that trade mark. As this provision was only introduced in March 2016, there is at the time of writing no guidance as to the level of similarity required to meet this threshold. However, it seems likely that the mark and the sign will have to be almost identical and a similar test to that discussed in Chapter 12, section 3.2 is likely to apply;
- the EUTM registration must cover goods identical to those in respect of which the sign is used. There is no leeway here and almost identical goods are not sufficient; and
- the plaintiff can prevent the use of the sign on and in relation to the relevant goods in the country the goods are destined for (ie, their final destination, not another temporary stop in transit).

The burden is, as would be expected, on the plaintiff to prove that the first three conditions are satisfied. However, the burden is on the defendant to prove that the plaintiff is not entitled to prevent the defendant putting the goods on the market in the country of final destination (ie, that the use of the sign on and in relation to those goods in that country does not infringe the plaintiff's rights in that country).

5.2 Preparatory acts

Another new restricted act was introduced into the Regulation in March 2016, relating to packaging, labels, tags, security or authenticity features or devices or any other means to which a mark is affixed that could be, but are not yet, used in relation to goods and/or services. These items are referred to in this section as 'preparatory items'.

Before the introduction of this provision, it was often difficult for plaintiffs to prevent the use of their marks on preparatory items if it was unclear what type of goods those preparatory items were going to be used for (unless the plaintiff had a registration that specifically covered the preparatory items in question). The introduction of this provision should allow the owners of EUTM registrations to fight counterfeiting more effectively, by stopping infringing products getting on the market in the first place: the plaintiff does not need to wait until goods have been placed on the market with the preparatory items attached before it can take action.

For a plaintiff to rely on this provision on the basis of an EUTM registration, the following conditions must be met:

- the sign must be affixed to the preparatory items;
- the sign used must be identical with, or similar to, the mark protected by the plaintiff's EUTM registration;
- there is a real risk that the preparatory items could be used in relation to goods and/or services; and
- if so used, the use would be an infringement of the plaintiff's rights.

If these conditions are satisfied, a plaintiff is entitled to prevent a defendant from doing either of the following in the course of trade:

- affixing the sign to preparatory items; or
- offering or placing on the market, stocking, importing or exporting preparatory items to which the sign is affixed.

5.3 Reproduction in dictionaries

The proprietors of EUTM registrations are entitled to take action to prevent the use of their marks as generic terms in dictionaries, encyclopaedias or similar publications.

If the proprietor of an EUTM registration discovers its mark being used in such a way as to give the impression that the mark is a generic term, it can require the publishers of the relevant work to indicate that the mark is a registered trade mark. Where the relevant work is a printed publication, this indication must appear in the next edition of the published work at the latest. Where the relevant work is an electronic publication, the work should be changed without delay to indicate that the mark is registered.

5.4 Use of a registered mark by an agent or representative

Where an agent or representative of a plaintiff obtains an EUTM registration for a mark of which the plaintiff is the 'true proprietor' without the plaintiff's consent, the plaintiff is entitled to prevent its agent or representative using that mark. For a plaintiff to rely on this provision in respect of an EUTM registration, the following conditions must be met:

- the proprietor of the EUTM registration (ie, the defendant) is or was an agent or representative of the plaintiff;
- the EUTM registration was obtained without the plaintiff's consent;
- the plaintiff is the true proprietor of the mark covered by the EUTM registration; and
- the defendant is unable to justify its actions.

This provision is equivalent to the 'agent/representative ground' of opposition as discussed in Chapter 12, section 8 and the discussion in that section is equally applicable here. Where the requirements of this ground are made out, the 'true proprietor' can demand that the EUTM registration be assigned to it from the agent or representative.

Further reference

Regulation – Articles 9-11, 14, 18

Arsenal Football Club Plc v Matthew Reed, CJEU decision in Case No C-206/01, judgment dated 11 November 2002 and English Court of Appeal decision [2003] ETMR 19 ('*ARSENAL*')

Directive 2006/114/EC concerning misleading and comparative advertising ('the Comparative Advertising Directive')

Chapter 23: Defences and avoiding infringement

1. Introduction

This chapter looks at the various defences that can be raised in response to an infringement action, as well as related matters that can prevent an infringement action succeeding.

2. Overview of defences and related points

The Regulation sets out a number of specific limitations on the rights on an EUTM proprietor, each of which can be raised in response to an infringement action. These defences are discussed in section 4 below and relate to:

- use of the defendant's own name or address;
- use of non-distinctive or descriptive elements;
- referential use;
- exhaustion of rights; and
- reliance on an intervening right.

Before these defences are discussed, it is worth noting that there is no need for a defence if a defendant can prove it is not infringing the plaintiff's rights. As a result, before a defendant considers whether it has a defence, it should consider whether a lack of infringement can be shown. This can be done by showing either of the following, which are discussed in section 3 below:

- the requirements for use to be an infringement discussed in Chapter 22 are not made out; or
- where the plaintiff is relying on a mark that has been registered for more than five years, the plaintiff cannot prove use of the mark and so is not entitled to rely on that registration.

The starting point in all infringement proceedings is that the plaintiff's EUTM registration is valid. However, an EUTM registration that no longer exists cannot be infringed, so a defendant can avoid infringement by successfully challenging the validity of the plaintiff's EUTM registration. The validity of the plaintiff's EUTM registration can be called into question by taking any of the following actions, which are discussed in section 5 below:

- raising a counterclaim for revocation of the EUTM registration;
- raising a counterclaim for a declaration of invalidity of the EUTM registration; or

- where the plaintiff has not issued proceedings yet, filing either an invalidity action or a revocation action at the Office (as discussed in chapters 17 and 18).

3. Proving that there is no infringement

This section discusses the ways in which a defendant can prove there is no infringement of the plaintiff's rights.

3.1 Where the requirements for the use to be an infringement have not been made out

The rules relating to when use amounts to an infringement are discussed in Chapter 22. There are a number of ways in which defendants can argue that their use is not an infringement, including that:

- *the sign used is not similar to the plaintiff's mark* – if this is shown, there can be no infringement under the Regulation on any ground;
- *the goods and/or services offered by the defendant are not similar to the goods and/or services covered by the plaintiff's EUTM registration* – if this is shown, there can be no infringement, unless the plaintiff is relying on a registration with a reputation;
- *the allegedly infringing use was not made in the course of trade* – if the defendant can show that the use is private and that no goods and/or services have been placed on the market, there can be no infringement;
- *the allegedly infringing use was made with the consent of the EUTM proprietor* – if the use has been consented to, so long as the defendant does not use in a way that exceeds the consent given, there can be no infringement. Such consent may be express or implied, and may be written or oral. In practice, express written consent is of course much easier to prove than implied and/or oral consent and the more concrete the evidence, the greater the chances of the defendant being able to rely on the consent; or
- *where the plaintiff is relying on a registration with a reputation, the allegedly infringing use was made with due cause* – an example of where this might be shown is where a defendant begins using a sign in good faith before the filing date of the plaintiff's EUTM registration in relation to goods and/or services dissimilar to those covered by the plaintiff's registration. Again, the more concrete the evidence that can be provided, the greater the chances of success in relying on this point.

3.2 Where the plaintiff cannot prove use of its mark

This is only an option for a defendant where the plaintiff is relying on a mark that has been registered for more than five years. In these circumstances, a defendant can require that the plaintiff prove use of the mark in relation to the goods and/or services covered by the relevant registration. If the plaintiff cannot do this, it is not entitled to rely on that registration in infringement proceedings.

The rules relating to proof of use are considered in Chapter 13, section 6 and those rules apply equally here.

4. Defences

The following specific defences are set out in the Regulation:

- the defendant is a natural person and is using his own name or address (***'own name defence'***);
- the defendant is using non-distinctive or descriptive signs (***'non-distinctiveness/descriptiveness defence'***);
- the defendant is using the plaintiff's mark for the purpose of identifying or referring to goods and/or services as those of the plaintiff (***'referential use defence'***)
- the plaintiff's rights in the mark have been exhausted (***'exhaustion of rights defence'***); and
- the defendant is entitled to rely on intervening rights (***'intervening rights defence'***).

4.1 Honest practices in industrial or commercial matters

This requirement applies to the own name defence, the non-distinctiveness/descriptiveness defence and the referential use defence. A defendant can only rely on these defences where the use made of the mark is in accordance with honest practices in industrial or commercial matters.

Whether use is in accordance with 'honest practices' is judged objectively and not in accordance with the subjective views of either the plaintiff or the defendant. It is worth noting that the same conduct may be viewed in different ways, depending on the defence being relied on. For example, use that might be seen as honest practices where a defendant is using his own name might not be seen as honest where the defendant is relying on the referential use defence.

4.2 Own name defence

Following changes to the Regulation in March 2016, this defence now applies only to natural persons. As discussed in Chapter 22, use of a company name is now specifically listed as a type of infringing use. At the time of writing, the effect that this shift will have on corporate parties who successfully relied on the own name defence prior to the change in the law is unclear.

The 'own name' defence is designed to allow individuals to make use of their own name and/or address in offering goods and/or services for sale, without having to be concerned with infringing the rights of others. This defence is often relevant where the name of an individual is itself used and perceived as a brand, as often happens, for example, in the case of fashion designers. The need for the use made to be in accordance with honest practices tempers this defence somewhat, which can be of particular relevance in the case of multiple family members seeking to make use of the same family name following a family or business falling-out.

4.3 Non-distinctiveness/descriptiveness defence

There are two different limbs to this defence, which are considered separately in this section.

The use of descriptive indications: Prior to the changes to the Regulation in March 2016, this defence only covered the use of descriptive indications. The Regulation lists the following types of indication that are covered by this defence:

- *the kind of goods and/or services* – eg, using the sign 'ROSES' in relation to bouquets of flowers containing roses;
- *quality* – eg, using the sign 'PREMIUM' in relation to lager of a high quality;
- *quantity* – eg, using the sign 'LITRE' in relation to drinks bottles containing a litre of liquid;
- *intended purpose* – eg, using the sign 'RELAX' in relation to massage services;
- *value* – eg, using a sign that indicates the price of the relevant goods and/or services;
- *geographical origin* – eg, using a sign that is the name of the town in which the defendant offers the relevant goods and/or services;
- *time of the production of goods or of the rendering of services* – eg, use of the sign '24/7' to indicate that the relevant goods and/or services can be purchased at any time of day or night; and
- *other characteristics of the goods and/or services* – the inclusion of this wording means that the list of characteristics is not exhaustive. In practice, however, virtually all use of this defence relates to one of the characteristics listed above.

The use of non-distinctive elements: From March 2016 this defence also covers the use of non-distinctive elements. A good example of where this might occur is where a plaintiff's registration is for a non-distinctive word in conjunction with a stylised logo and the defendant uses the word element but not the logo.

Prior to the introduction of this defence, defendants accused of infringing a registration containing non-distinctive elements had to try and avoid infringement through some other means, often having to file a counterclaim for a declaration of invalidity.

The manner in which the allegedly non-distinctive term is being used is relevant in considering whether this defence applies, bearing in mind that marks which have achieved registration are presumed to be validly registered. This fact, together with the need for the use in question to be in accordance with honest practices in industrial or commercial matters for the defence to apply (see section 4.1 above), is likely to mean that in many cases the nature of the use will have to be in some way descriptive for a defendant to be able to rely on the defence.

4.4 Referential use defence

The wording of this defence was also changed as part of the reforms introduced in 2016. The previous version referred only to uses that were necessary to indicate the intended purpose of the goods and/or services in relation to which the allegedly infringing mark was used. The updated version speaks of "identifying or referring to goods or services as those of the proprietor", although it still remains the case that the use should be "necessary" to indicate the intended purpose of the goods and/or services at issue.

This defence is intended to enable those who provide spare parts, accessories or related goods and/or services to refer to the brands/products for which they provide such goods and/or services. Much of the case law surrounding this defence has arisen from disputes in the automobile industry, where there is a large market in spare parts and accessories. As discussed above, this defence is subject to the requirement that the use in question should be in accordance with honest practices in industrial or commercial matters, meaning that parties cannot use it as a means of free-riding on a known brand name, eg, by making it appear there is an official connection with the EUTM proprietor where this is not the case.

4.5 Exhaustion of rights defence

The proprietor of an EUTM registration is not entitled to prohibit the use of its mark in relation to goods that the proprietor itself put on the market in the EEA, or which were put on the market in the EEA with the proprietor's consent, unless there are legitimate reasons for the proprietor to oppose further commercialisation of the goods.

A detailed discussion of the exhaustion of rights rules is outside the scope of this book, but it is worth noting that:

- for goods to have been 'put on the market', they must have actually been sold. Offering those goods for sale is not enough;
- the territorial scope of the exhaustion rules is the EEA, and so slightly wider than the Union;
- exhaustion does not apply to goods put on the market outside the EEA, so that a plaintiff can prevent goods sold legitimately in, for example, the United States from being resold in the Union, unless it can be very clearly demonstrated by the defendant that the plaintiff consented to those goods being imported into the Union; and
- there are a number of reasons why a plaintiff may have 'legitimate reasons' for preventing goods from being resold. The most common example is set out in the Regulation itself: "where the condition of the goods is changed or impaired after they have been put on the market".

4.6 Intervening rights defence

This defence can be used where, although the plaintiff has the earlier rights, the defendant owns an EUTM registration (or national registration) (referred to as the 'intervening right') that the plaintiff cannot invalidate on the basis of its earlier rights. If this is the case, the defendant's use of its registered mark cannot be prevented.

The key point here is the reason why the plaintiff cannot use its earlier rights to invalidate the defendant's intervening right. Owning an EUTM registration is not in itself a defence to infringement, so for a defendant to rely on the intervening rights defence, one of the following special circumstances must be shown to apply:

- *the plaintiff could not have used its earlier right to oppose the defendant's EUTM application* – eg, because it had not yet acquired a sufficient reputation to be used as the basis of a reputation-based opposition (such that it cannot be said that the later right should never have been allowed to proceed to registration due to the existence of the earlier registration);

- *the plaintiff expressly consented to the defendant's EUTM application* – the consent has to be unequivocal for the defendant to rely on it;
- *the plaintiff acquiesced in the defendant's use of the later mark* – for a detailed discussion of acquiescence, see Chapter 18, section 10.7;
- *the plaintiff could have invoked its right in an earlier action, but did not* – if a plaintiff brings an action based on one right, and loses, it cannot then bring a second action relying on a right that could have been, but was not, relied on in the first action (see Chapter 18, sections 7 and 10.5); or
- *the plaintiff cannot prove use of its earlier right in both the five years before the date of the current infringement proceedings and the five years before the application (or priority, if claimed) date of the defendant's EUTM application* – this point is particularly important and is the provision that is most likely to be relied on by defendants. It covers the situation where a plaintiff owns a registration for a mark that, for whatever reason, is not used for an extended period of time (at least five years). In these circumstances, the plaintiff's non-use means that it cannot prevent the defendant registering the same (or a similar) mark. If the plaintiff starts to use its mark again, the defendant cannot raise a counterclaim for non-use in infringement proceedings (as the plaintiff's use re-validates the registration for its entire lifespan). However, it would be very unfair if the defendant's use and registration could be challenged after the event when it could not have been challenged at the outset. This was in fact the case in some circumstances prior to the Regulation being changed in 2016 and the introduction of the intervening rights defence is a very welcome addition to the Regulation.

Although the above discussion refers only to the situation where a defendant owns an EUTM registration, there are equivalent rules covering the situation where a defendant owns a national registration (although, of course, in those circumstances the defence is restricted to the Member State covered by the defendant's national registration).

Where this defence applies, the owner of the later registration cannot use that registration to bring infringement proceedings against the owner of the earlier registration.

5. 'Attacks' on the validity of the allegedly infringed EUTM registration

Any EUTM Court dealing with an infringement claim must treat the allegedly infringed EUTM registration as valid unless the validity is called into question by the defendant, by way of a counterclaim either for revocation or for a declaration of invalidity. Where a revocation or invalidity action is filed at the Office after infringement proceedings have been issued (without any counterclaim being filed), the court hearing the infringement action should still treat the EUTM registration in question as valid. As a result, a defendant should not file a revocation or invalidity action at the Office if it has been served with infringement proceedings: instead, a counterclaim should be filed in those proceedings.

As discussed in Chapter 21, section 9, if the defendant files an invalidity or revocation action at the Office before infringement proceedings have been issued, the EUTM Court dealing with the infringement action stays those proceedings pending the outcome of the action before the Office, unless there are special reasons why the infringement proceedings should continue. This is the so-called 'EUIPO torpedo', which can be employed by a potential defendant as a defence mechanism if it becomes aware that infringement proceedings may be brought against it.

Where a counterclaim for revocation and/or a declaration of invalidity has been filed in infringement proceedings, the EUTM Court can, following a request from the EUTM proprietor, order the defendant to file an equivalent action at the Office. In this situation, the Court stays the case before it pending the outcome of the proceedings at the Office. This rarely happens in practice, however.

If a defendant is able to cancel an EUTM registration on which infringement proceedings are based, it cannot be held to infringe that registration from the effective date of cancellation. The effective date of the cancellation varies: if a registration is invalidated, it is deemed to have never existed (and so can never have been infringed). If, however, a registration is revoked, it is possible for the defendant to be found to have infringed it up to the date on which the revocation is effective, though the remedies available to the plaintiff would be limited in these circumstances (and it is very unlikely that an injunction would be awarded). The grounds and consequences of revocation actions are discussed in Chapter 17, while the grounds and consequences of invalidity actions are discussed in Chapter 18.

It is possible for a defendant to challenge the validity of an EUTM registration in multiple ways in the same infringement proceedings – eg, counterclaims for both relative grounds invalidity and for non-use revocation against the same EUTM registration. Various common scenarios are set out below, together with the available options for each situation:

- **The allegedly infringed EUTM registration had been registered for more than five years at the time the infringement action was brought, and does not appear to have been used in the past five years:**
  - counterclaim for non-use revocation;
  - file a proof of use request in the course of the infringement proceedings.

  A successful counterclaim results in the EUTM registration being removed from the Register, whereas the plaintiff's failure to prove use only means that the registration is ignored in the infringement proceedings (so that it remains on the Register). For this reason, it is usually prudent to file both a counterclaim for non-use revocation and a proof of use request.
- **The defendant considers that the allegedly infringed EUTM had become generic or misleading before the infringement action was brought:**
  - counterclaim for revocation.
- **The defendant considers that the allegedly infringed EUTM registration should never have been accepted, because the mark is not inherently distinctive:**
  - counterclaim for a declaration of invalidity on absolute grounds.

  Depending on the circumstances, it may be the case that the issues raised in a counterclaim for a declaration of invalidity on absolute grounds are similar to those raised where a defendant seeks to rely on the non-distinctiveness/ descriptiveness defence discussed above. There may, therefore, be merit in arguing by way of defence that the complained-of use was descriptive in nature and at the same time filing a counterclaim for a declaration of invalidity on the basis that the mark in question is descriptive of characteristics of the goods and/or services for which it is registered and should never have been registered (subject of course to any potential acquired distinctiveness points). Only one of these routes would need to succeed for the defendant to defend its actions.

- **The defendant owns an earlier right that predates the allegedly infringed EUTM:**
  - counterclaim for a declaration of invalidity on relative grounds.

Owning an EUTM registration is not in itself a defence to infringement. As a result, a defendant needs to raise a counterclaim as opposed to being able to rely on its own registration as a defence. If follows from this that where a defendant owns an EUTM registration that post-dates the plaintiff's rights, this does not assist. In such circumstances, the plaintiff is likely to apply to invalidate the defendant's later registration.

Where a defendant does own an earlier right, this can be any of the earlier rights on which an invalidity action can be brought, as discussed in Chapter 18. However, it should be borne in mind that, as with all invalidity actions, consent, *res judicata* and acquiescence are potential defences (see Chapter 18, sections 10.4, 10.6 and 10.7).

In addition, a counterclaim for a declaration of invalidity cannot be brought if the defendant has already filed an unsuccessful invalidity action (either through the Office or by way of counterclaim) on the basis of earlier rights that could have been invoked in support of the first action but were not. If the defendant filed an invalidity action at the Office on the basis of an EUTM registration, but that action failed, it cannot then file a counterclaim for a declaration of invalidity on the basis of a second EUTM registration that it owned (and thus could have relied upon) when filing the first action (see Chapter 10, sections 7 and 10.5).

6. Other issues

The issues below can be of assistance to defendants facing the threat of infringement proceedings.

6.1 Prior rights applicable to particular localities

The provisions in this regard are often described as a quasi-defence to infringement, as they prevent the owner of an EUTM registration from opposing the use of a right that applies only to a particular locality where:

- that right pre-dates the plaintiff's EUTM registration; and
- under the national law of the Member State of the particular locality, the defendant is able to prevent the use of the mark protected by the plaintiff's EUTM registration.

Acquiescence provisions apply to such local rights, such that if the owners of the local rights acquiesce in the use of the mark covered by the EUTM registration in question for a period of five years, they can no longer rely on such rights to prevent use of that mark. Even where this is the case, however, the EUTM proprietor is still prevented from taking action in relation to the use of the earlier local right.

6.2 Applying for a declaration of non-infringement

Where a defendant is threatened with infringement, or wants to have clarity as to whether its use (or intended use) will be an infringement, it may be possible for the defendant to ask an EUTM Court to rule on whether its activities or planned activities infringe a particular EUTM registration. Such actions can only be brought before an EUTM Court if they are permitted under the national law of the Member State in which that court is located (see Chapter 21, section 4.2).

6.3 Groundless threats

In some Member States, it is possible for a defendant facing a threat of infringement to bring an action against the plaintiff alleging that the threat is unjustified, or 'groundless'. This type of action is in some ways similar to an action requesting a declaration of non-infringement, as the defendant (who brings the action) is asking a court to rule that its use (or intended use) does not (or would not) infringe the plaintiff's rights. However, a groundless threats action is different in scope, in that specific remedies are claimed against the plaintiff, such as an injunction preventing the plaintiff from making further threats and damages to compensate the defendant for losses suffered as a result of the threat. The rules relating to groundless threats vary between Member States, and it is not possible to bring an action in relation to some types of threat, but again this is something a defendant should consider when accused of infringement.

Further reference

Regulation – Articles 12-13a, 99-101, 104
Office Guidelines – Part E, Section 6

Chapter 24: Seniority

1. What is seniority?

Seniority is a unique feature of the EUTM system that promotes the replacement of national registrations by EUTM registrations. It is only relevant when a proprietor owns both:

- a registration (or registrations) giving rights in individual Member States of the Union; and
- an EUTM application or registration for the same mark.

When the EUTM system started in 1996, there were, of course, a very large number of pre-existing national trade mark registrations in place across the Union. A successful seniority claim allows the rights given by national registrations to be maintained without the proprietor having to renew them: the earlier rights are effectively subsumed within the EUTM registration, enabling proprietors to make substantial savings on renewal fees, without any loss of rights.

In addition, proprietors who make use of seniority benefit from the other advantages of owning EUTM registrations rather than multiple national registrations (see Chapter 3, section 6). As a result, seniority makes the EUTM system more attractive to the owners of existing national rights in the Union than it may otherwise be.

2. How does seniority work?

The basic operation of seniority is very simple. Once seniority has been successfully claimed, the proprietor of an earlier registration can surrender that registration (or allow it to lapse) and continue to have the same rights as if the earlier registration were still in place.

Seniority can be claimed from multiple registrations for the same EUTM registration, whether at the same time or separately. For example, consider a proprietor owning national registrations in Austria (filed in 1994), Germany (filed in 1998) and Italy (filed in 2002), and an EUTM registration filed in 2014 for which seniority has been claimed from the earlier national registrations. If the national registrations are allowed to lapse or are surrendered, the EUTM registration will give rights dating back to 1994 in Austria, 1998 in Germany and 2002 in Italy. In the remainder of the Union, the EUTM registration will give rights as of its filing date in 2014.

The earlier rights obtained through claiming seniority can be relied upon in both national and EUTM proceedings. Staying with the example given above, suppose the proprietor wants to oppose an EUTM application filed a week before its EUTM application in 2014. Once seniority has become effective, this can be done using the EUTM registration, despite it having been filed after the application that is opposed (as the national rights that have become part of the EUTM registration could have been relied upon if they had remained independent rights).

3. When does seniority become effective?

Seniority is not effective unless and until the earlier registration(s) from which it has been claimed are surrendered or allowed to lapse. There is no time limit within which seniority must become effective once it has been validly claimed.

There are a number of reasons why a proprietor might decide to maintain an earlier registration. These include the following:

- there is pending litigation based upon the earlier national registration, in which case it is easier (and probably necessary) to maintain the national registration until the litigation is concluded;
- given the UK's decision to leave the Union, it would seem prudent to maintain UK national registrations rather than let them lapse prior to the date the UK leaves the Union; and
- EUTM registrations do not give protection in some dependent territories. For example, a national registration in Denmark gives protection in Greenland and the Faroe Islands, whereas an EUTM registration does not.

4. Requirements for a valid seniority claim

For seniority to be validly claimed the owner, the trade mark, and the goods and/or services must all be identical for both the EUTM and the national registration(s). This is known as the 'triple identity' rule. In addition, the national registration must give rights in the relevant Member State from an earlier date than the EUTM registration does.

4.1 Identity of owner

The applicant for seniority must ensure that the owners are the same as this will not be checked by the Office. If the owners are different, the seniority claim will be accepted, but will not be valid. The effect of this is that, if the national registration is allowed to lapse, the earlier filing date in the relevant country will be lost (though of course there will be no effect on the EUTM registration itself).

The important thing is that the actual owner of the EUTM right and the earlier registration are identical, even if this is not reflected in the relevant register when the claim for seniority is made. For example, there may be an assignment that has not been recorded, or the proprietor's name may be shown in different forms on different registers, such as a French company referred to as 'Société Anonyme' on one register and 'SA' on another.

For seniority to have effect, the owner of the EUTM right and the earlier registration must be the same both when the claim to seniority is made and when it becomes effective (ie, when the earlier registration is surrendered or allowed to lapse). If the earlier registration and the EUTM registration are assigned separately after seniority has been claimed, but before it becomes effective, the claim will cease to be valid (unless both have returned to the same ownership at the point at which the seniority becomes effective).

4.2 Identity of marks

It is only possible to claim seniority if the marks covered by the EUTM registration and the earlier registration are identical. When assessing whether marks are 'identical' or not, the Office ignores insignificant differences that a reasonably observant consumer would only notice upon examining the marks side by side.

There are particular issues as to whether figurative marks or logos filed in different colours are identical. This is considered in the context of priority claims in Chapter 5, section 12. Two examples of when seniority would be refused due to the marks not being identical are shown in the table below.

Earlier registration	EUTM registration	Decision
H/H HellyHansen	H/H HELLY HANSEN	Case R 1157/2009-1, HELLY HANSEN AS Seniority refused due to differences in terms of colours, typeface and shape. Refusal upheld on appeal.
Great changes in education PLC	Grate changes in education PLC	This is an example from the Office Guidelines. Seniority would be refused due to the difference in the spelling being a significant change that would be noticed by consumers.

4.3 Identity of goods and/or services

It is only possible to claim seniority for goods and/or services that are contained within both the EUTM registration and the earlier registration. The specifications for the EUTM registration and the earlier registration do not, however, need to be identical. Rather, seniority can be claimed to the extent there is an overlap between the goods and/or services. Examples of how this works in practice are shown in the table on the next page.

The relevant rights will be maintained automatically and an applicant does not have to specify the particular goods and/or services for which seniority is claimed. As with the requirement that the owner of the EUTM registration and the earlier registration are the same, the Office does not check whether the goods and/or services overlap: an applicant for seniority should check carefully to ensure that rights are not lost inadvertently by allowing a national registration to lapse where the specification of that national registration is broader than the specification of the EUTM registration.

Goods in earlier registration	Goods in EUTM registration	Effective seniority
Shirts, shorts, trousers	Clothing	'Shirts, shorts and trousers', as they all fall within the wider term 'clothing'.
Clothing	Shirts, shorts, trousers	'Shirts, shorts and trousers', as the rights maintained cannot be wider than the EUTM specification. As a result, the protection for other types of clothing covered by the earlier registration would be lost.

4.4 Existing registration(s) must give earlier rights in a Member State

A claim for seniority is only possible in respect of registrations having effect in individual Member States. It is possible to claim seniority from both national registrations (including Benelux registrations) and IRs designating individual Member States. It is not possible, however, to claim seniority from an earlier EUTM application or registration or a Union designation in an IR.

Ordinarily, the registration from which seniority is claimed will have a filing date that is earlier than the filing date of the EUTM registration. This is not necessarily the case, however, as things become slightly complicated when new Member States join the Union.

It is possible to claim seniority from a national registration that post-dates the EUTM registration, provided that the national registration was filed prior to the date the relevant Member State joined the Union.

By way of example, Croatia joined the Union on 1 July 2013. If a proprietor owns an EUTM registration filed in 2008 and a Croatian registration filed in 2011, it can claim seniority from that Croatian registration. The EUTM registration would give rights in Croatia from 2011 rather than (as would normally be the case) the date of Croatia's accession on 1 July 2013.

5. Process

5.1 Making a claim for seniority

To be valid, a claim for seniority must include:

- an indication of the Member State in, or for which, the mark is registered;
- the filing date of the relevant registration;
- the number of the relevant registration;
- the goods and/or services covered by the relevant registration; and
- evidence of the existence of the relevant registration. This evidence can be either a copy of the relevant registration or renewal certificate, an extract from the relevant register or national gazette, or an extract from an official database. Extracts from private or commercial databases are not accepted. It

should, however, be noted that no documentary evidence needs to be provided if the Office can access details of the registration online at the relevant national IPO. Having said that, the Regulation contemplates a new implementing Regulation stipulating the information to be provided, so this may change.

Everything except evidence of the existence of the relevant registration must be included with the request for seniority. Evidence of the relevant registration must be provided within three months of the seniority request being filed.

No fee is payable for making a seniority claim.

5.2 Timing of a seniority claim

A seniority claim can be made:

- when an EUTM application is filed;
- within two months of an EUTM application being filed; or
- at any time after an EUTM becomes registered.

If a seniority claim is made more than two months after an EUTM application is filed, but before it is registered, a deficiency notice is issued and (unless there has been some error) the claim to seniority will be refused. This does not, however, prevent a new seniority claim being made once the EUTM application becomes registered.

5.3 Language to be used

A seniority claim made when an EUTM application is filed, or within two months of the application, should be made in one of the two languages of the application. (See Chapter 5, section 10.)

Seniority claims made post-registration can be filed in any of the Languages of the Office.

5.4 Examination of a seniority claim

The Office examines seniority claims to ensure the marks covered by the earlier registration(s) and the EUTM registration are the same. The Office does not, however, check whether the owners or the goods and/or services are the same. It is for the applicant to ensure that these details are correct.

If the Office believes the marks are not identical, a deficiency notice is issued. Unless the Office can be persuaded that the marks should be seen as identical, the claim to seniority will be refused.

The other thing the Office checks is the evidence of the existence of the earlier registration(s) provided by the applicant. If no such evidence is filed, the Office initially attempts to obtain the necessary information from the database of the relevant national IPO(s). If this is not possible, a deficiency notice is issued and the applicant is given an opportunity to file the necessary evidence.

5.5 Once seniority has been accepted

Details of accepted seniority claims are published in the *EUTM Bulletin* and are recorded in the Register. In addition, the Office informs the IPO(s) of the relevant Member State(s) about the seniority claim.

6. Losing the rights obtained through seniority

There are a number of circumstances in which a seniority claim can be lost once it has been accepted.

6.1 There is no longer 'triple identity'

This may happen because the earlier registration and the EUTM registration have been assigned to different owners or because the overlapping goods and/or services have been removed from either the earlier registration or the EUTM registration prior to the seniority claim becoming effective (see section 4 above).

6.2 The EUTM rights are lost

If an EUTM application does not go through to registration, for whatever reason, the claim to seniority will be of no effect. The same applies if an EUTM registration is invalidated or revoked. In these circumstances, if the seniority claim has become effective (because the earlier registration has been surrendered or allowed to lapse), all rights in both the earlier registration and the EUTM application or registration will be lost. The only means by which rights can be maintained is if the EUTM application or registration is converted into national applications (see Chapter 25), in which case the seniority rights are maintained in the relevant Member State(s) in which conversion takes place.

6.3 The earlier registration is lost

It is important to ensure the earlier registration is not surrendered or allowed to lapse prior to the EUTM registration process being completed. If this happens, the claim to seniority will be lost. Similarly, if the earlier registration is invalidated or revoked prior to the seniority claim becoming effective, the seniority claim will be lost. Seniority will not, however, be lost where the effective date of revocation is after the filing date (or, where priority has been claimed, the priority date) of the EUTM registration.

7. Claiming seniority in IRs

Most of the rules applicable to claiming seniority for EUTM registrations apply equally to Union designations of IRs. There are, however, some specific points that should be noted.

7.1 Timing and method of seniority claims

Seniority may be claimed either:

- when the Union designation is filed, using WIPO Form MM17 (sent to WIPO with the designation request); or
- after the final acceptance of the Union designation has been published (by applying to the Office in the same way as with a direct EUTM application).

This differs from direct EUTM applications, in that it is not possible to claim seniority within two months of filing the Union designation. If a seniority claim is made in the period between the filing of the Union designation and the publication of its final acceptance, the Office treats the claim as having been made on the date of publication of the final acceptance. See Chapter 32 for more information on Union designations of IRs.

7.2 Supporting documents

If a seniority claim is made when the IR is filed, the deadline for filing supporting evidence is three months from the date WIPO notifies the Office about the application.

7.3 Representation

If the representative on record for the IR is not able to represent the applicant before the Office (see Chapter 2, section 10), a deficiency notice is issued. It will then be necessary for the applicant to appoint a suitable representative. For further information, see Chapter 32.

Further reference

Regulation – Articles 34, 35, 153 and 153a
Implementing Regulation – Rules 8 and 28
Office Guidelines – Part B, Section 2
TMDN, *Common Communication on the Common Practice of the Scope of Protection of Black and White Marks*
LTJ Diffusion SA v Sadas Vertbaudet SA (Case No C-291/00), CJEU decision dated 20 March 2003

Chapter 25: Conversion

---

1. What is conversion?

Conversion is a process that involves an EUTM application or registration being turned into national applications in one or more Member States. It allows proprietors to maintain rights at the national level in circumstances where, for whatever reason, it is not possible to (or the proprietor has decided not to) maintain the unitary, Union-wide rights given by an EUTM registration.

Conversion can be either total or partial. Partial conversion occurs where an EUTM application or registration is maintained in part but some of the goods and/or services are (for whatever reason) deleted from it. In the case of a partial conversion, only the goods and/or services that have been deleted can be converted: the goods and/or services that remain within the EUTM application or registration cannot be included within the conversion request, as they still give Union-wide protection.

2. The effective date of conversion

Ordinarily, a national application resulting from conversion will have the same effective filing date as the EUTM application or registration that was converted (taking into account any priority and/or seniority claims that may be relevant).

This is not necessarily always the case, however. Where conversion is requested in a Member State that was not part of the Union when the EUTM application was filed, the filing date of the national application might be different to that of the EUTM right that was converted. This is because the filing date of a converted national application cannot be earlier than the date a Member State joined the Union. For example, if an EUTM registration dating back to 1 April 1996 were to be allowed to lapse and converted into national applications in France, Estonia and Romania, the effective filing date of the national applications would be 1 April 1996 in France, 1 May 2004 in Estonia and 1 January 2007 in Romania.

National applications resulting from conversion give rights as soon as a valid conversion request is filed. This means that these rights can be used as the basis of EUTM opposition and cancellation actions even before the relevant Member States allocate application numbers (or take any other action) in relation to the conversion request. In the same way, pending EUTM opposition and cancellation actions can continue if they are based on an EUTM application or registration that is subsequently converted.

3. When can conversion be used?

There are four separate circumstances in which conversion can take place.

3.1 Where an EUTM application is refused

Conversion is possible whether the refusal arises as the result of objections raised on absolute grounds or as the result of a successful opposition. It is, however, only possible to convert in Member States in which the ground for refusal was not expressly found to exist in the relevant decision.

Where an EUTM application is refused on absolute grounds, if the refusal relates to a particular Member State or States, conversion will only be possible in the other Member States. For example, if a mark is refused registration because it is found to be non-distinctive in a particular language, it is not possible to convert in any Member State in which that language is an official language (see Chapter 8, section 4).

Conversely, if a mark is refused registration Union-wide (for example, if the application is for a single colour or a smell, which has no language relevance), conversion is not possible anywhere.

Where an application is refused following an opposition, whether conversion is possible or not depends on the earlier rights on which the opposition decision is based. If the decision is based on an EUTM right, conversion is not possible anywhere. If, however, the decision is based on rights in one or more Member States, conversion is possible in the other Member States.

It should be noted that the Office does not necessarily base opposition decisions on all the opponent's earlier rights. There are many cases in which the Office has only based its decision on one of multiple earlier rights included as the basis of the opposition. As a result, it may be that conversion is possible in a Member State in which it is known that earlier rights (which could form the basis of a successful opposition) exist. In these circumstances, an applicant should consider whether conversion is worthwhile in such Member States.

3.2 Where an EUTM application is withdrawn

Conversion is possible in every Member State in circumstances in which an EUTM application is withdrawn, no matter when in the application process the withdrawal takes place. This is subject to the caveat that the EUTM application must have been validly filed (that is, the basic requirements for obtaining a filing date – including payment of the necessary application fees – must have been met: see Chapter 5, section 2).

Conversion in these circumstances often occurs where an opposition is filed against an EUTM application and the proprietor realises that the opposition is going to be successful. Rather than have the application refused, the applicant instead voluntarily withdraws the application before an adverse decision is made. If the opposition is based on national rights, only the applicant may decide to convert in territories other than those in which the national rights exist.

3.3 Where an EUTM application is deemed to be withdrawn

Currently, the only circumstance in which an application is deemed to be withdrawn is where additional class fees (that is, fees payable because the application covers more than one class) are not paid.

The same rule would apply if an EUTM registration fee were not paid. No registration fee is, however, currently payable for any EUTM application and it seems very unlikely that such a fee will be reintroduced in the foreseeable future.

3.4 Where an EUTM registration ceases to have effect

A EUTM registration ceases to have effect in four separate circumstances:

- *where the registration is surrendered* – in such a case, conversion is possible in every Member State;
- *where the registration is not renewed and is instead allowed to lapse* – in such a case, conversion is possible in every Member State;
- *where the registration is declared invalid (either by the Office or by an EUTM Court)* – in such a case, conversion is not possible in Member States in which the reason the registration was declared invalid applies. This may be Union-wide (so that it would not be possible to convert anywhere) or could relate to only one or several Member States. The same considerations apply as discussed in section 3.2 above; and
- *where the registration is revoked, whether by the Office or by an EUTM Court* – in such case, conversion is not normally possible, unless the proprietor can prove that the ground for revocation does not apply in certain Member States. For example, where an EUTM registration is revoked for non-use, it will be possible to apply for conversion in Member State(s) in which sufficient use has been made to justify maintenance of a registration under the laws of those Member States. It is very rare that such circumstances will exist and this provision is hardly, if ever, used.

4. Process

4.1 Time limit for requesting conversion

The time limit for requesting conversion is three months. This deadline is not extendable. This time period begins to run from different dates, depending on the circumstances:

- *where an EUTM application has been refused* – the three-month period runs from the date on which the decision of the Office becomes final (that is, on the expiry of the appeal period, or the date of the decision if no further appeal is possible);
- *where an EUTM application is withdrawn* – the three-month period runs from the date on which the Office receives the withdrawal request;
- *where an EUTM application is deemed to be withdrawn* – the Office sends a notification to the applicant fixing the three-month period;
- *where an EUTM registration is surrendered* – the three-month period runs from the date on which the Office receives the surrender request;
- *where an EUTM registration is not renewed and is instead allowed to lapse* – the three-month period runs from the day following the last day of the period

within which a renewal request could have been filed (that is, the end of the six-month grace period within which late renewal is possible). For example, if an EUTM registration is due for renewal on 15 January, the grace period expires on 15 July, so that the three-month conversion period runs from 16 July to 16 October;
- *where an EUTM registration is declared invalid (whether by the Office or by an EUTM Court)* – the three-month period runs from the date on which the decision of the Office (or EUTM Court) becomes final. This is either the expiry of the appeal period or the date of the decision if no further appeal is possible; and
- *where the registration is revoked (either by the Office or by an EUTM Court)* – the three-month period runs from the date on which the decision of the Office (or EUTM Court) becomes final. Again, this is either the expiry of the appeal period or the date of the decision if no further appeal is possible.

4.2 Contents of a conversion request

A conversion request must contain the following information:
- the applicant's name and address;
- the number of the EUTM application or registration to be converted;
- the ground on which conversion is requested, together with the date the right to convert started (so that the Office can ensure the conversion request was filed within the relevant three-month period);
- the Member State(s) in which conversion is requested;
- the goods and/or services for which conversion is requested (it is possible to request conversion for different goods and/or services in different Member States, in which case it is necessary to set out the goods and/or services separately for each Member State);
- where conversion is requested following a decision by an EUTM Court, the date on which the decision became final must be indicated and a copy of the relevant decision must be submitted (the decision can be filed without translation, no matter what the language of the conversion request may be);
- the name and address of any representative appointed in the Member State(s) in which conversion is requested; and
- details of any priority or seniority claims that are relevant.

The easiest way to make a conversion request is to complete the online form, which can be found on the Office's website. Use of this form is not, however, compulsory.

4.3 Language to be used

The language a conversion request must be filed in depends on the circumstances:
- *if the conversion relates to an EUTM application* – the conversion request must be filed in one of the two languages of the application (Chapter 5, section 10); or
- *if the conversion relates to an EUTM registration* – the conversion request can be filed in any of the Languages of the Office.

4.4 Fee payable

The current fee for conversion is €200. This fee is not expected to change in the foreseeable future.

A conversion request is deemed not to have been filed unless and until the fee is paid. As a result, the fee must be paid within the relevant three-month conversion period. If the fee is not paid within this period, the conversion request will not be valid. The only exception to this is where the rules for late payment of fees apply (as to which, see Chapter 2, section 9).

4.5 Examination of a conversion request

The Office examines conversion requests in relation to the following matters:

- *fees* – if the fees are not paid in time, the Office informs the applicant that the conversion request is deemed never to have been filed;
- *timing* – a conversion request filed outside the relevant three-month period will be rejected;
- *language* – if the conversion request is filed in an unacceptable language, a deficiency notice is issued and the applicant is given an opportunity to correct the error;
- *formalities requirements* – if some of the required information (as set out in section 4.2 above) is missing, a deficiency notice is issued and the applicant is given an opportunity to provide the missing information;
- *grounds* – if it is not possible to convert the EUTM application or registration on the ground claimed in the request, or into one or more of the Member States listed in the request (see section 3 above), a deficiency notice is issued; and
- *partial conversio*n – if conversion is requested for goods and/or services in respect of which conversion is not possible (for whatever reason), a deficiency notice is issued.

If a deficiency is not overcome within the time period set by the Office, the conversion request will be rejected. It is possible for a conversion request to be partially rejected, normally on the basis that conversion is only possible in some but not all the Member States listed in the request or that conversion is only possible for some of the goods and/or services listed in the request.

If a conversion request is refused, an appeal can be filed against this decision, though it is unlikely (unless the Office has made a clear error) that such an appeal will be successful.

Where a conversion request is refused because of late payment of fees, any fees paid are reimbursed. If a conversion request is refused because of any other deficiency, the fees paid are not reimbursed.

4.6 Publication

If the conversion request relates to an EUTM application that was never published, no details of the conversion request are published either.

For all other EUTMs (ie, registrations and applications that have been published), once a request for conversion has been accepted, details are noted in the EUTM Register and published in the *EUTM Bulletin*.

4.7 Transmission to national IPOs

The final stage of the conversion process is for details of the conversion request to be sent by the Office to the national IPO(s) of the Member State(s) in which conversion has been validly requested. The Office informs the applicant of the date on which this was done.

Once a conversion request has been received, each national IPO will normally require the applicant to:

- pay the relevant fee due for an application in that Member State;
- give an address for service in that Member State;
- file a translation of the conversion request and accompanying documents into one of the official languages of that Member State if they have been filed in a different language; and
- provide further representations of the mark if the representation in the conversion request does not meet local requirements in that Member State.

Each national IPO is also entitled to ask for any additional information it feels is necessary to allow the converted application to be examined in that Member State.

Once the necessary information and documentation have been obtained, the national IPO examines the converted application in the same way as it would examine any other national application. The converted application cannot, however, be subjected to formal requirements of national law that are different from, or additional to, those provided for in the Regulation. This only applies to formal requirements: it is possible for the national IPO to raise an objection that was not previously raised by the Office.

5. Conversion of Union designations in IRs

Comparable rules exist when dealing with the conversion of Union designations in IRs. Several specific points should, however, be noted, as set out below. Further information on Union designations may be found in Chapter 32.

5.1 Choice of how to convert

An applicant converting a Union designation may choose to convert that designation:

- into national applications in the same way as for EUTM applications and registrations;
- into subsequent designations within the existing IR (so that, effectively, the designation of the Union is replaced by a designation of one or more Member States). This is known as 'opting-back'; or
- into a combination of the above options (although each Member State can only be designated once).

Opting-back is not possible unless the relevant Member State was a party to the Madrid Protocol ('the Protocol') on the filing date of the Union designation being converted (as otherwise rights could be obtained from a date before the relevant Member State joined the Madrid system).

5.2 Grounds for conversion

It is possible to convert a Union designation in the following circumstances:

- where the Union designation is refused by the Office;
- where the Union designation is invalidated by the Office or by an EUTM Court;
- where the Union designation is renounced and the renunciation has been recorded on the International Register; and
- where the entire IR is cancelled (in which case opting-back is not possible as there is no IR into which to opt-back).

5.3 Language to be used

If a conversion request is made prior to the Statement of Grant of Protection for the Union being issued, the conversion request must be filed in one of the two languages of the Union designation (see Chapter 32, section 3). After the Statement of Grant of Protection has been issued, a conversion request may be filed in any of the Languages of the Office.

5.4 Form of the request

The Office has produced a specific form covering the conversion of Union designations. While it is not mandatory to use this form, it is advisable to do so, so as to ensure all relevant and necessary information is given. In addition, where the opting-back option is chosen, WIPO form MM16 can be used.

5.5 Method of conversion

Particular care should be taken to ensure the conversion request is very clear as to whether the Union designation is to be converted into national applications and/or subsequent designations.

6. Conversion of certification marks

EU certification marks will be introduced from 1 October 2017. For further details, see Chapter 29.

The rules permit the conversion of EU certification marks in the same way and on the same basis as with ordinary EUTM applications and registrations. The TM Directive does not, however, require all Member States to have certification mark systems. As would be expected, conversion of an EU certification mark will not be possible in those Member States that do not have national certification mark systems.

Further reference

Regulation – Articles 74k, 112-114
Implementing Regulation – Rules 44-47
Office Guidelines – Part E, Section 2

Chapter 26: Restitutio in integrum

1. What is *restitutio in integrum*?

In the EUTM context, *restitutio in integrum* is a process that allows a party who has lost rights as a result of a failure to comply with a time limit set by the Office (but through no fault of its own) to have those rights reinstated. It is normally referred to simply as '*restitutio*'.

It is very difficult to succeed in a *restitutio* action, as the applicant for this remedy must prove that it took "all due care required by the circumstances." As a result, *restitutio* is only possible where the time limit was not met due to an issue that was outside the applicant's control.

2. The effect of *restitutio*

If an application for *restitutio* succeeds, the deadline that was missed is treated as if it had been met. This means that any rights lost by the applicant will be reinstated (and deemed never to have been lost). Any decision taken by the Office as a result of the missed deadline will become void.

Rights reinstated as a result of a successful *restitutio* action cannot, however, be used against a third party who, in good faith, began to use an identical or similar trade mark in the period between the loss of rights and publication of the successful outcome of the *restitutio* action.

To give an example of this limitation on the effect of *restitutio*, consider the scenario where an applicant does not respond to objections raised in the examination process and its EUTM application is refused. A third party notes the refusal and begins using an identical mark for goods covered by the refused EUTM application. Even if a *restitutio* application is successful, the EUTM registration that results cannot be used against the innocent third party who began using its mark in the intervening period. It is also possible for third parties to bring proceedings against the decision to allow *restitutio* (see section 6 below).

3. When is *restitutio* possible?

Any party that misses a deadline in proceedings before the Office is able to bring an action for *restitutio*. It is possible to apply for *restitutio* in all types of proceedings before the Office, whether *ex parte*, *inter partes* or appeals.

Only parties to proceedings can apply for *restitutio*, however (so that, for example, third parties that miss the opportunity to file observations cannot apply for it).

It is possible to apply for *restitutio* in respect of any deadline that is missed in proceedings, with the exception of the following (for which such an application is never possible):

- the three-month deadline for filing an opposition against an EUTM application and paying the associated opposition fee (see Chapter 11);
- the two-month deadline for applying for continuation of proceedings (see Chapter 27);
- any deadline which, if missed, does not directly lead to a loss of rights or means of redress – eg, a failure to request an extension of the cooling-off period in opposition proceedings; and
- the deadline for applying for *restitutio* itself.

4. When will an application for *restitutio* succeed?

Restitutio is only possible in very limited circumstances. The applicant must prove that it was unable to meet the missed deadline "in spite of all due care required by the circumstances having been taken."

The expression "all due care required by the circumstances" has been interpreted very strictly by the Office and by the CJEU. In the *AURELIA* decision, the General Court held that *restitutio* should only be permitted where there are "exceptional events, which cannot therefore be predicted from experience." In that case, it was stated that human errors are not "exceptional or unforeseeable events which cannot be predicted from experience", meaning that *restitutio* is not possible where a deadline is missed due to human error.

The *AURELIA* decision also made it clear that, where trade mark renewals are "entrusted to a specialised company using a computerised renewal reminder system", errors in the system (eg, the corruption or loss of data) are foreseeable errors. It was stated that there should be "a parallel reminder system" or, at least, that frequent checks should be carried out to ensure errors in the system are corrected. This means that *restitutio* is not possible where a deadline is missed due to errors in a computerised database.

In the same way, the breakdown of an internal procedure (even if that procedure has never failed previously) is not in itself enough to allow an application for *restitutio* to succeed. This seems very harsh and, as stated by the Fédération internationale des conseils en propriété intellectuelle (FICPI) in a submission of 2012, "out of proportion to the circumstances of the failure [that led to the deadline being missed]" and "contrary to the intentions and reasonable expectations of the proprietor of the IP right."

Nevertheless, under the current rules, it is unlikely that an application for *restitutio* will be accepted in most circumstances where a system breaks down. One situation in which *restitutio* has been allowed, however, is where a deadline was missed due to a breakdown in the postal service (see the Board of Appeal decision in *SUN PARK HOLIDAYS*). In the same way, *restitutio* is likely to be allowed where there is a late delivery of documents by an otherwise reputable courier company.

5. Process

5.1 Time limits for applying for *restitutio*

An application for *restitutio* will only be considered if it is made within the following timescales:

- *the application must be filed within one year of the time limit that was not complied with.* It should be noted that the one-year period for failure to file a renewal runs from the renewal date, not from the end of the six-month grace period (so that, for renewals, *restitutio* is only really a consideration once the six-month grace period has expired, as that period can be used during the first six months of the relevant period. For more information, see Chapter 15, section 3);
- *the application must be filed within two months of the reason for non-compliance being removed.* This will not necessarily be the date on which the applicant (or, if a representative has been appointed, the applicant's representative) discovers that the deadline was missed. For example, where a deadline was missed due to the applicant's representative being away from the office as a result of illness, the reason for non-compliance is deemed to have been removed on the date the representative returns to the office (and the two-month period will run from that date), irrespective of when they actually discover that the deadline was missed; and
- *the act that was not carried out before the missed deadline must be completed within two months of the reason for non-compliance being removed* (ie, the same deadline by which the application for *restitutio* must be filed). This means the necessary response/materials will generally be filed along with the application for *restitutio.*

5.2 Fee payable

The current fee for an application for *restitutio* is €200. This fee must be paid within the deadline for filing the application, otherwise the application is deemed never to have been filed.

5.3 Language to be used

An application for *restitutio* must be filed in one of the languages that could have been used in the relevant proceedings (but not necessarily the language that was actually chosen for those proceedings). As such, the application does not need to be filed in the same language as the proceedings to which it relates.

The choice of languages depends on the type of proceeding in which *restitutio* is sought, some examples of which are shown in the following table.

Choice of languages in *restitutio* proceedings

Proceedings in which the time limit was not observed	**Language of *restitutio* application**
Application filed in English with French as the second language	English or French
Opposition filed in German relating to an EUTM application filed in Portuguese with German as the second language	German or Portuguese
Revocation action filed against an EUTM registration filed in Italian with Spanish as the second language, where the parties agree that the language of the proceedings is Swedish	Swedish, Italian or Spanish
EUTM renewal	Any of the Languages of the Office

5.4 Content of an application for *restitutio*

An application for *restitutio* must contain:

- the grounds on which the application is based, including a detailed explanation of why the deadline was missed; and
- witness statements and evidence in support of the application, explaining why *restitutio* should be permitted.

In addition, as noted in section 5.1 above, the necessary documents to meet the deadline that was missed need to be filed before the deadline for requesting *restitutio*. These documents are, however, normally filed along with the application.

5.5 Where to apply

An application for *restitutio* must be filed with the tribunal or department of the Office dealing with the proceedings in which the relevant deadline was missed. Thus, for example, if a deadline is missed in an opposition, the application for *restitutio* should be filed with the Opposition Divisions.

5.6 Examination of an application for *restitutio*

Once an application for *restitutio* has been filed, it is examined by the competent body. If the application relates to *inter partes* proceedings, the other party (or parties) in those proceedings does not have an opportunity to comment on the application. If *restitutio* is allowed, that party's only recourse is to begin third party proceedings (see section 6 below).

5.7 Decision

If *restitutio* is permitted, any other parties to the relevant proceedings are notified. They cannot, however, appeal against that decision. In order to challenge the decision to allow *restitutio*, they must appeal instead against the final decision in the relevant proceedings.

If *restitutio* is refused, the applicant cannot appeal against that decision until the end of the relevant proceedings. At that point, an appeal against the decision not to award *restitutio* can be included as part of an appeal against the final decision. The rationale behind this is that the decision to allow or refuse *restitutio* may not affect the final outcome in the relevant proceedings, so to allow interim appeals on the issue of *restitutio* alone would merely prolong the proceedings and increase costs in a way that may be unnecessary.

5.8 Publication of decision

Where a missed deadline leads to a change in the status of an EUTM application or registration, the successful application for *restitutio* is published in the *EUTM Bulletin*. This is because the change in status will itself have been published in the *Bulletin* and, as a result, any third party relying on the change of status needs to be made aware that the change in status no longer applies. This allows the effect of a successful application for *restitutio* to be challenged in third party proceedings.

6. Third party proceedings

It is possible for a third party who is affected by a decision to allow *restitutio* to bring proceedings where:

- that party has put goods on the market or supplied services under a sign identical or similar to the relevant trade mark;
- that use began in the period between the loss of rights and the reinstatement of those rights as a result of the *restitutio* application; and
- the third party instigates proceedings within two months of publication of the decision to allow *restitutio* or, where there is no publication, the date on which *restitutio* takes effect.

There are no rules that apply to such third party proceedings. The competent body that decides on third party proceedings will be the body that decided to allow the application for *restitutio*. Any third party proceedings filed in these circumstances will be dealt with in the same way as opposition or cancellation proceedings.

Further reference

Regulation – Article 81

Office Guidelines – Part A, Section 8

International Federation of Intellectual Property Attorneys (FICPI) – *Re-establishment of Rights under Article 81 EUTMR and Article 67 CDR: Submission on behalf of FICPI*, dated 10 February 2012

Aurelia Finance v The Office (Case No T-136/08), Court of First Instance decision dated 13 May 2009 (*'AURELIA'*)

Ferienhäuser zum See GmbH v Sunparks Groep, NV (Case No R 1928/2011-4), Board of Appeal decision dated 25 June 2012 ('*SUN PARK HOLIDAYS*')

Chapter 27: Continuation and interruption of proceedings

1. What is continuation of proceedings?

Continuation of proceedings is a process that allows a missed deadline to be met retrospectively. It is normally referred to as 'continuation' and is also sometimes referred to as 'further processing'.

Continuation is only possible if the omitted act is carried out within two months of the missed deadline and an administration fee (€400 at the time of writing) is paid within the same period. It is possible to obtain continuation of most, but not all, time limits.

Continuation is granted automatically and no reasons or explanations have to be given as to why the original deadline was missed. As a result, where continuation is available, it is a much easier option than claiming *restitutio in integrum* (see Chapter 26).

2. Time limits that are excluded from continuation

Continuation is not available for all time limits. The following time limits are excluded from the scope of continuation:

- the one-month period within which the application fee for an EUTM application must be paid in order for a filing date to be maintained (see Chapter 5, section 2);
- the six-month priority period following an earlier trade mark application provided for in the Paris Convention (see Chapter 5, section 12);
- the six-month priority period following use of a mark at an international exhibition provided for in the Convention on International Exhibitions (see Chapter 5, section 13);
- the period within which deficiencies in an EUTM application (other than payment of the basic fee) must be rectified in order to obtain or maintain a filing date (see Chapter 5, section 2);
- the three-month period for filing an opposition (see Chapter 11, section 3);
- the three-month period within which the opposition fee must be paid (see Chapter 11, section 6);
- all deadlines set by the Office in opposition proceedings, namely:
    - the period within which the opponent must substantiate the opposition (Chapter 13, section 3);
    - the period within which the applicant can respond to the opposition (Chapter 13, section 5);

  - the period within which the opponent can file evidence and arguments in reply (Chapter 13, section 7); and
  - any other period granted by the Office for further exchange of arguments.

  Continuation is possible for all other deadlines in opposition proceedings (eg, time periods within which translations must be filed). These deadlines will not be excluded from the possibility of continuation after 1 October 2017. It is also worth noting that continuation is not excluded for any deadline set in invalidity or revocation proceedings:
- the period within which a registration can be renewed, although the availability of the late renewal period renders continuation irrelevant for this deadline (see Chapter 15, section 3);
- the six-month grace period within which late renewal of a registration is possible (see Chapter 15, section 3);
- the two-month period for filing a Notice of Appeal against a decision of the Office (see Chapter 20, section 2);
- the four-month period for filing a Statement of Grounds of appeal (see Chapter 20, section 2);
- the two-month period within which a Board of Appeal decision can be appealed to the General Court (see Chapter 20, section 13);
- all periods relating to an application for *restitutio in integrum* (see Chapter 26);
- all periods relating to an application for continuation;
- the three-month period within which conversion can be applied for (see Chapter 25, section 4);
- the three-month period within which the fee for conversion must be paid (see Chapter 25, section 4);
- the period after an EUTM application has been filed and during which priority can be claimed (see Chapter 5, section 12). The current period is two months, though from 1 October 2017 it will no longer be possible to claim priority after an application has been filed, so this period will no longer be relevant; and
- the period after an EUTM application has been filed and during which seniority can be claimed (see Chapter 24, section 5). The current deadline is two months and it is expected that this will remain the same when the new Implementing Regulation is published.

3. Process

Filing an application for continuation is very simple. A request for continuation is made in writing to the department of the Office dealing with the proceedings in which the deadline was missed. No official form is available and no explanation or evidence need to be provided: all that is required is a request for continuation.

Provided that the omitted act has been carried out, and the continuation fee (see section 1 above) paid within two months of the missed deadline, the application for continuation is accepted and the deadline is treated as if it had never been missed.

If the application for continuation is rejected for whatever reason, the continuation fee will be refunded.

Theoretically, it is possible to appeal against a decision refusing a request for continuation, though as this is such a simple process, it is very unlikely that such an appeal would be necessary (or, failing a clear error by the Office, successful).

4. Interruption of proceedings

Interruption allows proceedings to be effectively suspended if certain exceptional circumstances apply which mean that it becomes unclear who, if anyone, is authorised to continue with the proceedings. As a result, interruption is very rare.

The circumstances in which proceedings can be interrupted are as follows:

- where a natural person who is the owner of an EUTM application or registration (or the person authorised to act on his behalf, eg, a guardian or trustee in bankruptcy) dies or becomes legally incapacitated and so unable to act;
- where the owner of an EUTM application or registration is prevented from continuing the relevant proceedings for legal reasons resulting from action taken against his property. This applies equally whether the owner is a natural person (eg, where he is declared bankrupt and a trustee in bankruptcy is appointed) or a legal person (eg, where a company is declared insolvent and a liquidator is appointed); or
- where the above circumstances apply to the appointed representative acting in proceedings (eg, where the appointed representative dies).

The death or legal incapacity of the owner of an EUTM application or registration does not automatically cancel the authorisation of an appointed representative in most circumstances. This means that interruption is only possible where it is applied for by the appointed representative.

In the same way, where the owner of an EUTM application or registration is legally prevented from continuing with the proceedings due to, for example, insolvency, this will probably not automatically cancel the appointment of its representative. As a result, the proceedings will continue unless the appointed representative or the person designated to deal with the property of the owner of the EUTM application or registration (for example, a trustee in bankruptcy, a liquidator or a court) requests interruption.

Alternatively, in the circumstances set out in the first two bullet points above, it is possible that an appointed representative will decide that he can no longer act. If the representative resigns, the proceedings are automatically interrupted unless the Office is able to discover the identity of the relevant person who is able to continue with the proceedings (eg, a liquidator or trustee in bankruptcy). Where the owner of an EUTM application or registration is required to appoint a representative, failure to appoint a new representative does not give rise to grounds for interruption and is dealt with in the usual way (see Chapter 2, section 10).

Proceedings will be resumed once the reason for the interruption no longer applies – generally, when the Office is informed of the identity of the person able to continue with the relevant proceedings. The Office then writes to that person, and to any other parties to the proceedings, and indicates the date on which the proceedings will resume. All time limits are reset once proceedings are resumed following an interruption.

The situation is slightly more complicated in the circumstances described in the third bullet point above (ie, where a representative is no longer able to act). If the Office is not informed who the replacement representative is within three months, it writes to the owner of the EUTM application or registration and informs it that the proceedings will be resumed with that owner directly. If, however, that owner is required to appoint a representative to act on its behalf (see Chapter 2, section 10), the Office sets a two-month time limit for such an appointment to be made, failing which the relevant proceedings will be deemed to have been withdrawn.

Further reference

Regulation – Articles 82 and 82a

Implementing Regulation – Rule 73

Communication No 6/05 of the President of the Office of 16 September 2005 on restoration into missed time limits

Chapter 28: EU collective marks

1. What is a collective mark?

A collective mark is a special type of trade mark. It indicates that goods and/or services come from a member of a particular organisation, rather than from the trade mark owner itself. Put another way, collective marks distinguish the goods and/or services of members of the trade mark owner's organisation from the goods and/or services of non-members of that organisation.

Collective marks are therefore different in nature to ordinary trade marks and to certification marks. For a brief comparison of these three distinct types of mark, see Chapter 3, section 5. EU certification marks are considered in detail in Chapter 29.

2. What is an EU collective mark?

The EU collective mark system allows the owner of a collective mark to obtain Union-wide protection through a single registration.

The provisions of the Regulation apply to EU collective marks. This means that EU collective mark registrations give the same Union-wide rights and remedies as ordinary EUTM registrations, and most of the rules relating to EUTM applications and registrations apply equally to EU collective mark applications and registrations. There are, however, a number of differences and additional requirements, as discussed below.

One of the key additional requirements is that, as part of the registration process, an applicant for an EU collective mark must file regulations governing the use of the mark.

Examples of EU collective mark include DARJEELING (owned by the Tea Board, India, EU collective mark registration number 4325718), BAVARIAN BEER (owned by Bayerischer Brauerbund eV, EU collective mark registration number 9103367) and FIJI PURE (owned by the Government of the Republic of Fiji, EU collective mark registration number 10340586).

EU collective marks form only a tiny percentage (less than 1%) of the trade mark applications filed with the Office. Only 86 EU collective mark applications were filed in 2015 and 62 in 2014.

Before an EU collective mark application is filed, a potential applicant needs to ensure that the mark is definitely being used, or is going to be used, as a collective mark (rather than as an ordinary trade mark or as a certification mark). This is because it is only possible to change an EU collective mark application into an ordinary EUTM application if:

- the EU collective mark application is filed by an individual – as individuals are not permitted to own EU collective marks; or
- the Office is persuaded that an 'obvious error' was made when the application was filed: it is often difficult to prove that an obvious error was made, especially if the EU collective mark application was filed in the name of an association.

3. Who can own an EU collective mark?

There are two different types of owner of EU collective marks:

- *associations of manufacturers, producers, suppliers of services, or traders* – the association must exist as a distinct legal entity, with the capacity to have rights and obligations, make contracts, and sue and be sued in its own name; and
- *legal persons governed by public law* – the meaning of this phrase is interpreted broadly, so that all public bodies, of whatever nature, are covered. This includes the Union itself, the Member States and associations, corporations and other entities governed by public law at national or local level.

It is not necessary for the owner of an EU collective mark to be capable of operating across the entire Union. This allows associations and other entities which have a remit within only a single Member State to own Union-wide registrations. For example, the Institute of Trade Mark Attorneys in the UK owns an EU collective mark registration for M.I.T.M.A. (number 34322).

There is nothing to prevent the owners of EU collective marks from trading in the goods and/or services covered by their registrations. This is to be contrasted with EU certification marks, the owners of which cannot trade in the goods and/or services covered by their registrations.

An EU collective mark application or registration can be transferred to any legal entity that meets the definition set out above. Again, this is to be contrasted with EU certification marks.

4. Who can use an EU collective mark?

An EU collective mark can be used by anyone who meets the criteria set out in the regulations covering use of the mark. This normally means the members of the association that owns the EU collective mark registration.

Not all members of an organisation are, however, necessarily allowed to use an EU collective mark owned by the organisation. For example, the Chartered Insurance Institute owns a number of EU collective mark registrations, including FELLOW OF THE CHARTERED INSURANCE INSTITUTE (number 193672) and ASSOCIATE OF THE CHARTERED INSURANCE INSTITUTE (number 193631). Use of the first registration is, as would be expected, restricted to Fellows of the Institute.

There are also specific rules relating to geographic indications. The owner of an EU collective mark registration cannot prevent the use of a mark to designate the geographical origin of goods and/or services, provided that the use made is in accordance with honest commercial practices. This is examined in more detail below.

5. Fees

EU collective mark applications are more expensive than ordinary EUTM applications, presumably because of the additional requirements for the former, in particular the need for the Office to examine the regulations that form part of the application.

The application fees payable for EU collective mark applications are set out in the following table.

Table 1: Application fees payable for EU collective mark applications

Method of filing	Basic fee (one class)	Fee for second class	Fee for each class over two
E-filing	€1500	€50	€150
Paper filing	€1800	€50	€150

The renewal fees payable for EU collective mark registrations are also higher than for ordinary EUTM registrations, as set out in the following table.

Table 2: Renewal fees payable for EU collective mark applications

Method of filing	Basic fee (one class)	Fee for second class	Fee for each class over two
E-filing	€1500	€50	€150
Paper filing	€1800	€50	€150

6. Regulations governing use

It is a requirement of registration that regulations governing the use of the mark are filed by the applicant. These regulations must be submitted to the Office within two months of the filing date of the EU collective mark application.

The Regulation stipulates that the regulations governing use of an EU collective mark must indicate, as a minimum:

- the applicant's name and address (which is normally, but does not need to be, the same address as is shown on the Register);
- the objectives of the applicant (ie, the reasons the applicant organisation was created and what it is intended to achieve);
- the bodies (if any) authorised to represent the applicant;
- the conditions for membership of the applicant;
- the categories of person authorised to use the mark;
- any conditions governing use of the mark;

- any sanctions for misuse of the mark; and
- where the mark applied for is a geographical indication, a specific authorisation permitting any person whose goods and/or services originate in the geographical area concerned to become a member of the applicant.

The regulations are examined by the Office to ensure that they comply with the above requirements. In addition, the Office ensures that the regulations are not contrary to public policy or accepted principles of morality (though the authors are unaware of any objection ever having been raised on this basis).

If the Office believes that the regulations are not acceptable, a deficiency notice is issued and the applicant is given two months to amend the draft regulations so that they meet the relevant requirements.

It is also possible to submit amended regulations at any time, both before and after registration. Amendments will be accepted if the regulations still meet the requirements set out above.

7. Application process and examination

Applications for EU collective marks are made in the same way as ordinary EUTM applications, as set out in Chapter 4. Applications for EU collective marks cannot, however, be made through the Fast Track system, due to the requirement to file regulations.

Once filed, an EU collective mark application follows much the same process as an EUTM application, as detailed in Chapter 4. There are, however, a number of important differences.

7.1 Further absolute grounds of refusal

In addition to the criteria set out in Chapter 7, there are three further absolute grounds of refusal. The Office examines EU collective mark applications to ensure that:

- the owner is entitled to own an EU collective mark, as set out in section 3 above;
- the regulations meet the relevant criteria, as set out in section 6 above; and
- consumers will not be misled as to the significance of the mark: the Office needs to be sure that the mark will be seen as a collective mark, rather than as an ordinary trade mark or certification mark.

7.2 Observations

Observations by third parties can be filed on the same grounds as for ordinary EUTM applications (see Chapter 9, section 5). In addition, observations can be filed alleging that the EU collective mark should be refused registration on the basis of the additional grounds for refusal set out in section 7.1 above.

7.3 Geographical origin of goods and/or services

EU collective mark applications will not be refused on the basis that the mark indicates the geographical origin of goods and/or services. This is very different to ordinary EUTM applications for geographic signs and indications, which will be objected to on the basis that the mark is descriptive (see Chapter 7, section 5). It is accepted that geographic signs and indications can function as EU collective marks. This is subject to one caveat: an EU collective mark registration cannot be used to prevent the honest use of the mark to indicate that goods and/or services originate from the relevant geographical area. This is why, as noted in section 6 above, the regulations for EU collective mark applications where the mark applied for is a geographical indication must specifically permit any person whose goods and/or services originate in the geographical area concerned to become a member of the applicant.

8. Specifications of EU collective mark applications

Applications for EU collective marks do not need to be restricted to the goods and/or services actually provided by the applicant or covered by the regulations. As a result, EU collective mark applications can cover quite wide specifications.

For example, Asociacion de Productores de Papaya de Canarias Aspayacan (the Association of Papaya Growers of the Canary Islands) owns an EU collective mark registration for the logo shown below (number 12442273). The regulations filed indicate that the mark is used to show papaya and products derived from papaya originating from the Canary Islands. However, the registration covers terms that are a lot wider than this, including 'vegetables (including nuts and pulses)', 'bee products' and 'chocolate'.

Objections are not routinely raised by the Office against wide specifications in applications for EU collective marks (although it is possible for the Office to raise an objection if it is felt that the application is potentially misleading). This is to be contrasted with EU certification mark applications, which must be restricted to the goods and/or services to be certified.

9. Grounds for revocation

The grounds for revocation detailed in Chapter 17 are applicable to EU collective mark registrations, save that to maintain a registration, it is necessary to show use has been made by authorised members of the owner's association, as opposed to by the owner itself.

There are three additional grounds for revocation that are particular to EU collective marks. A registration can be revoked if the owner:

- has not taken reasonable steps to prevent the mark being used in a way that is incompatible with the regulations governing use of the mark;
- has used the mark in such a way that it is likely to be seen as something other than a collective mark (in particular, an ordinary trade mark or certification mark); and
- has amended the regulations governing use of the mark so that they do not comply with the requirements set out in the Regulation.

10. Grounds for invalidity

The grounds for invalidity detailed in Chapter 18 are applicable to EU collective marks. In addition, an EU collective mark registration can be cancelled if one of the additional grounds for refusal set out in section 7.1 above was applicable when the application was filed.

11. Infringement actions

Infringement actions can be brought by the owner of an EU collective mark registration. In addition, unless this is specifically prohibited by the regulations, it is possible for authorised users to bring infringement actions if the owner consents. To ensure the owner has conduct and control of any infringement actions, it is recommended that the regulations prohibit authorised users from bringing such actions.

Damage suffered by authorised users can be taken into account in infringement proceedings. The owner is entitled to claim compensation on behalf of authorised users who have suffered damage as a result of infringing use.

12. Conversion

The Directive requires every Member State to protect collective marks and it is possible to do so at the time of writing in each of the current 28 Member States. As a result, it is possible to convert an EU collective mark in every Member State (subject to the normal rules on conversion, as discussed in Chapter 25).

The rules relating to what has to be included in regulations governing the use of collective marks vary, however, between Member States, so that regulations accepted by the Office may need amendment (in addition to translation) before they are acceptable to national IPOs following conversion.

Further reference

Regulation – Articles 66-74
Implementing Regulation – Rules 42, 43
Office Guidelines – Part B, Sections 2 and 4

Chapter 29: EU certification marks

1. What is a certification mark?

A certification mark is another special type of trade mark. It indicates that goods and/or services have particular characteristics rather than indicating their trade origin.

Certification marks are therefore different in nature to both ordinary trade marks and collective marks. For a brief comparison of these three distinct types of mark, see Chapter 3, section 5. EU collective marks are considered in detail in Chapter 28.

Examples of well-known certification marks include the WOOLMARK logos (which indicate that products contain a certain percentage of wool) and the CE mark (which indicates that products satisfy certain health, safety and/or environmental requirements).

2. What is an EU certification mark?

The EU certification mark system allows the owner of a certification mark to obtain Union-wide protection through a single registration.

The Regulation lists the main types of characteristic that are likely to be certified, namely the "material, mode of manufacture of goods or performance of services, quality, accuracy or other characteristics" of the goods and/or services.

There is no limit on the characteristics that can be certified by an EU certification mark. However, the Regulation specifically excludes EU certification marks from indicating the geographical origin of goods or services.

The Regulation introduces EU certification marks with effect from 1 October 2017. As a result, there are no examples of EU certification marks that can be given at the time of writing.

The provisions of the Regulation apply to EU certification marks. This means that EU certification mark registrations give the same Union-wide rights and remedies as ordinary EUTM registrations; further, most of the rules relating to EUTM applications and registrations apply equally to EU certification mark applications and registrations. There are, however, a number of differences and additional requirements, which are discussed below.

One of the key additional requirements is that, as part of the registration process, an applicant for an EU certification mark must file regulations governing the use of the mark.

It is likely to be difficult to change the type of mark from a certification mark to a collective mark or ordinary trade mark after an application has been filed, so applicants need to be sure that what they are applying for really is a certification mark.

3. Who can own an EU certification mark?

It is possible for any natural or legal person to be the owner of an EU certification mark. There is, however, an important restriction on ownership: the owner of an EU certification mark cannot operate a business providing the goods or services certified by the mark. The reason for this restriction is that the owner of an EU certification mark has to be capable of independently verifying that the relevant goods and/or services meet the particular characteristics being certified.

This also restricts the assignment or other transfer of EU certification marks. It is only possible to transfer the ownership of an EU certification mark to a new owner if that owner meets the above criteria.

4. Who can use an EU certification mark?

An EU certification mark can be used by anyone providing goods and/or services that satisfy the criteria and characteristics set out in the regulations governing use of that mark.

This is very different to an ordinary EUTM registration, where the owner has exclusive rights to use the mark in the absence of a specific licence or permission being granted. The owner of an EU certification mark cannot prevent anyone from using the mark if the relevant criteria and characteristics are satisfied.

5. Fees

EU certification mark applications are more expensive than ordinary EUTM applications, presumably because of the additional requirements for the former, in particular the need for the Office to examine the regulations that form part of the application.

The application fees payable for EU certification mark applications are set out in the following table.

Fees payable for EU certification mark applications

Method of filing	Basic fee (one class)	Fee for second class	Fee for each class over two
E-filing	€1500	€50	€150
Paper filing	€1800	€50	€150

The Office has not published the fees that will be payable for renewal of EU certification mark registrations. It is expected that the renewal fees will be the same as for EU collective mark registrations (see Chapter 28, section 5). However, as the first EU certification mark registrations will not be due for renewal until 2027, the renewal fees that will be payable are impossible to estimate at the time of writing.

6. Regulations governing use

It is a requirement of registration that regulations governing the use of the mark are filed by the applicant. These regulations must be submitted to the Office within two months of the filing date of the EU certification mark application. The Regulation stipulates that the regulations governing use of an EU certification mark must indicate, as a minimum:

- who can use the mark;
- the characteristics certified by the mark;
- how those characteristics are to be tested;
- how the use of the mark is to be supervised;
- any conditions relating to the use of the mark; and
- any sanctions that apply for non-compliance with the regulations and/or misuse of the mark.

The Office examines the regulations to ensure they comply with the above requirements. In addition, the Office ensures the regulations are not contrary to public policy or accepted principles of morality.

If the Office believes that the regulations are not acceptable, a deficiency notice is issued and the applicant is given two months to amend the draft regulations so that they meet the relevant requirements.

It is also possible for the applicant to submit amended regulations at any time, both before and after registration. Amendments will be accepted so long as the regulations still meet the requirements set out above.

7. Application process and examination

Applications for EU certification marks are made in the same way as ordinary EUTM applications, as set out in Chapter 4. Applications for EU certification marks cannot, however, be made through the Fast Track system, due to the requirement to file regulations.

Once filed, an EU certification mark application follows much the same process as an EUTM application, as detailed in Chapter 4. There are, however, a number of important differences.

7.1 Further absolute grounds of refusal

In addition to the criteria set out in Chapter 7, there are four further absolute grounds of refusal. The Office examines EU certification mark applications to ensure that:

- the applicant is capable of owning an EU certification mark: that is, it does not operate a business trading in the goods or services to be certified;
- the regulations meet the relevant criteria, as set out above;
- the mark does not attempt to certify the geographical origin of the goods and/or services; and
- consumers will not be misled as to the significance of the mark: the Office needs to be sure the mark will be seen as a certification mark rather than as an ordinary trade mark or collective mark.

7.2 Observations

Observations by third parties can be filed on the same grounds as for ordinary EUTM applications (see Chapter 9, section 5). In addition, observations can be filed alleging that the EU certification mark should be refused registration on the basis of the additional grounds of refusal set out in section 7.1 above.

8. Specifications of EU certification mark applications

The specifications of EU certification mark applications are likely to be narrower than many ordinary EUTM applications. This is because of the need for all the goods and/or services in the application to be capable of certification according to the criteria set out in the regulations filed as part of the application.

The Office raises an objection if it appears that the characteristics in the regulations cannot be certified for all the goods or services in the application. As a result, proprietors should avoid using broad terms to which the characteristics being certified cannot be relevant. For example, if an EU certification mark indicates that drill bits are made from a particular grade of steel, a specification containing "drill bits made from titanium carbide" will face an objection.

9. Grounds for revocation

The grounds for revocation detailed in Chapter 17 are applicable to EU certification mark registrations, save that to maintain a registration it is necessary to show use has been made by traders authorised under the regulations governing use of the mark, as opposed to by the owner itself.

There are four additional grounds for revocation that are particular to EU certification marks. A registration can be revoked if the owner:

- is no longer capable of owning an EU certification mark, on the basis that the owner is trading in the supply of goods or services of the kind certified;
- has not taken reasonable steps to prevent the mark being used in a way that is incompatible with the regulations governing use of the mark;
- has not taken reasonable steps to prevent the EU certification mark being used in a way that is not compatible with the regulations governing use of the mark; or
- has amended the regulations governing use of the mark so that they do not comply with the requirements set out in the Regulation.

10. Grounds for invalidity

The grounds for invalidity detailed in Chapter 18 are applicable to EU certification marks. In addition, an EU certification mark registration can be cancelled if one of the additional grounds for refusal set out in section 7.1 above was applicable when the application was filed.

11. Infringement actions

Only the proprietor of an EU certification mark registration, or someone given a specific authorisation by the proprietor, can bring an action for infringement of an EU certification mark. This means that authorised users of the mark do not have any right to bring, or call upon the proprietor to bring, an infringement action. Damage suffered by authorised users can, however, be taken into account in infringement proceedings. The owner is entitled to claim compensation on behalf of authorised users who have suffered damage as a result of infringing use.

12. Conversion

Under the TM Directive, it is not compulsory for Member States to permit the registration of certification marks. As a result, it is not possible to convert an EU certification mark application or registration in every Member State. For further discussion of conversion, see Chapter 25.

At the time of writing it is possible to register certification marks in the following 16 Member States: Bulgaria, Croatia, Cyprus, Denmark, Estonia, Finland, France, Hungary, Ireland, Latvia, Malta, Portugal, Romania, Spain, Sweden and the UK.

This means that, if there is a problem with an EU certification mark, it may not be possible to use conversion to maintain rights in Austria, Belgium, the Czech Republic, Germany, Greece, Italy, Lithuania, Luxembourg, the Netherlands, Poland, Slovakia and Slovenia. The wording "may not be possible" to maintain rights is used because the terms 'collective mark' and 'certification mark' are not used in an entirely consistent way across the Member States. In the Benelux countries, for example, 'collective mark' is used to refer to certification marks. It remains to be seen whether it will be possible to convert an EU certification mark into a 'collective' mark in the Benelux, but this is, in theory, a possibility.

In addition, the rules relating to what has to be included in regulations governing the use of certification marks vary between Member States, so that regulations accepted by the Office may need amendment (in addition to translation) before they are acceptable to national IPOs following conversion.

Further reference

Regulation – Articles 74a-74k inclusive
At the time of writing, no rules or guidelines relating to EU certification marks have been published.

Chapter 30: Introduction to the Madrid Protocol

1. Introduction

The Madrid Protocol ('the Protocol') is an international treaty relating to the registration of trade marks. Together with the Madrid Agreement ('the Agreement'), it provides for the Madrid system, otherwise known as the IR system. This system enables applicants who own trade mark rights in their home territory to obtain a bundle of rights in other territories through the filing of a single application administered centrally by the World Intellectual Property Organisation ('WIPO') in Geneva.

In chapters 30-32 inclusive, a registration obtained under the IR system is referred to as an IR and an application filed under the IR system is referred to as an 'International application'.

As the Union is a member of this system, EUTM rights can be used as 'home' or 'base' rights by those seeking protection in other countries that are also part of the IR system, which can also be used by those seeking Union-wide protection.

This chapter provides a brief overview of the IR system, with a particular focus on the Protocol. The mechanics of obtaining protection on the basis of existing EUTM rights are considered in Chapter 31, and the steps involved in using the IR system to obtain Union-wide protection are considered in Chapter 32.

2. History and overview of the IR system

The IR system was first introduced with the entry into force of the Agreement in 1892. Comparatively few countries signed up to the Agreement, however, limiting its impact and effect. Although it cannot be used to obtain Union-wide protection, the Agreement is still in force and a number of Member States of the Union are contracting parties to it. In light of this, as well as the influence that the Agreement has had on the development of the Protocol, it is worth some further consideration.

2.1 The Agreement

Under the terms of the Agreement, an International application has to be filed in French, and can only be filed once the home application has matured to registration. The application must be filed at the IPO that issued the home registration, which then passes it to WIPO.

A formalities examination is carried out at WIPO, following which the application is forwarded to the IPOs of each of the designated contracting parties. The IPOs then have a period of 12 months to carry out their normal examination procedures and raise any objections. If no objections are raised, protection is granted.

An IR is, however, dependent on the home registration for the first five years of its life. If the home registration ceases to exist during this time, the IR also ceases to exist. Any attack on an IR in this manner is referred to as a 'central attack'.

While of interest to some, the system provided for by the Agreement was seen as unattractive by a number of countries. In particular, those countries with substantive examination procedures saw the 12-month timeframe for completing such procedures as too onerous. The need to file the application in French, the five-year dependency period and the fee structure also contributed to low levels of participation. The low take-up in turn hindered the ability of the system to provide the administrative convenience that was originally intended.

Over the years, numerous attempts were made to address the perceived weaknesses of the Agreement. The Protocol was signed in 1989, offering an alternative means of obtaining protection through the IR system, though the Agreement still remains in force. The two treaties operate side-by-side and a large number of territories (including a number of Member States of the Union) are contracting parties to both.

2.2 The Protocol

The Protocol entered into force in 1995 and it has been possible to file applications under this system since 1 April 1996.

The main advantages of the Protocol when compared to the Agreement are as follows:

- *applications can be based on home applications (as well as registrations):* applicants do not have to wait until they have a registration before they can file using the Protocol);
- *applications can be filed in any one of English, French or Spanish:* the Protocol is therefore more attractive for those who do not speak French;
- *transformation is available:* although applications filed under the Protocol are still dependent on the home registration for five years, the effects of central attack are tempered by a process known as 'transformation'. This allows the attacked IR to be converted into direct applications in the designated contracting parties, while maintaining the application or priority date of the IR (see section 6 below); and
- *longer examination period:* the Protocol gives the IPOs of the designated contracting parties the option of extending the 12-month refusal period to 18 months. The Union has exercised this option. It is also possible for the IPOs to notify WIPO during the examination period that objections may be raised after the end of that period (eg, by way of opposition).

The inherent flexibility of the Protocol, compared to the Agreement, led to a much higher level of interest and, at the time of writing, there are 97 contracting parties to this treaty. A full list of the current contracting parties to each of the Agreement and the Protocol can be found on the WIPO website at www.wipo.int/export/sites/www/treaties/en/documents/pdf/madrid_marks.pdf.

2.3 The Protocol and the Union

Crucially for trade mark owners based in the Union, and for those seeking Union-wide protection, the Protocol allows international organisations to join the IR system, which had previously been open only to individual countries.

The Union became a contracting party to the Protocol in 2004, paving the way for owners of EUTM applications and registrations to file International applications on the basis of these rights (see Chapter 31), as well as enabling trade mark owners to obtain Union-wide protection under the IR system by virtue of a single Union designation (see Chapter 32).

The territories an applicant can designate when using the IR system depend on the treaty or treaties to which its home territory is a contracting party. As the Union is a contracting party, it can constitute a home territory.

A home territory that is a contracting party to both the Agreement and the Protocol means that an IR applicant can designate:

- territories that are contracting parties to the Agreement only;
- territories that are contracting parties to the Protocol only; and
- territories that are contracting parties to both treaties.

A home territory that is a contracting party to only one of these treaties allows only for the designation of territories that are contracting parties to the same treaty (this, of course, includes territories that are contracting parties to both).

The application of both the Agreement and the Protocol is governed by the Common Regulations. In situations involving contracting parties that have signed up to both treaties, the rules of the Protocol apply insofar as there is any inconsistency between the two treaties – eg, the 18-month period provided for by the Protocol for notifying WIPO of the outcome of examination applies, rather than the 12-month period provided for by the Agreement.

As the Union is a contracting party to the Protocol only, EUTM rights can only be used as base rights when protection is sought under the Protocol. In addition, Union designations can only be made when the applicant's home territory is a contracting party to the Protocol only or to both the Protocol and Agreement. As the Agreement is largely irrelevant to considerations involving International applications and registrations based either on EUTM rights or designating the Union, the focus of the remainder of the this chapter and chapters 31 and 32 is on the Protocol.

3. Who can use the Protocol?

To be eligible to file an application under the Protocol, an applicant must satisfy the entitlement criteria. This means it must:

- be a national of a state that is a contracting party to the Protocol; or
- be domiciled in a state that is a contracting party to the Protocol; or
- have a real and effective industrial or commercial establishment in a state that is a contracting party to the Protocol.

For the purposes of the IR system, the state for which the entitlement criteria are met is the applicant's 'home' country. It is, of course, possible for any given applicant to have more than one possible 'home' country. For example, an applicant may be a national of Egypt, be domiciled in Egypt, and have commercial establishments in Tunisia, Iran and Kazakhstan, all of which are contracting parties to the Protocol. The applicant is free to choose any one of these four territories as its 'home' country.

An applicant is required to own an application or registration for the mark of interest in its 'home' country. The Protocol application must be filed through the IPO of the 'home' country, which is then referred to as the 'Office of Origin'.

In the case of an applicant wishing to rely on EUTM rights as its 'base' or 'home' rights, it needs to be a national of, domiciled in, or have a real and effective industrial or commercial establishment in at least one Member State of the Union. The International application is filed through the Office, as detailed in Chapter 31.

It is possible for applicants who are nationals of, domiciled in and/or have a real and effective industrial or commercial establishment in a Member State that is itself a contracting party to the Protocol and/or the Agreement to utilise the IR system on the basis of national trade mark rights. The fact that the Union is also a contracting party to the Protocol does not preclude this. Indeed, with the exception of Malta, all Member States of the Union are contracting parties to the Protocol. A number are also contracting parties to the Agreement.

Nationality, domicile and real and effective industrial or commercial establishment are matters to be determined by each contracting party. Nationality and domicile are generally fairly straightforward matters. With regard to 'real and effective industrial or commercial establishment', the key factor is that the establishment should not simply be a sham or shell presence.

4. When can the Protocol be used?

The Protocol can be used by trade mark owners who:

- meet the entitlement criteria; and
- own a home application or registration for a trade mark for which they wish to obtain protection in the territories of other contracting parties to the Protocol.

For these purposes, the following criteria must be identical in both the home application or registration and the International application:

- the mark;
- the goods and/or services – the specification does not have to be strictly identical; it can be narrower but not broader; and
- the owner.

The Office of Origin is required to certify that the triple identity requirements have been met when forwarding an International application to WIPO for processing (see Chapter 31, section 4).

It is possible for an International application to claim priority from the first filing of the same trade mark, provided the usual priority requirements are met (see Chapter 5, section 12) and that the International application is filed within the six-month priority period. In light of the need for a base application or registration, an IR itself can never amount to a first filing. It is, however, possible (and often advisable) to claim priority from the base application or registration when filing an International application.

5. Overview of the registration process

A summary of the process for obtaining protection under the Protocol is set out in the diagram below. The Office acts as Office of Origin for International applications based on EUTM applications and registrations (see Chapter 31). Where Protocol applications are based on rights other than EUTM rights, Union designations are possible (see Chapter 32).

The process for obtaining protection under the Protocol

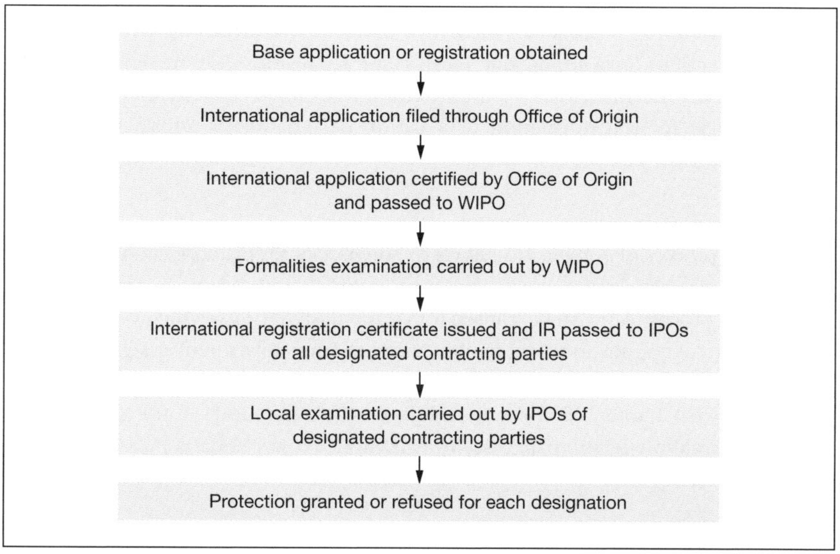

The International application is filed through the Office of Origin, which then passes it to WIPO, where a formalities examination is carried out. WIPO issues an International registration certificate once all formalities are in order, and then forwards details of the registration to the IPO of each designated contracting party. Each IPO carries out a local examination, applying the same process and criteria as are applied to direct trade mark applications. The IPOs have a period of 12 or 18 months from notification by WIPO within which to inform WIPO of any issues raised during the examination process (12 months is the default, but contracting parties can opt to extend this to 18 months, and many have done so). If no issues are raised, protection is granted in each contracting party at the end of the examination period. Certain IPOs issue Statements of Grant of Protection. Where this happens, protection in the territory concerned usually runs from the date of issue of this document, rather than the end of the 12- or 18-month examination period.

Additional designations can be added to an IR at any point during its life, through the process of subsequent designation, and the IR can be renewed for any designations of continuing interest for periods of 10 years. The renewal date is calculated from the original filing date. This is the case for all designations, irrespective of whether they were designated in the original International application or are subsequent designations.

6. Transformation

An IR is dependent on the base application or registration for the first five years of its life. If the base right ceases to exist during this time, the IR also ceases to exist. In light of this effect, any attack on the base mark during this period is known as a 'central attack'.

The effects of a central attack can, however, be minimised by making use of the transformation mechanism, which enables the IR to be transformed into direct applications in some or all of the designated contracting parties (subject to the payment of local application fees). These applications are treated as if they had been filed on the filing date of the IR and any priority claims are also maintained. The process for transformation of a Union designation is considered in Chapter 32, section 10.

7. Conversion

The process of conversion allows the owners of EUTM applications and registrations to turn their Union-wide rights into national applications in certain circumstances. This process can also be utilised for Union designations, which can be converted into national applications in Member States or into subsequent designations of the IR in question, or a combination of both.

See Chapter 25 for full details of the operation of the conversion process. Information relating specifically to Union designations is provided at Chapter 25, section 5.

8. Replacement

Another unique feature of the IR system is 'replacement'. This is where a pre-existing national trade mark registration in a contracting party is replaced by a designation of that contracting party in an IR, without prejudice to the earlier acquired rights.

Replacement takes place automatically without the holder, WIPO or the local IPO having to take any action. The requirements for replacement are that:

- the marks are identical;
- all the goods and/or services listed in the specification for the designation of the IR are listed in the specification for the direct registration;
- the owners are identical; and
- the direct right was registered before the date on which the designation was filed.

Replacement is in many respects similar to the process of seniority (see Chapter 24). Many contracting party IPOs (including the Office) have a procedure whereby replacement can be recorded in the national trade mark register. WIPO does not, however, require that replacement is recorded in national registers.

In the case of Union designations replacing pre-existing EUTM registrations, a request for replacement may be filed at the Office. There is no fee and the Office carries out a formal examination to ensure the criteria listed above are all satisfied. If the Office is satisfied, a note of the replacement is made in the Register. The Office also informs WIPO of the replacement. WIPO in turn records and publishes details of the replacement and notifies the holder of the IR.

After the replacement is recorded, the EUTM registration remains on the Register for as long as it is renewed by the proprietor. If the EUTM registration is allowed to lapse, the rights in the Union designation are theoretically deemed to date back to the effective filing date of the EUTM registration (taking account of any priority and/or seniority claims). These dates are included in the information published by both WIPO and the Office where a successful replacement request is made. It is, therefore, highly advisable to make such requests where there is an interest in actively taking advantage of replacement.

Given, however, the uncertain status of replacement at national level, and the fact that most EUTM Courts are unlikely to be greatly familiar with it, it is safer, where there is an ongoing interest in maintaining the filing date of an existing EUTM registration, simply to keep the EUTM registration in question live.

Both transformation and conversion remain possible for Union designations that replace EUTM registrations, and the priority and/or seniority dates of the replaced EUTM registration are again maintained.

9. Benefits of using the IR system

There are many benefits to using the IR system when seeking to obtain international trade mark protection. These benefits apply equally whether an IR is based on an EUTM application or registration, or includes a Union designation.

9.1 Administrative convenience

By using the IR system, an applicant seeking protection in multiple countries only needs to file a single application, rather than separate direct applications in each territory of interest. Filing one application clearly involves less work than filing multiple applications, even where each of them contains the same information.

Even after filing, an IR usually involves a lower administrative burden than separate direct trade mark registrations. An IR has a single renewal date for all designated territories. The renewal request is filed centrally through WIPO and the proprietor simply has to indicate the territories for which renewal is required.

It is possible to add further countries to an IR after filing, through subsequent designation, adding a further practical convenience to the system (see Chapter 31, section 7). The renewal date for all designations, including those added through the subsequent designation process, is the same – ie, 10 years from the filing date of the IR.

9.2 Certainty of timing

Under the terms of the Protocol, the IPO of any designated contracting party must inform WIPO within 18 months of being sent an IR by WIPO of any objections raised during its national examination process (or within 12 months in the case of contracting parties that have not opted for the 18-month option). There is no obligation to tell WIPO if there are no issues, although some IPOs do so. In the event that any given IPO does not contact WIPO within this period, protection is automatically deemed to be granted in that contracting party at the end of this period.

It is possible for IPOs to contact WIPO and inform it that oppositions may be filed after the end of the relevant examination period, due to the timings of opposition procedures for Protocol designations (which are generally the same as the timings of national opposition procedures for national applications).

Given the differing times taken for examination of trade mark applications in different territories, the IR system can be a useful means of obtaining certainty for applicants. For certain contracting parties, it can take longer to obtain protection for a Protocol designation than for a direct trade mark application. For many others, however, the IR system is more expedient and provides more certainty than direct systems in which the time to obtain protection generally depends to some degree on the workload of the relevant IPO.

9.3 Cost

The application fees for an International application vary, depending on factors such as the number of classes covered, the contracting parties designated and whether the mark applied for is in colour. For some territories, it can be less expensive to obtain protection through the Protocol than it is to file a separate direct application. Fluctuations in currency exchange rates can also have an effect in this regard.

A major cost saving, however, can be the possibility of not needing to engage local counsel. While most national (and regional) trade mark systems require applications to be filed by an authorised representative in the territory in which protection is sought, the Protocol only requires the involvement of local counsel in the event the IPO of a designated contracting party raises an issue during the examination process. Where this is the case, any response must be filed by local counsel.

Further reference

Office Guidelines – Part M, Section 1

WIPO, *Guide to the International Registration of Marks under the Madrid Agreement and the Madrid Protocol* (2014): www.wipo.int/export/sites/www/madrid/en/guide/pdf/guide.pdf

Common Regulations under the Madrid Agreement Concerning the International Registration of Marks and the Protocol Relating to that Agreement (as in force on 1 April 2016) ('the Common Regulations'): http://www.wipo.int/wipolex/en/treaties/text.jsp?file_id=397995

Chapter 31: The Office as Office of Origin

---

1. Introduction

This chapter describes the steps involved in filing an International application through the Office and further outlines the other responsibilities of the Office when it acts as Office of Origin under the Protocol.

2. Overview of the registration process

The Office is Office of Origin when an EUTM application or registration is used as the home or base mark for an International application. Where this happens, the steps in the application process are:

- the International application is filed through the Office;
- the Office carries out some basic checks and then passes the application to WIPO;
- WIPO carries out a formalities check, and informs both the Office and the applicant about any issues;
- once any formalities issues are resolved, WIPO issues the International registration certificate and passes the application to the IPOs of the contracting parties; and
- protection is granted or refused in each designated contracting party within a period of 12 or 18 months (subject to potential oppositions after this time in certain territories).

3. Filing an International application through the Office

To be able to file an International application through the Office, an applicant must own a base EUTM application or registration and must be entitled to hold an IR under the Protocol. This means it must be a national of, be domiciled in, or have a real and effective industrial or commercial establishment in a Member State of the Union (see Chapter 30, section 3).

Where these requirements are met, the International application can be filed through the Office, which is then referred to as the Office of Origin. There are strict requirements in terms of the form and content of the request for protection, as well as the fees that are payable. There are also important considerations with regard to language and representation requirements.

3.1 Application form

The application must be filed using either:

- the official form provided by WIPO (Form MM2, available in English, French and Spanish); or
- the official form provided by the Office (Form EM2, an adapted version of Form MM2 available in all Languages of the Union).

The Office recommends the use of Form EM2 as it is tailored specifically for Protocol applications based on EUTM rights. For example, the Office of Origin section is pre-populated and the Union is excluded from the list of possible designated contracting parties (as it is not possible to designate the contracting party whose IPO is the Office of Origin for an International application).

As it is not yet possible to file International applications electronically through the Office, the duly completed Form MM2 or EM2 must be filed by fax, by post or by hand.

3.2 Language

Any application under the Protocol must be transmitted to WIPO in one of WIPO's official languages (English, French or Spanish). Where Form MM2 is used, this should be completed in the same language as the form itself – eg, if the French language version of the form is used, it should be completed in French. The applicant should also indicate its preferred language for correspondence with WIPO, which must be one of WIPO's official languages but does not have to be the language in which the form is completed. If no language is indicated, WIPO communicates with the applicant in the language of the form.

Form EM2 is available in all Languages of the Union. Again, the form should be completed in the same language as it is written. The Office needs, however, to transmit the application to WIPO in one of the latter's official languages. Applicants using language versions of Form EM2 other than the English, French or Spanish versions must therefore indicate which of the three WIPO languages they wish the Office to use when forwarding the application.

When using Form EM2, an International applicant should also indicate its preferred language for correspondence with WIPO. This must be one of WIPO's official languages, but does not have to be either the language in which the form is completed or the language in which the International application is sent to WIPO. Where Form EM2 is used in a language other than English, French, or Spanish, the applicant must indicate the language in which it wishes the Office to correspond with it, which should either be the language of Form EM2 or the language chosen for the Office to transmit the application to WIPO. If no choice is made, the Office corresponds with the applicant in the language of Form EM2.

When transmitting the application to WIPO, the Office must include a translation of the specification covered into the language in which the application is transmitted. If the International applicant does not do so, it must specifically authorise the Office to produce such a translation; failing this, the Office issues a deficiency notice.

3.3 Fees

Two sets of fees are payable when filing an International application through the Office:

- the handling fee (paid directly to the Office, €300 at the time of writing); and
- the International application fees (paid directly to WIPO).

The handling fee can be paid to the Office by means of an Office current account, credit card or bank transfer (see Chapter 2, section 9). The International application is not deemed to have been filed until the handling fee is received by the Office. Where the base mark is an EUTM application, the applicant can indicate that the International application is to be based on the EUTM right once it is registered, in which case the handling fee is due on the date the EUTM application proceeds to registration. Provided that the handling fee is received on or before this date, the International application is treated as having been filed on the day on which registration of the base EUTM right is granted.

The International application fees can be paid to WIPO by means of a WIPO current account, by payment into the Swiss postal account of WIPO (this is a basic type of banking account with the Swiss postal service – WIPO is based in Switzerland) or to any of the specified bank accounts of WIPO. Both Form MM2 and Form EM2 contain a copy of WIPO's fee calculation sheet, which includes sections to instruct and identify payments to WIPO. The fee calculation sheet is an important part of the International application and should be completed in the same language as the application form. The Office does not check the fee calculation sheet when it examines the application form but, if the form is not completed correctly, WIPO raises an irregularity.

Any WIPO fees paid to the Office rather than to WIPO are returned to the applicant. The Office does not forward any such fees to WIPO, even where the applicant indicates that they are intended for WIPO.

3.4 Representation before WIPO

Although it is possible for an International applicant to appoint a representative to act on its behalf before WIPO, it does not have to do so. An appointed representative does not need to satisfy any particular requirements in terms of professional qualifications, nationality, residence or domicile and there is no need to provide a power of attorney. An applicant wishing to appoint a representative before WIPO needs only to provide the name, address and contact details for that person in the International application form. If an email address is provided, all correspondence sent by WIPO to the representative is sent electronically.

Where a representative has been appointed, WIPO sends any communications that would have been sent to the applicant directly to him. However, it sends the following types of notification to both the applicant and the representative:

- a finding that the appointment of the representative is irregular;
- renewal notifications; and
- notifications that insufficient renewal fees have been paid.

Where the representative asks for his appointment to be cancelled, WIPO sends communications to both the applicant and the representative until the cancellation becomes effective.

3.5 Representation before the Office

Where an EUTM applicant is domiciled in, has its principal place of business in or has a real and effective industrial or commercial establishment in the EEA, there is no requirement for a representative to be appointed at the Office when filing an EUTM application (see Chapter 5, section 9). As a result, it may be the case that a base EUTM application or registration used for an International application does not have a recorded representative at the Office. Where this happens, the Office corresponds directly with the applicant (or its WIPO representative, if it has one) in relation to the International application. Where a representative has been appointed for the base EUTM application or registration, the Office corresponds with him.

If no representative is listed for the base EUTM application or registration and the applicant falls into the category of parties who must be professionally represented at the Office (ie, the applicant is not domiciled in, does not have its principal place of business in or does not have a real and effective industrial or commercial establishment in the EEA) the Office corresponds with the WIPO representative. If, however, the applicant's WIPO representative cannot act as a representative before the Office, the Office contacts the applicant directly and sets a deadline for appointment of a representative before the Office (see Chapter 2, section 10 for discussion of who can act as representatives before the Office).

Form EM2 includes a section for the applicant to provide details of a representative before the Office. It is highly advisable to include such information at this stage if the applicant must be represented before the Office and no representative has been recorded for the base EUTM right.

3.6 Content of the application form: mandatory requirements

The following indications and information must be included in the International application form when seeking protection under the Protocol on the basis of an EUTM application or registration:

- the mark for which protection is requested;
- the goods and/or services for which protection is requested;
- the applicant;
- the entitlement of the applicant to use the Protocol system;
- the official number(s) of the base EUTM right(s); and
- the designated contracting parties.

The Office performs checks to ensure all this information is included and raises a deficiency notice if any of it is missing, incomplete, or inaccurate.

3.7 Mark

The mark applied for in an International application must be identical to the mark covered by the base EUTM right(s). Multiple base applications and/or registrations can be relied upon, but in all cases the marks must be identical. The base applications and/or registrations must all have been accorded filing dates and they must be in force at the time of filing the International application. Multiple base rights can only be relied upon where they cover goods and/or services that are different to each other – ie, it is not possible to rely on two base EUTM rights where the only difference between them is the filing dates.

Where Form EM2 is used, there is no need to include a reproduction of the mark, as the Office includes the representation available in its own database when it transmits the application to WIPO. Where Form MM2 is used, however, the applicant must include a representation of the mark. The Office checks that this corresponds to the base EUTM application or registration and issues a deficiency notice in the event of any inconsistency.

Where the mark is a word mark, the section of the form declaring that the applicant wishes the mark to be considered as a mark in standard characters should be completed.

Where the mark covered by the base EUTM application or registration contains colour, and the Register entry includes an indication of the colour(s), the same claim should be indicated in the International application. If the EUTM right is in colour but does not contain a colour claim, the applicant has a choice over whether to include such a claim in the International application. In such a case the colours listed must, of course, be the same as those shown in the reproduction. As the Office now treats any EUTM application as implicitly including a colour claim, and thus requires the EUTM applicant to indicate the colours claimed, it is usually the case that an International application based on an EUTM application or registration filed in colour also has to include a colour claim.

Where the base EUTM application or registration is for a colour mark (ie, the mark consists exclusively of a colour or combination of colours as such), a three-dimensional mark, a sound mark, a collective mark, or a certification mark, the International application must be for the same type of mark, which should be indicated in the International application form. In the case of sound marks, the Office only transmits the graphic representation to WIPO, as the latter does not accept electronic sound files.

Where the base mark consists of or contains non-Latin characters, a transliteration of the mark must be provided. This is a WIPO requirement and, as such, is examined by WIPO rather than the Office. Failure to include a transliteration is not picked up during the Office's examination but results in an irregularity notice from WIPO during the latter's examination stage.

3.8 Specification

The specification claimed in the International application must be the same as, or encompassed within, that of the base EUTM right. Form EM2 includes an option for the applicant to indicate that it wishes to use the same specification as in the base right. If Form MM2 is used, the specification to be covered by the International application needs to be set out even if it is identical to that covered by the base EUTM application or registration.

While a specification has to be indicated for the International application itself, it is possible within this to have different specifications for different designations. Normally, a different specification is only indicated for territories that have very particular national practices on specifications, such as the United States. Any differences for particular contracting parties must be clearly indicated on the International application form.

Where an International application is based on more than one EUTM application or registration, there must be a direct overlap between the specification covered in the International application and those covered by the base rights when considered collectively.

3.9 Applicant

The International applicant must be the same as the listed owner of the base EUTM application or registration. Any discrepancy in this regard results in a deficiency notice from the Office.

3.10 Entitlement

The International applicant must be a national of, be domiciled in or have a real and effective industrial or commercial establishment in a Member State of the Union.

Where entitlement is based on nationality, the Member State of which the applicant is a national should be indicated; where entitlement is based on domicile or establishment, the address of the domicile or establishment within the Union should be specifically indicated (if different to the applicant's address details).

3.11 The base EUTM right(s)

The details that need to be provided depend on whether each base EUTM right(s) is an application or a registration:

- *EUTM registration:* the registration number and registration date;
- *EUTM application:* the application number and application date. The International applicant can also indicate that the International application is to be based on the EUTM right once it is registered; this effectively puts the progress of the International application on hold until the base application proceeds to registration.

3.12 Designated contracting parties

The International application form must include an indication of the contracting parties in whose territory protection is sought. Both forms MM2 and EM2 include a list of the territories that can be designated in an International application under the Protocol, namely, the contracting parties to the Protocol. As noted above, however, it is not possible to self-designate – ie, the contracting party of the Office of Origin cannot be designated.

For most contracting parties, all that is required is a tick in the relevant box to show they are designated. In the case of the United States, however, a signed declaration that the applicant intends to use the mark at hand in the United States must also be provided. This is done by annexing a completed and signed Form

MM18 to the International application form. This form is only available in English and must be signed by the applicant directly (irrespective of whether it has appointed a representative).

3.13 Content of the application form: optional requirements

In addition to the representative information discussed above, there are a number of further pieces of information that can be included in or with a Form MM2 or Form EM2, which include the following.

Miscellaneous indications: If the base EUTM right includes a description or disclaimer, this can also be included in the International application. A description cannot be included in the International application if it is not included in the base EUTM right. By contrast, a disclaimer can be included in the International application even if the base EUTM right does not include one.

Other indications that can be included in the International application form include a translation of the mark into any or all of the official WIPO languages (or an indication that the words within the mark have no meaning and thus cannot be translated) and an indication of any word elements within the mark (in the case of marks other than word marks, such as logo or figurative marks that include word elements). These indications are optional but may be required during the national examination stage in certain designated contracting parties, so including this information when an application is filed can sometimes be useful and save time later.

Signature: Both forms EM2 and MM2 include a section for the applicant and/or the applicant's representative to sign. WIPO rules stipulate that the form only has to be signed if the Office of Origin requires this. As the Office does not require a signature, the form does not need to be signed.

Priority: If a priority claim is made, the following information should be provided for each of the earlier filings from which priority is claimed:

- office of earlier filing;
- application number of earlier filing (if available);
- date of earlier filing; and
- the goods and/or services to which the priority claim relates (if not all the goods and/or services covered by the International application).

There is no need to include any supporting documents with the priority claim. Any such documents sent to the Office together with the International application will not be passed on to WIPO. (See Chapter 5, section 11 for a general discussion of priority.)

4. Examination by the Office

When acting as Office of Origin, the Office is required to forward to WIPO any International applications that are based on EUTM rights. When doing so, it must provide a declaration certifying:

- the date on which the International application was received by the Office;

- that the applicant, mark and specification covered by the International application are all identical to those for the base EUTM right(s);
- that any indications provided in the International application with regard to type of mark and mark descriptions correspond with the information in the base EUTM right(s); and
- where colour is claimed, that the same colours are claimed in the base EUTM right(s), or, where the base right(s) does not include a colour claim, that the mark in the base right(s) is in the colour or combination of colours claimed.

With regard to identity in applicant, mark and specification, the Office applies strict criteria, as in the cases of seniority (Chapter 24), priority (Chapter 5) and conversion (Chapter 25).

If the Office cannot make the necessary declaration, it issues a deficiency notice and sets the applicant a deadline by which to correct the problem and/or provide the missing information. The Office typically sets a one-month deadline in such circumstances and, if the applicant fails to provide the requisite information, the Office can refuse to forward the application to WIPO.

Where all necessary information is provided by the applicant, either in the original application form or following a request for further information, the Office is required to forward the International application to WIPO as soon as possible. If this happens within two months of receipt of the application at the Office, the resulting IR is deemed to have been filed on the date the application was received at the Office, so long as the Office had also received the handling fee by that date.

If the handling fee is not received together with the International application, the Office issues a deficiency notice and informs the applicant that the International application shall only be deemed to have been received by the Office on the date the handling fee is received. If the handling fee is not received within two months of the deficiency notice being issued, the Office considers the application not to have been filed.

The Office also issues deficiency notices in the circumstances set out below and imposes a deadline (typically one month) by which the applicant must remedy any problems. Again, if the applicant fails to do so, the Office does not forward the International application to WIPO and the handling fee is not refunded.

A deficiency notice is issued where:

- the applicant has failed to use Form MM2 or Form EM2;
- the mandatory requirements of Form MM2 or Form EM2 have not all been met;
- the applicant has used Form EM2, but failed to indicate the language in which the International application should be submitted to WIPO;
- on the basis of the information provided, the applicant does not appear to be entitled to file an International application through the Office under the Protocol;
- the applicant has used Form EM2 in a language other than English, French or Spanish but has not provided a translation of the specification into the language in which the application is to be transmitted to WIPO, or has not specifically authorised the Office to provide or create such a translation;

- it is unclear on which goods and/or services the International application is to be based; or
- the International application includes a priority claim and it is clear to the Office that the priority claim is invalid. The Office does not examine priority claims in any detail and simply ensures the necessary information has been included in the priority section of the Form MM2 or Form EM2. If there is clear evidence that a priority claim is invalid, the Office asks for the claim to be deleted.

5. Formalities checks by WIPO

Once WIPO receives an International application from the Office, a series of formalities checks are carried out. If any irregularities are detected, WIPO issues a notification to this effect and sets a deadline by which they must be remedied. The notification is sent to both the Office of Origin and the applicant (or its WIPO representative, if appointed).

Full details of the types of irregularity (and the responsibility for remedying them) can be found in WIPO's *Guide to the International Registration of Marks*, available at www.wipo.int. Only the most common irregularities are discussed here.

Certain irregularities should be remedied by the applicant/the applicant's representative directly with WIPO, whereas others must be remedied by the Office of Origin. Where the irregularities are not remedied by the deadline set (typically three months), the International application is treated as abandoned. The only exception is in the case of specification queries, in relation to which WIPO proceeds with its own suggested amendments (or deletions) in the absence of a response. Where an International application is treated as abandoned, WIPO refunds any fees paid, after deducting a sum equal to half the basic application fee for an application in black and white (even if the application in question was filed in colour and thus attracted a higher fee).

The majority of irregularities issued relate to specification queries and to fee payment.

With regard to specifications, WIPO may issue an irregularity notice relating to the classification of the goods and/or services (ie, querying whether the terms indicated do indeed fall within the classes indicated) or the description of the goods and/or services (ie, querying the wording of terms used in the specification and whether they are sufficiently clear for classification purposes). Such irregularity notices can usually be remedied fairly easily, either by accepting the alternative classes and/or terms suggested by WIPO, by explaining why the goods and/or services were correctly classified in the original application form, or by deleting the queried terms.

Although it is technically the responsibility of the Office of Origin to respond to any such issues, in practice the applicant must file a response through the Office. The Office does not respond to WIPO of its own motion. Where the applicant files a response, the Office forwards that response on to WIPO in the form received. Any response sent directly to WIPO by the applicant is disregarded by WIPO. In any event, final responsibility for the classification of goods and/or services lies with

WIPO. If WIPO's suggested classification requires the payment of additional class fees and such fees are not paid (or terms are not deleted such that no further fees are required), the International application is treated as abandoned.

With regard to fee payment, while an irregularity notice is sent to both the Office and the applicant (or its WIPO representative), the Office's view is that the applicant is responsible for the payment of fees to WIPO. Thus, if the applicant mistakenly pays fees intended for WIPO to the Office, the Office does not forward those fees to WIPO. Rather, it refunds the fees to the applicant, whose responsibility it is to ensure that the fees are sent directly to WIPO.

Where an irregularity notice relates to the failure of the Office to provide the necessary declaration certifying the information contained in the International application, or where it relates to information that has been improperly certified by the Office, the responsibility for correcting the error lies entirely with the Office. However, depending on the information in question, the Office may need to liaise with the applicant in order to complete the application.

6. Issuance of International registration certificate by WIPO

Once WIPO is satisfied that the necessary formalities have all been properly completed, it issues an International registration certificate and notifies the IPO of each designated contracting party of the request for protection in its territory.

When WIPO issues the International registration certificate, it also publishes the particulars of the IR in the WIPO *Gazette*. The issuance of the International registration certificate does not indicate that protection has been granted to the mark in question. Rather, it simply confirms that WIPO's role in the filing process is complete and that the IPOs of the designated contracting parties have been notified of the request for local protection. The date on which WIPO contacts the local offices is known as the 'notification date'. It is from this date that the 12-month or 18-month period runs for the IPOs to inform WIPO of any issues during the local examination process.

When any individual office raises an issue, it must notify WIPO directly. WIPO then sends a copy of the notification directly to the applicant (or the applicant's WIPO representative, if one has been appointed). The applicant normally needs to appoint a local representative in the territory in question, who must file a response with the local office within the deadline it has set. There are, however, some issues that can be dealt with without the need for a local representative to be appointed, eg, if a specification query is raised, a response can be filed directly with WIPO without the need for local counsel. The local office ultimately informs WIPO of the final outcome of the local examination, the rule being that, in the absence of any correspondence from a given local IPO within the 12-month or 18-month period, protection is automatically granted in the territory of that contracting party.

7. Filing a subsequent designation through the Office

One of the benefits of the Protocol system is the ability to include additional designated contracting parties after the registration of the initial International application – ie, after the issuance of the International registration certificate by WIPO.

A subsequent designation request can only relate to contracting parties that are parties to the Protocol and cannot duplicate protection already afforded by the IR (ie, it is not possible to file a subsequent designation in respect of a contracting party that is already covered by the IR unless the coverage of the subsequent designation is different to that of the original designation).

It is not necessary to file a request for a subsequent designation through the Office of Origin. In practice, it is generally better to file such requests directly with WIPO, as this speeds up the overall process through to protection. A subsequent designation, once granted, takes effect from the date of receipt of the request by WIPO (or the date of receipt of the request at the Office if filed through the Office), unless a specific request is made that it should not take effect until either the IR is renewed or a particular change to the IR is recorded in the International Register. It should be noted that, irrespective of when the subsequent designation takes effect, the renewal date for this designation is the same as that for the IR. Thus, where there is an interest in filing a subsequent designation in a particular territory but the IR in question is shortly due for renewal, it can often be sensible to request that the subsequent designation does not take effect until the IR is renewed.

Where the Office is the Office of Origin for an International application, a subsequent designation request can be filed through the Office, unless the IR has been transferred to a party who is not entitled to file International applications through the Office. Where this is the case, the subsequent designation request must be filed directly at WIPO.

WIPO Form MM4 should be used when filing a request for subsequent designation at WIPO. This form is available in English, French and Spanish and can also be used when filing a subsequent designation request through the Office. Alternatively, Form EM4 can be used when filing a request through the Office. This form, which is the Office's modified version of Form MM4, is available in all Languages of the Union, other than English, French and Spanish (and any subsequent designation to be filed in one of those languages should be filed on Form MM4).

Any subsequent designation request should be filed in the same language as the original International application. In the case of subsequent designation requests filed on Form EM4, the IR owner must request that the subsequent designation request is transmitted by the Office to WIPO in one of WIPO's official languages. The applicant does not, however, need to choose the same language as was chosen for transmission of the original International application.

Where a subsequent designation request is filed through the Office, there is no handling fee. The only fees that need to be paid are the WIPO fees. A request for a subsequent designation, whether filed through the Office or directly at WIPO, should include a fee calculation sheet. The Office does not check whether the fee sheet is included or completed correctly. If there are any issues, including where the fee sheet is completed in a language that is not the language in which the subsequent designation request is transmitted, WIPO issues an irregularity notice.

Where a subsequent designation request is filed through the Office, checks are made by the Office before the request is forwarded to WIPO. The Office confirms that either Form MM4 or Form EM4 has been used and completed properly. If there are any issues, the Office issues a deficiency notice and sets a deadline by which the problems must be remedied. If the issue is not resolved, the Office does not forward the subsequent designation request to WIPO. Where a subsequent designation request is filed through the Office by a party not entitled to do so, the Office simply refuses to forward it on to WIPO.

8. Other tasks of the Office as Office of Origin

The other key tasks the Office is responsible for when acting as Office of Origin are informing WIPO of changes to the base EUTM right(s) and informing WIPO of other changes that affect the IR.

8.1 Notifying WIPO of changes to the base EUTM right(s)

The Office is only obliged to inform WIPO of changes to the base EUTM right(s) during the first five years of the life of the IR – ie, the five-year period from the filing date of the IR. This effectively amounts to a requirement to inform WIPO of any central attacks on the IR. If, during this period, the base EUTM right(s) ceases to exist (in whole or in part), the IR ceases to exist to the same degree. The Office is therefore required to inform WIPO when a final decision has been issued in this regard.

The Office must also notify WIPO where, at the end of the five-year period, any of the following proceedings remain pending against the base EUTM right(s):

- absolute grounds objections;
- opposition proceedings;
- cancellation proceedings; and
- counterclaims in infringement proceedings.

The Office must then inform WIPO when a final decision is taken in such proceedings or, if they are withdrawn, be sure to draw WIPO's attention to the extent that the base EUTM right(s) ceases to have effect.

The only other instance in which the Office is obliged to inform WIPO of changes to the base EUTM right(s) during the initial five-year period is where there is a division or partial transfer. Such a change has no effect on the validity of the IR itself and the requirement to keep WIPO informed is simply a record-keeping exercise.

8.2 Forwarding to WIPO details of changes that affect the IR

The following types of request can be filed either directly at WIPO or through the Office of Origin:

- change in ownership;
- specification limitation;
- renunciation of one or more contracting parties;
- full or partial cancellation of the IR;
- change in name or address of the IR owner;
- licence recordal;
- licence cancellation; and
- security interest recordal.

Where a request is filed by the IR owner at the Office as Office of Origin, using the correct WIPO form, the request is simply forwarded to WIPO. There is no fee to be paid to the Office for forwarding the request and the Office does not check that the request was correctly filed with it (on the basis that the request could have been filed directly at WIPO in any case).

If a request to record a change of ownership, a request to record a licence or a request to record a security interest is filed at the Office by a party other than the owner of the IR, the Office carries out basic checks to ensure that there is proof of the transfer, licence or security interest. If no such proof is provided, the Office does not forward the recordal request to WIPO.

Further reference

Office Guidelines – Part M

Regulation – Articles 145-150

Implementing Regulation – Rules 102-107, 125, 126

WIPO, *Guide to the International Registration of Marks under the Madrid Agreement and the Madrid Protocol* (2014): www.wipo.int/export/sites/www/madrid/en/guide/pdf/guide.pdf

Common Regulations under the Madrid Agreement Concerning the International Registration of Marks and the Protocol Relating to that Agreement (as in force on 1 April, 2016) ('the Common Regulations'): http://www.wipo.int/wipolex/en/treaties/text.jsp?file_id=397995

Chapter 32: Union designations

1. Introduction

This chapter describes how to obtain Union-wide protection by means of a single designation in an International application or a single subsequent designation in an IR. While in many respects the process through to protection is the same as that for direct EUTM applications, there are some important differences.

2. Overview and timeline

Whether a Union designation is filed in an International application or by means of a subsequent designation in an IR, the procedure at the Office through to grant of protection is the same, as shown in the diagram below.

Process for filing a Union designation at the Office

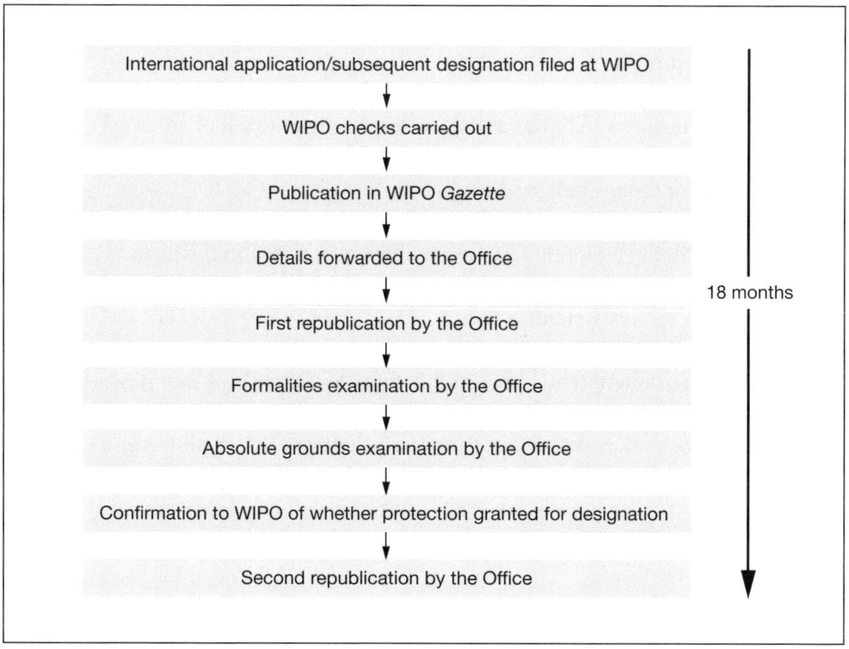

3. Filing and formalities

The general requirements for an International application or a subsequent designation are set out in chapters 30 and 31. There are, however, some additional points to bear in mind when filing a Union designation or subsequent designation.

3.1 Language

Like any International application under the Protocol, one that designates the Union must be filed in one of WIPO's three official languages (see Chapter 31, section 3). As with direct EUTM applications, the Office's requirement for two languages to be indicated must also be satisfied. At least one of these must be a Language of the Office (see Chapter 5, section 10).

WIPO's official languages are all Languages of the Office. As a result, the first language of any Union designation is always one of the Languages of the Office. As the second language indicated in a Union designation must also be one of the Languages of the Office, there are in practice only ever four possible choices of second language. This means that the two languages of a Union designation are both always Languages of the Office.

WIPO forms MM2 (International application form) and MM4 (application for subsequent designation) both include specific sections to indicate the second language when filing a Union designation. Failure to indicate a second language results in a provisional refusal of protection being issued by the Office and delays the progress of the designation.

3.2 Representation

As discussed in Chapter 5, when an EUTM applicant is domiciled in, has its principal place of business in or has a real and effective industrial or commercial establishment in the EEA, there is no requirement for a representative to be appointed. The same applies for Union designations.

In practice, where the application for a Union designation does not meet the above criteria, a representative only has to be appointed where:

- a provisional refusal is issued by the Office; or
- a seniority claim is filed.

If a representative is required before the Office and one has been appointed at WIPO, the Office considers the WIPO representative to be the representative before the Office if that person appears on the Office's list of professional representatives. In all other cases, when notifying the applicant of a provisional refusal, the Office also sets it a deadline by which it must appoint a representative.

3.3 Notification date

This is the date on which the Office is notified by WIPO of the designation or subsequent designation of the Union. The 18-month period during which the Office must notify WIPO of the outcome of the examination process begins on this date.

3.4 First republication by the Office

When the Office receives a request for protection by means of a Union designation, it immediately republishes the IR in the *EUTM Bulletin*. The only exception is where a second language has not been indicated, in which case a deficiency notice is issued and the applicant is set a deadline by which to indicate a second language for the Union designation.

In all other instances, the republication takes place immediately, before formalities checks or substantive examination of the designation are carried out. The date of the first republication is equivalent to the date of publication of a direct EUTM application. It is the relevant start date for potential compensation claims in the event of infringing activity that takes place before grant (see Chapter 22) and is the date from which the opposition period is calculated (as discussed in section 5.2 of this chapter).

3.5 Search reports

As with direct EUTM applications, those seeking protection by means of a Union designation can request that the Office carry out a search of the EUTM database. Any such request must be made directly to the Office within one month of the notification date.

It is also possible to request that national searches be carried out by the national IPOs of the Member States that participate in the national search system. An additional fee is payable if this request is made; both the request and the fee must be sent directly to the Office within one month of the notification date.

These searches are carried out for information purposes only and the Office cannot refuse protection on the basis of rights identified by them, in the absence of oppositions based on those rights. For further information, see Chapter 4, section 5.

3.6 Seniority

The EUTM system allows for pre-existing national registrations to be subsumed into EUTM registrations under a process called seniority (see Chapter 24). It is equally possible to claim seniority for Union designations.

Seniority is claimed by applying to the Office, either when the Union designation is filed or after publication of the final acceptance of the designation. The possibility of claiming seniority within two months of filing a direct EUTM application is not available for Union designations. If a seniority claim is made in the period between filing and final acceptance of the Union designation, the Office treats the claim as being made on the date of publication of the final acceptance.

Where a seniority claim is made at the time of filing a Union designation, WIPO Form MM17 must be used and should be attached to the International application form or subsequent designation form. Any supporting documentation must be sent directly to the Office within three months of the notification date. Any supporting documentation sent to WIPO rather than to the Office is not forwarded to the Office by WIPO.

4. Examination

The Office carries out a formalities examination before proceeding with examination on absolute grounds.

4.1 Formalities examination

As discussed in Chapter 31, WIPO carries out its own formalities examination for all International applications, which includes checks on the classification of the goods and/or services. In light of this, the formalities checks carried out by the Office for Union designations are more limited than those carried out for direct EUTM applications. For example, priority claims for Union designations are examined by WIPO and are not checked by the Office.

Given this, the Office checks whether:

- a second language has been indicated;
- the application is for a collective or certification mark (see section 4.2 below);
- a seniority claim has been made; and
- the terms used in the specification are sufficiently precise (see section 4.3 below).

If there is a problem in any of these areas, the Office issues a deficiency notice and sets a deadline by which a response must be filed by the applicant. The deficiency is in the form of a provisional refusal of protection and the time given to file a response is usually two months.

If the applicant falls within the category of parties who must be represented before the Office, the need to appoint a representative is communicated in the notification of the provisional refusal (see Chapter 2, section 10). If a representative is not appointed by the deadline, the designation is finally refused irrespective of whether the other formalities issues have been resolved.

4.2 Collective and certification marks

When filing Form MM2 (international application form) or Form MM4 (request for a subsequent designation), it is possible to indicate that the mark for which protection is sought falls into the category of 'collective mark, certification mark or guarantee mark'. However, neither form allows for an indication of which specific type of mark is being applied for.

Where such an indication is provided, the type of mark for which protection is requested should be the same as the base mark. Both collective marks (see Chapter 28) and (as of 1 October 2017) certification marks (see Chapter 29) can be filed under the EUTM system. Union designations can therefore be for collective marks or certification marks, in which case the requirements in terms of entitlement to hold the type of mark, higher fees and the need to provide regulations governing use all need to be complied with in the same manner as for direct EUTM applications.

4.3 Specification queries

While carrying out checks on the specification covered by a Union designation, the Office can only raise queries with respect to the wording of terms used. It cannot raise issues as to whether the terms are in the correct class; such issues will have been considered during the WIPO formalities checks.

The purpose of any query raised by the Office is to ensure that the terms used are sufficiently precise and the assessment is the same as for direct EUTM applications (see Chapter 6). However, the tests applied by the Office are not always the same as those applied by WIPO. As a result, terms deemed acceptable by WIPO may encounter objections from the Office, including some of the standard terms included within the class headings.

4.4 Absolute grounds examination

The Office performs examination as to absolute grounds for Union designations in the same manner as for direct EUTM applications (see Chapter 7). The same tests and case law are applied in determining whether the mark applied for is inherently registrable in relation to the goods and/or services in relation to which protection is sought.

If the Office believes the mark is not inherently capable of registration for the goods and/or services applied for, it issues a provisional refusal of protection. This is sent by the Office to WIPO, which forwards the provisional refusal to the applicant (or its WIPO representative). A deadline is set for a response to be filed at the Office. If the applicant is required to appoint a representative before the Office, this is mentioned in the notification of provisional refusal and a representative must be appointed by the deadline. As with direct EUTM applications, it is possible to file legal arguments and/or evidence to try to convince the Office to waive any absolute grounds objections raised.

If the Office believes the mark is capable of registration, either because no issues were raised or because any deficiencies or objections have been successfully overcome, it sends an interim status notification to WIPO. It informs WIPO that examination is complete, but that oppositions and third party observations are still possible.

If any deficiencies or objections raised are not overcome, the Union designation is finally refused, as discussed further in section 6 of this chapter.

5. Third party observations and oppositions

Both third party observations and oppositions can be filed against Union designations. Persuasive third party observations can result in the Office raising a provisional refusal, while an admissible opposition automatically results in a provisional refusal of protection.

The rules relating to observations (see Chapter 9, section 5) and oppositions (see chapters 10–14) apply to Union designations in the same way as they apply to direct EUTM applications, subject to the points set out in the following paragraphs.

5.1 Observations

Observations can be filed at any point between the notification date and the end of the opposition period. If an opposition is filed, observations can also be filed while the opposition is pending, provided that they are filed no later than 18 months after the notification date (ie, the period during which the Office has to inform WIPO of any issues raised during examination).

Observations are only mentioned to WIPO by the Office if they are received after the Office has informed WIPO that examination is complete and the Office is raising a provisional refusal as a result of the observations. Otherwise, they are simply forwarded to the applicant by the Office.

5.2 Opposition

There are a number of important differences in the opposition procedure for Union designations when compared to direct EUTM applications.

Opposition deadline: For a Union designation, the opposition period commences one month after first republication by the Office, so that the opposition deadline falls four months from the date of first republication. Any opposition filed in the one-month period between first republication and the commencement of the opposition period is treated as having been filed on the first day of the opposition period. If an opposition is filed during this period but is withdrawn before the opposition period actually commences, the official opposition fee is refunded by the Office.

As the first republication by the Office takes place almost immediately after the notification date, it can be the case that all absolute grounds issues have not been resolved (or indeed even raised) by the end of the opposition period. Potential opponents can therefore be faced with a situation whereby the Union designation they are seeking to oppose could potentially be refused on absolute grounds. If, however, they take the chance that such a refusal will be issued, they may find that it is not and that they have missed their opportunity to bring opposition proceedings.

In such a situation, potential opponents are always recommended to file a Notice of Opposition. What happens if an absolute grounds objection is raised after an opposition has been filed is discussed below.

Admissibility Checks: The admissibility checks carried out for an opposition against a Union designation are the same as those for oppositions against direct EUTM applications, as set out in Chapter 11, section 9. If an opposition is filed but is deemed inadmissible (either because the opposition fee is not paid or the other admissibility requirements are not satisfied) the Office informs the applicant but no provisional refusal is issued.

Language of proceedings: The language requirements for oppositions against Union designations are the same as those set out in Chapter 11, section 7. When communicating with the parties to the opposition, the Office always uses the language of the proceedings. However, when communicating with WIPO in relation to the opposition, the Office uses the language of the IR, just as it does for any other matters relating to provisional refusals.

Representation: As it results in a provisional refusal being raised, an opposition against a Union designation requires the applicant to appoint a representative if it cannot represent itself before the Office (see section 3.2 above).

Issuance of provisional refusal: For every admissible opposition filed against a Union designation, an official notification of provisional refusal is sent to WIPO by the Office and this is recorded on the International Register. The extent of the provisional refusal (ie, partial or total) corresponds with the extent of the opposition.

Suspension of opposition: If an opposition is filed and absolute grounds objections are raised by the Office after the end of the opposition period, or if an opposition is filed before an earlier-issued provisional refusal is finally resolved, the opposition procedure is suspended pending the outcome of the outstanding issues.

If the Union designation is finally refused as a result of the formalities or absolute grounds issues, the opposition procedure is closed and the opposition fee is refunded to the opponent.

If, however, the designation is accepted by the Office following the final outcome of formalities and absolute grounds examination, the suspension is lifted and the opposition proceedings continue as normal. The only exception to this is where the Union designation is only partially accepted and the opposition is directed at parts that have been refused, in which case the opposition procedure is closed and the opposition fee refunded to the opponent.

Amendments to the (opposed) designation: Where an opposed Union designation is renounced, or an IR as a whole is voluntarily cancelled, the opposition fee is reimbursed if the adversarial stage of the opposition proceedings has not yet commenced (as in the case of opposed EUTM applications withdrawn before the start of the adversarial stage of opposition proceedings – see Chapter 14). The owner of an IR that includes an opposed Union designation which it does not want to pursue must file a renunciation or cancellation request directly with WIPO or with the Office of Origin for the IR. If it only tells the Office that it no longer wishes to continue with the designation, the Office does not tell WIPO and the opposition proceedings continue.

If an IR as a whole ceases to exist as the result of a central attack, and there are pending opposition proceedings against the Union designation, the opposition fee is not refunded.

6. Notification of final outcome of examination

If a Union designation passes the formalities and absolute grounds checks without any problems, and no oppositions are filed, no provisional refusals are issued. In these circumstances, the Office sends a Statement of Grant of Protection to WIPO for all goods and/or services in the Union designation on expiry of the opposition period.

If one or more provisional refusals are raised, the Office must inform WIPO once a final decision is issued. The possible outcomes are that the Union designation is either fully accepted, fully rejected or partially accepted.

In the event of full or partial acceptance of a Union designation, the Office sends a Statement of Grant of Protection to WIPO with details of the goods and/or services for which the Union designation is accepted.

7. Second republication by the Office

Once the Union designation is granted, the Office proceeds with a second republication in the *EUTM Bulletin*. From the date of second republication, the Union designation has the same effect as an EUTM registration and can be relied upon in infringement proceedings.

The expiry of the five-year non-use grace period for the purposes of revocation actions (and proof of use in other proceedings) is calculated from this date. Post-grant seniority claims can also be filed after the second republication takes place.

8. Cancellation

As with an EUTM registration, a Union designation can be the subject of revocation or invalidity proceedings, or indeed the subject of a counterclaim for invalidity and/or revocation in infringement proceedings.

An invalidity action cannot be filed until after a Statement of Grant of Protection has been issued by the Office and a non-use revocation action cannot be filed until five years have elapsed since the second republication of the Union designation by the Office. The Office must inform WIPO if a Union designation is partially or wholly cancelled as a result of revocation and/or invalidity proceedings.

Revocation and invalidity proceedings against Union designations otherwise take the same course as proceedings against direct EUTM registrations (see chapters 17 and 18).

9. Transfer

Following the issuance of a Statement of Grant of Protection, a Union designation is effectively equivalent to an EUTM registration. It can be assigned either with the IR or independently of the other designations (provided that the assignor is able to hold IRs under the Protocol).

Applications to record the assignment of a Union designation should be filed either directly at WIPO or through the Office of Origin. They should not be filed through the Office.

Just like a directly-filed EUTM, a Union designation can also be transferred prior to grant.

10. Conversion and transformation

As discussed in Chapter 25, one of the unique features of the EUTM system is the possibility of converting an EUTM application or registration into national applications in one or more Member States. It is possible for Union designations to be converted in the same way, subject to the points set out in Chapter 25, section 5.

The key difference between Union designations and direct EUTM registrations is that Union designations can be converted into either national applications or subsequent designations within the IR in question, the latter option being known as 'opting-back'. It is in fact possible to elect for a mixture of both options, subject to any given Member State for which a subsequent designation is requested being a party to the Protocol (which is currently the case for all Member States other than Malta).

As discussed in Chapter 30, one of the key features of the Protocol system is the possibility of transformation. If an IR ceases to exist following a successful central attack on the base application or registration, it is possible to transform a Union designation into a direct EUTM application. The resulting EUTM application is treated as if it had been filed on the filing date or subsequent designation date of the Union designation.

To apply for transformation of a Union designation into an EUTM application:

- the EUTM application must be filed within a period of three months of the date on which the IR was cancelled;
- the goods and/or services covered should be the same as or subsumed within the specification of the original Union designation; and
- the following information about the IR must be provided in the EUTM application:
  - the IR number;
  - the date on which the IR was cancelled;
  - the date of the original Union designation; and
  - the date of any priority claim.

If these requirements are not met, the Office issues a deficiency notice and sets a deadline by which those deficiencies must be remedied. If they are not remedied before the deadline, the transformation fails and the application proceeds as a normal EUTM application (ie, without the benefit of the filing/priority date of the IR).

There is no fee for requesting transformation. The normal EUTM application fees must, however, be paid. If the transformed application is to have the date of the original Union designation, the application fees need to be paid within one month of the filing of the EUTM application.

If the Union designation had not been examined prior to the cancellation of the IR, the EUTM application proceeds in the same manner as a normal EUTM application.

If the Union designation had been accepted and there had been a second republication, the examination and opposition stages are omitted and a registration certificate is issued following translation of the specification into all the Languages of the Union.

If a successful seniority claim had been made as part of the Union designation, this is included in the transformed application, and no further steps are required.

Further reference

Regulation – Articles 14, 151-161

Implementing Regulation – Rules 108-126

Office Guidelines – Part M

WIPO, *Guide to the International Registration of Marks under the Madrid Agreement and the Madrid Protocol* (2014): www.wipo.int/export/sites/www/madrid/en/guide/pdf/guide.pdf

Common Regulations under the Madrid Agreement Concerning the International Registration of Marks and the Protocol Relating to that Agreement (as in force on 1 April 2016) ('the Common Regulations'): www.wipo.int/wipolex/en/treaties/text.jsp?file_id=397995

WIPO, *Making the Most of the Madrid System: Information and Practical Tips on How to Use Specific Forms*: www.wipo.int/export/sites/www/madrid/en/forms/docs/making_the_most_of_the_madrid_system_mm_forms.pdf

About the authors

Mark Holah
mark.holah@twobirds.com

Mark Holah is a partner in the intellectual property practice at Bird & Bird, based in London. He is dual-qualified in the UK as a solicitor (England and Wales) and Registered Trade Mark Attorney and is also qualified as a solicitor in Ireland.

Mark has been advising clients on intellectual property issues since 1994. His practice focuses principally on brand protection issues, both contentious and non-contentious, and he has a particular expertise in European Union trade mark law and practice. Mark has been advising on the EUTM (then CTM) system since it began in 1996 and has acted on thousands of EUTM applications, oppositions and cancellation actions.

The legal directories have consistently ranked Mark as an expert. In addition, he is listed as a leading individual in the *Guide to the World's Leading Trade Mark Law Practitioners* and the *International Who's Who of Trade Mark Lawyers*.

Mark is a member of ITMA (the Institute of Trade Mark Attorneys) and INTA (the International Trademark Association) and currently sits on the INTA Public Information Committee. He has also spoken on branding issues at a wide range of conferences and events.

Patricia Collis
patricia.collis@twobirds.com

Patricia Collis is an associate in the intellectual property practice at Bird & Bird, based in London. She holds an MA (Cantab) and an LLM, and is a Registered Trade Mark Attorney. She has specialised in the field of trade mark law for the past 10 years and has extensive experience of all aspects of brand protection and trade mark portfolio management.

Patricia advises high-profile companies in a range of sectors, including telecommunications, fashion, food and beverages, financial services and media and regularly acts for clients at the European Union Intellectual Property Office, at both first instance and Board of Appeal level. She also has experience of appeals from the European Union Intellectual Property Office to the General Court, and is a frequent user of the Madrid Protocol system on behalf of clients seeking multi-jurisdictional trade mark protection.

In addition, Patricia has considerable experience of the national trade mark system in the UK as well as cross-proceedings at national and EU level. She is a member of ITMA (the Institute of Trade Mark Attorneys) and of ECTA (the European Communities Trade Mark Association), and sits on the ECTA Design Committee.

Index